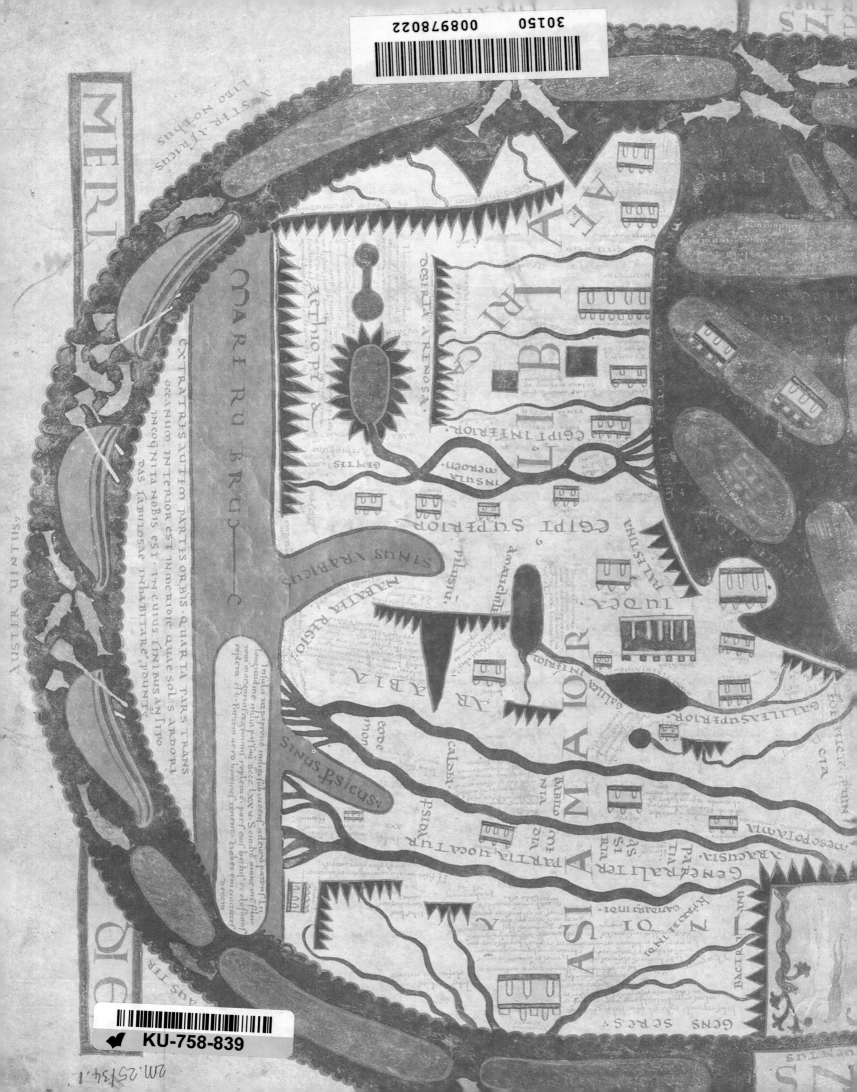

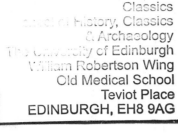
Atlas of MEDIEVAL EUROPE

Editor Graham Speake
Art editor Andrew Lawson
Text editor Robert Peberdy
Map editors Liz Orrock, Zoë Goodwin, Nicholas Harris
Picture research Diana Morris
Design Adrian Hodgkins
Production Clive Sparling
Index Jennifer Drake-Brockman

AN EQUINOX BOOK
Published by Phaidon Press Ltd,
Littlegate House, St Ebbe's
Street, Oxford, England, OX1
1SQ

Planned and produced by
Equinox (Oxford) Ltd, Mayfield
House, 256 Banbury Road,
Oxford, England, OX2 7DH

British Library Cataloguing in
Publication Data
Matthew, Donald
Atlas of Medieval Europe.
1. Geography, Medieval—
Maps
2. Europe—Historical
geography—Maps
I. Title
911'.4   G1792
ISBN 0-7148-2302-3

Origination by MBA Ltd,
Chalfont St Peter, Bucks,
England; Hongkong Graphic
Arts Service Centre; Sivier
Smith Ltd, Birmingham;
Colour Direction Ltd,
Hertfordshire

Maps drawn and originated by
Lovell Johns Ltd, Oxford,
England

Filmset by Keyspools Ltd,
Golborne, Lancs, England

Printed in Italy by
Amilcare Pizzi s.p.a.

Frontispiece Wooden statuettes
(height 55 cm) from the tomb of
Isabella of Bourbon (died 1465) at
Antwerp. From left to right
(identifications uncertain): Philip
the Good, Mary of Burgundy,
Emperor Louis IV of Bavaria,
Margaret queen of Sicily, John
IV of Brabant, overleaf Jacoba of
Hainault, Albert of Bavaria,
Anne of Burgundy, Philip of
Nevers, p. 6 Margaret of
Burgundy.

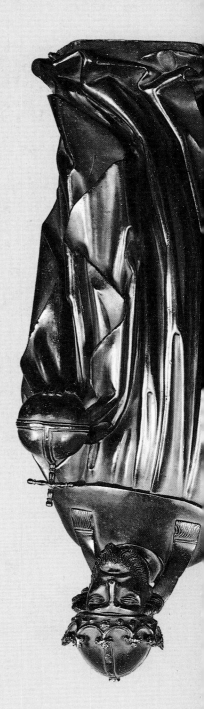

Atlas of MEDIEVAL EUROPE

by Donald Matthew

Phaidon · Oxford

List of Maps

CONTENTS

Special Features

CHRONOLOGICAL TABLE

	300	400	500	600	700	800
ARTS		Christian basilicas built in Rome, Jerusalem, Constantinople	532–37 St Sophia, Constantinople c.550 Ravenna mosaics	c.650 Sutton Hoo treasure c.698 Lindisfarne Gospels	735–804 Alcuin	Skellig Michael, Ireland c.870 *Codex Aureus*

Diocletian and Maximian, c.300.

St Sophia, Constantinople, 532–37.

The emperor Charlemagne, crowned 800.

Viking ship from Oseberg, 9th century.

	300	400	500	600	700	800
CHRISTIAN CHURCH	313 Edict of Milan granting toleration to Christians	430 death of Augustine at Hippo Regius 451 Council of Chaceldon	526 death of St Benedict 560– Irish missions to continent 590–604 Gregory I pope			817 Benedict of Aniane reforms monasteries 860 Cyril and Methodius sent to Moravia
ROMAN EMPIRE	395 division of the empire	438 *Codex Theodosianus*	533 Africa restored to Roman empire 534 *Codex Justinianus*	610–41 Heraclius emperor	716–17 Muslim siege of Constantinople 717–41 Leo III emperor 730–843 iconoclasm	867–86 Basil I, first emperor of Macedonian dynasty
ISLAM				622 Muhammad goes to Medina; the Hejira 636 Muslims defeat Roman army at Yarmuk 661–80 Muawiya, first Umayyad caliph at Damascus	762 foundation of Baghdad as Abbasid capital	
SPAIN		409 Vandals, Alans and Suevi enter Spain	509 Visigoths defeated at Vouillé and fall back on Spain 589 Reccared converted to Catholicism		711 Muslims invade Spain	c.860 serious Viking assaults on Spain
FRANCE		486 Clovis defeats Syagrius	c.507 conversion of Clovis to Catholicism	687 Pepin of Austrasia defeats Neustrians at Tertry	732 Charles Martel defeats Saracens at Poitiers 751 Pepin III becomes king of the Franks	888 Odo count of Paris becomes king
ITALY		476 Odovacar king of Italy	536 Belisarius reconquers Rome 568 Lombard invasion of Italy	668 Constans II killed at Syracuse	774 Charlemagne becomes king of Italy	
GERMANY		406 Germans cross the Rhine	509 foundation of see of Constance		754 death of St Boniface 772–804 Saxon wars	800 Charlemagne crowned emperor 843 Treaty of Verdun: empire divided
EASTERN EUROPE	341 Ulfila begins conversion of Goths 376 Goths cross the Danube		Slavs begin to infiltrate Balkans			864 conversion of Bulgars
BRITAIN AND IRELAND			563 St Columba in Iona 597 Roman mission to England	664 Synod of Whitby	Mercian supremacy 731 Bede completes *Ecclesiastical History* 793 first Viking raids on England	836 Danes established at Dublin 899 death of Alfred Wessex kings of England
SCANDINAVIA						860 Danes established in Iceland

900	1000	1100	1200	1300	1400	1500
c.985 *Beowulf*	c.1063 San Marco, Venice	1120–30 abbey church, Moissac *Chanson de Roland* 1194–1220 Chartres cathedral	c.1225–74 Aquinas c.1240 *Roman de la rose* 1265–1321 Dante 1266–1337 Giotto	1304–74 Petrarch 1345–1400 Chaucer 1377–1446 Brunelleschi 1386–1466 Donatello c.1390–1441 van Eyck	c.1400–74 Dufay 1452–1519 Leonardo da Vinci 1471–1528 Dürer	

The Tower of London, c.1080.

Sculptures from Chartres cathedral, 1134–50.

The town hall, Siena, 1297–1376.

David by Donatello, 1430.

900	1000	1100	1200	1300	1400	1500
911 foundation of Cluny	1046 Synod of Sutri – beginning of reform in Roman church	1115 foundation of Clairvaux 1179 Lateran Council III	1209 Franciscan order approved 1215 Paris university receives first statutes	1309–77 papacy at Avignon 1378 schism begins	1415–17 Council of Constance	
963–69 Nicephorus Phocas emperor	1018 final defeat of Bulgars 1071 battle of Manzikert	1176 Manuel I defeated by Seljuks at Myriokephalon	1204 4th crusade; capture of Constantinople 1261 restoration of empire		1453 capture of Constantinople	
909 foundation of Fatimid caliphate in N. Africa	1055 Seljuks capture Baghdad 1071 after Manzikert Seljuks occupy Asia Minor 1095 1st Crusade	1171 Saladin conquers Fatimid Egypt 1187 Saladin recaptures Jerusalem	1218–21 5th Crusade 1250–1517 Mamluk dynasty in Egypt 1291 last Latin states in Holy Land conquered by Mamluks	1326 Ottomans take Bursa 1389 Ottomans defeat Serbs at Kosovo	1402 death of Timur the Lame 1453 Muslims capture Constantinople	
929 Umayyad caliphate in Spain	1031 end of Cordoban caliphate 1085 Christians capture Toledo	1137 count of Barcelona becomes king of Aragon 1147 Lisbon captured from Muslims	1235–48 Catholics conquer Cordoba and Seville	1369 Trastamara dynasty in Castile	1479 marriage of Ferdinand V of Aragon and Isabella of Castile 1492 discovery of ''New World'' 1498 Vasco da Gama reaches India	
911 Rollo installed in Normandy 987 Hugh, first Capetian king of the Franks	c.1020 truce of God introduced		1204 Philip II conquers many Plantagenet lands in France 1210–29 Albigensian wars 1226–70 Louis IX 1284 war begins between kings of England and France	1337 war begins between Philip VI of Valois and Edward III	1431 Joan of Arc burned 1477 death of Charles the Rash, last Valois duke of Burgundy	
962 Otto I crowned emperor	1030 Normans established at Aversa	1130–54 Roger II king of Sicily	1212–50 Frederick II emperor and king of Sicily 1252 first florins struck in Florence	1347 plague reaches Genoa from Crimea 1385 Gian Galeazzo unites Visconti lands	1434 Cosimo de' Medici returns to Florence 1454 Peace of Lodi	
955 Otto I defeats Magyars at the Lech	1075 beginning of investiture dispute	1122 Concordat of Worms 1159–77 imperial-papal quarrel	1273 Rudolf of Hapsburg elected king of the Romans 1291 first Swiss alliance	1338 Declaration of Rense 1348 university founded at Prague	1419–36 Hussite wars	
966 foundation of Poland 989 Vladimir of Kiev becomes Christian	1000 Otto III establishes archdiocese at Gniezno 1001 kingdom of Hungary established		1241 Mongols defeat Christians at Legnica	1320 Polish kingdom reunited 1386 Poland ruled with Lithuania	1478 Ivan III takes Novgorod	
973 first recorded coronation of an English king	1017 Canute becomes king of England 1066 Norman conquest of England	1154 Henry II first Angevin king of England	1215 Magna Carta 1284 English king establishes rule over Wales 1296 war with Scotland	1381 peasants' revolt	1483 Henry Tudor made king	
995–c.1000 Olaf I king of Norway		1104 archbishopric of Lund founded 1152 abric of Nidaros 1164 abric of Uppsala		1397 Norway, Sweden and Denmark united by Kalmar Union		

PREFACE

There was a time when history was a branch of literature devoted to the evocation of the past by purely verbal means. Though words may still be indispensable for presenting some aspects of the past, the invention of photography made possible a different kind of historical record which has created a voracious appetite for pictures of the past. No period of European history has been found more photogenic than the much-maligned Middle Ages. The splendors of Versailles, designed to impress crowds, are demeaned by photography, whereas cathedrals, even if their great facades suffer, positively welcome prying photographers creeping along their galleries to find details unsuspected from the ground of sculptures or painted glass made centuries ago for God rather than men's eyes. Photography has revealed the marvelous detail of medieval workmanship not only in large-scale works, but in such small objects as illustrated manuscripts once known only to a handful of specialists. These objects, great and small, are so generously distributed across Europe that there are few parts of the continent where they do not make the idea of the Middle Ages a familiar one, and their infinite variety and superlative quality never fail to exceed all expectations. When history was mainly a matter of words, historians wrote of a Middle Ages lorded over by warriors where only religion was worth thinking about. Now that the past can be made visual, the Middle Ages appear to us in quite a different guise.

The historian's attitude to geography and mapmaking still reflects more his own view of the subject than any external imperative. In France the educational system has promoted the close cooperation of history and geography, which the English system of making them alternative disciplines has just as naturally frustrated. Teachers alive to the importance of spatial relationships in history only too often find it necessary to make constant reference to geographers' atlases, because the historical books they use provide only the most rudimentary maps. A book that aims to provide history through maps and pictures recognizes the legitimate needs of many students. Mapping the Middle Ages presents, however, some peculiar difficulties that deserve consideration.

To map the Roman empire, a territory with frontiers, is a comprehensible project. The term "Middle Ages" has no such territorial connotation. With some historians it has become an abstract term of art as esoteric as "Baroque." More pedestrian writers define the period by dates, but within such wide limits that it inevitably carries different geographical implications. The rapid expansion of medieval studies in western Europe in the last 40 years has tended to transpose the present divisions of Europe into the remote past. The Carolingian frame of the original EEC, without Spain and with an eastern frontier well west of the Elbe, yields on occasion to the geography of the Latin (Roman) church, though its eastern extremities in Poland and Hungary receive only the most perfunctory notice. Ignorance of their affairs, as of their languages and geography, even at the present time, is still so great in the west that it can hardly cause surprise if they get scant mention in accounts of medieval Europe.

The extension of ecclesiastical power across Europe invites cartographic treatment, but the church had none of the real geographic problems of an empire and to map Christian outposts across Asia as far as Peking can create a very misleading impression by a seemingly legitimate visual device. A church that was inextricably implicated in the affairs of its fellow Christians to the east cannot be mapped as though the eastern (so-called Byzantine) empire was a separate civilization, even if our academic disciplines pretend that it was. And what about Islam which touched Christendom along its whole southern front? Should this be treated as though it belonged to another subject? Must it not also be taken into account when writing of the Middle Ages? Admittedly medieval specialists are themselves ill-equipped to deal with the multifarious nature of the medieval world, but their problems are not unfamiliar in the modern world itself.

There is one other aspect to mapping the Middle Ages that deserves notice. Men did not then disregard mapmaking from ignorance of the required skills, but because territory and frontiers had no significance for them. Their loyalties were to individuals, lords and masters, not to states or nations. To map even a single town might require the identification of special enclaves. For many lands of Europe, to fence off ownership would have been impossible, since every territory supported a great number of different men with their own distinct and overlapping rights. Sophisticated modern mapmaking, if it tried to do them all justice, would bewilder the eye rather than assist understanding.

Thanks to the skills and dedication of the cartographers (Liz Orrock, Zoë Goodwin and Nicholas Harris) and those responsible for the visual effects (Andrew Lawson and Diana Morris), the reader should be able to appreciate the text as the author devised it to be read. Though I hope the text is coherent, it was not intended to be a summary of a long and complicated period of history, but to set the visual assets of the atlas in context. Topics were selected which required presentation in map form or were thought likely to benefit from it, so that when assembled they would provide a general survey of the period.

It remains only for me to thank others who have helped with the preparation of this book, especially Christopher Brooke for his invaluable comments and characteristically generous advice, Sir Richard Southern for his support and encouragement and Dr Graham Speake who has masterminded the operation.

THE IDEA OF THE MIDDLE AGES

In 14th-century Italy there were German kings who claimed to be Roman emperors. They drew on the notion that the Roman empire had continued from antiquity to their day, but for some this had become absurd. When Petrarch (1304–74) and scholars after him began to take a serious interest in the history of Rome, inexorably it seemed to them as though Rome had at some point entered on a decline in its fortunes. Their studies inspired them to recover at least the lost spirit of antiquity. The rebirth or Renaissance which followed notably did nothing to restore the political realities of ancient Rome – it remained a cultural phenomenon with at best only superficial effects on the management of public affairs – but historians working in this revival and those who followed in its cultural tradition accepted the notion that there had been a middle age, between the old cultural world and its modern revival. The very concept of the Middle Ages was based on little better than an original scholarly prejudice, with no basic intention of solemnly dividing history into periods at all. Thus all attempts to define this period by other criteria must founder; historians who try to justify the 14th-century scheme simply fall into a trap.

From the first talk of the Middle Ages, they were looked down on by the superior Latinists of the Renaissance as a period of barbarism. At a time when the values of Latin scholarship dominated Western culture this convention about medieval barbarism became received wisdom. Intense study of the Middle Ages only began in the 19th century. Still more recent is the belief in the relativity of cultural values, which has undermined the prestige of classicism. Though a new assessment of the Middle Ages has therefore now become possible, the term itself has become so well established that attempts to prove its absurdity have not successfully eliminated its use. So it is retained as convenient and stands with its equally absurd colleagues, ancient and modern, as mere labels for the tripartite division of history.

The Renaissance, which bequeathed us the concept of the Middle Ages, made one outstanding contribution to the definition of the subject when Giorgio Vasari's *Lives of the Most Eminent Italian Architects, Painters and Sculptors* (1550) set out to show how artists had recovered the lost arts of painting, sculpture and architecture. The arts of the Middle Ages were for centuries spurned as crude and primitive; artists who knew nothing of the laws of perspective or the classical canons of human beauty merited no attention. Medieval architecture was labeled "Gothic" to signify its barbarous northern origin. This term has since acquired a more restricted meaning, but it remains singularly inappropriate, for example, for the work of 12th-century French architects. When Gothic was rehabilitated by 19th-century enthusiasts, full appreciation of its technical achievements was thwarted by a misplaced emphasis on its religious and social connotations. Once again changes in modern taste have been chiefly responsible for doing justice to its importance as one of the few genuinely original creations in architecture. In painting too the collapse of the academic tradition, with its emphasis on figure drawing, perspective and elevated subject matter, made it possible for the first time to judge medieval art without classical prejudices. As a result the Renaissance can no longer be accepted on its own terms as a period of artistic "rebirth." Its self-consciousness makes it an artistic movement without parallel in the Middle Ages, but its different "style" was only the last of many changes now recognizable in medieval art, which was far from being uniform and worthless. The Renaissance prejudice against medieval art, however excusable for its own day, has lost all power to sway modern sensibilities.

Hard on the heels of the Renaissance, the Reformation created its own influential and aggressive body of scholars, persuaded that church history too could be divided into three: early, middle, and contemporary, when the church was to be restored to primitive perfection. Though the dates of the middle period were somewhat imprecise, it could be defined as the era of papal, rather than imperial, Romanism, during which the papist clergy held men's minds in superstitious subjection. The Catholics could not take quite the same dismal view of the period as the Protestants, but their attempts to defend and justify the medieval order did nothing to shake confidence in this periodization of church history. In the 20th century the Ecumenical Movement and the Second Vatican Council (1962–65) have between them generally blunted the knives of religious polemic and have at last rescued the history of the medieval church from sectarian controversy. But though modern scholars of the Middle Ages reckon to have dispensed with the older prejudices of Latinists, connoisseurs and theologians, the legacy of these well-established cultural attitudes for medieval studies has been very profound. Most information about the western medieval world comes in Latin, written by clergy, so historians cannot avoid the problems of assessing the trustworthiness of the writers or their degree of Latin culture.

Modern specialists may be keen to discard outmoded assumptions, but it is impossible to deny that the whole basis of the medieval idea comes from the 16th century, when men first sensed a break between their own times and their immediate past. Obviously those who lived in the 10 or more medieval centuries of western European history, since lumped together with scorn or dismay as a period of regrettable human retrogression, had no impression of their common fate. To treat them all as part of one period is to start with the preoccupations of the 16th century. The medieval millennium was as varied, dynamic and creative as any millennium known to science.

Historians and the Middle Ages

Before historians took an interest in the Middle Ages, antiquaries had at least begun to conserve relics of the medieval past: manuscripts, charters and religious objects after the Reformation; evidence for ancient lineage; old buildings for the glory of noble families. Such antiquaries were not merely collectors, they were also students of the past. Their combined labors resulted in the publication of much useful material (some lost since) and in preparing indispensable handbooks like the "Art of establishing Dates," or the "Medieval Latin Dictionary" of Charles Du Cange, and in the beginnings of the study of Old English. The distinguished contribution of these scholars began earlier than, and drew upon a different inspiration from, that of the historians. Medieval studies are still branded with the double sign of their dual origin. If ever historians should lose interest in the Middle Ages, the archivists, archaeologists, heralds, numismatists, paleographers and others would not falter in their medieval loyalties. Medieval objects demand attention, whether their period is thought "relevant" or not.

The work of the antiquaries was inspired by the wish to rescue something from the destructive zeal of religious reformers. The dissolution of the monasteries in England destroyed or dispersed the treasures accumulated in them for many centuries. There alone had been nursed the will to preserve at least some objects deemed precious, though several centuries old. In a few years these ancient treasure-houses were plundered under the approving eye of those who considered themselves and their beliefs vastly superior to the monks. At the time this arrogance seemed not vandalism but enlightenment. But within a generation this mood had already passed. A few men could be found, ready to look back, to regret the pillage and to salvage something, not as "Old Believers" but with a dim sense of what can be lost from the human record by unthinking endorsement of current intellectual fashions.

In Catholic countries the destruction caused by disturbances was less. The Council of Trent (1545–63) restored faith in much of the Catholic tradition. Monasticism itself recovered its self-confidence. In France the so-called Maurist scholars in particular used the resources of the old monastic libraries that survived the Wars of Religion (1562–98) to lay the foundations of medieval scholarship. Jean Mabillon (1632–1707) learned how to read the ancient documents of the Benedictine order and expounded the rules for testing the authenticity of medieval records. He published texts and wrote about the history of his order. The Jesuits began to test the stories of the

The political and physical geography of Europe today Human settlement across the whole continent of Europe was first achieved in the period between the collapse of the Roman empire and the European discovery of the rest of the world. To do this, northern peoples from beyond the empire exploited resources of the Mediterranean world. By this means the cultural divide in Europe between civilization and barbarism was obliterated. Europe became more than a mere geographical term: it carried cultural implications. But this culture was sustained by a new kind of physical support. The ancient civilizations had been shaped within the Mediterranean basin, as one kind of physical unit. With medieval culture the physical environment of the European continent itself first acquired significance.

Byland abbey, Yorkshire, England, begun after 1177 and finished in the 13th century. The picturesque quality of such ruins was already apparent to John Milton and had a profound effect on the Romantic imagination. Historically it is necessary to imagine how monasteries looked in their prime. As busy centers of work and prayer they would not stir the same kind of emotional response. The buildings appear to have been designed for a complement of 36 monks and 100 lay brothers.

saints by serious study of the texts. Throughout western Europe scholars began to publish narratives and documents relating to the medieval period, well before historians even tried to write about it. The great Edward Gibbon (1737–94) was the first to write an important medieval history, and typically enough it was on the decline of the Roman empire. His technique he learned from the study of ancient history and his work is marked by an intolerable condescension to the Middle Ages. His studied skepticism about the virtues of religion, characteristic of the age of the Enlightenment, prevented him, and his contemporaries, from penetrating to the heart of medieval sensibilities.

The certainties of philosophy were swept away in the aftermath of the French Revolution and it was in the subsequent generation that historians first took up their own study of the Middle Ages in earnest. The manifest failure of the modern man's rational mind to correct the errors accumulated in the centuries of ignorance and the inability of purely rational solutions for human problems to command universal assent drove historians back to study periods where the nonrational depths of the human mind seemed more in evidence. Religion itself was no longer seen as an illogical tissue of intellectual propositions but as an expression of men's deeper emotional experiences. To some it seemed worthwhile to try and restore European order in terms of pre-Enlightened verities, the church and the monarchy in particular; the study of the past and the origins of the European world itself therefore required investigation. In Germany, where Napoleon had provoked a national rebirth, an understandable wish to rediscover the remote German past before French fashions had corrupted

the German princely courts drove scholars back to the Middle Ages. The heroes of the earliest times, who had also overthrown a great empire across the Rhine, came back into their own. Medieval Germans had not been abashed to assume the burdens of the Christian empire; 19th-century Germans took heart from their medieval past as to their own civilizing role. Taken up enthusiastically in Germany, medieval studies rapidly became popular in all the countries of the west where Germanic invaders had once broken down the imperial barriers. These "barbarians" were drawn as men of virtue, combating the corruption and decadence of Rome, renewing the physical stock of Europe, laying the foundations for the nations of modern Europe. The beginnings of the Middle Ages now appeared to owe everything to the beneficial purge made by these heroes; there was no need to deplore the sack of Rome: the empire's blood lusts had been punished in kind. Latin culture, oppressive and elitist, thus lost the virtue seen in it by Gibbon's contemporaries. To understand the real nature of the Germanic peoples it was necessary to study the Middle Ages.

The French Revolutionary period and the Romantic Age also inspired a new interest in the old national literatures and languages, which had flourished particularly in the "medieval" period. Literary works lacked self-evident historical information but nevertheless gave insights into the cultures of the past, without apparently exhibiting ecclesiastical prejudices. Stimulated by their readings of heroic poetry and legend, Europeans not only began to form a different impression of medieval barbarism, but planned a new program of mass education in the vernacular languages of Europe, which, realized by our own day, has

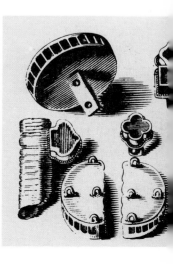

deprived the classical tradition of its centuries-long hold over education. In the place of classical literature have been put the national literatures and histories of the European states. Several modern states have been "revived" politically because of their medieval origins, and their nationalist pre-occupations of the present have forced medieval studies to explain the sources of national inspiration for educational purposes.

Partisan enthusiasms have sustained years of painful investigation into the past – the problems of interpreting medieval records, of producing new editions of chronicles and charters and all the countless but necessary works of reference, dictionaries and atlases. Even now medieval scholars have not caught up with the classicists, who had nearly four centuries' head start. But already, as appreciation of the medieval past has developed, the academic contrast between Germans and Romans is seen to be exaggerated and misleading. The Middle Ages were not a long battle between men of different races and cultures. The Romans were not so corrupt, nor the Germans so exemplary, as legend would have it.

The study of the Middle Ages, of medieval literature, art and architecture cannot, however, so easily escape the cocoon spun around them in the Romantic Age. Studies from that age have helped to create the kind of cultural world we still take for granted, with its taste for the primitive, the exotic, the exalted and the emotional. Writers as close to us in time as Voltaire or Gibbon would find un-palatable our taste for the Romantic imagination, which lies behind our ideas of the Middle Ages as a land of mystery, imagination and grandeur. The Middle Ages of Walter Scott, Richard Wagner, Emmanuel Viollet-le-Duc, the brothers Grimm, John Ruskin or William Morris, for all their faults, inevitably still point out to us a way backwards to their original medieval inspirations. Those who follow such leads and try to come to fresh terms with the Middle Ages may escape from Romantic interpretations, but they continue to owe to Romanticism itself the wish to rediscover a misunderstood world. The Middle Ages only "exist" in the modern imagination as a proper place for the human mind to explore its own full potential because in the Middle Ages the minds of most men were not forcibly subjected by education to the arbitrary ideals of the few. Many men achieved positions of influence without being formally educated at all. As a result there was in some way more opportunity for wayward human imagination to assert itself.

In this sense the Middle Ages are not to be confined by boundaries in time or space, for they are a product of the historical imagination. Inspired perhaps by certain peculiar features of a phase in the western European past, the concept has been transferred to quite different cultures, such as Japan. The stirrings of the modern romantic impulse drive us to the unknown and its wayward inspiration may also explain the great variations of interpretation about the "real" nature of the Middle Ages. The pull of the ancient world on modern sensibilities has been traditionally through litera-ture – Homer, Virgil or *the* book, the Bible. The attraction of the Middle Ages has been altogether less coherent. It is more like the lure of a fabulous

island for visitors, all of whom are capable of finding something to please their fancy and return with different accounts of all they saw. For some an age of faith, for others of craftsmanship, of feudal oppression; for others still a primitive society somehow galvanized into life, containing the secret of the European preeminence in modern times which, if known, might enable other primitive societies to "take off" in their turn. To touch on the history of Europe for more than a thousand years is still to rake over a storehouse of treasures in the hope of a fabulous find. The idea of hidden secrets and wonderful mysteries remains an inescapable part of what is expected of the Middle Ages.

The definition of the medieval period here accepted deals with the miscellany of events that fell between the collapse of the Roman empire in the west and the maritime discovery of the rest of the world in the 1490s, the period between the invasion of the empire by the "barbarians" and the invasion of America and Asia by "Europeans." Not everyone would now regard these European invaders as "civilized" or less "barbarous" than their ancestors a millennium earlier, but they were obviously very different in their accomplishments and their ideals. They had already passed through and profited from great vicissitudes of fortune.

The western European focus implied by the triad ancient – medieval – modern blurs the image of the Roman empire based on Constantinople and darkens that of Islam, though by modern worldly standards the empires of the Greeks and Muslims in this period merit attention as world powers, in the way that medieval European states do not. In Constantinople and Baghdad the medieval period cannot be made to seem a justifiable term; their histories are inevitably distorted by fitting them to western categories. Better this, however, than to leave them out altogether. Taking into account their coexistence with medieval Europe helps us to resist specious simplicities but creates complications for historians. Few of them, if any, ever have been, or in foreseeable circumstances ever will be, familiar enough with the three cultures in question to write of their complex interaction without bias. The scholarly equipment necessary to do justice to all the communities of the west is elaborate enough, even before the extra burden of eastern European languages and the different traditions of Islam and the Orient are considered. The Middle Ages must be accepted as a basically western European cultural concept, devised in one phase of its own history as it was trying to come to terms with its own past. For men living in those troubled times, however, western Europe constituted no favored region insulated from hostile influences. On the contrary, it was highly vulnerable to attack and recognized its own position of inferiority with regard to both the empire of the Romans at Constantinople and the civilization of Islam to the south. Hence the concern to insist on the purity of its own religious practice, for here it was unassailable. To speak now of studying the Middle Ages as though the period did have definable coherence must create distorting effects not only for the rest of the world but on a thousand years of momentous events and dramatic changes. The Middle Ages must not be regarded as homogeneous. Every century cries out for recog-nition of its individuality.

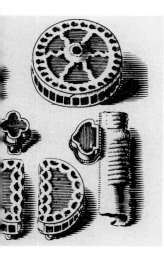

Childeric died at Tournai in 481. His tomb was opened in 1653 and the grave finds rapidly published by Chifflet (1655). It is one of the most spectacular medieval deposits, important also because accurately datable. Most of the pieces of jewelry were stolen from the Cabinet des Médailles in Paris in 1831. Chifflet's drawings are therefore still valuable. The jewelry was decorated with garnets set in cells.

MEDIEVAL THEMES

Faith and the primacy of local power

Renaissance and Reformation judgments on the Middle Ages no longer command historians' respect, but their concern with the affairs of church and empire put the emphasis in the right place. Modern experience proves how important governments can become in the lives of every community. Our evidence for the Roman empire shows its government to have been capable of creating comparable conditions of life across its whole extent, against which there could be only local, intermittent resistance. Not all inhabitants of the empire enjoyed the same advantages, but the government influenced and framed their expectations of life. The collapse of the empire meant above all that "government" ceased to be effective, so that all societies depended for their direction on individuals known to them, rather than on officials acting for the state. Henceforth for most men, lords personally known to their vassals and dependants remained more significant until the various states of Europe began to assert the claims of the public good and oppose feudal, that is private, power in what are called modern times. The security offered by private lordship extended, at best, no further than a lord's reputation and the system was obviously incapable of deterring distant marauders from raiding. Once the universal government itself failed to keep out disorderly barbarians, the only hope of any political control over events lay with great landowners discharging public duties at a local level. The Middle Ages was to define itself as a period that did not recognize the right of sovereign authorities to promote civil society or to exercise responsibilities for defending frontiers against hostile neighbors. This could also mean that brutal men rampaged without fear of government correction, since no lord's arm reached as far as his pretensions. However there were other restraints, for during this period strong men were at least hampered by their inability to claim that their might was right. The authority to pronounce on "right" had been separated from the state, where it rests in some places today. Then it was the prerogative of the church. In the Middle Ages the only acknowledged "sovereign" was God.

Monotheism became established in the Roman empire in the 4th century. The universal emperors themselves bowed to the consequences of this well before barbarian rulers found that they had to do likewise. The latter, though obviously enjoying much more limited real power than the emperor, showed much more reluctance to accept the constraints of monotheism. Until they did so, however, they remained "barbarous," living on the fringes of medieval society, denying the values of the "civilized" world. Faith that God would prevail over injustice gave men strength to endure hardship and violence at a time when there was no powerful state to restore right. But at a human level men had perforce to put their trust in their kin, their

A wheel of fortune of the late 14th century from Florence. Fortune turns the wheel lifting one king to eminence while the presiding king, with orb and scepter, already looks after his declining predecessor. The image, which here serves the moralist making points about human prosperity and adversity, was however a medieval cliché on the transitoriness of all things human.

neighbors and their patrons, and experienced the inevitable disappointments and betrayals. Their religion did not permit them to aspire by heroism to the status of gods. They had to come to terms with their humanity, for all its limitations, as never before. When they defined the seven deadly sins they thought the worst to be pride, a concept that bewilders modern men who are not ashamed of their proud humanity. (Typically, for us, sexuality is our greatest problem because it proves how ungodlike we are; the Christian Middle Ages appears to have been quite uncomplicated in this respect.)

Faith in God, or the Unseen, was not always and everywhere as orthodox as the Christian clergy required, but the church acquired a comfortable authority in dealing with religious matters that was not challenged except occasionally at a local level. And there are no good grounds for believing that the majority of men then doubted the church's teaching, however irksome they recognized its ministers could be: they certainly knew no rational or intellectual arguments for skepticism.

The church's doctrines were in general terms acceptable, because plausible and comforting, and because they confirmed that wrongdoing would certainly be punished with suffering in the next life if not actually avenged in this. Submission to the divine law and acceptance of the church's direction gave hope of divine favor now, and in the future. The miseries of the present life paid the necessary price for sin. Human weakness and error made men incapable of much understanding, but from revelation at least they learned that God was sovereign and had saved his people. They could therefore appeal to him with confidence to intervene in their affairs, through his saints and their miracles. The earth was believed to be at the center of his universe. The church was his faithful community. It did not seem improbable that God had extended his loving care for eternity even if the life of any one individual was short and uncertain. Such teaching strengthened those who worked for the church; it weakened any aspiration to work for earthly power and glory, since these would rapidly fade away. Kings and emperors, blessed by God in the church's ceremonies, obtained thereby a special destiny and had even less motive to think of denying God's sovereign power. His glory necessarily overshadowed theirs. Their rivalries blatantly demonstrated their earthly limitations. The self-assertiveness of some individuals, notably rulers, though it might make a great stir in the world, lasted but a little time. Characteristically, during this period no schemes were conscientiously pursued across generations which were capable of undermining this belief in the vanity of earthly glory. Experience therefore confirmed that human efforts were not sustainable, that sons did not live up to their fathers' heroic achievements. Charlemagne was followed by Louis the Pious, who broke up the empire, and Robert Bruce, Savior of Scotland, by the unhappy David II. Medieval chroniclers could easily demonstrate that the history of human societies was uncertain, a matter of fortune and not of effort rewarded. Men's individual destinies would only be resolved beyond the grave.

The limitations of ambition

The spectacle of the way great men were toppled from their eminence probably gave much satisfaction to those who did not try to rise above their station in either church or state. Anonymous and uncounted, the majority who worked in their communities over the generations were the real makers of the Middle Ages. The shortness of individual life and the frailty of human achievements never weakened belief that men's lot in this imperfect world was to labor, and that mainly for the purpose of finding the means to stay alive: agriculture. The only works of men's hands made to last were those dedicated to God. With his idealism

Illustration to the calendar month of August from a mid-15th-century French Book of Hours showing peasant with a flail. Despite the conventional element, there is a certain realism about the drawing of the face, the rakish poise of the straw hat and the boots, stockings, under-linen and surcoat, which gives an impression of rustic affluence.

focused on God, man was able to enjoy life for what it was and without illusions. Hence the paradox, as it seems now, of men at once exalted in spirit and coarse in conduct. Life was undoubtedly very hard for most men, most of the time, but since even the rich had no expectation of how it might be rendered very comfortable there was no alternative but to live according to immediate circumstances, responding to abrupt changes of mood or situation, without stoic pride in consistency, seizing chances to feast and make merry in company or enjoy the more brutal pleasures of quarrels, violence and vengeance. They accepted their need for one another, for human warmth and society, with no idea of living solitary lives in search of personal fulfilment. Hermits were exceptional creatures and curiosities worth visiting. For most men lived and worked in the same place, with familiar people all their lives, committed during daylight to their occupations, day in day out. The Christian dispensation at least imposed rest from labor on Sundays throughout medieval Europe, though the acceptance of the week as a seven-day cycle must have started in the pagan period. The church also tried to enforce observance of rest on numerous holy days throughout the year. Dedication to labor over the generations, as men multiplied in numbers, began to effect a transformation of the environment. They extended the land, tilled for food. They congregated in towns to manufacture and trade with neighbors. Eventually the commercial network brought Europe into touch with remotest China and India. Despite these successes, however, no political coherence comparable to the Roman empire ever grew out of the social-economic order, because political power had in the Christian period lost its claim to ultimate significance. The transformation of the European environment, which was the real achievement of the period, did not, however, strike contemporaries as much as it has impressed modern writers. Those who worked hardest in their own region barely looked up to see what was happening beyond the horizon. And the educated were naturally more involved in the special preoccupations of cultured people everywhere. At a time when writing itself played no essential part in the ordinary work of men, not even of the politically prominent, those who could write did not intend to use their talents to describe everyday occupations. As God was sovereign, writing was to serve him.

The restricted use of writing in the Middle Ages was not a legacy of either the empire or the church. Within the empire the church had naturally extended its influence on men down to the humblest level by allowing the use of the many widely disseminated languages. Its scriptures were written in demotic Greek. Its early liturgies appeared in Syriac and Coptic, not only in Greek and Latin. In the empire literacy, if not universal, was certainly esteemed. The functioning of the empire depended on all its servants and supporters recognizing the importance of an educated understanding. Such an awareness did not survive the collapse of Roman imperial administration in the west. From that time government ceased to rest on the availability of literate aristocrats and citizens, on written instruments of government, on the existence of schools and libraries. Not before the

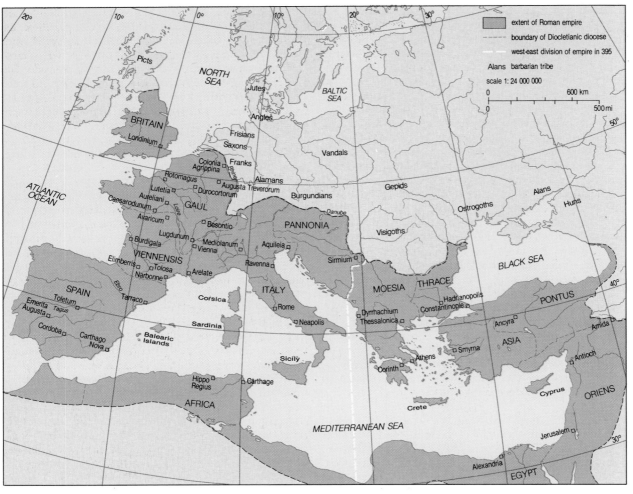

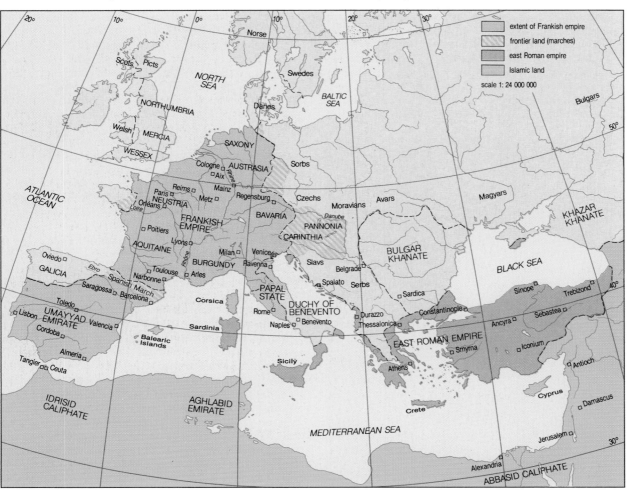

Left: Europe in 350
The four maps on this page are designed to sum up the theme of this atlas in a visually provocative manner. The contrasts were never so stark, nor the implied development so steady, as the maps suggest. Yet they make a dramatic point about universal history in a way that only theater can. Centuries, even millennia, of human civilization had by the beginning of the Christian era enabled a single government to prevail across the Mediterranean and further north in Gaul and Britain. Northern and central Europe had eluded its grasp. The first map shows that the empire could not by the 4th century resist encroachment and occupation from barbarian peoples not to its liking. If the forms of civilization were thereafter preserved, the initiative no longer lay with the Romans. Only the Christians somehow retained their cultural links with the past and, by sentiment, with the Mediterranean lands of Palestine and Rome. The map itself gives the appearance of a venerable painting, with its glaze cracked and stained by alien bodies, to all appearances on the verge of disintegration and decay.

Below left: Europe in 800
The second map immediately suggests that in the intervening period the potentially viable elements of European or Roman civilization had concentrated their strength in a limited part of western Europe, with barely a stake in the Mediterranean at all. The map might provoke the idea that the aim of Mediterranean unity was more properly continued by the Muslims, for even if Rome and Constantinople eluded their grasp, their presence at sea and on all but the northern shores of the Mediterranean gave them the upper hand, even over the east Roman empire. But Islam did not draw its strength from the civilization of the Mediterranean world but from a religion of desert peoples and the culture of Persia. It used the learning of the Greek world in translation. It had no interest in making the old Mediterranean culture its own. Though overshadowed by Islam, therefore, the Christian peoples of Europe in the eastern and western empires were justified in clinging to their faith in themselves as true heirs of the Roman legacy. In the time of Charlemagne there can have been no expectation that the west would garner more of that harvest than the east. Indeed, in the century after Charlemagne, the eastern empire proved what powers of recuperation it disposed of at a time when even the limited revival of the idea of empire attempted in the west could not be sustained.

Right: Europe in 1150
By now western Christendom no longer aspired to Mediterranean dominion, though it showed its strength by assaults on Islam in the south, in Spain and in the east. Its advance from Germany into eastern Europe more significantly showed to what extent Christendom was now confidently based in a northern European territory. It was expanding from its northern French cultural centers, even to the far north. It was not, however, any longer a united political force. The eastern rump of the Carolingian Roman empire had become the nucleus of the most powerful state in the west, but its vitality depended on its new German members, not its Roman legacy. The spiritual energies of the west, not so easily plotted on the map, had been recharged by the ideal of a restored Christendom, which enabled the crusading expeditions to take place, despite western diffidence about the seas between. The eastern empire, whose revival in the 10th century is not shown by these maps, had since become weak enough to value aid from fellow Christians in the west. If this map creates the impression that the new energies of the west, capable of decisive action in the east, might eventually enable the west to reimpose unity on the Mediterranean, this proved to be an illusion.

Below right: Europe in 1500
The last map shows that the optimistic possibilities of the mid-12th century were doomed to disappointment. The eastern empire, at first aided, then taken over, and finally abandoned by the west, ceased to be a Christian state at all. The Holy Places, protected by western Christians for a time, passed irrevocably into the orbit of Islam. Several crusading expeditions from the west could not prevent the setting up of the Ottoman empire, which finally succeeded for the first time in Islamic history in uniting the whole of the eastern Mediterranean area. Only to the north did Catholic energies continue to expand, pushing their dominion firmly onto Orthodox peoples of Lithuania and Russia. Europe was now divided, as never before, into east and west. The west had access to the European seas and the Atlantic routes leading them far overseas. Political unity in the west was still not achieved, but political diversity turned out to be a condition of western European vitality. The three major kingdoms on the extreme west, Spain, France and England, now set the pace and duly acquired worldwide empires. Germans and Italians failed to assert the influence their wealth, culture and education deserved, though they were an important source of religious, artistic and intellectual inspiration. Where was once the unity of the Roman empire, there was now the Babel of European culture on the eve of its encounter with America and the east.

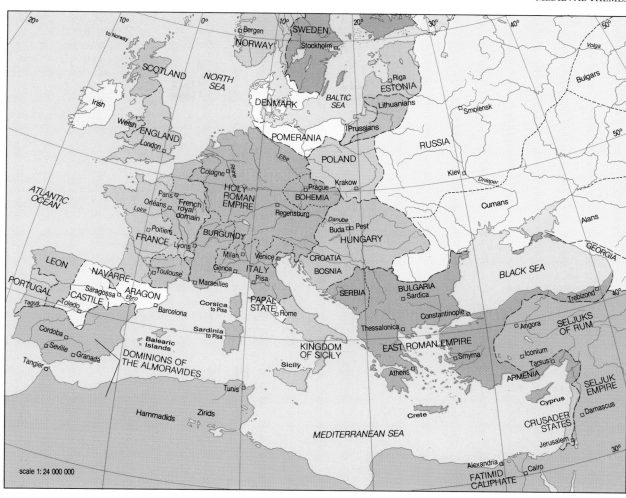

scale 1: 24 000 000

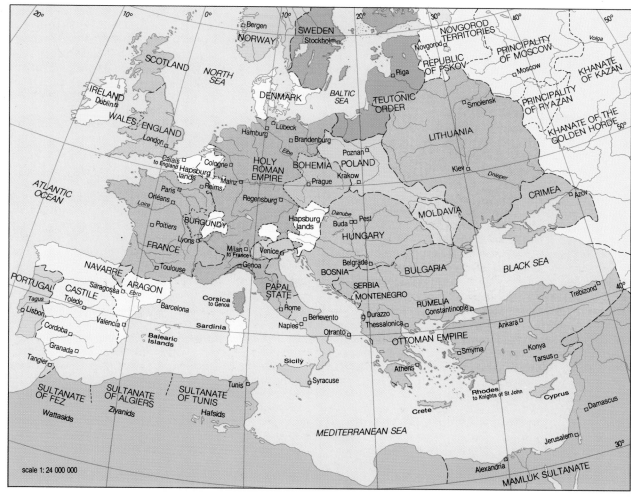

scale 1: 24 000 000

13th century or the 14th did they again become common or prominent features of public life. The clergy of the Christian church and some monks retained a sense of the importance of literacy, first because the Christian revelation was known to them through the scriptures with their more or less learned patristic commentaries, and secondly because, as the clergy became increasingly submerged in a non-Latin-speaking world, special efforts had to be made in schools for clergy to learn the Latin language. The diminished range of literature consulted encouraged the use of codices (books) into which the few basic texts could be copied and consequently the abandonment of the rolls or scrolls that had been common in antiquity. For the clergy and their bookish culture literacy remained indispensable, but increasingly the Christian majority of laymen happily left literacy to the clergy, recognizing that clerical books were of precious little value to their concerns. In noble households, in particular, there was originally no understanding of the value of written literature either for government or for culture, as had been the case in the Roman empire.

The deadening effects of the Roman literary education should not be forgotten, but on balance the collapse of literacy not only signified the disintegration of the imperial inspiration, it proved a misfortune for civilization. However small the number of literate persons, they had by their learning acquired a sense of the continuity in time of the human community and a sense of the place of books in the transmission of culture from one generation to another, so that even the achievements of one man could be made available in writing for anyone. From this had been derived some notion of the universality of knowledge, some sense of what could be learned from the past and an appreciation of the length of time in which the civilization of the Mediterranean basin had been developed. The Germanic peoples had no use for writing, either for communicating across the generations or with other peoples. They had other means for transmitting their culture down the generations; this probably kept their cultural legacy more vivacious and personal, but it narrowed its scope and its range. The culture of the west was thus fragmented, leaving Latin to serve only for the formally educated. Secular cultures in the vernacular necessarily had very local diffusion, since vernacular speech varied so much according to region. The invention of printing which overcame some of these disadvantages made others worse. It has perpetuated the division of the west into compartments by "national" languages, in a way unknown in the Roman empire. Latin itself became dispensable for the purposes of learning once translations and original learned writings in the vernacular created the possibility of monoglot cultures. There have therefore been profound consequences for the west in the collapse of Roman literacy. By contrast, in China, despite troubles, linguistic and literary unity survived.

Written records in Latin and the vernacular hardly bear on the major activities of the ordinary people of this period. And if most men's occupations dropped out of literary sight, only a tiny fraction of the artifacts then produced survive to give an inkling of the full extent of human activity.

Conditions of medieval life, outside venerable churches at least, militated against both the construction of magnificent buildings and the preservation of valuable articles. Our view of the ancient world obviously owes much to the imposing evidence of its great cities which suggest how much Mediterranean civilization was linked to political life. Human societies were organized in such a way as to wrest a living from the land and sea with sufficient surplus to support a higher level of intellectual culture for citizens, though even slaves might enjoy such benefits. Medieval cities give quite a different impression. Magnificence was played down. Christian society, which increasingly responded to the idea that manumission of slaves was meritorious, began to dispense with slave labor. In time this produced a working force of free men, as for example on medieval building sites. Such a society could support only a modest number of nobles and almost no "officials." The majority of men lived and worked in the countryside; the town, though it survived, fulfilled quite a different role from that in antiquity. Life in towns, if preferred by townsmen, no longer shaped general expectations of life's possibilities. The change has nothing to do with the development of an otherworldly religion. The church set more store by cities as Roman institutions than its barbarian parishioners did. It was the barbarians who either had no time for town life, or no knowledge of how to regenerate activity there when the responsibility for government fell to them. Everywhere within the empire the old Roman cities, much shrunk in size, at least remained seats of ecclesiastical authority. By the early 12th century the revival of economic, industrial and commercial activity brought about some renewal of urban energy, but medieval cities never recovered the place of the ancient ones as centers of civilization, and, except in Italy, the countryside of Europe was not subjected politically to cities. It looked to them only for its economic needs. In this respect too, modern industrial towns are obviously heirs of the medieval, not the ancient, tradition.

By contrast, it was during the medieval period that the countryside came fully into its own. Had the Roman empire simply been taken over by nomadic raiders like the Huns, as China was by the Mongols, the consequence could have been the survival of an imperial-type regime. Nomadic raiders caused the least permanent damage to the Roman empire. In the long term it was the steady encroachment of barbarian cultivators into the Roman empire that changed its character. Some barbarians for a time simply stepped into the positions of Roman landlords as owners of great estates. But the prevailing system of Roman cultivation eventually disappeared, to be replaced in most parts of Europe by a pattern of landholding that allowed peasants to collaborate in cultivating lands around small villages. For centuries most men of western Europe were born into such rural communities, where they were brought up and from which few of them ever departed for careers elsewhere in towns or in the church. The steady pressure of these groups on the land made it worth clearing more forest and draining marshes. By their cooperative efforts the good, and the less good, soils of northern Europe were put under the plow. Mediterranean culture continued to attract the

The 14th-century Pont de Valentré which carries the main Bordeaux–Lyons road over the Lot at Cahors. With its seven ogive arches, imposing pillars with spurs and battlement parapets, and three square towers it is typical of the need to fortify potentially exposed places in unsettled times.

The Franks casket, made in Northumbria about 700 of whalebone and measuring 10·5 × 1·23 × 18·5 cm. The front panel with runes and Latin inscription shows the adoration of the Magi combined with a mythological scene of Wayland the smith. The combination of Christian with pagan stories illustrates how the new religion could be assimilated in barbarian Europe. Despite the writing and the detail of the narration, it is not easy to interpret.

leaders of northern society and deck them with coveted ornaments. Yet from the beginning of the Middle Ages, the new power of the northern peoples was proved by their ability to bring down the empire and create a new order of their own without it. In the nature of things this rural achievement went almost unobserved, or at least without anyone realizing what it meant.

The church between Rome and paganism

For all the achievements of ancient Mediterranean civilization it was in many ways an austere, even ascetic one. The original city-states were small without extensive rich soils to cultivate. Grain yields were often poor and erratic. The vine needed skilled attention and favorable conditions. Even the olive needed nurture, though from poor soils it provided the main source of light and fuel as well as food. The sun and temperate seasons gave suitable conditions for a mainly outdoor public life. Once simple wants were supplied there was time left from the fields for leisure and conversation in the open. The Romans themselves found difficulty in taking this style of life to the northern provinces, and after the conquest of Britain they made no further effort to carry their civilization to other northerly peoples. The barbarians had to force their way into the empire to obtain any of its benefits. They were not immediately concerned to acquire those virtues of civilization valued most by the Romans themselves. Work on the heavier, moist soils of northern Europe was more arduous, more exacting and more time-consuming. There was less leisure and few men could enjoy the privilege of it. In time, of course, as northern Europe became better cultivated and the boundaries of civilization were pushed well beyond the frontiers of the old empire, the northern peoples reacted more positively to what they could of the Mediterranean world. Symbolically this may be indicated by the acceptance of Christianity and its Mediterranean ceremonies – baptism with the water of life, anointing with oil, and the eucharistic meal of bread and wine – by the country peoples of northern Europe, who had no experience of drought and who normally drank beer. In the Roman empire, before the barbarian invasions, Christianity had barely begun to penetrate beyond city walls. The countryside remained "pagan." Over the next few centuries the new religion was taken to all the village communities of the north. It took root there so strongly that western Christianity lost its preeminently urban, sophisticated and polemical traditions. But what it lost in one direction it gained in another. Europe was made by the Christians, whereas in the empire they had won only recognition from a state that was older and more self-confident than the church.

The church was, however, much changed in the process. By the end of the 4th century the Roman empire had succeeded in taking over the Christian church and turning it into a department of state, an arrangement actually welcomed by the clergy because of the advantages that accrued to them and their activities. When the barbarians arrived in the empire few clergy looked upon them with favor. Many of the early barbarian leaders had accepted "Arianism" and Catholics hated their heresy. Catholic bishops who shouldered the responsibility for the care of Catholic congregations normally came from the ranks of the senatorial governing class. From the first they stood for continuity of the old Roman values. The eventual conversion of the barbarian leaders was due to their influence. The Roman stamp on Christendom, reinforced by the

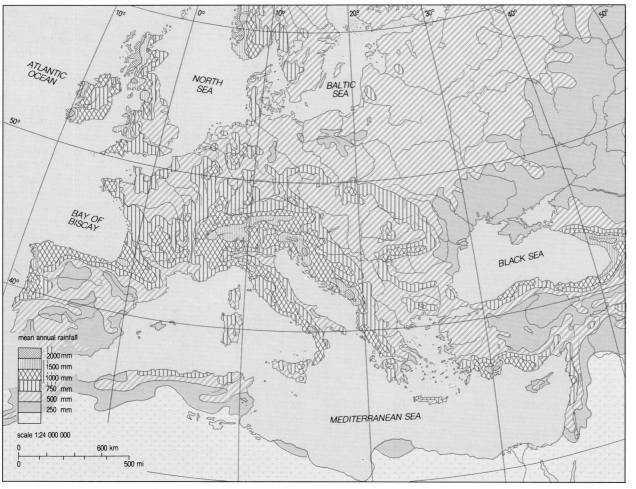

mean annual rainfall

	2000 mm
	1500 mm
	1000 mm
	750 mm
	500 mm
	250 mm

scale 1:24 000 000

0 — 600 km

0 — 500 mi

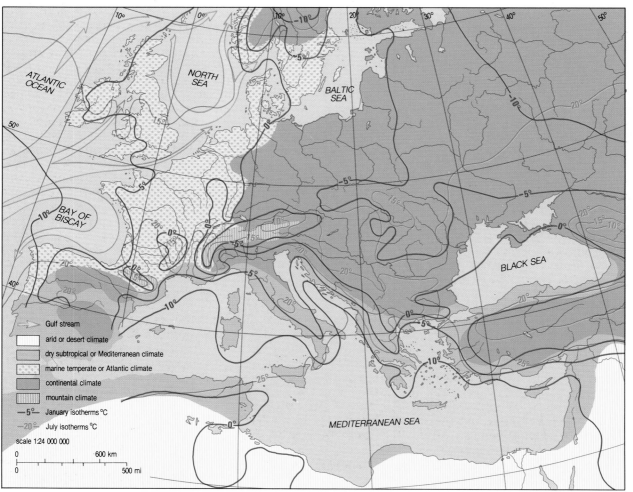

→ Gulf stream

arid or desert climate

dry subtropical or Mediterranean climate

marine temperate or Atlantic climate

continental climate

mountain climate

—5°— January isotherms °C

—20°— July isotherms °C

scale 1:24 000 000

0 — 600 km

0 — 500 mi

Left: The climate of Europe
Above: Mean annual rainfall
Below: Seasonal temperature and climatic zones

Modern research has established that the climatic conditions now prevailing in Europe have themselves been subject to changes over time, even if the causes are not agreed. Evidence for very severe conditions in the 17th century has persuaded historians that climatic conditions probably deteriorated over a long period from the later Middle Ages. Earlier still, historical geographers now believe that Europe enjoyed conditions more benign for agriculture, particularly in northern Europe, over a period of several centuries. The beginnings of this phase may roughly be correlated with the period of Scandinavian expansion which ventured to colonize Iceland and Greenland. The onset of adverse conditions from the 14th century contrariwise had the effect of snuffing out these colonies' prosperity. Though fluctuations of this order are now accepted, they cannot be used to explain many specific historical events. The climate of Europe obviously has a bearing upon the nature of the human settlement patterns, as upon the distribution of animals and vegetation. Contemporaries who were not aware of these climatic changes experienced their effects and had to adapt their behavior accordingly.

Quite apart from such changing circumstances, it should be noted that Europe anyway enjoys an exceptionally favorable climate for settlement by contrast with regions in comparable latitudes in other parts of the world north and south. This means that the inhabitants of Europe benefit from a climate that combines certain features of normally distinct zones – high latitudes with marked differentiation of seasons, together with the benefits of warmer conditions generated by the Gulf Stream. This is normally responsible for preventing the freezing over of northern European rivers in winter and keeping the northern lands warm enough to ripen crops like grain and grapes. Europe is composed not of one but of three climatic zones – Mediterranean, Atlantic and continental. The Mediterranean zone was one of the most immediately attractive for settlement, its major disadvantages for agriculture being limited to occasional droughts. Long before the northern parts of the continent were extensively colonized it had nurtured many civilizations. Their example was one of the chief incentives operating later in the north. There the interaction of the three zones gave further advantages, though they were only realized at a later date.

The tempering effect of the seas that surround three sides of Europe means that, until the broad band of land is reached where Europe joins Asia, Europe does not experience such great extremes of temperature between summer and winter as to disrupt the four-season cycle altogether, as it does in Russia. Avoiding extremes of cold and hot, as of wet and dry, Europeans, particularly in the Middle Ages when they had few resources for countering nature's defects, made good progress with the settlement of this ideal and temperate zone. Populations not being very dense could ignore the mountains and the marshes, whereas in the Orient this was otherwise. If there was competition for the best lands, many colonists were happy to cultivate anew, though there was always room for siting settlement carefully in the more attractive areas. The climate did not condemn any of these efforts beforehand and over the centuries the size both of the cultivated territory and of the population grew to prove it.

Gregorian mission to England (597), led, from the 8th century onwards, to a move for papal direction of the western church, particularly through the efforts of English missionaries in Germany and their impact on the Carolingian empire. When Christianity was taken to the barbarians it became more pointedly ''Roman'' than it had ever been in the empire itself. Rome in the 4th century had had many cultivated pagan families and was not even the western emperor's capital seat. Christianity itself was stronger in the eastern than in the western Mediterranean. Once the Christian clergy came to be recruited from barbarian peoples they openly professed a ''Roman'' allegiance. Their education in the Latin language, and to some extent in Latin culture, at least put some distance between them and their lay kinsmen. When reform of the church imposed clerical celibacy, all clergy had perforce to enter holy orders from secular life. They joined a privileged order of bachelors, ruled by leaders from their own ranks. This international body of literate men claiming special rights, endowed collectively with great wealth, not surprisingly excited envy and resentment. In spite of this, the church played a remarkable role, unlike that of the early church before and after Constantine, and one that was often inconsistent with some of its professions of belief.

This role for the Christian church in the west might have come about anyway, irrespective of the collapse of the empire, but by analogy with what happened in the eastern empire it seems much more likely that such a privileged status for the church would not have been tolerated had the lay aristocracy continued to be cultivated and educated. The barbarian leaders of the west made so many concessions to the clergy because they wished to gain clerical support and because they felt themselves too alien in spirit from the clergy to run the church's affairs with confidence. As a result, western Europe was subjected to an experience from which it has never fully recovered, namely a separation of *potestas* (power) and *auctoritas* (authority), not known in old Rome and barely tolerated at Constantinople. The Christian church which acknowledged the claims of both God and Caesar found it difficult in practice to live with both and was often tempted to simplify the problem by a variety of means. Its special privileges in the west enabled it to act independently, up to a point. Barbarian political power, for the most part wielded without deference to any imperial tradition, could not therefore be infiltrated by men of education, but only influenced indirectly by the church's monopoly of moral exhortation. In time the Christian rulers were brought to ways that churchmen at least found more tolerable. Whereas the eastern emperor, for all his Christianity, remained confident in the nature of his ancient rights to rule and did not have to acknowledge that only the church knew the meaning of culture, learning or principle, in the west the undeniable and unwelcome facts of barbarian kingship could only be excused and justified by the churches. The search for these justifications began with reference to the kings of Israel in the Old Testament; they led directly to the revival of political theory in the late medieval schools. The Middle Ages were over when secular powers felt confident enough to dispense with such ramshackle scaffolding.

Lay and local values

Throughout this period the evidence of Christian writings tends to thrust from our attention aspects of the past that must have counted for much. Rather obviously, the rule of celibacy for the priesthood, though much respected in medieval society, was never assumed by the majority. The values of a predominantly uneducated lay society cannot be easily understood in our own modern secular world. Our secular society depends on the powers of indoctrination by universal, obligatory education – the secular counterpart of Christian teaching. Historians of the Middle Ages rely overmuch, for want of better evidence, on the values extolled in surviving vernacular literature: heroic and aristocratic. Medieval writers' preoccupations with war and love, duty and loyalty, kinship and honor; their assumption of a social hierarchy, always thought to be ancient and natural; the rather unimpressive, seemingly ornamental role played by the clergy in such stories: these features may all suggest the outlook of a very small charmed circle of nobles without giving any clues as to more popular values. Enough is known about these societies to suggest that dividing them by classes falsifies their essentially local character. Lords may have shared an international ideal, but their pride was in their names, their lordships. If they chose brides from other lordly families, they also made war on one another: they had no ''class'' interest against other classes. Though separated in rank from their immediate neighbors, they belonged with them in other respects – speaking the same vernacular, defending with arms the same territory. If their basic assumptions were mainly military, it is in modern armies that their social bonding has comparable features; in the separation of men by rank and in the promotion of *esprit de corps*.

The great senatorial families of the Roman empire had had possessions throughout its extent; they lost them when from the 5th century they accepted the facts of local barbarian protection that confined their movements. From that time the universal was swamped by the local. The Carolingian nobility was thinly spread around the empire as a governing group, but it was rapidly absorbed into the localities it governed, to constitute feudal principalities. Norman lords in England and Ireland totally replaced old loyalties with new ones. Local and personal connections invariably prevailed in the long term over all attempts to set up an international order. This was bound to happen among peoples without formal education. In modern times, when education has become the preferred means to social advancement, the absence of formal schooling in the Middle Ages seems highly damaging. But at that time formal education, being only the form of apprenticeship reserved for the clergy, had no such desirable status, except in clerical eyes. The well-being of society more obviously rested upon the willingness of each community to work together effectively, in the village, estate or town. Every local society had to promote its own interests and seek outlets for its own talents. There was no hope of rescue or encouragement from outside. Each individual recognized that the group wielded more power and carried more weight. The lone voice was not that of the righteous prophet, but heretical vainglory. In modern times the contrary is true and

Two details from the Devonshire hunting tapestries, designed c. 1420–30 at Arras or Tournai. Noble families acquiring tapestries for comfort and color in their houses appreciated designs showing their favored pastimes, such as hunting. Against a decorous background of dogs, boars, birds and flowers, the fashionably dressed huntsman and lady show how display prevailed over practical considerations. The search for elegance in clothing had become as international as the market for Arras tapestries by the early 15th century.

the modern sympathy with heretics and eccentrics in the Middle Ages makes it more difficult to understand their standards of value. The communal circumstances of men's working lives proved the value of cooperative effort. The origin of this social attitude may be traced back to barbarian conditions, where cultural values could only be transmitted orally. Barbarian tribal society cannot, however, have been without individualistic elements. The most ancient reflections of its ideals in heroic poetry single out great warriors for their personal prowess. If they are folk heroes, symbols of their nations, the effects of their inspiration must have left a personal mark. The barbarians bore only one name, personal to themselves, whereas by their names civilized Romans declared their membership of clan and family. If single personal names at first sufficed, the social units must themselves have been small. When the social group expanded, there grew up the modern system of fixed surnames, derived from father, provenance or trade, simple devices appropriate to medieval conditions. These ancestors of modern Europe have also bequeathed us the basis of modern costume, with men in trousers and women in skirts; Roman garb disappeared even in the Mediterranean region. By the 15th century at the latest the basic shapes were already vulnerable to the spread of international fashions and the wit and extravagance of artful designers. The variations possible at a less sophisticated level are nonetheless revealed by peasant costumes, even homespuns, which remained distinctive by locality.

The enrichment of every locality capable of it eventually generated a new kind of political and economic order, in which the old local organizations became restrictive. Such medieval communities, however large or small, hampered all schemes for reviving an effective universal empire, secular or clerical. And modern Europeans have never been able to live down their medieval past or reestablish the concept of universal citizenship on which the old Roman empire depended. The different histories of these long-lived communities show by what varied means, from what different dates and over what lengths of time their peoples attained political coherence. No formula can explain all cases. For every general rule there will be exceptions. Commonly, however, each group expressed some unity in terms of vernacular speech, and in the use of that speech in writing. The use of the vernacular owed much to the encouragement of the learned clergy, such as preachers, who by the late Middle Ages had everywhere undertaken a massive program of public religious instruction, by sermons, by schooling and by the writing and dissemination of works of edification. The clergy, who learned Latin to master the profoundest studies of human science, saw fit to communicate the most valuable parts of it to others. The unlearned, stimulated to some degree, began to educate themselves at least to read books in the vulgar tongue. Though the most resolute disciples would go on to master Latin, a decent level of attainment did become possible in many vernacular languages (though not in all) and so prepared the way for the eventual collapse of the preeminence accorded for centuries to both Latin and the clergy. To this extent the Middle Ages marks not only the period of clerical dominance in education, but also, by the clergy's encouragement of the vernacular, of a popular language culture too. In this respect the medieval period differs radically from that of the Roman empire, where in most parts of the west the old languages disappeared and were replaced with popular speech derived from imperial Latin itself. Medieval civilization failed therefore to impose a language of its own: it only set up an order within which all the peoples of Europe learned how to use their tongues.

PART ONE
DISINTEGRATION OF THE ANCIENT WORLD

THE ROMAN WORLD AND ITS ENEMIES

The substance of Rome's empire

The Roman empire of the 4th century gave political unity to the basin of the Mediterranean. To the south it was bounded by the Atlas mountains and the desert. To the east, likewise, the desert acted, along with the effective power of the Persian empire, to define the reach of Roman government. To the north the frontier could not be so easily defined by unalterable facts of life, but since the time of Augustus (23 BC–14 AD) the limits had been drawn from the North Sea to the Black Sea along the line of the Rhine and Danube. To this empire were subsequently added only the provinces of Britain, Mauretania, Arabia and Dacia by the early 2nd century. The impulse to extend the empire had notably dried up from the time of Augustus himself, for the very obvious reason that a Mediterranean civilization which had already brought together in one government all the shores of the inner sea could have no motive to expand beyond the limits required for its own security. It had no interest in the possibilities for conquest or colonization beyond those limits, which were, to the north, as was proved in Britain, rather further than nature had intended the Mediterranean style of life to reach.

Political unity achieved in the last resort by military means proved to be enduring because it put an end to the political competition and rivalry that had beset the Mediterranean for centuries. With Roman government was spread the veneer of Roman civilization, but the empire was composed of many peoples with civilizations older than Rome itself and in two or three centuries Roman peace had not necessarily gone very far towards undermining older cultures. The imperial system affected most the great landed families of the senatorial class who held lands all over the empire and regarded themselves as the main beneficiaries of the system. Their cultural ideals and models they took from Rome itself at its cultural apogee in the Augustan age. Even for them, however, the Latin language and Roman law had to acknowledge the prestige of Greek as the language of intellectual culture and commerce, particularly in the eastern Mediterranean. Throughout the empire other local languages were in general use for unofficial purposes. The advantages of the empire could not be denied, but political unity had not even tried to eradicate differences, only to superimpose a means of managing the whole.

An empire that had continued to grow, if only fitfully, by military means was ill-prepared for a mainly conservative role, in which soldiering became a matter of frontier patrols or the suppression of civil disorders. Changes in the army and attitudes to its role had to be matched by civilian adaptations as well. If ideals had served to establish the imperial system, idealism turned in other than a political direction once a peaceful world-order had been established. The empire that ceased to expand could not be frozen into immutability. For Edward Gibbon the imperial government of the Antonines (96–180) had achieved a system which was unique because the emperors were dedicated to the service of humanity; if this was the apogee of political perfection, it could only be followed by decline and fall. But this is to impose a criterion both anachronistic and unreal. The empire continued to change from within as human communities necessarily must. Its problems would have been no fewer if it had continued with conquests into unpromising and uncoveted lands. Nor could it attempt to stifle changes within for fear of enemies taking advantage of its weaknesses. Its enemies without seemed remote and contemptible. This is not to deny that the military, civil and imperial authorities may have shouldered their burdens less conscientiously and intelligently than their dependants had reason to require. Due allowance must also be made for the difficulties of adapting to a new situation by persons whose education and ideals tended to make them look back rather than forward. The problems facing the empire could not be solved by great men, however virtuous or wise. Roman civilization had entered a critical phase. In a sense the empire had completed one task: that of bringing into fruitful contact the many civilizations of the Mediterranean. It then inevitably became involved in the process of gestating another, one that would admit the peoples beyond the frontiers to some of the benefits. As time was to show, the empire itself was not necessary to or even compatible with the completion of that process.

Barbarian irruptions, wanderings and ephemeral kingdoms

The peoples who most earnestly desired to share in the advantage of Roman peace lived beyond the northern frontiers. Their first breach of the frontier came in 166 but was resolutely opposed. In the mid-3rd century a much more serious and protracted Germanic invasion occurred all along the northern frontier, which the army could not counter. The empire was overrun by barbarians: Belgium (259), Gaul (268–78), Italy (260–70), Thrace, Greece and Asia Minor (258–69). About the same time the Persians defeated and captured the emperor Valerian (260). The empire appeared to have reached its term. Yet it not only survived; it went on under the emperor Diocletian (284–304) to effect a radical reorganization of its government, and under Constantine (313–36) to establish a new capital at Constantinople and come to a new understanding with the Christian church. The 4th-century empire appears therefore to be in some respects in a very vigorous condition.

Twentieth-century historians, who not surprisingly tend to be impressed by the evidence for the serious economic difficulties of the empire, are inclined to believe that draconian measures for enforcing tax payments alienated the local digni-

Europe's natural advantages
The Mediterranean basin had been settled and exploited by many peoples over several millennia before the Roman empire took shape. North of the Alps the possibilities of the land for settlement had not been tested to the same degree. Less sedentary peoples, still more dependent on hunting for their food and resources, seminomadic by inclination, initially preferred to settle in the Roman empire rather than civilize their forests. The extent of the forest cover cannot be mapped precisely, though there is no doubt of its importance and its steady exploitation throughout the Middle Ages. Medieval towns, even Venice, were built of more wood than stone. By modern standards human settlements were small distinct communities, separated from one another by the natural reserves from which they lived. The siting of their villages, towns and churches required careful consideration of the elements necessary for defense, water supply and cultivation. Sites were changed if found to be unsuitable. The settlements were vulnerable, not only to enemies, but to natural disasters and conflagrations. Their resources for bullying nature were limited, so they had to be quick to spot the natural advantages of each place, if their efforts were to be crowned with success. They were not usually tempted into high mountains, which became refuges rather than barriers. Otherwise they gradually spread everywhere. The many rivers draining into different seas offered opportunities for many different societies to prosper. Every part of Europe proved to be capable of sustaining settled agriculture – even the Magyars accepted it in place of their old nomadic life. When the continent's population became numerous enough to penetrate every part of it, the nomadic life of the steppe was also arrested on the eastern limits of European culture.

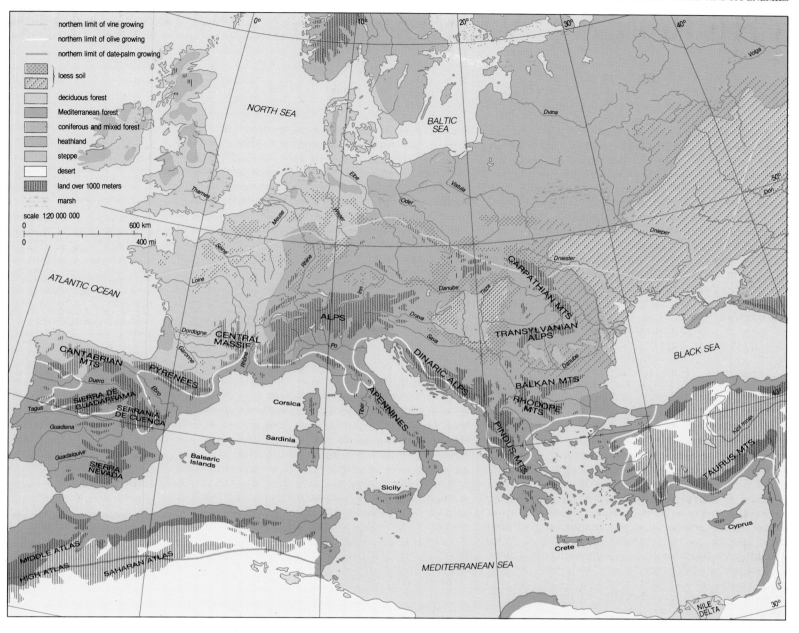

taries they burdened. Looking for reasons to explain the fall of the empire exposes all its points of weakness to scrutiny. The empire in the 4th century was no more perfect than in preceding centuries, but it showed considerable powers of recuperation. Inasmuch as the empire continued to function for centuries in the east, and to inspire for a long time to come in the west, it was thanks to the work of Diocletian and Constantine. The strength of their reforms was put to the test after 376 when barbarian pressure on the northern frontier was resumed. Though historians may trace the collapse of the western empire from this point, contemporaries, not knowing the future, were impressed rather with the capacity of the empire to deal with the barbarians as they arrived, in contrast to the situation in the previous century.

This period of barbarian migrations into the western empire, which extended over two centuries, is rather better known than the shorter and very destructive generation of barbarian turmoil in the 3rd century, not only because its consequences have earned it intense historical investigation, but also because the flourishing condition of imperial

letters and history has left far more evidence about it. The scale of our information enables us to measure the size of the problem without answering most of our questions.

One of the major difficulties is that, given the belief of the civilized within the empire that there were only barbarians outside it, the period is initially described in terms of incompatible peoples set in opposition. One of the barbarous aspects of the invaders was their indifference to writing and formal education, so that historians are obliged to see them mainly from the point of view of literate Romans. Of the invaders' own outlook, motives and history, even of their common barbarian features, it is difficult to speak with confidence. Most of those who appeared in the western empire during the period 376–568 did so, however, under acknowledged leaders, usually seeking to settle inside the empire with imperial blessing, or at all events with political objectives and some political skills: they were not savages. To this extent it appears that after the barbarians had been pushed back beyond the frontiers by emperors Valerian (253–60) and Probus (276–82) they had then learned something during the century of their exclusion from the empire. But whereas the transformations wrought by Diocletian are known to us, those of his German contemporaries can only be inferred.

The movements of Germanic peoples within the northern lands beyond the Roman frontiers cannot be described with any precision, though there are enough indications to suggest that they were both frequent and important. However, after their irruption into the empire in the mid-3rd century, the Goths, to whom the emperor Aurelian abandoned Dacia in 271, appear to have settled to a more ordered kind of life to the north of the river Danube, and for a century to have lived as neighbors to the empire without notable incident; like other peoples across the frontiers these Visigoths provided recruits for the Roman army. In 332 a treaty between the Romans and the Goths

regulated relations for 35 years, during which Ulfila, a Goth, began the conversion of his people to (Arian) Christianity, providing them with both writing and a vernacular Bible. There was nothing untoward in this conversion since Arianism at the time enjoyed the support of the emperor in the east. Its condemnation in the west eventually secured a victory for Orthodoxy over Arianism after 381 which permanently damaged the reputation of the Arians and gave them a name for religious crudity that is probably quite unfair. (Arius, an Alexandrian priest, had raised questions about the nature of the relationship between God the Father and God the Son in the Trinity. This controversy led to the formulation of the creed at the Council of Nicaea (325) and provoked the minds of the greatest theologians of the age, such as Athanasius. Whatever the rights and wrongs of Arius's

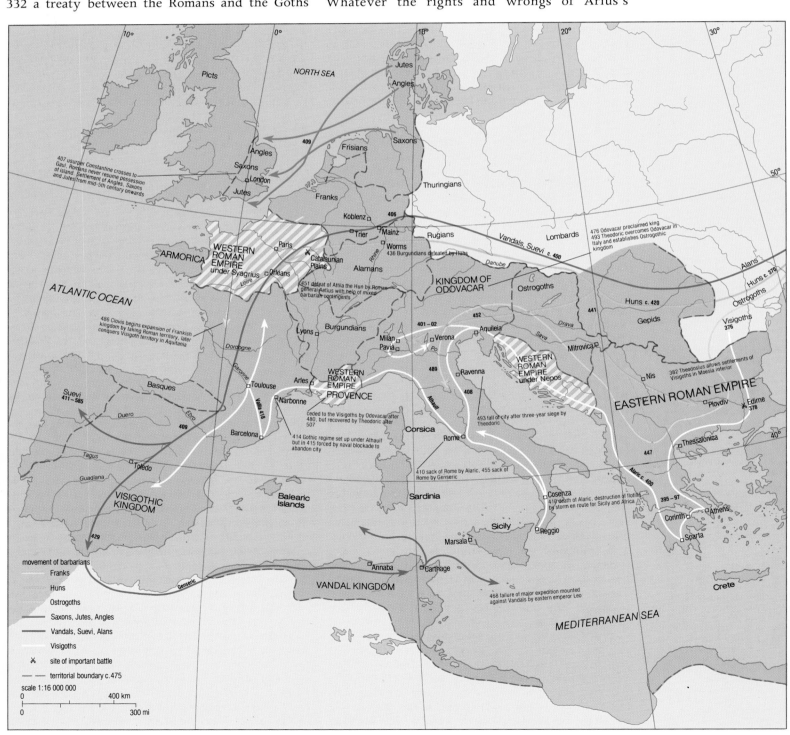

teachings, the issues involved were far from trivial.)

Other Goths (Ostrogoths) appear to have established a settled life on the lower Don, of which almost nothing is known until 375 when the Huns destroyed their state. Panic-stricken, the Ostrogothic remnant streamed to the west where they inspired the Visigoths with their fears of the Huns. Here the Gothic refugees divided into two groups: the smaller, moving north, lived in submission to the Huns; the larger preferred to seek asylum within the empire and were received and settled in Thrace (376). They remained strong enough however to react violently against the treatment to which they were subjected; once outcasts, they rapidly became terrible enemies of the empire, defeating and killing the emperor Valens at Adrianople (Edirne) in 378. They immediately proceeded to the siege of the capital city, Constantinople, and though this was saved by the emperor Theodosius, who also reestablished the Danube frontier, the Visigothic army was left to wander through the Balkans. This was the origin of the Visigoth problem for which the government found no better remedies than treaties of settlement which failed to keep them in Moesia (382) or Epirus (397).

The Visigoths' chief, Alaric, obtained the imperial office of *magister militum* (master of the soldiers) in Illyricum as the eastern emperor tried to shift him to the west out of his own jurisdiction. In 401 Alaric led his people into Italy. For 11 years they pillaged in the peninsula, and even sacked Rome (410) before resuming their march westwards under Alaric's brother-in-law, Athaulf. Frustrated in their hopes of an imperial commission in Gaul, they seized Narbonne, Toulouse and Bordeaux (413), and Athaulf married the emperor's sister whom he held as a hostage. Although a Visigothic regime was set up at Bordeaux, Athaulf's people remained restless and they were tempted into Spain by an imperial proposal to attack the Vandals there. After this the Visigoths did give up their wanderings. An agreement with the empire negotiated in 416 brought them back into Gaul where their barbarian kingdom was installed in the region between Bordeaux and Toulouse with official approval, and they restored Narbonne to the empire, thus providing the government with a corridor between Spain and Provence. This Visigothic regime survived in Gaul for nearly a century, expanding into Spain on its own account in the late 5th century and eventually taking refuge there after the Frankish victories over them in Gaul. In Spain the Visigothic kingdom lasted till 711. The Visigoths were the first barbarians to trouble the western empire and their power lasted longest.

By the time the Visigoths arrived in Gaul the western empire had already experienced the devastating consequences of other Germans breaking across the Rhine frontier and across Gaul into Spain. In this situation the Roman army in Britain crossed to Gaul proclaiming a new emperor, Constantine III, who was soon tied down by responsibilities there. From this point Roman government may have been suspended in Britain, even if relations across the Channel were not. In 395 the empire was divided between the two young sons of the emperor Theodosius, and actual power was wielded by their military leaders. In practice,

whether the politicians and generals were incompetent, treacherous or unlucky, they failed to master events or barbarians; but to describe what ensued as the fall of the Roman empire explains nothing. The Visigoths played as large a part in the process as any group, yet they never set out to destroy the empire, defy the emperor or subvert the state. Their case is however instructive, for it shows the extraordinary ability of their group to blunder about in the empire for 40 years without breaking up, their unwillingness to settle for long in one place and their ability to live by pillage within the empire that protected them from their original enemies, the Huns. Their leaders could only aim for imperial recognition as military leaders, or through treaties of settlement, which their peoples or themselves were reluctant to respect. The government for its part tried to avoid commitments with them: it was the emperor Honorius's refusal to negotiate for the safety of Rome that drove them in exasperation to sack the city in revenge in 410. In a sense the government must have anticipated or simply hoped that the Visigothic band would wear itself away, possibly on Alaric's death. Neither side expected them to settle down in a barbarian kingdom within the empire, for such a course was unprecedented. Indeed by the time this was achieved, they had compromised their own position and become Roman military allies. Their first king, Theodoric I (ruled 418–51), died fighting with the Romans against Attila, ruler of the Visigoths' great enemies, the Huns.

The Visigoths had shown no interest in acting politically except on behalf of their own group, but just what really kept this group together is difficult to say. An exile army wandering in the empire for 40 years must have recruited new members over the years. It is unlikely to have been satisfied with its own Visigothic women. Culturally it may have kept its distance from the Roman population to preserve its Arian Christianity, but the main cohesion to this force must have been provided by its leadership, and its Visigothic character rested essentially with

The funerary stele of a warrior from Hornhausen near Magdeburg, c. 700. Despite its barbaric and pagan provenance, the idea of commemorating a dead warrior in stone funerary sculpture comes from the Mediterranean world and the craftsman's skill in depicting both warrior and horse has no parallel in barbaric art.

its royal family and its noble leaders. The Goths as a whole had thus acquired some political coherence in the century before 376, for it was essentially this that kept their force in being within the empire and shaped the Visigoths' destiny after 418. To what extent they otherwise insisted on maintaining their tribal purity is unknown, but it is likely that they accepted recruits and followers from whatever quarter they came.

Despite their years of peaceful settlement along the Danube, the Visigoths once within the empire hardly behaved as though agriculture attracted them more than soldiering. The Germans of the northern frontier region however were known to the Romans both as soldiers and as farmers and which of their activities loomed larger would depend upon many variables in the local situation. When in 406 a great body of mixed Germans forced

the Rhine crossing near Koblenz, some of them quickly streamed across Gaul into Spain; others with different ambitions settled down within the frontier to cultivate rather than pillage. The mounting pressure of these many German groups on the frontier in the late 4th century is most plausibly explained by their fear of the Huns who had installed themselves in Pannonia beyond the Danube c. 390, though there can be no proof of this. At this stage the empire itself feared little from the Huns, people of the steppe, amenable to imperial suggestions about cooperating against the Germans, who showed no inclination to settle in the empire and whose raiding could normally be controlled. On the other hand the Germans beyond the frontier were more vulnerable to Hun attacks and preferred the security of the empire, though some, by streaming into Spain, thought no distance too great to put between themselves and the Huns.

The most successful peoples who crossed the frontier in 406 were the Vandals and the Burgundians, both of whom established barbarian kingdoms lasting over a century. The Vandals, threatened with a Roman offensive in southern Gaul, escaped into Spain (409) where civil unrest facilitated their conquest. They divided up the country among themselves and their allies, the Suevi and Alans, but the arrival of the Visigoths, first on their own account and then as Roman allies, rapidly changed the situation. The Vandals were crushed, leaving forces only in the northwest. From there they later escaped to the south (419) and took to the sea, embarking on the conquest of Africa, together with the remnant of the Alans, which, of the original barbarian invaders, left only the Suevi in the west. The Suevi established their own kingdom with its base at Braga. Though this lasted till 585, its history is quite obscure after their expansion had been checked by the Visigothic invasion which drove them back into the far west in 464. Far more impressive was the Vandal kingdom set up in Africa, from which Genseric menaced Italy. The emperor Valentinian III bought peace by recognizing the position in 442, but Genseric until his death in 477 kept up the pressure on Rome and the Roman Christians in North Africa, expropriating the landlords and bishops for the benefit of his army. The Roman province furthest from the Rhine frontier became the most ruthlessly governed by any of the barbarians.

By contrast, the Burgundians made only a modest showing after they crossed the frontier in 406. Like the Vandals they had lived for a long period across the northern frontier and unlike them they appear to have been more receptive to Roman influence. After 406, instead of joining the Vandals, they rapidly took service with Romans in the empire, first with a short-lived usurper, Jovinus, then under the emperor Honorius. With him they made a pact (413) which granted them part of Gaul near the Rhine. This kingdom lasted till 436 when the Roman general Aetius used the Huns to destroy it, in order to frustrate its ambitions in the lower Rhineland. The Burgundians had shown themselves to be relatively unadventurous, and were easily disposed of when they looked dangerous. However, Aetius still valued their services as soldiers and used them to the east against the Alamans. Then in 443 they were transferred to the region of Geneva. For a number of years they served as Roman auxiliaries both against the Huns (451) and against the Spanish Suevi in the campaign led by the Visigoths in 456. On their return however they finally appear to have taken the initiative in Gaul by seizing the imperial provinces of Lyons I and Vienne. The brief campaign (in 457) of the emperor Majorian was insufficient to act as more than a temporary check on them and after his departure they occupied the town of Lyons itself. From their bases at Lyons and Geneva they created a sizable kingdom for themselves, but one in which they obtained the willing support of the Gallo-Roman aristocracy. By then they were regarded as traditional friends of Rome offering the locals their best hope of protection in the absence of the emperor. Although their kings were Arians, they even remained on good terms with the Catholic bishops of the kingdom, notably

Avitus of Vienne, until Clovis the Frank became a Catholic (507), when the clergy turned without scruple to him as an even more acceptable protector. This kingdom, where the Romans and Burgundians enjoyed almost equal status, lasted just as long as it suited the Roman, Catholic populations and it disappeared altogether under Clovis's sons in 534.

Both the Vandal and the Burgundian kingdoms came to an end in 534. Both proved incapable of establishing more than an ephemeral kingship over populations which, whether treated well or badly, remained by religion and culture hostile to the barbarians and confident, if not of their military power, then of their superior civilization. In their different ways the Vandals and the Burgundians demonstrate the extremes open to the invading Germans: hostility and self-aggrandizement or amenability to Roman manipulation. The Germans had not the resources to remake civilization. For them the main hope of advancement was by soldiering. They would fight their Germanic enemies with greater alacrity than they fought the Romans. Neither as barbarians nor as Arians did they consider that they had more in common with one another than with the population in the empire. In their groups they acted for their own limited advantage. Faced by such people, the Romans did not fear for the long term, even if the barbarian presence was disagreeable, costly and destructive.

The dilution and displacement of Rome in northern Europe

The ability of the populations in the empire to retain their old culture despite the barbarian breakthrough appears most obvious in matters of religion and language, for only in the case of Britain did a whole province of the empire eventually become dominated by people of Germanic speech. By contrast the great German thrust across the Rhine after 406 carried the frontier of German speech no deeper than a hundred kilometers to the west, and Germans who penetrated more deeply were eventually absorbed linguistically into the local population. Of the Germans whose main purpose after 406 was to settle in large numbers within the empire, but not under any Roman protection, rather maintaining their hold on the German side and living under their own leaders, the main group were the Alamans, a name that implies a mixed group of peoples (from which the French acquired their own general word for Germans). They called themselves Swabians and their pressure to the southwest has been kept up for centuries, as the gradual shift of the language frontier can show. They were not just peaceful farmers or colonists, for their strength was a formidable cavalry force armed with a long two-edged sword. But little of the stages of their advance is recorded. Aetius used the more docile Burgundians against them, but after his death (454) they consolidated their hold on the Palatinate and Alsace across the Rhine. Expansion to the north then ran up against the Frankish rulers of Cologne and the Merovingian Clovis. The Merovingians routed the Alaman king and extended a protectorate over the northwestern part of their territory. The main thrust of their colonization now developed to the south where already they had previously raided into the Franche-Comté. After 500 they settled south of the Rhine and advanced also in Raetia with the assent of Theodoric in Italy, the Roman population moving back into the protection of the mountains. Throughout the 6th century they consolidated their hold so that by 610 they were able to occupy central Switzerland, overcoming Frankish opposition there. Only from this time were they susceptible to pressure for conversion to Christianity. The see of Constance, founded c. 590, served as a basis for an operation in which the Irish missionaries of Columbanus's school took the lead. The Alamans were thus comparable to the Anglo-Saxons in being able to pursue their colonization into Roman lands for a long time without having to make any serious compromise with Rome.

Further north in the lower Rhineland the Franks also drove out the Roman inhabitants, but the consolidation of a Frankish power, based first at Tournai and then at Soissons, meant that the rulers of these Frankish peoples took the Roman presence into account, as is proved by the fact that they were the first pagan barbarians to accept Catholic Christianity. In other respects, however, the Franks of Chilperic and Clovis, who became the military arm of the north Gallo-Roman populations, rather imitated the Burgundians who had already taken up this role after 456. These armies, like the "Roman" forces they superseded, in effect represented what was left of imperial authority, and granted that Roman armies had been recruited heavily from barbarian peoples since the 3rd century, to emphasize the contrast between the two may obscure the similarities. However, whereas a Roman general like Stilicho was a Vandal, his army was heterogeneous. It was not his people and his force that he led, whereas barbarian leaders who sought employment for their warband under the emperor could certainly count on the loyalty of their force in a way that the emperor could not. The difference between a Roman army recruited from Germans and a barbarian army with an imperial mandate was thus crucial. And until the second half of the 5th century, even in the west, the Roman armies had retained their own coherence.

The collapse of the Huns and the revival of the empire's fortunes

One of the enduring elements in this continuing engagement between the empire and the barbarians was the position of the Huns, the people who had originally pressed upon the Goths in 375. Though they did not threaten the empire from the inside, from beyond the frontier they could press upon both groups at will, relying on their horsemen to spring surprise raids. As nomadic people from the steppes, they were first mentioned in Ptolemy's *Geography* (c. 172 AD) as living by the river Dniester near the northwestern shores of the Black Sea. But they were not well known to the Romans before they fell upon the Gothic kingdom and destroyed it in 375. From southern Russia they spread into the lands north of the Danube during the next generation and, because they seemed to take no interest in settling in the empire, the emperors were happy to use them against the much more troublesome Visigoths, already within the frontiers. A few Huns did settle in Thrace and the Roman general Rufinus used them for his bodyguard. Stilicho used Huns against the Goths in Italy in 406. These Huns were drawn from a state existing under

King Uldin which stretched at least as far west as the Hungarian Danube and east into Muntenia. The Huns were perfectly capable of exploiting Roman weaknesses, as by raiding in the Balkans about the same time. They always chose their moment well and their intelligence services were obviously superior.

The internal history of their kingdom for the next two decades is obscure, but raiding continued across the Danube into Moesia, even while other Huns served with Roman leaders in the west, particularly with Aetius on occasions after 425. Aetius had been a hostage among them and knew their language and how to contract for their services, but he was not necessarily their "friend" as his enemies alleged. The Huns may actually have lacked effective leadership at this time and the successful war waged by the Romans on them in Pannonia bears out this impression.

In Attila the Huns found their most effective leader, but his power lasted less than a decade. At the time of the empire's preoccupation with Genseric's attack on Sicily (442) the Huns broke into the Balkans and pressed into Thrace. They were probably bought off with the promise of tribute, but the empire repudiated the settlement as soon as it felt free to do so. Only in 447 did Attila, who in the meantime had become sole ruler of his people by murdering his brother, demand the arrears of tribute and make war on the empire, so that the emperor had to beg for terms. Apart from tribute, Attila required the evacuation of a large territory south of the Danube from Pannonia to Svishtov, which left the empire defenseless. From there he directed his forces into Gaul, where however he was defeated by Aetius and a motley army of barbarians in 451.

The next year Attila attacked Italy, being obliged to capture Aquileia in order to advance further; however, having crossed the Po and devastated Emilia, he turned back to attack Milan and Pavia rather than press south. In northern Italy his forces contracted such wasting illness that after barely a month they withdrew. Attila had failed. When he died the next year, his kingdom fell apart. The customary dispute about the succession this time gave the subjugated Germans the opportunity to throw off three-quarters of a century of Hun control. The Ostrogoths recovered their autonomy, and their leader Valamer could think of nothing better to his purpose than a pact with the empire. This allowed him to settle in the region of Lake Balaton in Pannonia. Such an arrangement hardly suggests any serious deterioration of imperial prestige after half a century of trying to cope with insubordinate barbarians.

In one sense the optimism and patience of the imperial government were justified, for the barbarians within had no real alternative political solution to offer: though parasites on the empire, they would eventually be digested. The emperor Valentinian III made a humiliating peace (442) with the intransigent Genseric of Africa, but having acquired his son Huneric as a hostage, married him to his own daughter, expecting to make of Huneric in the next generation the instrument of Romanization among the Vandals. There are many comparable examples. To deal with barbarians beyond the frontiers had become impossible since the frontier

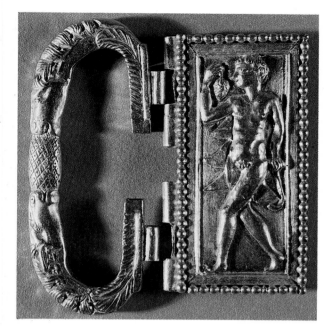

Part of the Thetford treasure, discovered in Norfolk, England, in 1979, an astonishing collection of gold and silver objects possibly deposited by a merchant in the late 4th century. The gold objects belonged to a temple of Faunus and were of continental working. The most handsome piece is this buckle, 5 cm high. The hinge is decorated with horses' heads and the rectangular plate shows a satyr with a bunch of grapes. The deposit may be explained by the disturbed conditions of the time.

in the old sense had been broken down; but in one sense the Romans had placed between them and uncertainty friendly barbarians like the Burgundians or Franks who were already trying to contain the pressure of such as the Alamans on their own account. After the unexpected collapse of the Hun empire, there were in fact no further peoples eager to invade the Germans, and when it was safe to do so the emperors would return. Though the Roman counterattack was long delayed, Justinian at last proved the good sense of Roman patience when in 533, after a hundred years of the Vandals, Africa at least reverted to the empire, like a dog to its master.

The end of imperial government north of the Alps

Roman rule was never restored to the whole of Spain, Gaul or Britain, and the reasons for this must now be considered. For though the emperors might scorn the barbarians' political abilities, they had not reckoned with the possibility that changing circumstances could permanently damage the chances for Roman recovery. The barbarians themselves became so familiar with a situation in which the imperial government proved weaker and their own hesitant authorities more confident, that they began to act with less deference. The Roman populations in the west also became adept at dealing with a situation for which the government offered no speedy remedies. Some form of accommodating both sides, barbarians and landowners (the governing class of the empire), served most principal interests at stake, though at the government's expense. The less desirable alternative to compromise was military dictatorship.

Until the middle of the 5th century the responsibility resting on Roman generals to defend the structure of the empire had been discharged adequately. There had been no persistent attempts to throw off imperial government, to create satrapies or indulge civil war. But the burdens falling on the generals were very great and the government was neither grateful nor helpful. The western emperor himself needed to be active and effective. For a time the imperial family had retained its own limited sense of the unity of the empire, despite the division of the empire into east and west between imperial brothers (395) and then cousins. With the deaths of Valentinian III in 455 and of Marcian (457) in the east, even this family nexus was rent. In the east the new emperor Leo was promoted by the Alan general Aspar. In the west Avitus was put up by the Visigothic king Theodoric II, but was soon obliged by Ricimer, the military commander of Italy, to renounce the glory; his valiant successor, Majorian, also appeared too successful to Ricimer who had him assassinated (461). After Majorian the emperors of the west had no effect on its government, whether sent from the east or, as was more normal, nominated by the generals. After Majorian no emperor had authority in Gaul, still less in Britain or Spain.

Without support in Gaul the empire of the west stretched no further than Italy. By the time of Majorian's death the Roman Lyonnais had already chosen the amenable Burgundians as their protectors. Further north the authority of Aetius (assassinated 454) passed to Syagrius who for 25 years ruled independently. His "kingdom" was annexed by Clovis after battle. When Clovis became a Catholic, the Romans of the Lyonnais cheerfully preferred him to the Burgundians. They had learned to consult their own interests and make what terms they could without recourse to the emperor at all. Individuals who suffered losses and indignities in the process are likely to have been heavily outnumbered by others who came to terms with the barbarian rulers. In Gaul at least they were spared the worse fate of the Romano-British, who had to abandon their best lands to the English invaders and settlers. The advance of that settlement was delayed by a Romano-British victory at Mons Badonicus, but the invaders were neither repulsed nor assimilated and after a time the English resumed their pressure on the Roman remnant. Nothing so ignominious happened in Gaul. But Roman civilization was not salvaged by the empire, by political, administrative or military means. It was salvaged by the landowners through their villas and their churches. The empire no longer mattered. The Visigothic king of Toulouse had shared in the defeat of Attila and had supported the Roman emperorship of Avitus. After the death of Majorian the kingdom under the brothers Theodoric II (453–66) and Euric (466–83) resented efforts to contain it. Euric extended his lands to the Loire (470), across the Rhône into Provence (477) and across the Pyrenees into Spain, which he subdued. Only the Arianism of the Visigoths justified their expulsion from Gaul by Clovis and their isolation thereafter in Spain. But Gaul itself had begun to fall apart and the successor states impeded all chance of restoring Romanism in the west. Except in Italy.

The fate of Italy

Italy itself experienced the worst barbarian invasion under Alaric in 401, but after the Visigoths left for Gaul it suffered only the brief invasion of Attila in 452 and had managed therefore to continue the modes of Roman life. Its well-being was most threatened by the belligerence of Genseric, operating from North Africa after c. 440. Difficulties about the imperial succession after 461 gave barbarian generals in charge of the Roman army in Italy fresh responsibilities. Ricimer (Suevus), Gondebaud (Burgundian) and Oreste (from Pannonia) discharged their duty, or covered their usurpations, by nominating shadow emperors not acknowledged at Constantinople. When Constantinople sent a new emperor, Anthemius (467–72), to the west, his bodyguard was Odovacar, who was elected king by the army of Italy in 476. He deposed the nominal emperor of the west, who had anyway not been recognized at Constantinople (476), and was eventually recognized as patrician by the emperor of the east, Zeno. For more than 50 years Italy then enjoyed such benefits of stable government as a military dictatorship could provide, with only one disruptive period lasting three and a half years (489–92), when Odovacar fought to retain his authority against Theodoric the Ostrogoth, his eventual successor. Theodoric and Odovacar were involved in a family vendetta that gave personal animus to their rivalry, but the main reason for Theodoric's invasion of Italy was the emperor Zeno's desire to rid the eastern empire of the Ostrogoths by whatever means and the pleasure of disposing at the same time of Odovacar. Zeno was himself a "barbarian," an Isaurian brought in to deal with Aspar the Alan general who aimed to rule in Constantinople. Theodoric himself later enjoyed no better favor at Constantinople than his predecessor, but he lived out his time because the eastern empire had finally dealt with all the undesirable barbarian groups in its own lands and had no more to banish to the west. After Theodoric's death the eastern empire felt strong enough to set about the recovery of Italy in earnest.

Theodoric's reputation rests upon the achievements of his own reign (493–526), better documentation (his advisers and administrators included Cassiodorus and Boethius, both famous as scholars and writers) and his place in Germanic legend. As a result Odovacar has been rather overshadowed. In essence their manner of government was identical. Theodoric's army of Ostrogoths was as composite a band of barbarians as Odovacar's. Both were kings, but not of nations. Kingship was for their soldiers; to the emperor they were only generals: *magistri militum*. Odovacar had obtained lands for his troops on the familiar basis of "hospitality." Landed proprietors in Italy assigned a third of their lands to the barbarians or paid a third of their revenues to the state for maintaining the army. The Romans and their barbarian "hosts" were legally associates, *consortes*, but whether the barbarians were cultivators or only beneficiaries is not clear. Their lands were chiefly in the Po valley, around Ravenna, in Tuscany, Picenum and Samnium with a few garrisons in Campania and Dalmatia. This system was used by Theodoric for his Germans, and not unnaturally he attracted recruits for his army from all over the Germanic world, where in more than 30 years of rule he achieved an unprecedented reputation as the successful Germanic leader. He aimed to keep his Germans apart from his Roman subjects by administrative dualism. By remaining faithful to the Arianism of his people he made it impossible for the Romans to believe completely in his professions of respect for Roman civilization. His Roman officials, notably Cassiodorus, served him and their own interests as best they could by

rhetoric. As a builder Theodoric also modeled himself on his Roman predecessors. His regime proved to be difficult to eradicate after his death, though it had never become popular. Its basic intention of protecting separate Roman and German peoples betrays a fear that without such an artificial system the Germans would inevitably be absorbed and emasculated by the superior numbers and culture of the Romans. This may reflect Theodoric's own personal anxieties, for he had been sent as a child hostage to Constantinople where he had learned to appreciate Roman civilization, but without wishing to give up his innate Germanness. Odovacar had allowed the Visigoths to occupy Arles in 477 and received the refugees who left Noricum in 488, renouncing therefore remoter outposts for the defense of Italy. He had however profited from the death of Marcellinus, the leader of a Dalmatian army comparable to his own, by dividing up its force in conjunction with Zeno. Theodoric's empire therefore included lands beyond Italy, extending into Dalmatia, Illyricum, Pannonia and Raetia, though in places it was a protectorate rather than the exercise of direct authority.

When the Visigoths were defeated by Clovis, Theodoric took over the management of Provence on behalf of the threatened kingdom of his Visigoth grandson, though he was himself married to Clovis's sister. Theodoric, like most Germans, took little interest in maritime power. He abandoned the islands, except eastern Sicily, to the Vandals, whose ruler Thrasamund (496–523) married Theodoric's sister and in policy imitated his brother-in-law. Theodoric's alliances with the great barbarian rulers of his day and his own central position in Italy made him alive to the possibility of building up a quasi-imperial position for the Germans in the west. It is however also possible that the heterogeneous character of his German force prevented him from adopting the nationalist manner of most barbarian kings. His Ostrogoths had suffered many reverses of fortune in the hundred years before he had led them to a kingdom within the empire. His forces in Italy lacked the cohesion acquired by the Franks, Visigoths and Vandals from their spectacular achievements in war and diplomacy. Theodoric achieved a personal prestige only paralleled later by Charlemagne among barbarians, but his people basked in no reflected glory. Above all, to cultivate his image as a Roman betrayed the inveterate weakness of the Germans within the empire: politically they could do no better than imitate the Romans. Within the empire they were so outnumbered and outclassed that they could neither set up autonomous communities nor impose their own type of regime. German kingships might suit Germans, but Romans required something more and were still sufficiently strong to make sure they got it. The Roman empire, admittedly, was no longer what it had been, but it had not disappeared into historical limbo. In Italy at least it still set the standard for political organization and in Constantinople gave every sign of still acting effectively.

Endurance and change in the eastern empire

The history of the eastern empire during the 5th century may appear uneventful by comparison with the west, but by the end of the century it could

Top The Probianus diptych, from the abbey of Essen-Werden, c.400. In this second part of the diptych Probianus is shown installed as Vicar of the Roman Prefect, wearing tunic and chlamys, office attire of Roman civil servants. He carries the act of his appointment and signs it with his stylus. He is accompanied by two scribes and congratulated by two officials below. In the background is a tablet with portraits of the emperors Arcadius and Honorius. The continued functioning of the Roman empire is here encapsulated.

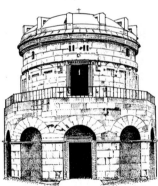

Above Theodoric's tomb at Ravenna, c.526. The dome, a single block of limestone, covers the great ruler in a traditionally Germanic manner. For the rest the building is in the Roman manner, though the workmen probably came from Syria. Originally a gallery on the upper story must have made the mausoleum more impressive than it now appears, but art historians have long disputed what exactly it looked like.

Top The church of St Simeon, c.470. At the time this was the most grandiose church ever built in Syria. Cruciform in plan, with each of the four arms in the form of a basilica, the central crossing was originally covered by a timber dome, erected over the pillar where St Simeon Stylites had spent the last years of his life. This was a church built to celebrate his cult and accommodate his devotees.

Above A 6th-century gold plaque of St Simeon. The saint is shown on his column, with the ladder used by those who wished to consult him. The great snake was the form taken by the devil who tempted him.

be seen that its tribulations had been very great and to some extent similar. It was not cynicism that made emperors encourage the unruly barbarians entering the empire to leave for the west. The Visigoths caused more trouble to the emperors in their 26 years in the east than they did in the west, where they were eventually settled on what seemed a satisfactory basis within 18 years. The west was less densely populated and had fewer vulnerable cities than the east. But where the west was thickly populated, as in North Africa, Vandal occupation there aroused profound disquiet in the east. An expensive expedition was sent under the emperor Leo I in the late 460s to deal with it and, though the operation failed, the project to recover Africa was not forgotten. The east had also had to bear the brunt of Hun attacks, since it was not until 451/2 that Attila had turned on the west. The Ostrogoths who thereafter emerged from Hun tutelage did not take long to use their muscle against the empire. Their leader, Theodoric, though raised in Constantinople as a hostage, used his culture to drive a hard bargain. Alternately allies and bullies, the Ostrogoths wore out Leo I and Zeno before the latter found the chance of setting them against Odovacar, Theodoric's personal enemy and Zeno's independent general in Italy. The emperors themselves had been threatened in their capital, which was, unlike Rome in the west, the nerve center of the administration. In their palaces they had been overawed by their generals, from Rufinus tutor of Arcadius I to Aspar who had installed the emperor Leo I, much as Ricimer made emperors in the west. However, the eastern emperor could still find ways of asserting himself. To become his own master Leo I had his protector assassinated, after he had found an ally in the Isaurian chief who married his daughter,

took the Greek name Zeno and succeeded him as emperor in 474. As a foreigner Zeno was unpopular and was promptly overthrown, but within two years he was restored to live out his time (476–91). The eastern empire survived for another thousand years because it could attract and keep capable emperors of many diverse origins. The problems of the eastern frontier naturally committed the empire to more regular campaigning, against the power of Persia, than anything known on the Rhine-Danube frontier; the interests of eastern Anatolia were not unnaturally uppermost in calculations of policy. Imperial support of Armenia in the 4th century, although it protected Christianity there, did not suffice to create a military bulwark in the far northeastern corner of the empire.

The Greco-Roman element in the empire might have to make way for less civilized soldiers and emperors, but in other respects its "civilizing" power had lost none of its zeal. The separation of the east from the west tended to exalt Greek rather than Latin in the east, but the Roman cultivation of law was still vigorous. The first great codification of imperial edicts since Constantine was published in Latin in 438: the *Codex Theodosianus*. Nevertheless the main intellectual interests of the day concerned theology and the emperors could not, and did not try to, sidestep problems that excited both profound and popular attention. At Constantinople both emperor and patriarch intended to maintain the leading position of the church of the New Rome in the east, recognized in a decree of the Council of Constantinople in 381. But where in the west the unique prestige of Rome was unassailable, at Constantinople the patriarch had to contend not only with the pretensions of much older sees than his own, like those of Antioch and Alexandria, but also with the passions of monks and people, and the sophisticated speculations of theology. The teaching of the school of Antioch about the two separate natures of Christ was propounded at Constantinople when Nestorius became patriarch (428). It was immediately challenged by Cyril, the patriarch of Alexandria, who secured the condemnation of Nestorius as a heretic at the Council of Ephesus (431) and the preeminence of his own see till after his death (444). With the support of the Roman pope Leo I, the church of Constantinople then reacted against the "monophysites" of Alexandria and at the Council of Chalcedon (451) promulgated the doctrine of the two perfect and indivisible but separate natures of Christ. This theological victory alienated many of the eastern provinces of the empire from Constantinople, which at the same time forfeited its papal support, by securing a further declaration of its own equality with Rome. This left Rome with only a primacy of honor. The eastern empire was thus preparing in the 5th century both for its successful survival and for its metamorphosis into a predominantly Greek state. In the east Greeks and foreigners continued to respect the Roman name. Only the arrogance of the west could turn the vicissitudes of empire into dissolution of its nature. The Roman state survived like a force of nature. There was no other political creation on earth comparable to it and the barbarians who squatted within its territories were only temporary blemishes on the body politic of *Roma Eterna*.

THE AFFIRMATION OF FAITH

The empire from the 5th century to the 7th

No western Roman emperor was appointed after 476, so the sovereignty of the whole empire devolved upon the ruler at Constantinople. No eastern emperor for more than 50 years was, however, in any position to take on western responsibilities. In the meantime it certainly did not seem proper at Constantinople to conclude that the empire was finished in the west. Nor had western Catholics, including the pope, any intention of allowing their eastern brethren to leave them for ever in barbarian hands, particularly since most of the barbarians in power were, apart from the Franks, Arian heretics. Theodoric the Ostrogoth, king of Italy (493–526), could not afford to disregard the eastern empire or deny the emperor's authority, for even if he enjoyed practical independence, his Catholic Roman subjects bore his rule with ill-concealed dislike. His interventions in Gaul to prop up the Arians against Clovis naturally encouraged the eastern emperor to notice the Frankish king and do him honor. Emperor Anastasius's successor, Justin (518–27), felt that his government was strong enough to repress the heresies that had weakened the empire in the 5th century, including the Arians; Theodoric had begun to fear for the future before his own death in 526. Justin's successor, Justinian (527–65), was able to follow this initiative by military intervention in North Africa, Italy and Spain. North Africa was recovered from the Vandals in a matter of months in 533. After a century of fear Rome itself was delivered from Vandal power in the Mediterranean. From Africa Justinian's general Belisarius proceeded to take the islands – Sicily, Sardinia and Corsica. He landed at Naples and entered Rome (536). Theodoric had been dead 10 years and there had been no Ostrogoth to succeed him as an astute politician, still less to deal with the novelty of direct intervention. Even so the Goths, unlike the Vandals, did not collapse altogether. Like the emperor they called on the Franks for help; they even stirred up the Persians against Justinian. The emperor's cause was hampered by his own distrust of general Belisarius and complications caused in replacing him with Narses. For 17 years Italy was a theater of war. Only in 554 was Justinian able to take charge of the country and reorganize its government through an exarch based at Ravenna. By that time Justinian's troops had beaten back a Visigoth invasion of North Africa (544) and recovered southeastern Spain as their reward for exploiting the difficulties of the Arian Visigoths there.

Justinian's reconquests in the west restored imperial control of the Mediterranean and demonstrated the remarkable powers of recovery characteristic of the empire. They have, however, generally seemed in retrospect the results of excessively grandiose ideas pursued with scant regard for prudence or economy. Involvement in the west diminished the amount of attention he

could give to the Persian revival under Khusrau I (emperor 531–79), who was more frequently bought off than confronted. Justinian also spent much money building fortresses on the eastern frontier. The empire was invaded on the European side by Slavs (534, 547, 549, 551), Bulgars (534, 538) and Huns (539–40, 559). Constantinople itself was threatened. Barbarian ravages through Illyricum, Greece and across the Aegean into Asia Minor provoked much criticism against Justinian for compromising the security of the capital and of the whole eastern empire by his ambitions in the west. No part of the empire however was permanently lost as a result of these attacks and Justinian, faithful to the long-term concept of Roman empire, could feel well satisfied that his persistence had been rewarded. Allegations against him and his most famous minister, John of Cappadocia, for bringing on financial ruin cannot be substantiated from records and depend on the testimony of the malicious contemporary historian Procopius. Justinian's concern for the trading interests of his empire at least suggests that he had enough sense of

The empire of Justinian
This map should be compared with that on p. 28 to show what Justinian accomplished in reimposing the imperial presence in the west. More than a century of separation between the governments of the eastern and western empires had not encouraged eastern emperors to shrug off their continuing responsibilities for the west. The unity of the empire and civilization was taken for granted; the barbarians' own political shortcomings and lack of resource needed no urging when the time for reconquest had come. Justinian's pattern of government shows continuity with the old empire. For the future the metropolitan cities of the provinces already stand out as places with potential as ecclesiastical centers. The map can hardly do justice to the ecclesiastical problems of the empire, or the strength and diffusion of dissident theological opinions. It may help to emphasize how much more worrying they seemed to the emperor than military campaigns against mere barbarians. The weight of Christian numbers in the east, particularly in Asia Minor, earned that part greater attention. It was vulnerable to Persian ambitions and Justinian chose to buy peace there, a policy that has been criticized, though it is hard to see what other real option was open to him.

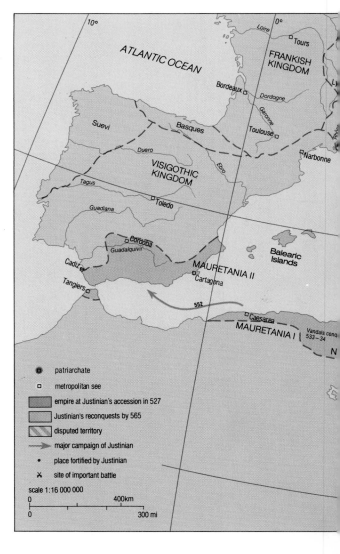

- patriarchate
- metropolitan see
- empire at Justinian's accession in 527
- Justinian's reconquests by 565
- disputed territory
- major campaign of Justinian
- place fortified by Justinian
- site of important battle

scale 1:16 000 000
0 ___ 400km
0 ___ 300 mi

economics to be capable of calculating the cost of military glory. The Persian wars interrupted commerce, particularly the China silk trade, so negotiations were started with Ethiopia in order to open up an alternative route (532). Twenty years later Justinian secured some silkworm eggs from China and began the process of silk manufacture in the empire. This rapidly became one of its most important and lucrative industries. It cannot be proved that the prosperity of the empire was compromised by the costs of war or by government actions. Justinian's personal reputation, enhanced by his responsibility for the codification of Roman law (529–34) and for building "the fairest church in all the world," the church of the Holy Wisdom (St Sophia in Constantinople, completed in 537), has consistently survived the diatribes of his detractors.

After Justinian's death in 565 his achievements did not immediately crumble, though fresh problems arose which severely strained the capacities of his less able successors. Justin II (565–78) declined to pay any more tribute to the Avars and broke with the Lombards whom his uncle Justinian had established in Noricum. While the Avars attacked the empire, the Lombards turned on the Gepids and then invaded Italy (568). The initial shock of the invasion enabled them to seize most of the Po valley by 572, but the future of their state was compromised by lack of leadership between 575 and 584 when many dukes shared power and continued the conquest piecemeal. The emperors did not resign

themselves to this new threat; once more they called on the Franks to help them in Italy. The coast and much of the interior south of the Po were defended. The Lombards were admittedly not dislodged and little by little began to gain ground. However, the empire did not lose all its lands in Italy until the 11th century, so the reimposition of imperial authority by Justinian was no transitory event in the history of the peninsula. It made it impossible for the Lombards to unite Italy under their rule as Theodoric had done; this had profound consequences for the future of that land.

In the east the fortunes of war gave the Persians occasional victories, but the empire was still capable of continuing the struggle and profiting from the Persians' own internal disputes until the reign of Phocas (602–10). Then Khusrau II defeated the empire in 604 and overran Asia Minor as far as Chalcedon opposite the capital (609); he also conquered in Syria, Jerusalem and Egypt. Only when the Persians turned back to menace the capital (619–20) did the new emperor, Heraclius (610–41), bestir himself. For six years (622–28) Heraclius was like a man inspired, driving back the Persians in Asia Minor and Armenia. Khusrau brought in the Avars to effect a joint attack on the capital, while Heraclius crossed the Black Sea to attack Persia directly. Defeated at Nineveh in 626, Khusrau could not save himself or his empire. Heraclius recovered all the territory lost in the previous 20 years. Yet by the time of his death in 641 the empire was beset

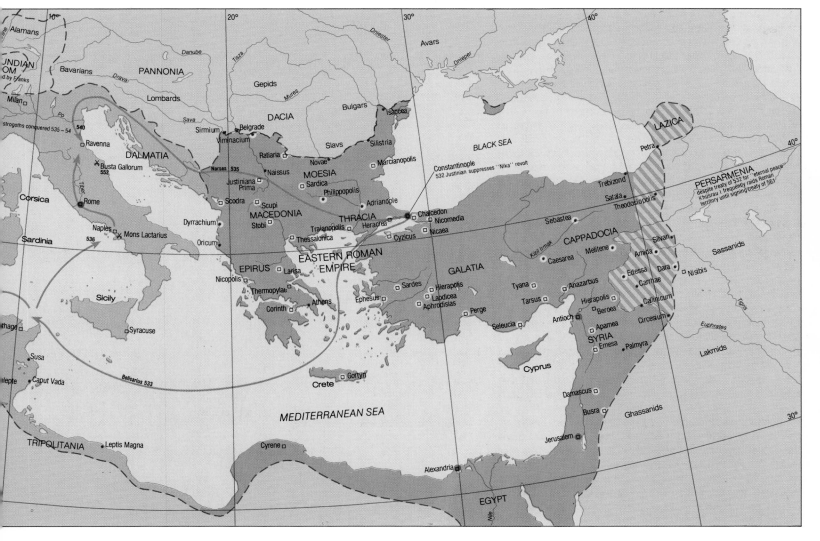

with a more terrible and durable enemy, for the Muslims had arrived in Syria in 634 (see p. 49). This time Heraclius could not stem the tide. By mid-century the Muslims had taken to the sea and captured Cyprus (649) and Rhodes. Constantinople itself was besieged three times (669, 674–80, 716–17). Though the Greek heartlands were preserved and the war carried into the Muslim camp for a time, the loss of North Africa (697) confirmed that the empire was in a parlous state. When the war was resumed in Asia Minor, the capital itself was only just saved by the first emperor of a new dynasty, Leo III (717–41). The loss of much of the most valuable, densely populated and longest-civilized parts of the empire, for example Syria and Egypt (where the three great Christian centers Alexandria, Jerusalem and Antioch passed into Muslim hands), not only depleted the empire's resources but accentuated its predominantly Greek character. In the time of Heraclius Greek had replaced Latin as the language of official acts. The empire would still recover some of its military power, but it never thereafter resumed its Roman universal mission.

Politics and the progress of faith

The spectacular collapse of the Christian empire in areas of powerful Christian sentiment has prompted historians to suspect that differences of theological opinion between the local populations and Constantinople caused them to regard the Muslims as welcome liberators, rather than as hated enemies of the faith. What is certain is that since the mid-5th century Christian orthodoxy as defined by the Roman church, even when upheld by the emperors, could not prevail against the teaching of mono-physitism which was prevalent in Egypt, Syria and Armenia (see p. 35). Several emperors took for granted a right and duty to find a religious formula to be imposed all over the empire, only to discover that it was impossible to formulate one acceptable to both Rome and Alexandria. Declarations of doctrine by emperors did not of themselves command respect. Patriarchs and even popes could be handled roughly, but their churches could not be coerced and persecutions were counterproductive. The Muslims' tolerance of Christians of all sects inevitably made their regime more acceptable to the devout than that of the orthodox emperors. The church in the west had since the 5th century shown greater powers of resilience than the empire; in the east it was the same in the 7th century. When the empire was effectively reduced to the territory of the patriarchate of Constantinople, other Christian churches preserved their own religious traditions unscathed, under Muslim rulers.

In the west the strength of Catholic religious affiliations had been shown up by the fact that when political authority had fallen into the hands of Arians the Catholic populations of Italy, Gaul, Spain and North Africa, though they had to bow before the wind, refused to be reconciled to heretics. With the conversion of Clovis the Frank to Catholicism their patience was rewarded. The subjugation of the Arian Burgundian kingdom was then followed by the defeat of the Visigoth Alaric II (507). His son Amalric was left with only the southern coast of Gaul and Spain under the protection of his grandfather Theodoric. The latter's death paved the

way for the return of the orthodox Justinian to Italy and Amalric, instead of falling back on an alliance with the Franks, managed to provoke a Merovin-gian invasion of Spain, allegedly by ill-treatment of his wife, one of Clovis's daughters. The Visigoths did not altogether lose their lands in southern Gaul, but they were obliged to make Spain the real basis of their kingdom. Their own feuding over the succession gave Justinian's forces the opportunity to reestablish Roman rule in Spain.

The Visigothic kingdom only began to retake recognizable shape under Leuvigild (567–86) who incorporated the newly converted Suevi into his kingdom. He also transferred his capital to Toledo, a provincial city in the diocese of Cartagena, which was itself held by the empire. Most of his subjects remained staunch Catholics, but he held so ob-stinately to Arianism that when his son, Hermeni-gild, became a Catholic the king refused to allow it; for him Arianism was the religion that held the Goths together as a people. Only after Leuvigild's death (586) did his successor, Reccared, make peace with the church and carry most of his people with him. Later reaction was ineffective. The alliance of interest between the Visigothic rulers (who es-tablished no royal dynasty) and the church was symbolized by an ecclesiastical ceremony of anointing the king. The Visigoths had been the most obstinate of the Arians and in an undistinguished manner the most enduring, but in the end they too had accepted that conversion and assimilation were

Above Sta Maria de Naranco, Oviedo, Spain. The palace, originally built by the Asturian king Ramiro I beneath the summit of Monte Naranco north of Oviedo, was dedicated by him as a church to the Virgin in 848. Both stories are vaulted and its construction excited considerable admiration at that time. Its proportions were inspired by those of the Camara Santa at Oviedo, built in the previous reign. However, a great many divergent interests are detectable and show the high level reached by Asturian culture at that time. The vertical emphasis and the perfect balance of the main features prove classical influence. The decorative roundels within and without use design elements derived from the east, Islam, Ireland and northern Europe. The harmony of the design blends all the diversities in a building of exceptional strength and refinement. The balustrades of the upper story balconies have fallen, but the intention of the building to afford pleasure to spectators within, as well as without, deserves to be remarked.

Isidore of Seville, from a Paris manuscript of c.800. This is the oldest known representation of Isidore, here presenting his book *Contra Judaeos* to his sister Florentina. The manuscript was copied in NE France at a time when Charlemagne had attracted many Spanish scholars to his court and when the achievements of Spanish 7th-century learning were acknowledged in the Frankish empire.

was no single Visigoth royal dynasty and few kings reigned for as long as 10 years, but the kingdom was held together; even Septimania (the Visigothic territory in southern Gaul) was retained despite some disaffection (672). The 7th century, generally so troubled in the east, in Italy and in Gaul, was for Spanish Christians remarkably successful, though darkened by repeated repression of Jews, who do not anyway appear to have been very numerous.

The growth of Frankish prominence

Clovis's conversion to Catholic Christianity, first described in the history of the Franks written by Gregory, bishop of Tours (573–94/5), may have occurred about 507 and later in his life than Gregory supposed. Its historical importance was momentous and it probably struck contemporaries even more forcefully than it has historians. Clovis was the first barbarian prepared to accept the religion of the empire, though in retrospect this seems the indispensable step for success. Unlike his Arian rivals Clovis began not as the leader of a whole people but as a minor ruler of the Franks settled around Tournai; other obscure Frankish kings ruled other groups of Franks in the regions of Tournai, Toxandria and the Middle Rhine. His people, the Salian Franks, had first been authorized to settle in Brabant in 358 and from there had penetrated into the better lands to the south. Clovis's father, Childeric, had been no more than a local Frankish king around Tournai, so Clovis had had to make his own way in the world. By defeating the Roman Syagrius (486) he won a kingdom based on Soissons; he went on to defeat the Burgundians (from whom he had married a Catholic wife) in 500 and the Visigoths in 507. He beat the Alamans at Tolbiac in 506, but only at the end of his life was he able to secure the Ripuarian Frankish kingdom of Cologne or deal with the other Salian kings, like Ragnachar of Cambrai. His conversion, which had certainly been accomplished by 507, brought him the enthusiastic support of all the Catholic clergy and recognition in Constantinople. If this did not necessarily impress his own peoples, it at least earned him unstinted praise from the Catholic bishops of Gaul and therefore the backing of the Gallo-Roman aristocracy.

If after Clovis's death in 511 the Frankish kingdom was not actually partitioned, it was administered by his four sons, each in charge of a block of territory and lacking a clear desire to cooperate in ruling or serving any Frankish ideal. Their violence towards one another and their opportunism admittedly served from time to time, for brief periods, to reunite all the lands of the family in the hands of one or other of them, but the more important development in this period was the emergence of the distinctive kingdoms of Austrasia in the old Frankish lands and Neustria in the new lands won by Clovis himself, who had made Paris his chief city. When, in 511, Clovis's sons divided the lands of his dominions, their shares did not thereby acquire any coherence. When Clodomir died in 533, his surviving brothers split his lands among themselves. The brothers also individually or in alliance extended their shares by conquest. Thuringia was conquered by the oldest, Theuderic; Burgundy was suppressed and divided between Childebert and Chlotachar; Provence, acquired by

preferable to holding out on their own in heresy. Even so it was not until the mid-7th century that King Recceswinth (649–72), whose father Chindaswinth had abolished the right of Goths and Romans to live under their own laws, could publish a single code of law, the *Liber Judiciorum* (Book of Judgments; 654). The Catholics appear to have been well satisfied with their Gothic royal protectors despite their domineering ways, in church appointments for example. During the 6th century the Spanish Catholic church had learned to look after its own interests without expectation of outside help. Good relations with Rome were hampered by difficulties of communication but the church was sufficiently well organized to be able to hold frequent councils and it was the Spanish collections of canons that supplied western Christendom with its most comprehensive statements of law before the Carolingian revival in the 8th century. At the time of Reccared's conversion the clergy were well prepared to take a preponderant place in the royal government. The king's uncle, Leander, bishop of Seville (died 600), a friend of Pope Gregory I, supervised the transitional period. Leander's more famous brother, Isidore of Seville, represents the apogee of Spanish scholarship in the barbarian period. The task of directing the Spanish church was assumed by the metropolitan of Toledo (610), originally a bishopric under the diocese (province) of Cartagena, which had been in Greek hands when Toledo became the royal capital. The embarrassments of the government at Constantinople shortly after enabled the Goths to clear out the imperial garrisons and to subdue the Basques, particularly under Swinthila, who was general before becoming king (623–31). His attempt to provide for the succession of his son provoked opposition. There

involvement in the affairs of Italy, was split between Theuderic and Chlotachar. The brothers willingly involved themselves in wars in Germany, Italy and Spain as a means of keeping themselves and their followers supplied with booty. Though the youngest brother, Chlotachar, eventually reunited all the Frankish lands and the recent conquests as the last survivor of Clovis's family (558–61), on his death his four sons proceeded to a different division of the inheritance. They still used the same four capital cities designated in 511, Reims, Orléans, Paris and Soissons, all reasonably close together, however awkwardly shaped their kingdoms, and all to be found in the territory of Syagrius before 486. In 567, when Charibert died without heirs, highly Romanized Aquitaine, the major part of his kingdom acquired from the Visigoths, was likewise happily cut up to satisfy his brothers. But eight years later Austrasia was not so casually disposed of. When Sigebert was assassinated and his violent youngest brother Chilperic expected to lay

hands on his kingdom, the powerful men of Austrasia thwarted his design. They defended their own independence by proclaiming as king Sigebert's five-year-old son, Childebert: the heart of the Frankish lands had resisted partition and annexation, unlike the southern part of Gaul.

Austrasia was the most German of the Frankish kingdoms, but its peoples and great men had no intention of turning their backs on their rights to the Roman legacy. Its rulers continued to show interest in campaigning in Italy and Childebert even succeeded his uncle as ruler of Burgundy, the most Roman of all the kingdoms. When in the early 7th century Chlothacar II of Neustria was left as sole Merovingian king, the Austrasians were strong enough to force the appointment of his son Dagobert as their own king and moreover extracted from him in 622 what they regarded as their share of Aquitaine and Provence, lands ruled by Sigebert nearly 50 years before. The Austrasians were not therefore preoccupied with defining a national

Dagobert's throne. This folding stool of bronze was used as the royal throne at St Denis and already in Abbot Suger's time was associated with the abbey's alleged founder Dagobert. Its folding legs with lion heads and paws were derived from an antique model and suggest that at least part of it was Carolingian.

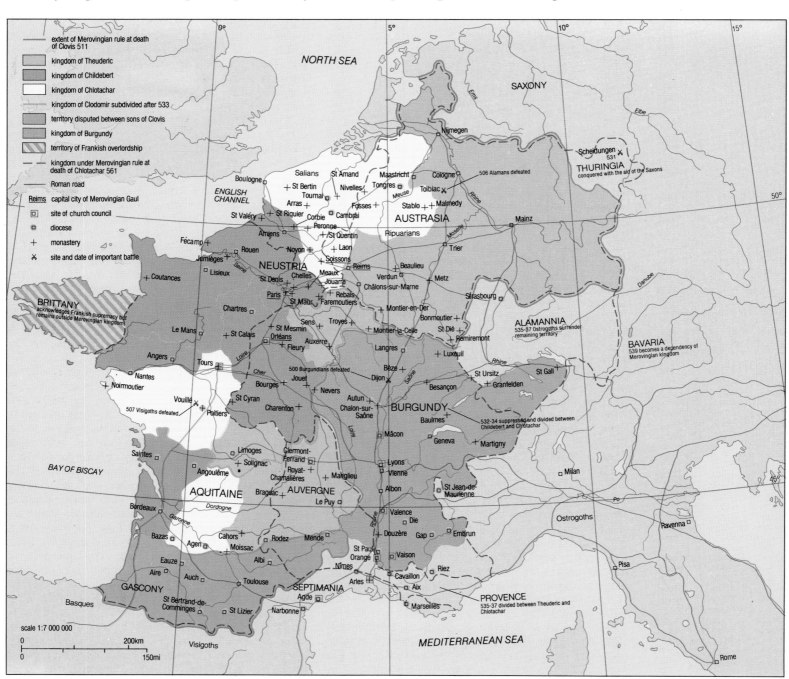

territory, but they had clearly acquired an idea of their own identity. Although they thwarted a Merovingian carve-up, these passions abetted the vicious violent wars between the rulers of the kingdoms, in particular under the Austrasian queen Brunehaut (died 613) and the Neustrian she-wolf Fredegonde (died 597).

The position of Austrasia may be contrasted with that of Burgundy which, by the 7th century, had acquired its own distinctive character through its powerful great families, though there was no separate king of Burgundy after 590. One family had aspired to build a kind of regency from the office of mayor of the palace; but after the mayoralty of Warnacher had made him powerful enough to stir up opposition, on his death in 626 the great men in the kingdom required Chlothacar II to leave the office vacant; they preferred to deal directly with the king themselves. The political contest in 7th-century Gaul was therefore limited to the two kingdoms of Neustria and Austrasia.

Under the Merovingian aegis a new grouping of local interests had achieved geographical coherence. The powerful men included not only Frankish military leaders but also the descendants of the old Gallo-Roman aristocracy, who had retained their preponderance in the episcopate and in local government. The end of Merovingian foreign adventures reduced the kings' capacity to reward their followers, except by alienating the lands of the Roman fisc. Now enriched, the great landowners of Gaul began to concentrate on their own properties. The last important Merovingian ruler, Dagobert I (628–38), was already reduced to trying to weaken the position of the great men of Austrasia and Burgundy by supporting the principalities to the east, for example Thuringia and Bavaria. In Dagobert's own Neustria the great men were no more easily tamed than in the other kingdoms, particularly when royal minorities obliged them to accept responsibilities in regencies. In both Austrasia and Neustria the mayors of the palace took charge. From Neustria Ebroin for many years kept Austrasia in check. After his assassination, however, the Austrasian mayor defeated the Neustrians at Tertry (687) and established the preeminence of his own house, though while the two kingdoms had been in rivalry their outlying territories had inevitably broken loose.

The Austrasian leadership in Gaul had shifted the basis of Frankish power from the Seine basin, where Paris was the Neustrian capital, to the territory between the rivers Meuse and Moselle, where the capital was Metz. From Austrasia the Carolingian family was to rule all the Merovingians' conquests from Rome and more, but its prime concern was to conquer, convert and colonize the lands immediately to the north and east of its new base. The Franks proved remarkable among barbarians for paradoxically combining two very different qualities. First, they were prepared to accept Roman influences, as over religion. Second, they did not abandon their own Germanic homeland and remained more faithful to it than any of the Goths ever did to theirs.

In the time of Clovis Theodoric had intervened in Gaul to save its southern littoral for the Visigoths and to take Provence for himself. After his death two sons of Clovis were soon drawn into Italian affairs and carved up Provence between them. It was, however, another two and a half centuries before Charlemagne actually made himself king of Italy, despite several successive Frankish interventions in the peninsula when circumstances allowed Frankish kings such adventures. Theudebert actually occupied lands in Venetia and Liguria in the mid-6th century. After his day Frankish influence in Bavaria gave additional access to Italy from the east. All these territories were then very closely linked by political events, for when the Lombards descended uninvited from Noricum into Italy in 568, they did not immediately penetrate far south and for several years thereafter they and their Saxon confederates made many violent incursions into Burgundy. Burgundian resistance effectively checked the Lombard advance. This impressed the pope and the emperor sufficiently to persuade them of the advantages of deploying the Franks against the Lombards in Italy. The Lombards, unlike other barbarian "invaders" of the empire, never had any authority to settle, and for nearly two centuries the pope in particular felt menaced by these savage peoples, some of whom were still pagan at the time of the invasion; others were Arian. Pope Gregory the Great (590–604) found that Theodelinda, Frankish and Catholic wife of King Autharis and king maker among the Lombards in the early 7th century, in no way bowed to his authority even in ecclesiastical matters; her Catholicism actually served to strengthen her political position with the north Italian episcopate. The Lombards backed the authority of the patriarch of Aquileia in northern Italy against the pope until 698. In the meantime the papacy's best political hope remained the surviving strength of the emperor's government in Italy; only the difficulties of the empire at Constantinople by the early 8th century, followed by the conflict over iconoclasm, deprived the papacy altogether of this support. By that time popes had long since reconciled themselves to the need for assistance from the Catholics of northern Europe.

The growth of Lombard power in Italy

By the end of the 6th century, while Gaul was subjected to Merovingian rule, Italy was effectively dominated by three quite separate powers: the empire, the Lombards and the papacy. For 1300 years Italy was not to know the hand of a single master, and the main reason for this was the failure of the Lombards to emulate other barbarian peoples and create a single united kingdom south of the Alps. At the time of their invasion the Lombards were still very uncivilized. The invading force was itself made up of peoples of many different kinds. It was led by Alboin, who, together with his father, had already served in Italy in the imperial army; only when subsidies from Constantinople were cut off did it seem opportune to pursue the attractions of Italy. Alboin had himself crowned king at Milan in 569 but he was not able to take even neighboring Pavia until 573. However, before Alboin was assassinated in the same year, the Lombards had overextended their political penetration of Italy as far as Spoleto. Alboin himself appointed a relation to rule the duchy of Friuli, and this was symptomatic of the Lombard approach to government. After 575 the Lombards dispensed with a king altogether. Various dukes (36 by tradition) shared power and

Merovingian Gaul
Here are summarized the vicissitudes of the Merovingian dynasty over about two centuries, between the death of Clovis and the ascendancy of Charles Martel. The Frankish territories of Clovis's predecessors, united by him with the Roman kingdom of Syagrius and the Visigothic kingdom south of the Loire, had been extended by his sons to include the Burgundian kingdom and Provence as well as conquests in Germany. These lands of the Merovingian family were successively partitioned in various ways before the three new kingdoms of Neustria, Austrasia and Burgundy emerged, with the duchy of Aquitaine eventually obtaining effective autonomy. Meanwhile the convinced Catholicism of the Franks was responsible for missionary activities in the east and north as well as monastic foundations throughout the land which in the 7th century witnessed to the fervor of both Irish and Benedictine inspiration. Across the Channel the Merovingians made contact with the English. The Merovingians thus proved to be more than mere barbarian warlords. Some political coherence gradually crystallized out of the violence and the partitions to prepare the Franks for their leading role in the succeeding period.

the responsibility of extending their ravages through the peninsula. Many inhabitants fled before the advance to evade their oppressors, though the Lombards simply bypassed the cities and the strong points of imperial government to ravage the rest. The Lombards thus put themselves in a very different position from the Ostrogoths before them.

At first their power looked predatory but temporary. The emperor Maurice called on the Franks to join him in suppressing the Lombards. Only the disagreement of the allies saved the Lombards, who began to appreciate the need for a concerted leadership. A new king, Autharis, grandson of Alboin, beat off the Franks and consolidated his realm north of the Po. He even pushed the limits of his rule to Reggio di Calabria and then, with the help of his Catholic wife, aped the Roman-style government of Theodoric. When he died in 590 his kingdom, surprisingly enough, did not crumble with him. But it was not territorially complete and Lombard dukes survived to pursue ambitions of their own, particularly from Spoleto in the Apennines and Benevento in Campagna. Once the crisis was past, the number of dukes left in local commands actually made it more difficult to dislodge the Lombards altogether. The imperial government, fully taken up with the Persians in the east, could only maintain a defensive front in Italy.

Theodelinda's second husband, Agilulf, duke of Turin, was able to go over to the offensive and take Mantua, Padua, Cremona, Parma and Piacenza from the Greeks in 603. His successes made it easier for him to discipline the northern dukes and to obtain the support of the north Italian bishops, who recognized the jurisdiction of the patriarch of Aquileia rather than that of Rome. The Lombards were being slowly won from Arianism. It was in his reign (590–615) that they acquired their national shrine at Monza (595) and that the Irish missionary Columbanus founded his final resting-place at Bobbio (c. 612). After Agilulf's death the kingship passed to his son and to his daughter's two husbands under whom further conquests were made from the Greeks both in the east (Oderzo) and in the west where the Ligurian littoral was at last acquired and entrusted to another duke. King Aribert, nephew of Theodelinda, was openly

Catholic (from 653); Arianism faded away.

By the mid-7th century, therefore, the Lombards had dug themselves into Italy and a century after their invasion had proved their capacity to turn a new situation to their advantage. Their ferocity and savagery had been softened by their responsibilities and King Rotharis was the first of a notable series of legislators (Edict issued in 643). Like their contemporaries in Spain the Lombards had clearly ceased to be uncivilized even by Roman standards, and once the Lombard kings had become Catholic the main impediment to their assimilation was removed. Disputes about the royal succession admittedly gave the emperor Constans II the occasion to intervene in Italy in person (663). He actually conquered more of the duchy of Benevento before his death, after which, however, the Lombard duke Romuald turned the tables on the Greeks and captured Brindisi and Taranto together with the rest of Apulia and Calabria.

But the Lombards were not able to dislodge the imperial administration in the south, and its band of territory across central Italy linking Ravenna to Rome kept the Lombard principalities divided. The emperor, though taken up with his problems in the east, had no fear of losing his control of Italy and generally overawed the papacy throughout the 7th century; it was probably only the iconoclastic controversy that forced the papacy for doctrinal reasons into opposition. Even then it was the Lombards' seizure of Ravenna in 751, taking advantage of the unpopularity of the empire, that precipitated a papal appeal to the Franks for aid.

Gregory the Great and the monastic transformation of the Catholic church

The balance of Lombard and imperial interests in 7th-century Italy had saved the weak popes of the period from the ultimate humiliation of being treated as mere Byzantine officials or as Lombard chaplains. In the meantime the Lombards were being culturally assimilated into the Catholic population while the Roman church itself, increasingly well endowed, was recognizing that it had important responsibilities outside the peninsula. The key figure here was Gregory I (the Great, pope 590–604). Gregory was the last of the four Latin doctors of the church; the only one of them to be pope. His piety and learning made him, after

Italy in the Ostrogothic and Lombard periods
Italy was the last province of the western empire to be subjected to barbarian rule, and the imperial presence was rapidly reasserted under Justinian. Thus with its longer history of Roman government Italy, not surprisingly, remained the most Roman and civilized part of the western world. The rule of barbarian military chieftains left only superficial marks on Italian geography. With the Lombards, however, began a more radical phase, for their rule was resisted, if not everywhere, at least from Ravenna and Rome, which impeded Lombard control of the peninsula. Effectively this successfully kept the Lombard kingdom of Italy separated from the Lombard duchies of Spoleto and Benevento. Still further south the eastern empire frustrated deep Lombard penetration. The Lombards thus provoked the division of Italy into distinct regions. The authority claimed by the Roman church throughout Italy admittedly gave some notion of unity, but in practice this too was curtailed by imperial control of Ravenna and the south, while the north tended to respect the claims of the patriarch of Aquileia or the archbishop of Milan to represent Catholic authority. For these reasons, though Italy was spared earlier barbarian destructiveness, its experience under the Lombards was eventually more harrowing than the experiences of other provinces which succumbed to more tractable barbarians.

Pannonia

BURGUNDY

Raetia

Noricum

L Balaton

Rhine

Rhône

L Geneva

Rhône

Rhine

Chiavenna

Bellinzona

L Maggiore

L Como

Bolzano

Drava

Mur

Danube

FRIULI

Aosta

Dora Baltea

Adda

Corno

Monza

Bergamo

L Garda

AUSTRIA

Trent

Ceneta

Cividale + Salto

Concordia 615

Grado

Ivrea

Novara

Vercelli

Milan

Brescia

Vicenza

Oderzo 640 Sesto

Treviso

Trieste

Liguria

Ticino

Leno

Verona

Sirmione

VENICE

Adige

ISTRIA

Turin

Pavia

Olonna

Cremona 603

Monselice 601

Padua 603

Venice

Asti

Po

Placenza 601

VIA EMILIA

Mantua 603

Chioggia

Pola

NEUSTRIA

Alba

Tortona

+ Bobbio

Parma

Ferrara

Comacchio

Po

Illyricum

Pagno +

Tanaro

Reggio

Nonantula

Modena

Canneto +

Alpes Cottiae

Berceto +

Bologna

Ravenna

+ Pedona

LIGURIA

Savona

Genoa 640

Emilia

Faniano

Imola

EXARCHATE OF RAVENNA

Faenza

DALMATIA
lost to Slavs

Zara

Albenga

Luna

Cesena

Rimini

Ventimiglia

Pistoia

Lucca

Flaminia

Pesaro

Fano

Spalato

LIGURIAN SEA

Pisa

Arno

Florence

VIA CASSIA

Urbino

Senigallia

Ancona

PENTAPOLIS

Cagli

Volterra

Arezzo

Umbria

Osimo

Siena +

Cortona

Tadino

Camerino

Fermo

Picenum

ADRIATIC SEA

Ragusa

Elba

Chiusi

Perugia

Nocera

Ascoli

Corsica
c.700

TUSCIA

Monte
Amiata

Todi

VIA FLAMINIA

Spoleto

Orvieto

Tiber

Narni

Rieti

Penne

Pescara

Viterbo

Farfa +

Chieti

Ajaccio

Civitavecchia

Sutri

Valeria

DUCHY OF
SPOLETO

Samnium

Tivoli

DUCHY OF
ROME

Rome

Albano

Campagna

Monte Cassino +

DUCHY OF
BENEVENTO

Siponto
c.642

Lucera

Canosa

Bari

Terracina

Cingla +

+ Benevento

Ofanto

APULIA

Torres

Gaeta

Capua

Acerra

Naples

Ischia

DUCHY OF
NAPLES

Salerno
640

VIA APPIA

Brindisi
c.670

Calabria

TYRRHENIAN SEA

Agropoli

Lucania

Taranto
c.670

Otranto

Sardinia

Policastro

Gallipoli

Bisignano

Rossano

Cagliari

Cosenza

IONIAN SEA

Bruttii

Squillace

Lipari Is

Messina

Reggio

MEDITERRANEAN SEA

Palermo

Taormina

Sicily

Enna

Catania

Agrigento

Syracuse

boundary of Roman province in Italy
under the Ostrogoths 493-553

Bruttii Roman province

lands of the Lombard kingdom in Italy c.600

division of the Lombard kingdom

territory still under imperial control c.700

territory lost from the empire 600-700

640 date of Lombard acquisition

▣ patriarchate

▣ archdiocese

+ monastery

road

scale 1 : 5 000 000

0 ——— 150km

0 ——— 100mi

VANDAL KINGDOM
534 reconquered by empire,
c.680 Muslim

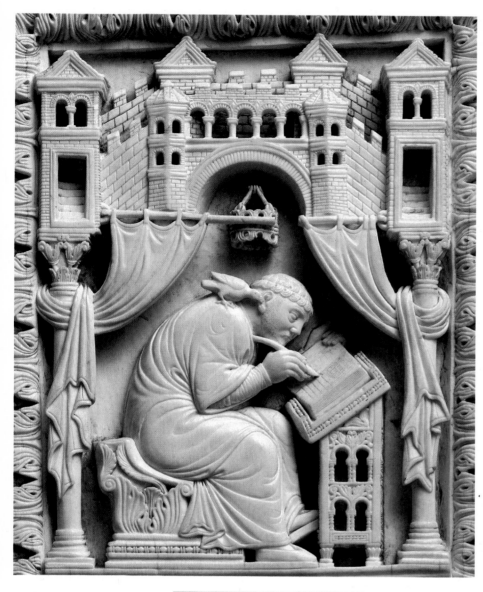

Augustine, the most influential of Christian teachers in the Middle Ages. But in his own day his position at Rome obliged him to take on the burden of transforming the nature of the Roman idea to suit barbarian conditions.

Despite his respectful attitude to the emperor at Constantinople Gregory believed in claiming autonomy for the Roman church in the west, in Spain and Gaul as well as in England where a mission arrived in 597. It was the success of this enterprise, followed too by a return mission to the pagan Germans of the continent, that provided the papacy by the early 8th century with Catholic subjects in the north, unquestioningly devoted to Rome; for these Christians this link had no political overtones: it was a purely religious commitment.

Gregory entrusted his English mission to monks from Rome, whereas hitherto the conversion of the barbarians within the empire had usually devolved upon the bishops surviving in the former Roman provinces. Monks as missionaries, who became bishops, transformed the character of the episcopate and the western church in the course of the 7th and 8th centuries. Gregory's monks in England were only the best known of a company who, from the mid-6th century, tackled the problem of converting the barbarians. From the provincial capital of Braga monks penetrated into Galicia and brought the Suevi to Catholicism (550–61); about the same time Columba planted a community on Iona (563) from which the Picts and the Northumbrians eventually received the faith. In 590 Columbanus arrived in Burgundy from Ireland and he and his disciples established monasteries from which the efforts for the conversion of Alamannia and Bavaria were sustained. During the 7th century a great number of monasteries were founded by royal and munificent patrons in Spain, the British Isles, Gaul and Germany. Their monks became courtiers and bishops as well as new generations of missionaries. In England monastic Christianity established a hold on the episcopate and on the cultural life of the church which it was not to lose before the Reformation; in Gaul it spiritually overshadowed the bishops drawn from the established aristocracy whose energies had saved the church in the 5th century.

Until the second half of the 6th century monasticism on the continent had been confined to the few who felt called to a life led in special dedication to God apart from the world. Monasteries grew up in the vicinity of particular masters of the spiritual life in various parts of the western empire. It is difficult to know whether a continuous monastic life was maintained beyond the life of the founder, even if, by writing a rule for his community, such continuation was anticipated. Bishops themselves tried to supervise such communities by drawing up rules, but few rules survive. It has however been estimated that there were over 200 monasteries in Gaul alone by 600. The most famous western monastic rule, that of Benedict of Nursia (died c. 526) for his monastery at Monte Cassino, was not widely known outside his own region before Gregory I wrote about him in his *Dialogues*. Knowledge of it spread through Gaul in the 7th century and it was even used as part of the rule at Columbanus's foundation at Luxeuil from 637. Later it was enthusiastically supported by

Above Gregory the Great and his scriptorium. Gregory is depicted here, on a 10th-century ivory book cover, with his symbol, a dove, perched on his right shoulder.

Left The dome mosaic from the Arian baptistery at Ravenna, dated to the reign of Theodoric (493–526). Modeled on the much more dazzling orthodox baptistery of the mid-5th century, the more modest proportions of the Arian building imposed a simplification of the decorative scheme. The artist seems to have tried to avoid copying, but the device of placing the cross on the cushion of the throne was ill judged. The river Jordan is here fully personified, but John the Baptist has been moved from Christ's right to his left. The decoration does not itself suggest any important doctrinal difference.

Right The monastery at Monkwearmouth in Northumbria was founded by Benedict Biscop in 674. The west front of St Peter's church is all that survives of the original buildings. The upper reaches of the tower are late Saxon.

Much of the early Christian building in Ireland was too crude and simple to survive into later times. It was mainly in the south and west that stone was used for early constructions, not always easily datable. Skellig Michael (*below right*) is an island 35 kilometers SW of Ireland with the best-preserved monastic site before the Viking period. On a south-facing precipice six beehive cells and two churches were erected for a community of ascetic monks. The beehive shapes (*far right*) were achieved by careful construction with stones to keep out the rain. The technique was adapted in the 7th century for building other shapes like the boat-shaped oratory at Gallarus on the Dingle peninsula (*right*).

Two buildings from eastern Ireland show that by the 9th century the value of more durable religious buildings was appreciated. The Iona community found refuge from Viking attacks at Kells and in the early 9th century constructed this church (*bottom*), known as St Columba's house, though it has no more personal connection with the 6th-century saint than St Kevin's church at Glendalough (*below*) has with that 6th-century saint.

Some 50 crosses survive from before 800 in Ireland. These two examples come from the Barrow valley where the local stone, granite, has determined the use of low relief. The Moone cross (*right*), 5 meters high, illustrates many religious subjects, most with simple doll-like figures which in their own assured way have the charm of folk art. The Castledermot cross (*far right*) is of slightly later date and its panels on Christ's Passion are worked with more detail, but the figures at the top are reminiscent of the Moone cross apostles.

Bishop Leger of Autun (bishop 663–79) who introduced the rule to all the monasteries in his diocese. But no drive for the uniformity of monastic life according to rule was contemplated before the reforms instigated by Benedict of Aniane for Louis of Aquitaine (later emperor) in the early 9th century. The use of the Benedictine rule then was to reform communities that had already flourished and decayed and needed discipline.

The effectiveness of monks in changing the nature of the church, particularly in the 7th century, depended not on the inspiration of a particular rule or saint but upon the capacity of monks to extend religious belief and practice into the countryside where on both sides of the frontiers of Christendom the populations were pagan. Catholic Christianity before and after the barbarian invasions had been the religion of the cities, where the bishops were installed. It was from the bishops that Clovis and the leading Franks had accepted Christianity. By the end of the 6th century, however, the cities had exhausted their capacity to Romanize the barbarians who were not for the most part city-dwellers. Their leaders, landowners or even colonizers of borderlands, needed Christian pastors who could bring religion to the countryside. As far as Gaul was concerned the most powerful thrust came in Burgundy, where there was an immediate need to consolidate the Frankish encroachment to the east and where the strong Roman traditions of southern Gaul could be harnessed for a new purpose. Monasticism from Arles and Marseilles had spread in the south, particularly through knowledge of the rule of Bishop Caesarius of Arles (469–542). The great men of Burgundy and Aquitaine could promote the work of conversion with monastic help. Lyons was in the 7th century one of the leading Christian cities, where the English monk and bishop Wilfrid was to spend three useful years (654/5–57/8).

It is however generally agreed that the main inspiration for the monastic renewal of Gaul came with the arrival of Columbanus, then about 50 years of age, in Burgundy c. 590. After about 20 years he was driven out by his disagreements with the aged queen Brunehaut. However, his disciples, for example St Gall, continued his work, and his most famous Burgundian monastery, Luxeuil, flourished after his death. Columbanus also extended his activities to the Lombards, founding a monastery at Bobbio where he died in 615. This movement depended not only on Irish emigrant monks but on the support of such men of these lands as Donatus, a monk of Luxeuil who became bishop of Besançon (627–58) and founded a monastery there, or Emmeran who was brought from Aquitaine to Regensburg as bishop where the burial place of his martyred body became the site of a powerful monastery from the mid-8th century. The monks accepted the task of extending Christianity into pagan areas beyond the reach of the secular arm. Irish efforts in southern Gaul were paralleled by efforts made in the northeast, as by Omer who from Luxeuil became bishop of Thérouanne (died 667). By the early 8th century English monks had extended the mission field from their own island into Frisia and Thuringia. As a result diocesan organization there was at first inchoate because the bases of the missionary effort were monastic.

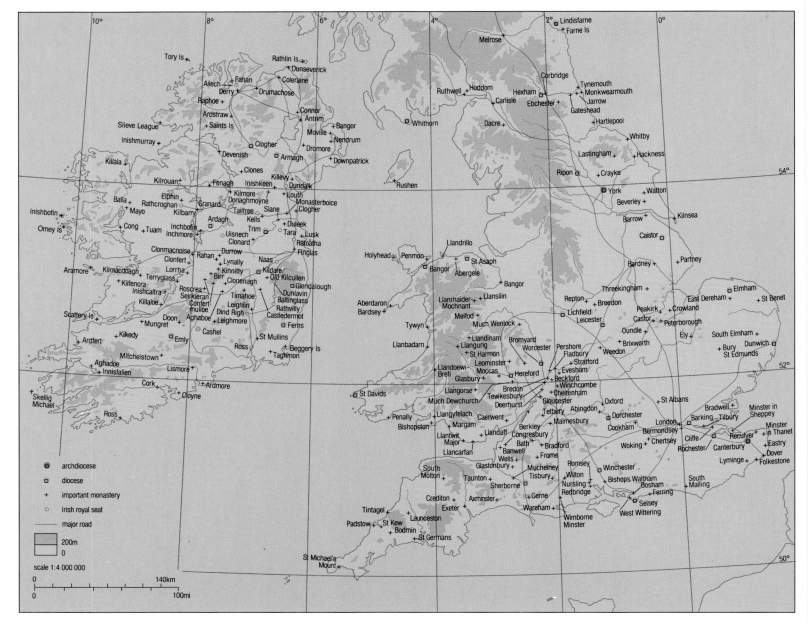

The original nature of the monastic inspiration had nothing to do with preaching the gospel; the change in the character of the institution in Gaul itself seems to depend on the injection into it of Irish monks. The Irish church itself had begun in the 5th century with the preaching of the bishop Patrick, but Ireland had had no Roman government and no cities. By the 6th century the monasteries had already become the focal points of Irish spiritual life, adapted both to life in the countryside and to the tribal organization of Irish society. Dating the early Irish monasteries is not easy but a number of communities had probably come into being well before Columbanus was born. By the time he left Ireland to lead a life of continuous "pilgrimage" or wandering as part of his asceticism, Irish monasticism itself had quite eclipsed the original episcopal establishment. It was the ascetic qualities and the spiritual discipline of the Irish that impressed their continental hosts, but Gallic Christianity did not succumb to all the Irish innovations. The Irish were grafted into a system that had already provided for the royal endowment of some great monasteries, like Clovis's house of St Geneviève at Paris. The new monasteries of the 7th century were not established in places connected with the cults of saints, but in the course of time their founders themselves became famous saints, like St Philibert (died 685), founder of the abbey of Jumièges. The monastic custodians of their relics naturally encouraged popular devotions at these shrines and the monasteries became rich, powerful and famous. King Dagobert built or revived a monastery for the apostle of the Gauls at St Denis near Paris – to establish his own links with the Roman past of Neustria and to be his burial place. The monastery at Fleury, founded in 672, acquired by stealth the body of the famous St Benedict from deserted Cassino before 705. By then the possession of relics had become almost indispensable. But the patronage of kings and the popularity of the saints and their cults helped to give monks a new place in the affairs of Christendom. The monks were themselves, as great landowners, responsible for carrying forward the work of opening up their land for cultivation. The extent of their influence in 7th-century society may be gauged from two very different kinds of evidence – charters which reveal how much benefactions had made them owners of extensive properties and saints' lives which give a

A page of Bede's *Ecclesiastical History*, written at Monkwearmouth before 747. This important manuscript of the *History* offers a very accurate text, porbably taken from the author's own copy, and its fine ornaments have therefore some claim to be considered authorized. This page from the beginning of Book 2 shows Gregory I, the originator of the English mission, who was much venerated there.

England and Ireland in the 8th century
The conversion of the English and the Irish indicates that enough stability and literacy was attained in both countries by this date to map their settlements on the eve of the Viking disruptions. Politically England accepted the rule of kings of Mercia, but the older local kingdoms can still be identified and sentiment for them still counted. Ecclesiastically the siting of bishops' sees and monasteries gives a clear indication of where the strength of Christianity could be found. The great days of Northumbria were numbered, but the map suggests how insouciant of danger from the North Sea it was. Beyond the reach of the English as yet, the Welsh too fostered their monasteries, and like the Irish recognized no political constraints on local autonomy. The lack of Roman-type diocesan organization in Celtic Christianity prevents the drawing of territorial boundaries, and it is hardly surprising if precision is impossible where political divisions are concerned. The original Patrician tradition of bishoprics had been swamped in Ireland by the exuberant proliferation of monasteries. The influence of these houses radiated over Ireland and on the continent, but it is not easy to map the nature of their spiritual bonds.

glimpse of the popular religious beliefs of the age.

Gallic missionaries were also to be found in England: in East Anglia Felix from Burgundy, the Frankish Agilbert among the West Saxons. But in England the influence of the Roman and Irish churches combined to produce in Northumbria a Christian culture specially well known from surviving illuminated manuscripts and from the many works of Bede of Jarrow (672/3–735). Bede, as the most distinguished scholar-monk of the dark ages, demonstrates what monasticism was capable of by 700. In his *Ecclesiastical History of the English People* he writes particularly about the English monasteries and nunneries but incidentally he also reveals the attraction of the monkish state for many of royal blood. He shows in the story of Caedmon (*fl.* 658–80) how the monastery of Whitby nursed a popular poet who wrote in the vernacular and thereby served God in ways undreamed of in the continental Catholic church. As a scholar with access to the learned literature available in his day from Ireland, Spain, Gaul and Rome, Bede was not content to distill his learning for monastic pupils. He turned his hand to vernacular translations of the gospel and shows how different were the effects of the English conversion for popular culture from what they were in Gaul. In Christian England someone also troubled to write down the poem *Beowulf* and to lift thereby a corner of the curtain that Christianity had generally lowered on paganism. Christianity established its centers in England according to the political circumstances of the day rather than, as in Gaul, in the surviving Roman cities. This capacity to deal with its real public indicates the virtues of early monasticism for barbarian society.

The new Mediterranean power: Islam

The monks were the soldiers of Christ in the western world. In the east, faithful soldiers of another kind appeared in the 7th century when the Arabs of the Arabian peninsula, united by Islam, invaded the empires of Rome and Persia. The prophet Muhammad had achieved in 10 years (622–32) the creation of a new religious society in submission to God. He himself fought as well as taught and the Arabs who abandoned their own internecine wars because of their new religious brotherhood did not give up fighting altogether. They raided in Syria in 629, before Muhammad's death, and were repulsed. Under his successor, the caliph Abu Bakr, they returned to a land well known to them from trading, the fertile crescent. Persians and Romans had recently clashed there, but Persian successes, however ephemeral, must have already alerted the Arabs to the weakness of the empire, where Roman power in the cities had never been very effective in the countryside. Roman attempts to repulse the invaders, now fully united behind the attack, culminated in the efforts of Heraclius in 636. His forces were devastatingly defeated at Yarmuk in 636, where the Arab forces were reinforced by a contingent that had come in haste across the desert from Iraq. The Romans were quite unprepared for warfare of this kind. Their desert frontier had become the Arabs' highway. The desert was a waste the Bedouin knew how to cross.

The Muslims' acquisition of Syria as far north as the Taurus mountains forced a wedge between the

emperor's base in Asia Minor and the African provinces. Egypt could not be saved from invasion (641) and Alexandria, the second city of the empire, was betrayed without a fight despite the strength of its maritime position. The conquest of both Syria and Egypt, which immediately put Islam in possession of some of the richest and longest-civilized parts of the world, had not been the goal of the caliph at Medina, but the result of the ambitious ardor of his generals and their skill in both warfare and diplomacy. They had offered favorable terms to local populations strongly dissatisfied with the imperial government's religious policies. Muslim terms guaranteed, provided customary taxes were paid, that these populations, as people of the book and therefore tolerated by Islam, could enjoy autonomy under their own religious leaders, who were predominantly monophysite rather than orthodox. At the time of the conquests the richest provinces of the Roman empire appear on religious grounds to have been satisfied with the change of regime. Caliph Umar I (634–44) laid down principles for the administration of this vast unexpected empire and for keeping his generals under surveillance. The army was settled in base camps to keep them away from the local populations and to keep them pure and unmixed. They were not even allowed to hold or cultivate land outside the Arabian peninsula: in conquered territories they had the monopoly and burden of military duties.

Even before the collapse of Roman power in Syria Arab forces had moved out of the peninsula against the Persians in Iraq, who were defeated at Qadisiya (636). The new Persian ruler, Yazdigird III, nevertheless put up a desperate resistance, though he was driven even further east until he was assassinated in 651. The Persians were driven from Iraq into Khuzistan and then into Persia proper. After Persia the Muslim armies advanced even further east, into Khurasan. The annihilation of Persia, though difficult, went beyond what the Arabs had done to Rome and added further complications to the problem of governing an empire on the basis of the Koranic rules for the new community. Umar's rules to safeguard the Arabs required the setting up of a military society in base camps at Kufa and Basra in Iraq as in those of Syria and Fustat in Egypt. The Muslims tolerated the Persian religion of Zoroaster as they had permitted Christians and Jews to worship freely. However, among the peoples of the east, in Syria and Iraq, the Arabs found peoples of similar speech and culture to their own. The fabulous riches of Ctesiphon dazzled the Arab soldiers as much as the new warriors impressed the subjugated populations. In due course a new cultural community grew out of the new situation. The frontiers of the empire had been pushed to Makran, bordering on India, by 643; in the north an expedition attacked Kabul and crossed the Oxus in the early 8th century before the movement for expansion eventually petered out on the Jaxartes river. Transoxiana was the last Islamic province towards China.

Strains on the new religion already appeared under Caliph Uthman (644–56), a member of the Quraysh tribe which had been dominant at Mecca in Muhammad's time and for long hostile to his teaching. Under Uthman their old aristocratic pretensions reappeared, and after his assassination

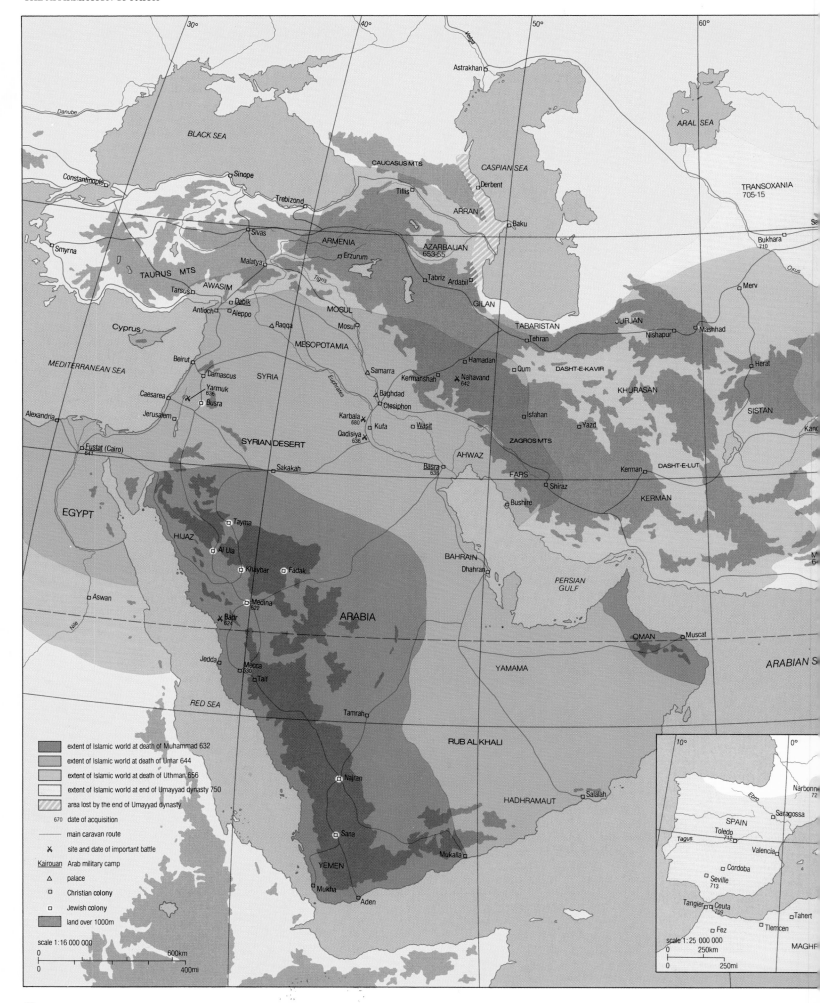

extent of Islamic world at death of Muhammad 632
extent of Islamic world at death of Umar 644
extent of Islamic world at death of Uthman 656
extent of Islamic world at end of Umayyad dynasty 750
area lost by the end of Umayyad dynasty
670   date of acquisition
       main caravan route
       site and date of important battle
Kairouan   Arab military camp
△   palace
□   Christian colony
□   Jewish colony
       land over 1000m

scale 1:16 000 000
0   600km
0   400mi

scale 1:25 000 000
0   250km
0   250mi

Left: The expansion of Islam
Unlike Christianity, Islam was a religion that gave its founder immediate political responsibilities. After his death his successors took charge not only of the faith but of the management of the enlarged community of the faithful. The making of peace among the warring tribes of Arabia was completed by carrying the new order into the lands of the Roman and Persian empires. To overcome the resistance put up by those authorities, Islamic armies swiftly conquered ever deeper into the empires. On the map these extensions of Islam appear like the advance of inexorable forces of nature. In the process Islam swept away the ancient political authorities of Rome and Persia, achieving more in less than a century than mere barbarians could do in the west over 250 years.

Above The mosque at Damascus, built by Caliph al-Walid in 706–14. This congregational mosque, the work of Syrian craftsmen, was magnificently decorated and intended to provide Islam with a new model for a place of worship. An existing church on the site was demolished, but the great enclosure of the even earlier 1st-century Roman temple was retained, on the four corners of which were raised the first minarets in Islam. In the Middle Ages it was regarded as one of the wonders of the Islamic world.

his kinsman Muawiya, governor of Syria, demanded his right of vengeance on the murderers, suspecting the new caliph Ali of complicity. By this time tensions within Islam had risen to the surface and it was many years before the new religion recovered sufficiently to enlarge upon its conquests. Both Ali and his successor Muawiya had however seen that the new empire made Medina an unsuitable place for the capital. Ali moved his to the new military city of Kufa in Iraq. Muawiya made Damascus, already an ancient capital city, the center of his Umayyad caliphate. In time he won recognition of his position, but meanwhile the religious unity of Islam had been disrupted over the position of Ali, the prophet's son-in-law: out of this dispute arose the sect of the Kharijites as well as the Shia. Without suppressing disaffection in the Hijaz (which actually survived till 692), Muawiya had nonetheless felt strong enough to reshape the government of the empire and resume the contest with the Romans. He had himself conquered Cyprus in 649 and developed a navy to combat the Romans at sea, where the Arabs had no experience. He also attacked Constantinople in 669 and 674–80. But Asia Minor was not conquered and the frontier with Syria was guarded with forts on all the main roads and mountain passes from the coast to the upper Euphrates. In the west his forces were able to extend Islamic rule out of Egypt to Kairouan by 670. The warrior Uqba's success there was concluded with a raid as far as the Atlantic, but these efforts were inconclusive and not until the end of the century were Berber opposition and Roman authority overcome. Carthage fell in 698. The Muslim

governor Musa, who was responsible in North Africa at the time of the Muslim invasion of Spain in 711, had already severed his dependence on Egypt and held his command directly from Damascus.

At the beginning of the 8th century Islam had reached its limits for the time being, not by steady successes but in two or three bursts of energy and in spite of serious difficulties experienced within its own community. It had shown its capacity to deal effectively both with its own men and with its conquests, and by the end of the 7th century the caliphs Abd al-Malik (685–705) and Abd al-Walid (705–15) could consolidate their empire. Al-Malik struck the first purely Arabic gold dinars in 695 and gave up authorizing or imitating the gold coinage of Rome and Persia. The public register of receipts and expenditures instituted under Caliph Umar and hitherto written in Greek or Persian by local officials was henceforward written in Arabic. The Muslim government had to reconsider its taxation policy to discourage conversion to Islam for purposes of securing the tax benefits enjoyed by Arab Muslims, particularly in Iraq and Khurasan. Communication with the provinces required an organization of the transport and courier services adequate to official needs. The Umayyad caliphs also countered the religious prestige of Arabia by promoting the Islamic significance of Jerusalem on the Dome of the Rock site and by the magnificent mosque they built at Damascus.

The Arab invaders from the south more quickly proved their capacity to take on the government of an empire than any of the barbarians who had penetrated from the north in the 4th and 5th centuries. The Muslims had acquired in Syria a more valuable prize and immediately took advantage of the services of the Christian officials in administration. The Muslims did not however settle in a particular corner of the empire. They had taken half of the Roman empire and added it to the whole of Persia's and more besides to make, in less than a century, the most considerable state in the world. They had disrupted the unity of the Mediterranean – so carefully built up over the centuries – and its southern and eastern shores have ever since been culturally part of a different world. The Bedouin by their capacity to cross deserts could hold together disparate lands more effectively than ever the Romans could do by water.

In the long term Islam itself began to penetrate the cultures of the many people brought together in the Umayyad empire, chiefly through the use of the Arabic language and the study of the Koran. In the short term the empire was the result of the expansion of the Arab tribesmen themselves, no longer fighting each other but turning on their enemies. They did not initially expect or demand conversion to their own faith but lived apart as dedicated warriors, disciplined enough to conquer effectively and not to disperse their energies in individual enterprises. But as they reached the limits of what they could acquire, different qualities became more important. The political realism and continuity provided by the Umayyads from Damascus, the old Roman provincial capital, proved that these southern barbarians had seen how to combine Arab and Roman talents in ways that had eluded the northern barbarians. They united the territory from within which Islam has ever since flourished.

Carolingian Europe

The empire of the Carolingian dynasty had some effective political existence for nearly a century and, though retrospective by concept, exercised a certain fascination thereafter. It was more than the realization of a Merovingian program to expand into Spain, Italy and Germany. It was held together for more than 40 years by the force of Charlemagne's own character. After his death a tradition of respect for him that inspired both chivalry and literature lived on among the Frankish nobility. Clergy from all over the empire, and beyond it, strove to make a reality of the return to Roman standards in literacy and learning. Political divisions of the empire, though projected from the first, were only realized belatedly, and when they came seemed rather superficial. The major achievements – the linking of Italy to the states north of the Alps, the Christian foothold on the southeast of the Pyrenees, the extension of Christianity in north Germany and the destruction of the Avars – were not compromised; nor was the attempt to enforce disciplined monasticism or to achieve goals in education, even during the disturbances that followed. With the disintegration of the political framework the monks and scholars acquired a new significance for handing on the cultural tradition. The Benedictine order here entered on the most influential phase of its history.

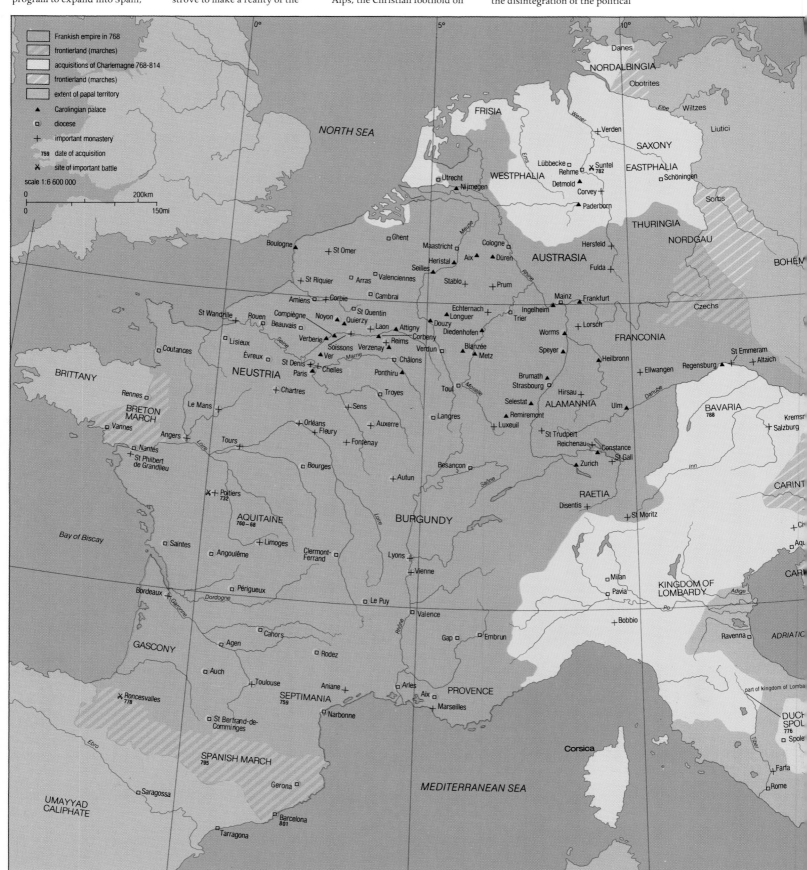

52

THE SELF-ASSERTION OF THE NORTH

A new empire in Europe

The 8th and 9th centuries were for Europe the period in the Middle Ages when the attractions of the Mediterranean regions counted least in northern calculations. The exuberant advance of Islam had swept across North Africa and now arrived in Spain, in 711. It crossed the Pyrenees and continued to cause flurries in the south of France long after Charles Martel defeated the Saracens near Poitiers in 732 and deflected them from reaching further north. At the other end of the Mediterranean, Constantinople itself was threatened. Preoccupied as they were with the survival of the empire, the eastern emperors barely had time for the affairs of the Balkans. However, the wedge of pagan Slavs between the Christians of east and west was less damaging than the imperial policy of iconoclasm which caused a breach that lasted more than a century (730–843). The emperor detached Illyricum and southern Italy from subjection to the Roman church and placed them under the aegis of the patriarch of Constantinople (731). In Rome the pope was obliged to look across the Alps for a protector able to take the emperor's place. Before the iconoclastic controversy was over, southern Italy fell prey to a fresh wave of Muslims from North Africa, which made the papacy even more desperate to retain Frankish support. In these conditions the peoples of Europe, who had been able to take for granted Rome or Romans as their inspiration, found that the onus of Christendom and the initiative in policy lay with them.

The most striking feature of European history in this period is the domination achieved by the Carolingian family, first as mayors of the Austrasian royal palace, then as kings of the Franks, finally as Roman emperors. There was however no consistent aim clearly seen and pursued generation by generation, and to the end of the dynasty the more far-sighted rulers were incapable of mastering their congenital pettiness. Nor was the prominence achieved by the Carolingians a matter of luck or even craft. They were thrust into a position where they had to act, because they were the only men of power in a position to do so. The energies left on the continent of Europe were concentrated in their lands of Austrasia straddling the Rhine and mainly German speaking, but comprising some lands of the old Roman empire. Here the Carolingian family had already established itself under the last really successful Merovingian ruler, Dagobert I (629–38), and in successive generations members of the family ruled as mayors of the palace or dukes, originally acting to cover the royal minorities. However after the death of Childeric II (675) no Merovingian exercised any real power. Pepin of Heristal became ruler of all the Frankish kingdoms after 687 but only as mayor of the palace (and master of the king), for the Merovingian kings, however impotent, could not be dispensed with. The Neustrians resented Austrasian dominance and in Alamannia and Bavaria, outlying territories of the Frankish empire, the royal dynasty seemed a valuable check on the ambitions of the mayors of the palace.

The Carolingian family was therefore obliged either to bridle its ambitions or to maintain the traditional respect for the house of Clovis and in these circumstances could do little to arrest the decay of the Frankish empire beyond the Rhine, except from their own bases. In Austrasia, however, they used their extensive lands to build up loyalties and reward service, providing their friends with bishoprics and encouraging monastic foundations in an effort to consolidate their advance into the lands of the still pagan Frisians and Saxons. In these efforts they were assisted by Irish monastic evangelists and then increasingly by English ones. The conversion of the English peoples in the 7th century promoted a new and regular traffic of Christians to Rome which inevitably crossed Austrasia. The ravages of the Saracens in southern Gaul also effectively blocked the old main routes from Gaul to Rome through Provence so that the main routes now passed across the Alps. The conversion of the northern peoples and the flow of travelers north, from the Alps, stimulated the recovery of the Rhineland. A new duty therefore devolved upon the rich and powerful rulers of Austrasia, whose enthusiasm for war and in particular for fighting pagans made them the only Frankish group capable of restoring crumbling Frankish fortunes.

Charles Martel (Charles "the Hammer") was the first Carolingian to achieve a European reputation, as victor over the Saracen Muslims near Poitiers in 732. He was the ruler to whom Pope Gregory III appealed in 739 for help against his Lombard enemies around Rome. Charles had had to build up his own position from nothing, for he was the illegitimate son of Pepin of Heristal and had had to fight his stepmother and the Neustrians to obtain the mayoral office. Not content with that he went further, by fighting the Frisians and the Saxons, in order to recover influence in the lands to the north lost at the time of his succession. The Saracen raids that had penetrated as far as Autun in Burgundy in 725 drove the duke of Aquitaine Odo to seek his aid, and after Odo's death in 735 Charles's reputation and power enabled him to recover the suzerainty of that land. Ravaged Burgundy and Provence were also open to him in the 730s, though the Saracens were not finally driven out, by his son, until 759. Charles was the first ruler since Dagobert I of more than local importance; he had not only reunited all the Frankish kingdoms in his hands, but had reasserted himself beyond the Rhine and acquired an unparalleled reputation abroad. His clergy regarded him as the stout defender of Christianity — overlooking the way he assigned church lands to his soldiers. His family had already acquired the *cappa* (cloak) of St Martin of Tours by 710 and with it the patronage of the church there, where his victory over the Saracens was particularly celebrated. He also began to supplant the Merovingians as patrons of St Denis, the greatest of Frankish monasteries. When the Merovingian Theuderic IV of Neustria died in 737, Charles did not trouble to take his place. The Merovingian dynasty seemed dispensable.

Charles Martel's sons, Carloman and Pepin III, were nevertheless faced after his death with risings against their authority in Aquitaine, Alamannia and Bavaria, so they found it prudent to raise up another Merovingian king, Childeric III, in 743. It was not until some years later that Pepin III, after the retirement of Carloman to the monastic life, sought papal authority to depose Childeric and become king himself (751). After being elected by the people, he was anointed king by Boniface, bishop of Germany. The first stage of Carolingian advancement was complete.

Carolingian power then made rapid advances. Pope Stephen II visited Pepin and besought him to intervene in Italy (754). In return for an everlasting alliance with the Franks the pope himself anointed the king again and his two sons at St Denis, confirming that the Carolingian race had been designated by God as kings of the Franks, just as Samuel had anointed the first kings of Israel. The same summer Pepin crossed the Alps and forced the king of the Lombards to restore the imperial lands of the Exarchate and Pentapolis to the "empire"; Pepin, who received them, gave them to the pope. Two years later he was obliged to return to hold the king to his promises, but showed no interest in extending the papal dominion in central Italy to please the pontiff. Instead he turned to the conquest of Aquitaine, taking Narbonne in 759, making himself protector of the Goths and then turning on Aquitaine from the north. In a succession of sustained campaigns Pepin became ruler of the whole territory from the Loire west to the Atlantic and south to the Mediterranean before he died in 768.

On his death his great empire was divided between his two sons, and their bad relations could have prejudiced the Franks' future had not the younger died in 771 leaving Charlemagne, Charles the Great, as sole ruler. His reign of over 45 years made him the most famous of all medieval rulers. He organized around 60 military expeditions and led half of them in person, which gives an idea of his energy and of the number of problems he dealt with. As Aquitaine had been more or less thoroughly conquered by his father, his main preoccupation throughout was the Saxons, with whom the Franks had been fighting for more than two centuries. Charlemagne brought these wars to an end, but not without great effort, savage slaughter and reversals of policy: his brutal methods failed to subjugate the Saxons to Christian obedience. Only in 803 could Charlemagne proclaim general pacification.

Charlemagne had not concentrated exclusively on the Saxons in the early years of his reign, but had accepted in 773 a further appeal from the pope to go to Italy, as a result of which the Lombard kingdom was annexed. His authority was accepted by the duke of Spoleto (776) and even in the southern principality of Benevento (786); a plan to conquer Muslim Sicily was considered. Frankish presence in Italy now made an understanding with the eastern empire imperative. When Charles was crowned

Above Charlemagne, a bronze of 860–70 from Metz, formerly gilded. This is the oldest known figure sculpture of the emperor but may not be intended as a likeness. The Frankish clothes and the beard, cut in the 9th-century style, however authentic, must be taken together with the fact that the king carries an orb in the one hand (and no doubt once carried a scepter in the other), a regal attitude first known from the time of Charles the Bald, his grandson, who may have inspired this image.

Left This marble throne in Aachen was used for the coronation of Otto I in 936 and thereafter by all German kings, and was traditionally considered to have been Charlemagne's. Within were deposited relics which could be visited and revered by the faithful.

emperor by Pope Leo III (800), he could be considered master of the west. His two sons Pepin and Louis had already been anointed respectively king of the Lombards and king of the Aquitainians (780). Bavaria had been deprived of its native duke (788) after more than two centuries of quasi-independence and, on being annexed to the Frankish kingdom, was divided up into counties. From Bavaria and Italy the Carolingian government accepted the gage of warfare with the dreadful Avars, who were finally crushed in 796 when their headquarters near the Tisza river was stormed and their booty appropriated by the victors. Having broken these pillagers of eastern Europe, Charlemagne became the protector of the neighboring Slavs and set up a number of margravates (military districts) to watch the frontiers, from Friuli in the south to Nordalbingia on the Danish border.

Charlemagne's ambitious conquests did not overextend Frankish power and the frontiers he established were therefore not pushed back after his death. He recognized, however, that military might would not suffice to maintain the Frankish empire. His administrative devices, like the new authority entrusted to the counts once the traditional dukes were dispensed with, indicate that the emperor recognized the need for political innovation. His reliance on the clergy was as traditional in his family as the proposed divisions of his lands between his sons. More remarkable was his interest in an educational or cultural renewal, which predated his actual imperial coronation and could be an expression of his personal character rather than calculated for political purposes. His capitularies (instructions to his officials on an extraordinary variety of subjects, in punctilious detail) were not platitudinous decrees for reform. The western empire had found at last a barbarian king with

Charles the Bald, from a manuscript written by Liuthard in gold uncials for Charles himself between 842 and 869. The king is shown sitting on a throne encrusted with colored stones. It is typical of contemporary work designed to exalt the prestige of the monarch, as the Carolingian empire began to face the succession of crises that was to bring it down.

power who was equal to the political responsibilities of imperial rule. It remained to be seen whether all the motley Christian peoples assembled within it could be held together in a revived empire after three or four centuries' experience of a different kind.

Divisions in the empire

Charlemagne's sole surviving son Louis intended to preserve the empire, for which his years of government in Aquitaine had given him due preparation. His intentions were not sufficient to overcome the innate difficulties of the task, particularly when his own sons (by his first wife), no longer committed as Charlemagne's had been to continual campaigning against outside enemies, concerned themselves above all with the lands they were assigned to govern and with their future prospects, particularly after the birth of a son, Charles (823), to Louis's second wife. Divisions in the Carolingian family and successive divisions of the empire between the family's members reduced the empire itself to a political fiction. The clergy, who were bound to be influential in advising an emperor of Christian subjects about an imperial program modeled on a vanished empire of history books, needed a ruler of independent mind; they could not themselves make good any defect there, particularly in preserving harmony between rival princes of the dynasty. Leaving aside the shortcomings of the princes and the heterogeneous character of the lands of their portions, the basic needs of government in the 9th century were necessarily very local. The Carolingians' repulse of hostile neighbors had created favorable conditions for the improvement of agriculture within the empire, but industry, commerce and town life remained backward. There was no longer booty to stimulate the

empire's economy. Its own growing agricultural prosperity and in particular its resplendent churches had begun to attract raiders, not by land but by water, on which the Franks were neither confident nor experienced. The division of the empire between the three surviving sons of Louis I in 843 ended neither their quarrels nor the sense of the unity of Frankish lands. In fact it encouraged all the rulers to improvise ways of building up military support and alliances with the great non-royal families of their lands which precluded all possibility of restoring unity.

The "middle kingdom" of the oldest brother, Lothar, which included all the key places of the empire, Rome, Pavia, Aachen, as well as much of the family land in Austrasia, was further divided between his three sons after his death in 855. Ten years later Louis the German divided his kingdom between his three sons. It was by luck rather than design that "Germany" was reunited by 882 when Charles the Fat was left as sole survivor. To the west Charles the Bald had difficulties in obtaining recognition of his rights in Austrasia where he saw fit in 852 to appoint his son Charles as king. Two of his other sons were made abbots in order not to divide his realm still further. Neustria was to be the portion of Louis the Stammerer. Again, it was only a matter of chance that Louis II inherited all his father's lands in 877, only to die himself in 879. Within a few years the defense of Paris against the Normans put up by one of the counts, Odo, secured his appointment as king of the Franks in 888. He was the most powerful lord in western Francia and his descendants were to be kings of France for many generations. But after his death in 898, Louis II's son Charles the Simple became king. The Carolingian hold had however been broken and no subsequent king of France would ever again claim the empire as well. The Carolingian empire had in effect been broken down. The old lands of the center and the west, with longer historical traditions, developed institutions of their own. Only in the east did the concept of Christian empire still have value, for without it the rulers of Germany risked falling victim piecemeal to their eastern enemies.

The effort of cultural renewal launched by Charlemagne survived his death and reached its peak in the middle of the 9th century. Nor were its achievements all ruined in the aftermath of imperial collapse, for the revival of some great schools, like that of Reims, was sustained over the generations and enriched later scholastic movements. Charlemagne brought together in his large court scholars from all over Christendom and pooled their experience, so that later generations worked from a broader basis than had previously been possible. Among the men of un-Frankish nations who served the Carolingian empire, the part played by Englishmen is even preponderant and calls attention to the rapid progress achieved by the English in the century after their conversion to Christianity.

Barbarian kingdoms in England

The other great state to emerge in northern Europe about this time was England. Thereafter it exerted a powerful influence throughout the Middle Ages. Much of its history in its formative years remains obscure and confused but two periods stand out as being comparatively well described: the conversion

The Carolingian Renaissance

The term "renaissance" came into historical use to describe the revival of learning in 15th-century Italy, when it was believed that this inaugurated a movement for the cultural transformation of medieval into modern Europe. Over the years the emphatic use of "*the* Renaissance" for this period has become an affirmation of this convention, though at the same time medieval historians applied the term, thereby weakening its force, to fit the intellectual changes of the 12th century and the renewed interest taken by the Carolingians in antiquity. The Frankish control of the west, their presence in Italy and their confidence in dealing with the eastern empire made them eager to claim for themselves what they could of the Roman legacy. This meant bringing architecture to Aachen from Ravenna, where the imperial court had left a more dazzling impression than in Rome itself. It meant, above all, copying books, from which the clergy could immediately (and their pupils in the long term) acquire the learning of antiquity. They studied "science" and profane literature as well as the church fathers like Augustine. They reformed their style of calligraphy in copying ancient texts and executed faithful imitations of ancient drawings in a bid for authenticity. The texts then copied ensured the survival of Latin literature for subsequent centuries, since some authors are now known by manuscripts no older than the 9th century. Whether this bookish renaissance really had a comparable counterpart in building and wall painting remains doubtful, given the destruction wrought so soon after by the Vikings and by subsequent rebuildings. The Carolingian rulers showed their ambition to effect substantial improvements throughout the empire by their monastic and administrative reforms, but the easiest part of the operation to carry through was certainly the reform of letters and education. The clergy had their own motives for persisting with it and adequate intellectual support came from Italy, Spain and England. The Carolingian renaissance achieved little in the short term, if it planned to restore the Roman empire. Its importance was to salvage so much of the threatened Latin literary past.

Right The Acts of the Council of Ephesus. An example of Carolingian minuscule, the clear script developed at the court of Charlemagne.

Below right The *Codex Aureus* of the four Gospels. This superb manuscript was made at Corbie c.870 and shortly after given by the Carolingian emperor Arnulf to St Emmeran monastery at Regensburg. Christ in Majesty in a mandorla is shown with the four evangelists writing in both codices and rolls.

Right The back cover of the Lindau Gospels is a great treasure of metalwork dating from Charlemagne's own day. Though designed as a whole, it required a variety of techniques in its execution: enameled cross and busts of Christ, champlevé and cloisonné. The cross is superimposed on four silver-gilt panels of engraved animal interlace. The link with Irish and English 8th-century decoration is striking. The gripping-beast medallions seem to be older than their earliest Scandinavian appearance on the Oseberg ship. The Gospels, of the late 9th century, were not originally bound with their present magnificent covers.

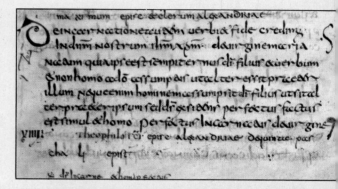

Above An early 9th-century enamel cross from the Capella Sanctorum of the Lateran, now in the Vatican. It is decorated with scenes from the early life of Jesus and set in gold filigree.

Right This important Saxon monastery at Corvey on the Weser was founded in 822. The west front, built on the model of the church of St Riquier in Picardy (c.800), created the first imposing facade for a church in western architecture. Though the middle of the facade was raised higher c. 1146, it gives the best impression surviving of the new style of Carolingian building.

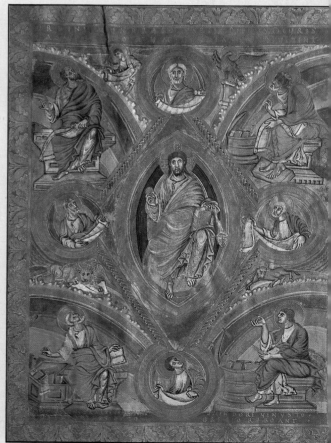

of the English peoples in the 7th century as told by Bede, and the construction of the united monarchy under the kings of Wessex in the 10th century. These two periods were separated by the time of Danish invasion and settlement, a belated replay of phenomena that had brought the English themselves to Britain four centuries earlier.

The marriage of Ethelbert, king of Kent, to a Merovingian princess, Bertha, which opened the way for the Roman mission to England in 597, proves that by then political relations had been reestablished between English settlers and the continent after a century and a half of silence. Only one contemporary British writer, the monk Gildas (c. 500–c. 570), gives any information about conditions in the country during that dark age and it is not easy to make his work, *The Ruin and Conquest of Britain*, yield precise, datable events. Yet when the English record does begin again after 597, it becomes obvious how much had changed in England in the two centuries since Roman administration was last vouched for.

In the first half of the 5th century the Romano-British peoples, left to themselves by the withdrawal of the Roman legions to the continent, had to deal in particular with invasions from the north, which came across what had been the best-defended frontier of the Roman empire: Hadrian's wall. The British probably employed German auxiliaries as was the practice on the continent. Some of these may have been settled with their families in enclaves even as early as the 4th century, but they and their successors were not absorbed into provincial society. We know that at least by the mid-5th century Germans wanted to settle independently of the Romano-British authorities; their appropriation of the more Romanized eastern part of the island could not be prevented. Some British enclaves remained there, some Britons were enslaved by the conquerors. But the Germans were not Romanized in language or religion, so Roman Britain was the only province of the western empire ever settled by the barbarians where the newcomers did not have to come to terms with survivors of Roman civilization. The Romano-British to the west spoke Celtic, but continued to write in Latin. They also remained Christian, though their bishops, unlike those in Gaul, left their cities in eastern England and did not attempt to convert the Germans, who were pagans, not Arians. For a time in the late 5th century the British succeeded in holding up the German advance westwards but never recovered sufficiently to evict their erstwhile auxiliaries from the island. By the mid-6th century several distinctive Germanic kingdoms had taken shape and they put pressure on the British, whose areas have continued to contract ever since.

These Germans came from the northern shores of Europe and were probably even more diverse in culture than is implied in Bede's division of them into Angles, Saxons and Jutes. A Jutish element has been identified with Frankish elements detected in Kent and the Isle of Wight. "Angles" established themselves in England, as distinctive groups in East Anglia, Middle Anglia and Northumbria. "Saxons" separated into western, southern, middle and eastern branches. The survival of some of these groups as distinctive kingdoms as late as the 9th century proves that there must have been several coherent groups well established by 600. But in part the kingdoms were a consequence of the way that the Germans had penetrated into different areas of Britain along several rivers and as distinctive groups. However, the later kingdom of Wessex, which is historically the best known, grew out of a union effected between Saxons, who had advanced from Southampton Water northwards and through into Wiltshire in the 580s, and another group of Saxons settled in the Thames valley who, having conquered Bath, Cirencester and Gloucester from the British c. 600, absorbed the Hampshire and Wiltshire Saxons by 680. The development of a powerful kingdom in Wessex took more than a century and was achieved as a result of historical circumstances in England itself, not as a result of invasion by one homogeneous group from the continent and not in the 5th century at all. It is highly probable that other kingdoms grew similarly in the long period for which we have so little information.

The small kingdoms were as often in conflict with one another as with the British to the west. There was no relentless drive against the British until the three most powerful English kingdoms, Northumbria, Mercia and Wessex, which in turn dominated in the 7th century, extended English military and colonizing ambitions from shore to shore. This inevitably forced the alien peoples of the west into the extremities of the island. Competition between the three great kingdoms for hegemony did not decline, though Northumbria, with considerable scope for activities to the north, tended to leave the two southern kingdoms alone. As early as the 7th century the midland kingdom, Mercia, aspired to dominate all the English; even the kingdom of Wessex, stretching through the south of England with the opportunity for further expansion towards Devon and Cornwall, could not resist Mercian overlordship when exercised by Ethelbald and Offa in the 8th century. Only briefly did Egbert of Wessex conquer England as far as the Humber. Disputes about preeminence remained politically significant and the position of authority exercised by one ruler over all the English, the *Bretwalda* (ruler of Britain), was a personal preeminence not transmitted to his kin, unlike the kingship, but fought for. By tradition the authority of *Bretwalda*, the only pathetic reminiscence of Roman Britain retained by the English, had been first exercised by English kings from the late 6th century, and it is significant that at that stage they found no word, like "English," to convey their common qualities.

The conversion of the English peoples to Christianity in the first half of the 7th century was the first stage in creating the English people, according to the scheme of Bede, the historian of the events. For contemporaries, however, their military struggles with one another no doubt absorbed more of their attention than the monastic historian suggests. All the same, fighting among English kings did not apparently hamper the Christian missions. The number of kings that had to be won over with their peoples made the conversion more complex than in Gaul or Spain, though the advantages of having several bases to work from should not be forgotten. The main kingdoms were converted in a comparatively short time: Kent by

Top The most spectacular medieval find of the present century was made at Sutton Hoo in Suffolk in 1939. The remains of a large clinker-built rowing ship 26 meters long were traced from rivets and stains in the sand, the timbers having rotted. No evidence of a body was found, but an astonishing collection of goods, appropriate to a pagan great man's grave, including loot from overseas and a collection of coins, suggesting deposit c.650/660. A king of East Anglia seems to be indicated, but no evidence of his identity has yet emerged.

Above One of a pair of gold clasps in cloisonné work from Sutton Hoo, set in patterns and fitted with thin slices of garnets, precisely cut to the shape of the cell. The pin has an animal-head top. The curved ends are shaped in the form of two boars interlocking from their hindquarters. This piece, probably of English workmanship, is the finest example of the skills shown by 7th-century craftsmen.

the initial Roman mission (597 onwards); Northumbria in two stages, first by the Roman bishop Paulinus (626) and then by monks from Iona (635 onwards). In East Anglia a bishop was established about the same time and the Saxons in the Thames valley had one bishop at Dorchester in the 630s, though another set up at Winchester before 664 actually became the permanent seat of the bishop of Wessex. According to the Northumbrian historian Bede, the king most hostile to Christianity was Penda of Mercia (king c. 632–55), but even before his death his son Peada was baptized and his subkingdom of the Middle Angles was opened up to the Christians from Northumbria. The mission that came also sent a detachment to revive a church feebly set up among the East Saxons much earlier. After the synod of Whitby (664) the new archbishop of Canterbury, Theodore of Tarsus (669–90), organized the administration of the English church. There were then bishoprics at Whithorn, Abercorn, Lindisfarne, Hexham, Ripon, York, Lichfield, Leicester, Dunwich, North Elmham, Winchester, Worcester, Hereford and London. Some proved shortlived; all had been founded to serve particular "tribes" and were quite unlike the diocesan structures of Gaul or Spain. At the time the South Saxons were still pagan. Only between 681 and 685 did Wilfrid establish a see for them at Selsey. Even

so, within a century of Augustine's mission the English had accepted Christianity in all the kingdoms. Paganism, if not eliminated, had long since proved incapable of resisting persistent Christian pressure.

Monasteries also became numerous in 7th- and 8th-century England, following Irish, Roman and Frankish example. Like contemporary Merovingian princes, English rulers founded monasteries. Some famous houses were founded by women, for example Whitby founded by Abbess Hild or Ely founded by Princess Ethelthryth. Others began modestly, like Crowland in the fens, or even Lindisfarne, a cell founded by missionaries from Iona opposite the royal stronghold at Bamburgh. The works of Bede are proof of the good use to which Abbot Benedict Biscop's foundations at Jarrow and Monkwearmouth in Northumbria were put, especially their splendid libraries of books acquired on Biscop's journeys to Rome. Bede himself reports, towards the end of his life (735), that unworthy motives inspired the fraudulent foundation of monasteries to avoid public liabilities on land. A church council held in 747 ordered bishops to supervise monasteries more closely to tighten discipline. Monasteries however had become part of the fabric of society; they were rich and influential. As in Gaul so in England the visible accumulation of riches to the glory of God in churches resplendent with gold, silver and bejeweled shrines and ornaments proved irresistible to plunderers.

Links with the continent mattered much in 8th-century England. The pious and the educated feared for the souls of their Germanic brethren overseas, laboring under pagan delusions, and felt themselves to be part of the universal church, over which the pope presided in Rome. The Carolingian empire owed much to the Englishmen who sustained the Frisian and the Thuringian missions. The contribution made by Boniface to bringing the papacy into alliance with the new Frankish royal dynasty has not been exaggerated. The learning of the school of York came into the main stream of the Carolingian cultural revival through the work of Alcuin (735–804). England was the only part of Christian Europe in the west not absorbed into the Carolingian empire, but it was culturally part of the same world.

By the 8th century Mercian ascendancy over the English had proved to be, if not continuous, at the least the norm. Offa of Mercia (king 758–96) even called himself *Rex Anglorum* (king of the Angles) by 774. He treated Charlemagne as from a position of equality. Both rulers protected the trading interests of their own peoples with the other and clearly stood to gain and lose much by commerce between the two countries. Silver pennies struck in southern England after 775 followed on from the reform of the Frankish coinage c. 755, just as the English had used, then imitated, Merovingian coins since the later 7th century. England might retain its political independence, but it played as integral a part in the economic life of northern Europe as it did in the cultural and religious spheres. During the 7th and 8th centuries the English appeared in European affairs as persons of some consequence, even if their own political unity was far more precarious than that of the Franks. If sources of information about

Mercia were better they might show that some steady progress towards the unity of England was being made across the whole period, but the probability is that the political divisions in the country still ran deeper than they did in 9th-century Gaul, when both lands were invaded by Northmen. The paradox of these invasions is that, whereas in Gaul they accelerated the process of political disintegration, in England they served to bring the whole country under one decisive and lasting leadership.

England, the Carolingian empire, and the onslaught from the north

The earliest raids on England, probably by Northmen, were made on the monastery at Lindisfarne and other places in Northumbria in 793. Danes appeared in Wessex in the reigns of Beorhtric (786–802) and Egbert (802–39) and were even defeated in battles on both land and sea. But they were not deterred. In 855 they wintered for the first time in England on the Isle of Sheppey, but English kings were not alarmed and made no preparations for dealing with Danes who were building up their experience and resources for a massive assault against the English kingdoms. By 865 they were ready for a decisive engagement. A great force arrived in East Anglia and, after browbeating the people there, turned north and captured York where they founded a kingdom. The Northumbrian kingdom became a dependency. The Danes killed Edmund the king of East Anglia in 869 and expelled the king of Mercia in 874. Of the English kingdoms, only Wessex held its own against the invader.

Even there the situation became desperate as Danes invaded and was only retrieved by Alfred ("the Great"; king 871–99) who forced the Danish leaders to terms. They and their followers were allowed then to settle in an area known as the Danelaw on condition they accepted baptism, which authorized English infiltration. The slow process of absorbing the new settlers did however speed up, with the military reconquest of the Danelaw by Alfred's son Edward ("the Elder"; king 899–924) and grandson Athelstan (king 924–39). The Danish settlement must have been massive for it had a profound influence on the development of the English language. If the Danes were absorbed into the English kingdom in the 10th century it was due to an unprecedented expansion in the activities of government, which the extraordinary circumstances of the time can alone have excused.

English kingship in the 10th century depended on the king's ability to lead troops into battle, to success, and this required the careful appointment of royal thegns (military noblemen), properly equipped, who secured social eminence as part of their reward. The kings also learned to develop a national strategy for dealing with the enemy. Alfred himself built defense points called burhs, and a surviving list of them proves that they were founded for military purposes. The organization of labor services for burh, bridge and road building, according to land held, made new demands on the humble population not called to battle. The burden of taxation had certainly become regular enough in the 10th century for kings to think of raising large sums to buy off Danish aggression when raids were

resumed. These later raids show that England was thought to be worth plundering again. But this time the Danes were not interested in plundering the monasteries, even if they had become numerous and prosperous again thanks to royal patronage. It was the monarchy itself they seized, in 1013. By that date the English monarchy had become the most powerful single state north of the Alps.

The king controlled the issue of a national coinage, though the coins themselves were struck in mint towns all over the country. The administration of the country was not generally based on the old tribes or kingdoms but on smaller divisions first used in Wessex and transferred systematically to the rest of the country as it was absorbed by the kings of Wessex from the Danes. The largest units, the shires, were territories formed around a leading town or fortified point from which it took its name. The shires were subdivided into hundreds, districts which had judicial, financial and probably military

Above This "Ezra" portrait comes from the *Codex Amiatinus*, a manuscript made at Monkwearmouth to the order of Abbot Ceolfrid (690–716) who intended it for the pope. It was modeled on a text of the Bible prepared by Cassiodorus which the abbot had brought back from Rome. Probably this manuscript contained an author portrait of Cassiodorus depicted as Ezra, the scribe who renewed the law. In this copy nine volumes of the Bible are shown on the shelves, as in Cassiodorus's edition. The 8th-century artist has reinterpreted his classical model, but his inspiration is clear.

Right A Pictish stone from Rhynie, Aberdeenshire, probably of the 7th century. The symbols of a fish and "elephant" may represent marriage agreements or land settlements.

Above This surprising find, bearing the name of "Offa Rex" on a gold coin otherwise imitating the Islamic dinar, complete with Kufic inscription, is the most extravagant demonstration of Offa's interest in coinage and suggests how far away 8th-century English trade might reach.

Above right A page from the so-called Book of Kells. Christ is here shown bearded, enthroned on a draped cushion, under an arch, flanked by a pair of peacocks with four angels below. Though at Kells since the early 11th century, this most lavish of all Irish manuscripts was more likely executed at Iona c.800. The portraits in the manuscript were all painted by one artist, one of three used in the decoration, which was never completed.

significance. The kings published codes of laws in the vernacular, at first excerpted from those of various English kingdoms, but which became increasingly responsive to changing conditions in the 10th century. They required men to have lords to vouch for them in legal business or to belong to collective security groups of 10 neighbors. The royal power to direct affairs did not permit the country to fall into the hands of territorial lordships or break up into localities. The kings obtained acknowledgment of their overlordship from the surviving Celtic principalities (Devon and Cornwall became part of Wessex); only in the north was their rule insufficiently masterful to dispense royal authority. This monarchy proved to be an institution so well established by a succession of not always very remarkable kings in the 10th century that it survived its tribulations in the 11th century to become the basis of the much more powerful Norman monarchy. No doubt the slow, unspectacular colonization of the country by generations of settlers since the original invasion period, which had by the time of Domesday Book (1086) extended settlement to its practicable and economic limits for that age, provided the massive countrywide backup for this powerful monarchy, but without the Danish invasions of the 9th century it is unlikely that the unification would have been brought about so quickly, and still less from the south rather than from Mercia. Moreover, the kings of Wessex who had in the 9th century so carefully noted the activities of Northmen across the English Channel in the Carolingian lands, naturally became apprehensive about the political sympathies of Normandy when Danish raids were renewed. In the south of England there was no illusion that the English Channel would act as a frontier, and this concern for their free access in the waters of the Channel remained an important element in royal policy for centuries. As Bede's *Ecclesiastical History*, written in the north, is to the conversion period, so the *Anglo-Saxon Chronicle*, begun in Wessex, is to the

great age of the 10th-century monarchy. Both sources emphasize the basic unity of the English peoples, while revealing incidentally how difficult it was to achieve institutional realization. In their own way their monastic writers contributed to the work of preparing the various peoples of the land to live as one nation, at both the ecclesiastical and the secular level.

The Danes played a prominent part in English history between the 9th century and the 11th. On the continent the effect of their presence was mainly negative. The extension of Carolingian domination along the shores of the North Sea had inevitably brought the empire to the attention of the Danes, and even before Charlemagne's own death raiding along the coasts began to present his government with unmanageable problems. The revival of Frankish military vigor and the value of mounted troops did not equip the empire to deal with maritime enemies. For more than a century the Danes therefore battened on to the empire, not in its weaker outlying territories, but where it was strongest, in the valleys of the rivers flowing into the North Sea and in the Loire valley. Here the Frankish traditions of the empire were strongest, the monasteries most thickly planted and enriched by two centuries of royal patronage. The political troubles of the imperial family after Charlemagne's death did not help to coordinate resistance to the new enemies. Even the energetic Charles the Bald was reduced to buying one band of enemies to fight another in 861–62. The invaders' skill on the water, their surprise attacks and their unscrupulous way of operating in small bands made them difficult for the Franks to deal with except at a local level. The imperial government was at its weakest there. Effective encounters with the invaders could only be achieved by local princes at the cost of causing the empire to disintegrate. Ironically it was the Carolingian king Charles the Simple's defeat of the mixed band of warriors led by Rollo at Chartres that brought the duchy of Normandy into being in 911, when Rollo was induced to make peace, become a Christian and stand guard for the Franks against other marauders in the Seine valley. Paris was spared another Danish attack like that of 885–86, but Normandy was to become the greatest of the northern principalities and the one that most hampered royal power.

The settlement of these northern peoples in the west was the last stage of their onslaught, when raiding, plunder and extortion ceased to yield enough booty or to satisfy their enlarged appetites. Nor were these settlements usually long-lived or successful. Several earlier "colonies" had already foundered before 911. One on the lower Weser lasted for less than 30 years (826–52); one in Frisia around Walcheren just over 40 (841–85); a colony at Nantes planted in 919 was eliminated in 937. The early history of Normandy was itself one of rapid expansion at first, followed by a serious crisis that nearly brought its independence to an end. Only in England had dense settlement in the Danelaw enabled the Danes to bring about a major change in the history of the whole country, but even there it was not because they survived as an independent political unit. Normandy survived its crisis to become one of the major "feudal" principalities within the Frankish kingdom.

The "Viking" embrace

The activities of the Danes in the 9th century were in no way inspired by their own kings. The pirates who descended on the Carolingian empire and on equally attractive England did so as bands of adventurers, probably under established local lords rather than as associated freemen. Their incentive was booty; only belatedly did they follow up raids by spending winters in the lands they plundered. If these experiences tempted them to think of settling, they were only induced to do so when their enemies managed to check their advances by giving successful battle. The Danes' assets were their hardy vigor and their marvelous ships. Their settlement in England in large numbers proves however that these pirates could become cultivators or could attract cultivators from their homelands, so there was clearly some desire felt in Scandinavia for more land, and perhaps therefore some pressure from population growth that drove men out.

From Norway at least it seems certain that colonists moved out into the Atlantic and reached the northern isles of Britain early in the 8th century. A century later the colonizing movement had reached the Faeroes. By the middle of the 9th century western Norwegian peoples had an organized lordship on Orkney and from there further colonists fanned out, towards Iceland in the north (860) and, to the south, through the Hebrides to Man and to Ireland where settlements were established at Dublin (836) and Limerick. In Ireland, however, the Norwegians found another rich land where their occupation was resisted. A brief period when they aimed at conquest was succeeded by another in which they settled for the occupation of key towns on the coast, from which they could control foreign trade. Though the Norwegians had no towns or trades to speak of in their native land, as colonists they adapted to their new circumstances and became the founders of Ireland's medieval ports. From there they raided even further out. As pirates they appeared before Lisbon and Seville in 844 and made further assaults on Spain c. 860.

Norwegian colonization in Ireland in the second half of the 9th century was not merely the consequence of the Norwegians' own political realism. Due to changing circumstances in Scandinavia – after the onset of Danish raids in the North Sea and Channel – the Scandinavian world itself had ceased to be, economically speaking, a closed one without towns and commerce. Raiding brought into Scandinavia much booty, including slaves, to be exchanged in emporia like Hedeby in Schleswig and Birka west of Stockholm. The Swedes, a people united around the shores of Lake Mälaren, were already expanding their activities across the Baltic into Kurland and through the Gulf of Finland to Lake Ladoga. Through the 9th century these thrusts into the interior were extended along the Russian waterways to bring the Varangians (a generic term for Scandinavians) to the Sea of Azov (839) and to Constantinople itself (860). These merchant-warriors apparently assumed political leadership in the great cities along their passage and by this means brought into one commercial and political network the settlements between the principal cities of Novgorod in the north and Kiev in the south. The Baltic thus ceased to be an economic cul-de-sac, but rather pumped trade from one end of

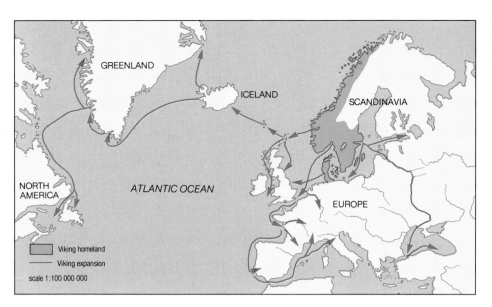

Europe to the other while Europe was clasped in the "Viking" embrace. The maritime waterways of the north and south, linked by the Varangian presence in Slavonic lands, tapped the resources of the Islamic world, which the Arab conquests of the 7th century had so long denied to the west.

The "Russians" made no less fearful impression on Constantinople in 860 than their northern fellows from the Carolingian world, but the empire in the east put up a better show in dealing with these pirates, from whom they were separated territorially by other peoples. But if the pirates did not have it all their own way, they did extort trading concessions in 907, when Prince Oleg of Kiev appeared before Constantinople with a large fleet, and by treaty established close commercial relations with the eastern empire. They supplied it with the furs and honey of the northern forests, but their chief traffic was in men; slaves gathered somewhere along the great Viking network, and valuable auxiliary sailors and soldiers for imperial campaigns. Renewed hostilities in 941 eventually turned to the Russians' disadvantage, since the empire had much improved its military strength in the interval. In 968 Emperor Nicephorus had no hesitation about calling on the Russians to deal with the Bulgars while he was otherwise engaged in Syria, but their leader Sviatoslav, having by that time also destroyed the Khazars (whom the Greeks had used as a check on the Russians), aspired to extend his influence to the Balkans and bypass his most serious enemies, the Petchenegs, on the lower Dnieper. The emperor Tzimisces (John I, 969–76) had no intention of having the Russians as near neighbors and forced them to return and confront the Petchenegs (971). As disciplined auxiliaries, however, the Russians were indispensable, and Basil II, in his hour of desperation in 988 called on them for help; thereafter Varangian soldiers, regularly recruited from the Northmen, counted among the foremost of imperial regiments. The Russian prince Vladimir of Kiev obtained as a reward for his alliance Basil's own sister in marriage on condition he accepted Christianity for himself and his people. In rather more than a century the empire had tucked the Russians into its cultural sphere and obtained valuable services from them, not without incident, but the empire was never

Viking expansion
The enterprise of the Northmen might seem an ideal topic for map makers to illustrate, but in fact maps of different kinds are required. Several general maps on a large scale would be needed to show all the places visited by them at different times, as well as many maps of the areas they came from and settled in. In England intensive study of place-names has revealed the distinctive settlements of Norse and Danes in different parts of the country. To generalize about Northmen or Vikings thus misrepresents important parts of the story. Those who left Norway to colonize Shetland or Iceland were obviously not in search either of booty or of well-cultivated agrarian lands, like Rollo and the partisans who settled with him in Normandy after 911. The conditions of Scandinavia in the 9th century that encouraged many emigrants also enabled many more men to develop a settled life in their homelands. All these people of Scandinavian origin had no more features in common than the pirates, colonists, East Indian men or gentry born in 18th-century England. Not only conditions at home, but opportunities abroad, need to be remembered when depicting the Viking world.

Viking enterprise owed most to their skills at sea. These were learned in the historical period. Archaeologists can trace their progress from the shapes of their ships. At first they had much to learn from others. They improved boats for rowing on the fjords. They added sails and learned to navigate on the open seas. From their journeys they brought back valuable cargoes and booty or news of lands suitable for settlement, trade or plunder. Their confident manipulation of their ships enabled them to travel deep inland up the main rivers of Europe. It gave them mastery of river ports such as Rouen, Nantes, Dublin, Limerick, Novgorod and Kiev. Though they are also said to have taken quickly to horses, this can only have been as an expedient before they were settled in a district.

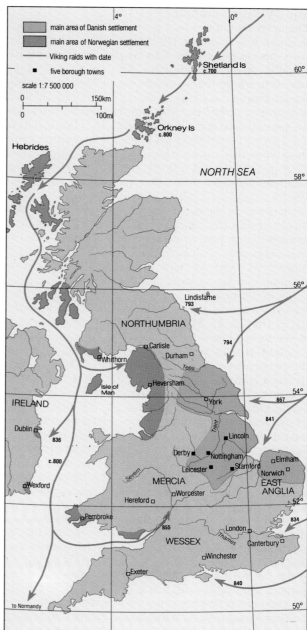

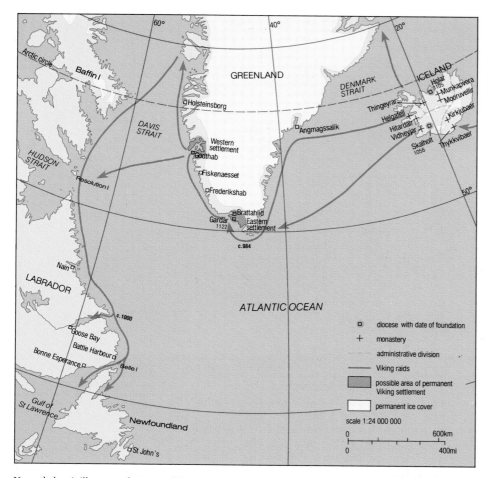

Nevertheless it illustrates their opportunism and venturesome character. They dared all. Once they had left home they had nothing to lose but their lives. The maps show the chief areas of their activities. The northern emphasis points to their settlements in unpropitious areas, more suitable for sheep farming than plunder. In Iceland they developed an abundant literature which, though not written down before the late 12th century, certainly gives us the most insight into these peoples. It shows them as hardy, passionate and violent, given to feuds and fighting. So simple sheep farmers were not necessarily far removed in spirit from the bands of marauders described by terrified monastic chroniclers.

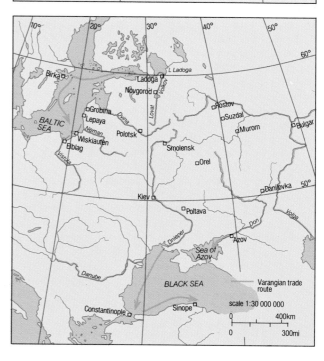

seriously shaken like the peoples of the west.

The resistance put up by the empire itself checked the capacity of the Russian leaders to rampage without hindrance and no doubt helped them to concentrate on organizing the great area their enterprise disposed of. It is certain that when Swedes broke into the northern river network and linked it to the Baltic there must already have been commercial links by river with the south, particularly down the Volga, through the territory of the Khazars and across the Caspian Sea for contact with Baghdad, but also down the Dnieper into the Black Sea. The facility of the Baltic peoples on the water enabled them to exploit the existing system very rapidly. Muslims had tapped northern forests for their supplies of slaves, furs, wax and honey; depots had grown up for trading purposes, both among the Slav populations of the forests and among the Khazars. The latter established a state on the lower Volga c.700, which was converted to Judaism about a century later. But the Slavs along the Dnieper were probably very ill organized politically when the Northmen arrived. There was little agriculture and towns there were basically fortified trading posts. When the Northmen arrived they must very quickly have taken the lead, either at the request of those who needed their military services or by imposing themselves. The leaders of the assault from Kiev on Constantinople in 860 were already Northmen. Within a few years the leadership of the city passed to Oleg from Novgorod who brought all the cities of the Volkhov-Lovat-Dnieper river system together. In this way the Northmen established their most enduring political community outside Scandinavia. Oleg's descendants, the Rurikovitch, ruled in Russia for centuries. By the mid-10th century their names were already Slav, as they were absorbed into the more numerous local population. They had already attacked and destroyed the Khazars, their commercial rivals to the south, before their occupation of Bulgaria and their conversion to Christianity. But it was only with the importation of Greek culture that reliable records of their activities began. By that time, inevitably, their more daring exploits had already come to an end. As settled, organized peoples, with their own metropolitan bishop at Kiev (from 1037), the chief city of the Russians, they had to deal in their turn with the constantly threatening Petchenegs who preyed on Russian links with Constantinople. Only in 1091 were they crushed by the eastern emperor. But after 1055 the Kievan cities suffered from both external enemies and internal rivalries, which hindered their prosperity at a time when western Europeans were finding their own way back to the Mediterranean.

The Baltic world itself settled down to the effects of Christian kingship, the drying up of Viking enterprise, the cessation of those raids that had sent enslaved men to the markets of the east through Russian waters. The era of unrivaled northern superiority was over. History had shifted into a new gear. The barbarians of Europe had been either converted to Christianity or dispersed, and Christian Europe could embark on other enterprises. The Russians themselves were not spared the effects of the last migration of peoples across Asia, that of the Mongols, but for the rest of Europe the migrations of peoples, so problematic for six centuries, had finally reached their term.

Above This 9th-century picture stone from Alskog, Tjängvide, Gotland, may be intended to depict Valhalla. A dead warrior, mounted on Odin's eight-legged horse, is welcomed to the other world by a woman offering him a drinking horn. Lower down is shown a ship with warriors.

Top This ship, built c.800 and used for the burial of two female bodies, was discovered beside Oslo fjord and is the oldest known northern sailing ship. The valuable jewelry deposited had been looted, leaving only more prosaic grave goods. It was fitted with 15 pairs of oars; the prow and stern bear elaborately carved panels.

PART TWO
BREAKING NEW GROUND

SHAPING NEW FORCES

The resurgence of the eastern empire

The period following the collapse of the Carolingian empire in the west – the mid-9th century onwards – has often struck observers as a particularly depressing one because it so abruptly and swiftly betrayed the hopes generated by the outstanding members of the Carolingian family. However the recovery of Europe was not in fact achieved by any imperial regime but by the capacity of local authorities to consolidate their own economies and societies to the point where they could be defended against recurrent predators. From that point of view this period must be regarded as one of very positive achievement. By the beginning of the 11th century Europe had become a recognizably stable community of peoples, no longer liable to be upset by waves of invaders or by intestine disputes. The Northmen themselves were absorbed into Christendom by their conversion; the Magyars on the periphery were more forcibly expelled and decided to abandon their nomadic way of life for agriculture in the empty lands of Hungary. Even the Saracens in the west retreated: their nest of piracy was suppressed in Provence; in Spain and Sicily the days of Islamic rule were numbered.

The Christian powers were not directly responsible for this, but they were preparing themselves to take advantage of it in due course. Europeans were no longer at the mercy of foreign conquerors. They had found the means to defend their own territories in the west without an emperor, though Charlemagne had at least shown the way and, in legend, provided inspiration for the future.

In the east however the empire still discharged the role of defender and at this stage entered upon its most glorious phase. It had been saved against the most persistent attacks of the Muslims by the emperor Leo III (717–41) and his successor Constantine V (741–75) who had also turned on the Bulgars and made them sue for peace (774). But their dynasty, the Isaurians, was also responsible for the iconoclastic controversy over the veneration of images in the church (726) which aroused popular and monastic hostility in the empire as well as creating difficulties with the papacy, so that during this period the Franks "usurped" imperial power in Italy. By the time the cult of images was restored in 842 the western empire, though not living up to its original promise, had acquired respectability. With the emperor Basil I (867–86) the eastern empire fell into the hands of the successful Macedonian dynasty which was to rule for nearly two centuries (867–1058). The greatest western success of the dynasty, finally achieved by Basil II (emperor 976–1025), was the domination over the Bulgars who had shown their ambitions in the Balkans as early as the 7th century. By 811 they had advanced from their original settlement in the Danube basin and encroached on imperial Thrace, as far as Constantinople itself where they killed the emperor

Nicephorus I in battle. During the 9th century their empire expanded into Macedonia where it acquired many new Slav subjects. Gradually the Bulgars gave up their own language and became Slav-speaking themselves. About this time the Greek church, under the patriarch Photius (858–67, 877–86), accepted that it was its duty to send missions for converting the pagans of the Balkans beyond the frontiers of the empire, and as Christianity spread among the Slavs the Bulgars feared they would lose their hold over them unless they too became Christian. The Bulgars revised their hopes of getting their Christianity from the west after the Greek emperor put on an impressive show of the empire's naval strength. So the Bulgars were converted (in 864) by the eastern church but this was not followed by meek submission to the authority of emperor and patriarch. The Bulgars' ruler Boris obtained in 870 from a Constantinople worried by his negotiations at Rome the semiautonomous ecclesiastical province he desired for his people, and despite the growing influence of Greek culture in their lands the Bulgars remained capable of defending their own interests. Boris's younger son Simeon (ruler 893–927) felt justified in attacking the territory of the empire in 894. The Greeks appealed to the Magyars for help which drove Simeon to call on the Petchenegs, who pushed the Magyars west into the Danube plain and thus separated the southern Slavs from those in Moravia. Simeon then defeated the Greeks and made peace in return for annual tribute (896). Later, taking advantage of the crisis at Constantinople when there was only a child as emperor, Simeon attempted to acquire the empire for himself (913) and at least succeeded in obtaining his own coronation from the patriarch, as "Basileus" (king) of Bulgaria, and the promise of becoming the child emperor's father-in-law. He was, however, frustrated in his plans for becoming the dominant power in Constantinople, and neither his territorial acquisitions in the Balkans nor the setting up of an independent patriarchate weakened Byzantine resolve to oppose his pretensions. After his death, his successors could not hold the Bulgar state together; disaffection grew even in the church, leading to the Bogomil heresy. Meanwhile the Greeks recovered their nerve, particularly in the east. The emperor Nicephorus called on the Russians to deal with the Bulgars when they became troublesome (968) with such effect that Nicephorus's successor, John Tzimisces, found the Russians more of a challenge than the Bulgars. In the process of expelling them he proceeded to annex Bulgaria and abolished its patriarchate (971). John's death in 976 not surprisingly produced a reaction and in Macedonia a new "Bulgar" empire began to take shape under the czar Samuel, who revived the patriarchate and established his political and ecclesiastical capital at Ochrida. At first Basil II failed to defeat Samuel as he expanded his rule into imperial territory, so that Samuel's empire came to

Revival of the eastern empire under the Macedonian emperors

The Greeks succeeded in saving their part of the Roman empire from the first century of Islamic attack but, until the advent of the Macedonian emperors in 867, were in no position to counterattack in earnest. It was during the next 150 years that the empire of Byzantium, or Constantinople, enjoyed its finest hours. The Muslims were pushed back into Syria, and Greek authority extended over Armenia. More lasting proved to be the new efforts made in the mission field to convert the Bulgars and the Slavs in the Balkans and beyond. The acceptance of Orthodox Christianity proved to be a means of bringing people who had hitherto eluded and defied the imperial government into the orbit of Macedonian influence. The territories were eventually divided into "themes" or military recruitment areas. With the final conquest of the Bulgars Basil II once more established the imperial frontier on the Danube. The Byzantines' confidence that the tide had turned in their favor encouraged later governments to economize on the army and trust to the rule of civilians. The result was that, when the Seljuk Turks arrived in Asia Minor, the Byzantine army was crushingly defeated at Manzikert in 1071. From this blow the empire never properly recovered.

Center right The great Macedonian emperor Basil II is here shown in armor, with prostrate Bulgars in the foreground. It gives a majestic impression of the aged ruler who dominates all the other figures, is blessed by Christ and receives the insignia of office from the angels. From a Greek Psalter written for the emperor (1017–25).

Below right This profusely illustrated manuscript, written in a monastery of Asia Minor in 1066, shows here incidents in the debate over images which had disturbed Byzantine society three centuries earlier. The monks and the laity in general had been hostile to the attack on religious images, which was ruthlessly pursued by emperors, for reasons not altogether clear. Muslim influence on Christianity has, improbably, been alleged. Hostility to monastic influence in the church is more likely. The prominence of Theodore the Studite monk, shown here, emphasizes the responsibility of bishops in attacking images of Christ and may reflect the personal enthusiasms of the copyist himself, Theodore of Caesarea.

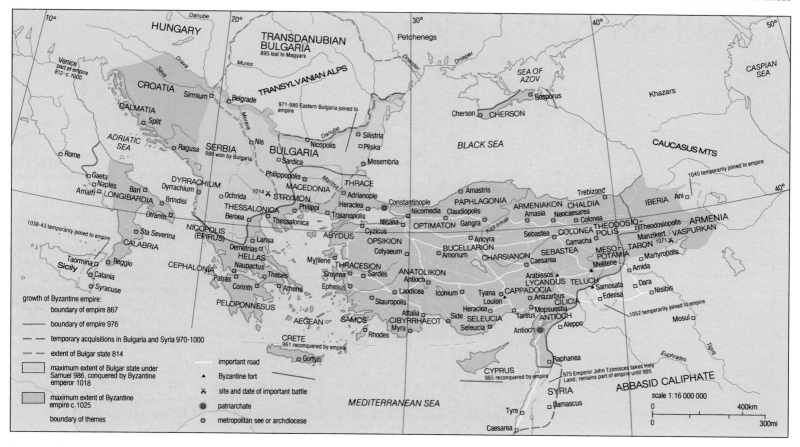

growth of Byzantine empire:

boundary of empire 867

boundary of empire 976

temporary acquisitions in Bulgaria and Syria 970-1000

extent of Bulgar state 814

maximum extent of Bulgar state under Samuel 986, conquered by Byzantine emperor 1018

maximum extent of Byzantine empire c.1025

boundary of themes

important road

▲ Byzantine fort

✗ site and date of important battle

patriarchate

metropolitan see or archdiocese

scale 1:16 000 000

0   400km

0   300mi

stretch from the Adriatic to the Black Sea. Basil II had to contend with difficulties both at Constantinople and on the eastern front, but even after 1001 when he fought regularly in the Balkans it took many years to bring down Samuel (1014) and his empire (1018) despite the massive resources of the Greek state. The result he sought, though inevitable, was slow in coming, but the only Balkan state that had dared to set itself up against Constantinople had been finally subdued.

The importance of religious organization in the Bulgar empire confirms the strength of the new influence of the Christian church in the Balkans soon after the launching of the missions in the second half of the 9th century. The Greek church, which had been reduced by Arab conquests to a comparatively small territory within the empire, began at this time to win members beyond the frontiers, as the Roman church had been doing since the 8th century. It was probably to avoid being entangled in the Roman-Carolingian net that Ratislav prince of Moravia appealed to Constantinople for Christian missionaries in 860. The dispatch of the brothers Cyril and Methodius as missionaries from Thessalonica led to the invention of the Cyrillic script for Slavonic languages and the translation of the Bible into Macedonian Slavonic. This inaugurated the missionary movement that converted the Slavs, even though Moravia itself eventually accepted Roman direction. Greek missionaries expelled from Moravia returned to the Balkans to work among the southern Slavs in Serbia and Macedonia. The power of the empire not only protected them there but was proving strong enough to reestablish its hold on Dalmatia, encroach on "Roman" areas like Croatia and resume campaigning in Italy. The empire had recovered its vitality with its orthodoxy.

The Dalmatian cities and the Serb princes of the interior contributed to the military requirements of the empire and the "theme" of Dalmatia was set up to complete the organization of the empire's military resources. The themes were large military zones, originally devised under the Roman emperor Heraclius to replace the Diocletian province and settled with troops, over which a *strategus* (state general) exercised supreme civil and military power. From Asia Minor the system was extended to other parts of the empire, as settlers including Slavs were sent in to colonize – cultivating land and discharging military responsibilities in return for their holdings. Building up reserves of men and improving the economy of the land, the empire duly nursed its strength and made good the losses inflicted by the Arabs in the 7th century and by the Slav infiltrations since the 6th. In the 8th century the Balkan themes had been increased from Thrace (against the Bulgars) and Hellas to include Macedonia and the Peloponnese; in the 9th century the Greek grip on the west was shown by the organization of themes for the Ionian islands, Thessalonica, Dyrrachium (Durrës) and Epirus, before Dalmatia was finally reached.

The empire's recovery of its hold on the west was bound to take second place in imperial calculations to the problem of dealing with Islam, for even if the Muslims did not renew the direct assault on Constantinople after 717, it was not until 740 that Leo III, by his victory over them at Acroinon, put an end to their annual ravage of Asia Minor. His successor Constantine V (emperor 741–75) raided in north Syria in 746 and captured the fortresses of Theodosiopolis (Erzurum) and Melitene (Malatya) which marked new frontiers until 781 when the young Harun al-Rashid led the army of his father, the Abbasid Caliph al-Mahdi, deep into Asia Minor. He only made peace in return for tribute. When the Greeks tried to recover from this humiliation, Harun, by then caliph, punished them by recapturing Heraclea and Tyana (806), both beyond the Taurus mountains in Cappadocia. But the Abbasid caliphate at Baghdad naturally took much less trouble with the imperial frontier than did the former Umayyad caliphate at Damascus and by the mid-9th century campaigning had become a matter of annual skirmishing along the frontier that kept the troops in training and brought some compensating booty. The Greeks nevertheless used their fleet to recapture Crete for a brief period (in 843) and to sack Damietta (853), though they could not prevent the Muslims of North Africa from conquering in Sicily. On the eastern frontier, however, the Greeks attacked from Samosata (Samsat) as far as Amida (Diyarbakir) (856) and the war thus renewed indicates that the Greeks were now ready to counterattack in earnest. Basil I failed to recapture Melitene but began an assault on the frontiers which little by little enabled the Greeks to push back the Muslims as well as bring into being a semiautonomous buffer state in Armenia.

While the Bulgar Simeon required attention, the empire could do little about the Muslims who took advantage of their strength at sea to complete their conquest of Sicily (902) and to raid in the Aegean at Demetrias (902) and Thessalonica (904). With Simeon curbed, the new emperor Romanus

Lecapenus strengthened the fleet and reopened the eastern war with the recapture of Melitene (931/4). This provoked a counterattack from the Hamdanid rulers of Mosul who advanced into northern Syria and fought against the Greeks from Aleppo. Nevertheless the campaign of 943 recovered Martyropolis, Amida, Dara, Nisibis (Nusaybin) and Edessa (Urfa) for the empire. The frontier constantly shifted in the recurrent campaigning and it was only under Nicephorus Phocas and John Tzimisces that reconquest was achieved on a large scale. Crete was recaptured in 961 and in north Syria Nicephorus advanced as far as Aleppo (962). His military success in forcing back the frontier from the Taurus mountains and the naval victory which gave him Cyprus (965) prepared for the spectacular capture of Antioch after a long siege and the submission of Aleppo, the Hamdanid capital. Tzimisces advanced from this position against the Fatimids (who had invaded Syria) and took the Holy Land as far south as Caesarea, when he decided that to capture Jerusalem itself was beyond his powers at that time (975–76). After his death the Fatimids returned, but Basil II made peace on terms that left him with possession of Antioch and Raphanea and a protectorate over Aleppo. Basil II also put part of the Armenian kingdom under his protection and annexed the rest. The whole new eastern frontier zone was divided into districts – under dukes in Antioch and Mesopotamia, under catepans at Edessa, Vaspurkan, Iberia and Theodosiopolis, and under the *strategus* of the themes of Teluch, Melitene and Taron. The eastern empire was therefore at its medieval apogee when Basil II died in 1025, having made a remarkable and unpredictable recovery as a major military and naval power against assault from every quarter.

Political collapse in the Islamic lands

Byzantine successes in the east demonstrate that the forces of Islam were no longer invincible. Islam had not altogether reached its medieval limits, except in the west, but the setting up of the Abbasid caliphate in 750 had not successfully solved the problem of governing the far-flung dominions of the new

The ancient citadel of Aleppo was restored by Nureddin and the great gate and entrance bridge built by Ayyubid rulers in the early 13th century. The gateway is the finest to be found in the east. It has been restored many times, particularly after the attack of Timur in 1400.

Islamic disintegration in the 11th century
The Umayyad caliphate was set up after political controversy and had difficulty in imposing its authority in Mecca itself. Its successor, the Abbasid caliphate, had from the first to reckon with the secession of an Umayyad state in Spain. If the political divisions of Islam did not carry religious implications, the religious differences between the orthodox Sunnis and various sects, including the Shiite Muslims, created other problems. It was the setting up of a separate caliphate by the Shiite ruler of Kairouan in North Africa (909) that first seriously challenged the integrity of Islam. When this caliphate was transferred to Cairo in 969, it became a formidable enemy to orthodox Islam in its heartland. By that time, however, the caliph of Baghdad was himself at the mercy of his Shiite protectors, the Buwayhids. The inability of the Abbasid caliphs to preserve the formal unity of Islam represents the collapse of the peculiar Islamic idea of the religious state. Effectively religion had become a separate concern. Power passed to military leaders, usually drawing upon the support of their own peoples and tribes, particularly Turkish ones.

religion. From its beginnings the Spaniards had rejected the caliphate in favor of a ruler from the Umayyad dynasty, and before the end of the century Morocco and the Maghreb also had independent rulers of their own. The transfer of the Islamic capital from Damascus to Baghdad, founded in 762, did not in practice make it any easier to dominate the Islamic lands further east despite the splendor and the cultural eminence of the Abbasid rulers. Possibly the intellectual awakening of Islamic scholars brought about by the 9th-century assimilation of non-Arabic learning, notably under al-Mamun (caliph 813–33), helped to diminish the political effectiveness of the caliphate. Harun al-Rashid had divided his empire between two of his sons on his death, and when the younger, al-Mamun, usurped his elder brother's position as caliph, his own principality in Khurasan was assigned to his victorious general Tahir (820). Tahir and his successors were nominally vassals of the caliph but they acted independently. In effect they

began the process of Islamic disintegration in the east. In Baghdad al-Mamun's successor, his brother al-Mutasim (833–42), introduced a Turkish bodyguard to protect himself against his own army. The Tahirid rulers of Khurasan were succeeded by the Safarids in 872, a dynasty originating in Sijistan who also made themselves masters of Persia and boldly threatened Baghdad itself, before themselves succumbing to usurpers, the Samanids, a dynasty descended from a Persian noble. As Persians they promoted their native literature as well as Arabic learning; the young philosopher-scientist Avicenna (980–1037) himself benefited from access to their library at Bukhara.

These dynasties proved that the divisions of Islam did not necessarily prevent Muslims from enjoying the fruits of Abbasid culture, but the eclipse of the caliphate deprived them of the benefit of any other legitimate form of government. In the early 10th century Islam was visibly rent when two new caliphates were set up. The first was the

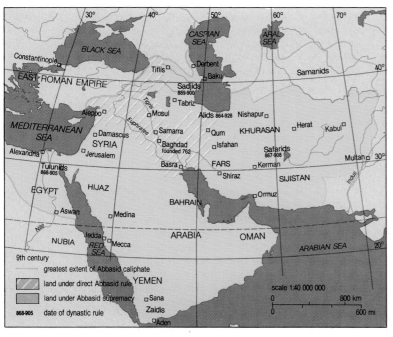

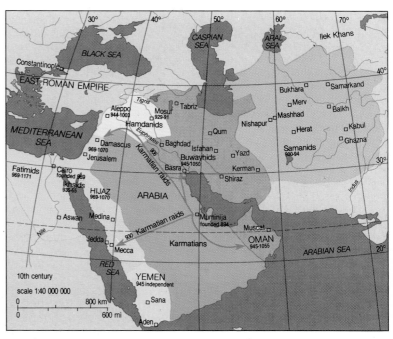

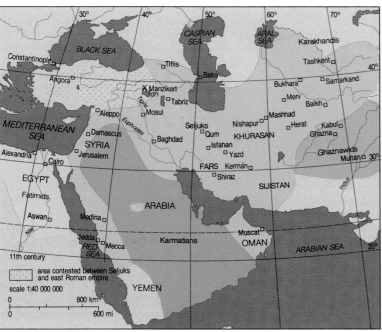

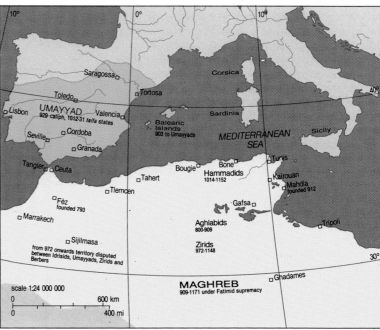

Fatimid "caliphate" founded by the Shiite Imam al-Mahdi at Kairouan in North Africa in 909, when he supplanted the Aghlabid dynasty. His rule was rapidly extended throughout North Africa and, after Egypt had been wrested from its ruling dynasty in 969, the capital of the Fatimid empire was transferred to the new city of Cairo.

For two centuries the heretical Fatimids ruled the most powerful Muslim state. From their Aghlabid predecessors they had acquired a powerful navy, but the basis of their power in Egypt was the century-old independent state set up there in 868. Its founder, a Turk called Ahmad ibn-Tulun, had

been sent to Egypt by the caliph, but then led the resistance to long-resented demands for taxation. Egypt became once again an independent state. Ahmad's power rested on his army and he extended his authority into Syria (877). For a short time the country reverted to Abbasid rule (905–35), and then again became the fief of another Turk, Muhammad ibn-Tughj, who revived the link with Syria and occupied the holy cities of Mecca and Medina across the Red Sea. His short-lived dynasty, the Ikhshidis, were ousted by the Fatimids, who found Egypt an admirable base for their activities. The improvement of the economic life of the country enabled the

Spain in the Visigothic and Umayyad periods
It was in this period that the Spanish church was first effectively organized, the distinctive importance of the northern regions emerged, and the south (Andalus) was developed by the Muslims as one of the gardens of Islam. The Christian survival in the north, together with their links across the Pyrenees, gave a new importance to that region and a new character to medieval Spain, which in the ancient world had been more open to influences from the Mediterranean.

Right The greatest mosque of the medieval world outside Mecca was begun by Caliph Abd al-Rahman I at Cordoba in 785. When it was extended by Abd al-Rahman II (833–48), the *mihrab* was moved further south to the site of what is now called the chapel of Villaviciosa, shown here. The enlargement of the mosque in the late 10th century once more removed the site of the *mihrab*. The 9th-century decoration rises above funerary slabs of the Visigothic and Arab periods.

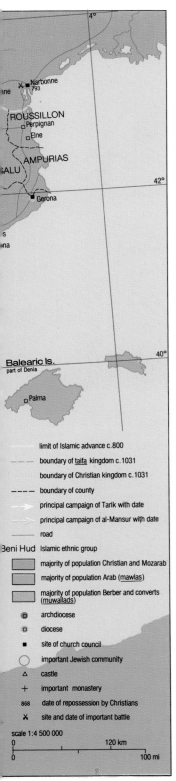

limit of Islamic advance c.800

boundary of <u>taifa</u> kingdom c.1031

boundary of Christian kingdom c.1031

boundary of county

principal campaign of Tarik with date

principal campaign of al-Mansur with date

road

Beni Hud Islamic ethnic group

   majority of population Christian and Mozarab

   majority of population Arab (mawlas)

   majority of population Berber and converts (muwallads)

◎ archdiocese

◻ diocese

■ site of church council

◯ important Jewish community

△ castle

✛ important monastery

868 date of repossession by Christians

✕ site and date of important battle

scale 1:4 500 000

0   120 km

0   100 mi

Fatimids from the first to set about a building program, vestiges of which survive to prove the confidence and splendor of the new regime.

The Fatimids, like the Abbasids, came to rely however on armies, importing Turks and Negroes as mercenaries. In 962 Alpitgin, a former Samanid governor of Khurasan, had captured Afghan Ghaznah which was to become the capital of a new empire extending both into the Punjab (conquered 1001–24) and over most of the Samanid dominions. Here however they came into conflict with an even more powerful family, the Buwayhids, who likewise owed their initial success to the patronage of the Samanids. The Buwayhids were also Shiites and had made themselves masters of Persia, before advancing on Baghdad in 945. The caliph's Turkish guard fled and Ahmad ibn-Buwayh was installed as his new schismatic protector, though Ahmad's own capital remained at Shiraz. The protectors in fact made caliphs at their pleasure for the century of their preeminence. Their own religious unorthodoxy and family quarrels narrowed the basis of their support over the territories they ruled, but they were only overthrown by the Seljuk Turks.

Shortly after the Buwayhids had occupied Baghdad, their eventual supplanters had arrived on the fringes of Islam and settled in the region of Bukhara where they became staunch Sunnis. The Samanids were ousted from Bukhara by the Ilek Khans from Turkestan, and the Seljuks, fired by this example, proceeded to take over Bukhara for themselves and to advance then through the lands of the Samanids and the Ghaznawids. The Seljuks' leader, Tugril Beg, occupied Merv and Nishapur in Khurasan in 1037. In the next 20 years the Buwayhids themselves were exposed to Seljuk attacks and, after Persia had fallen, Tugril and his Turkomen hastened to rescue the caliph from his impious masters. These fervent Muslims then revived the political power of Islam, recovered Syria and the Holy Places of Arabia from the Shiite Fatimids, and poured into Asia Minor where the Byzantine armies, defeated at Manzikert (1071), could not prevent a Muslim occupation. The glorious reconquests of the Macedonian period were thus lost by the revival of Islamic military might.

Rival faiths in the Spanish peninsula

The second caliphate set up in the early 10th century had a much less long-term impact on Islam than that of the Fatimids, though it is better known in the west. In 929 the Umayyad ruler of Spain, Abd al-Rahman III (912–61), took the title caliph, after he had recovered his full authority in Muslim Spain, asserted himself against the rulers in Christian Spain and obtained recognition of his authority in Morocco. With his navy he was now able to provide the only effective sea-borne challenge to the Fatimids; it was no doubt to represent his orthodox challenge to them that he took the title of caliph. His capital, Cordoba, became in this period one of the most wonderful cities of the world; its opulence, culture and power were unrivaled in western Europe. Its reputation was maintained by his successor and then by the vizir al-Mansur who emulated the first Cordoban caliph by his military exploits against the Fatimids in North Africa and against the Spanish Christian states. He sacked Barcelona in 985 and demolished the new pilgrimage church at Compostela in 997. Yet on his death in 1002 Islamic Spain fell to pieces once again, and was never fully restored. Like the other Islamic states of the east that achieved cultural and economic well-being under military leaders it failed to develop a cohesive body-politic and its fabulous reputation rested upon less than a century of achievement.

Still overawed by the rulers of al-Andalus (as the Islamic Spanish territory is called) in the 10th century the Christian rulers of Spain were nonetheless nursing the future of the peninsula in their separate states. The glories of the Cordoban caliphs in their heyday rather obscure the fact that even the Muslims in Spain were more often politically divided than united and that the plurality of political organization all over the country reflects the great geographical diversity of Spain. The Visigothic rulers had given a notion of unity from their capital at Toledo but their rule had rarely been uncontested in the whole country. Nor did the Muslim conquest after 711 immediately result in the establishment of an effective government for Spain as a whole. The Muslims, like the Visigoths before them, extended their government into southern Gaul. But nominally the Spanish ruler was an emir appointed from North Africa or Damascus. Only the capture of Cordoba in 750 by the Umayyad Abd al-Rahman I established a dynasty in Spain and by that time a Christian kingdom, Asturias, had managed to assert its independence. Raided and ravaged, it eluded Muslim domination, resistance being organized from its capital at Oviedo. Beside this Christian remnant should be mentioned the Spanish March set up by Charlemagne, out of which later developed both the county of Catalonia and a kingdom with its capital at Pamplona. For more than two centuries these small states of the northern Spanish mountains had to bide their time, but the

Muslims, even in the 10th century, could do nothing to dislodge them.

After the decline of the Carolingian empire these states had to fend for themselves. They were poor and isolated. In the early 10th century, however, the king of Asturias moved his capital south to León and the county of Castile that was set up soon claimed its independence. The new lands were settled with freemen attracted by the generous terms offered by kings in search of colonists. The kingdom of León was not organized as a valiant crusader-type state against the Muslims. It lived precariously on the periphery of the great caliphate and its own dissensions afforded frequent opportunity for the Muslims to intervene in its affairs. Likewise to the northeast the Muslims under Abd al-Rahman III raided the lands of the Christian king established at Pamplona, but had an only ephemeral effect on his determined advance out of the Pyrenees. By occupying Nájera and a large part of La Rioja, and by building fortresses, the new kingdom was preparing to become the principal Christian state of the peninsula, putting behind it its earlier dependence on the Carolingians and on the Muslim rulers of Tudela. Good relations with al-Mansur, the most influential Muslim in late 10th-

century Spain, spared the kingdom his hostility. Under Sancho the Great the kingdom came to include the county of Aragon, Sobrarbe and Ribagorza, and his influence stretched to Barcelona and Gascony before he incorporated Castile (1029) and León itself (1034). When he died in 1035 he was the most considerable Christian ruler seen in Spain since 711. After his death his sons inevitably divided his empire into four kingdoms, rapidly reduced to three: Castile, Aragon and "Navarre," and then to two (1076) when "Navarre" was divided between the other two. It was however restored in 1134, when this name first came into use.

By that time the Spanish caliphate itself had disintegrated into several successor (*taifa* or party) states. Their weaknesses gave the Christian kings of Castile and Aragon in particular the opportunity to intervene in the south and draw on the fabulous riches of the Muslims by selling their military "help." The new wealth of Christian Spain naturally attracted attention in the rest of Christendom, not merely through its connection with Gascony but as far away as Burgundy, where Cluny, the great monastery founded by William the Pious of Aquitaine (911), had become the mother-house of a great movement for religious renewal. A fervor for

The natural fortress of Loarre (which means rocky terrain) was in the 10th and 11th centuries in the frontier zone between the Pyrenean Christians and the Muslim rulers of Huesca. After it was definitively acquired by the Christians in 1070, King Sancho Ramirez made it a favorite residence and founded his royal chapel here. With the Christian occupation of Huesca, however, it ceased to have any further strategic importance.

conquest from the Muslims already unleashed in Sicily brought French recruits to the Spanish armies which now acted to extend the kingdom of León to Toledo (1085). Alarmed for their survival, the Muslim rulers of Seville, Badajoz and Granada sought help from Morocco where a militant Muslim movement, the Almoravides, had established a state based on Marrakech (1062). They defeated the Castilians in 1086 but failed to recapture Toledo, and their leader Yusuf ibn-Tashfin turned against his allies, the Spanish Muslims, and built up his own aggressive Muslim state in the south which eventually reunited all the *taifa* states under his son Ali (caliph 1106–43). The support provided by North African Muslims to the Spanish Muslims matched the support provided by the French for the Christians. Spain became a battleground for the rival faiths.

The long previous history of Christian involvement with Spanish Muslims and the fluctuations of the military battle line had the effect of drawing off the venom the Spaniards' coreligionists had tried to inject into the conflict. Twelfth-century Spain provided in fact an opportunity for Christian scholarship to catch up with superior Muslim learning, much appreciated by such men as Raymond, archbishop of Toledo (1125–51), and Peter the Venerable, abbot of Cluny, who both patronized translators of works from the Arabic. There were many bilingual Spaniards and the Jews also served as middlemen. On the Muslim side of the political divide the intellectual ferment produced both the great Muslim philosopher ibn-Rashd (known as Averroes; 1126–98) and the Jewish philosopher Maimonides (1135–1204).

The cultural achievements of this period probably owed much to the inability of political leadership, both Christian and Muslim, to hold together their people for concentrated action at the military level. The kingdom of Castile was divided after the death of Alfonso VII (1157) between León and Castile and had already been obliged to tolerate the appearance of the new independent kingdom of Portugal. In the northwest Navarre broke away from Aragon (1134) which became united with the county of Barcelona. The Catalans, who first appear under this name c. 1100, had a ruler whose dynasty had already flourished for two centuries in the lands of Charlemagne's Spanish March, and though at this point they became yoked to the Aragonese their own interests still stretched along the shores of the Mediterranean, north into Provence and south, by 1148, to Tortosa. Catalonia might well have remained under the French monarchy like its neighbor Gothia, from which it was only divided in 875. However, by the 11th century effective Frankish authority in southern Gaul had long since disappeared and indeed the possibility that Gaul itself might be divided among several "kings" was not so far-fetched, given the reality of powers exercised by the rulers of the provinces.

New states in Carolingian lands

Charlemagne had envisaged that his empire should be divided between his three sons so as to give his northern lands with Burgundy to the oldest, Charles, Italy and Bavaria to Pepin, and most of France west of the Alps and south of the Loire to the youngest, Louis. When the empire was actually divided, between the sons of Louis in 843, the results were quite different. "France" and "Germany" were established, separated by a "middle kingdom" assigned to the emperor Lothar; it included all the principal imperial cities. The eastern frontier of France thus established was to remain the formal boundary of the kingdom throughout the Middle Ages. The Carolingian rulers of France could not forget the ambitions and history of their house, but in an emergency in 888 the Carolingians themselves were kept off the French throne, by a former count, Odo, who having won his military reputation by the defense of Paris against the Danes (885–86) was made king (reigned 888–98). After his death, the Carolingian Charles the Simple obtained the crown of France, but lost it seven years before his death (in 929). Though his son, Louis d'Outremer, was eventually restored (936), the revived Carolingian line lived with the fear of being displaced again and for all its members' tenacity they failed to reestablish themselves permanently.

The power of the Capetian duke of the Franks, the military leader in the north, compared favorably with that of the kings. When the young king Louis V died in 987 the notables of the kingdom preferred to make the Capetian duke king rather than seek a "foreign" Carolingian ruler (from Germany). The Capetian dynasty ruled the kingdom of France until the end of the monarchy in 1792. Hugh Capet was the most imposing among French princes; he possessed great lands, church patronage, family connections – a following not easily matched. He had the support of great churchmen like the archbishop of Reims, who crowned him, and the ruler of Normandy, his vassal. The duchy of Burgundy was acquired for his younger brother Henry and kept in the family, but other lands in the old Burgundian kingdom did not accept Capetian rule.

Such strength as the Capetian monarchy enjoyed for the next two centuries depended on the domain lands of the family and their hold on the loyalties of the principal counts of northern France. Among these the most considerable was the ruler of the Normans, who from the time of Richard II (996–1025) styled himself duke. Normandy, originally a modest county based on Rouen assigned to Rollo in 911, had been extended to include Bayeux and the lands as far west as Mont St Michel by 933. Not all the Normans had accepted Christianity or an imposed ecclesiastical jurisdiction before the end of the 10th century, but from Richard II onwards the duke enjoyed an enviable Carolingian-like power over the fighting men and churches of his duchy. The vitality of his duchy is further confirmed by the evidence for pilgrims and exiles who made their way to Italy. There they won fame and fortune; they were French by speech, but Norman by character. Normandy was already deeply interested too in English affairs, but long before Richard II's grandson William the Bastard became king of England, his French royal overlord had ceased to play more than a nominal part in his affairs.

Comparable to Normandy was the principality of Flanders, where, by contrast, domination by Northmen had been successfully opposed through the efforts of the Carolingian counts. They had proceeded to enlarge their jurisdiction from the old *pagus* (district) of Bruges and the Yser estuary to include the Courtraisis, Boulonnais, Tournaisis and the counties of Ghent and Waas. Arnoul (count 918–65), profiting from the political discords of the last Carolingian kings and the Capetian dukes, built up the principality of Flanders, embracing people of both French and Netherlandish speech.

Conditions of life in the 10th century were sufficiently precarious to justify the exercise of real power by the counts, for they could deal effectively with the local problems that distant kings could not tackle. Uncertainties over the royal succession, which caused six changes of dynasty within a century (888–987), the raids of the Magyars and problems over Lorraine and with the German kings precluded the exercise of royal oversight. The functions of the kingship itself, which embodied the unity of the kingdom, necessarily changed. Counts neither ignored the king nor, after 987, aspired to usurp his place. But in effect they consolidated local powers, based on their capacity to build up local military strength, to attract military service and reward it, to build castles and to raise funds, by minting coins, levying tolls or even by selling protection to churches. They held the loyalty of their vassals to be basic to their political hold on their lands, but they sought no religious, as distinct from moral, sanction for their authority. Many of them were pious benefactors of monasteries, but few of them disposed of general powers sufficient to make episcopal appointments as the duke of Normandy alone did, and elsewhere too there was no real overlap between their actual jurisdiction and the ecclesiastical provinces. Churchmen did not approve of the new order which made them more vulnerable to local oppressors. They had to accept what terms they could and, by keeping alive the memory of Charlemagne, did their best to salvage belief in the ideal of kingship.

Capetian France meant little beyond the river Loire or in parts of Burgundy, where the collapse of Carolingian government allowed older Roman traditions to recover. These were the lands of written rather than customary law, where ideas of homage so esteemed in the north seemed to smack of servility. In Aquitaine, the duke Charles the Bald had set up as elsewhere to supervise the counts, did not even aim as in "France" or Burgundy to establish a "feudal" hold. His armies were not composed of vassals, but of faithful men paid for their services. From the south the Basques extended their influence to the Garonne, which kept out the claims of the counts of Poitiers. Though the latter styled themselves dukes of Aquitaine after 984, they were not able to rule beyond the Garonne until the duchies of "Gascony" and Aquitaine were united in 1052. The county of Toulouse, first set up in 817, became independent, enlarged by the acquisition of Albigeois and Quercy, which reduced Gothia to the region of Rodez and Narbonne. Aquitaine had suffered greatly from the Carolingian conquest of 760–68; after the collapse of the empire it happily reverted to its older traditions and restored its links across the Pyrenees. In the 11th century it enjoyed a remarkable period of cultural renewal, in poetry and architecture. Its leaders played a notable part both in the promotion of Cluniac monasticism and in the crusading movement to the Holy Land.

Unlike Aquitaine, the kingdom set up for the emperor Lothar in 843 had no geographical, linguistic or cultural coherence. After a mere 12 years it was divided into three parts for Lothar's sons. The oldest, Louis II, took the kingdom of Italy and the imperial title; the second, Lothar II, took the territories to the north which acquired from him their name, Lorraine, in the brief 14 years of his tenure; the youngest, Charles, who died in 863, received the southern part of the old Burgundian kingdom. On Charles's death and also in 869 when Lothar II himself died their lands were shared out among their covetous relations. It is remarkable that, despite these changes and Lothar's brief tenure, Lorraine itself survived as an entity, becoming a duchy (888) and even a kingdom for Zwentibold (895–900), son of Arnulf of Bavaria. In 911 it reverted to Carolingian overlordship by accepting Charles III of France, when Conrad of Franconia became king of Germany, but in 925 the Saxon king Henry recovered the lordship of the duchy. Under Otto I it came to be ruled by his brother Bruno, archbishop of Cologne, who divided it into two: Upper Lorraine on the Moselle; Lower Lorraine, from Luxembourg north (959). The suspension of ducal authority allowed several distinct ecclesiastical and secular principalities to establish themselves and Lorraine came to be the name of a small duchy bordering the larger county of Burgundy.

The protean character of the names in the Middle Kingdom lands is perhaps even better demonstrated by the case of Burgundy which had by 924 become a kingdom stretching from Basle in the northeast to Arles in the southwest. This kingdom had been cobbled together from lands of the Middle Kingdom first separated in 855. Much of it comprised the portion assigned then to Charles (duke 855–63) which had been reconstituted more or less by Boso, count of Vienne, for himself (880–87). His son Louis, grandson of the emperor Louis II, was attracted from there into Italy where he was crowned, but sent back in 905, blind. This kingdom of Provence was acquired by King Rudolf II of Burgundy

San Millan de la Cogolla (Logroño), a Spanish monk (died 574), was the most revered of Spanish saints after Santiago. His life, written by Braulco of Saragossa (635–40), was used to illustrate the ivory shrine designed for his relics when they were translated in 1067. Here is shown the realization of his prophecy that the Cantabrians would be destroyed by the Visigothic king Leuvigild. The craftsman, Master Redolfus, influenced by German traditions, shows the king in military harness reminiscent of the Bayeux tapestry.

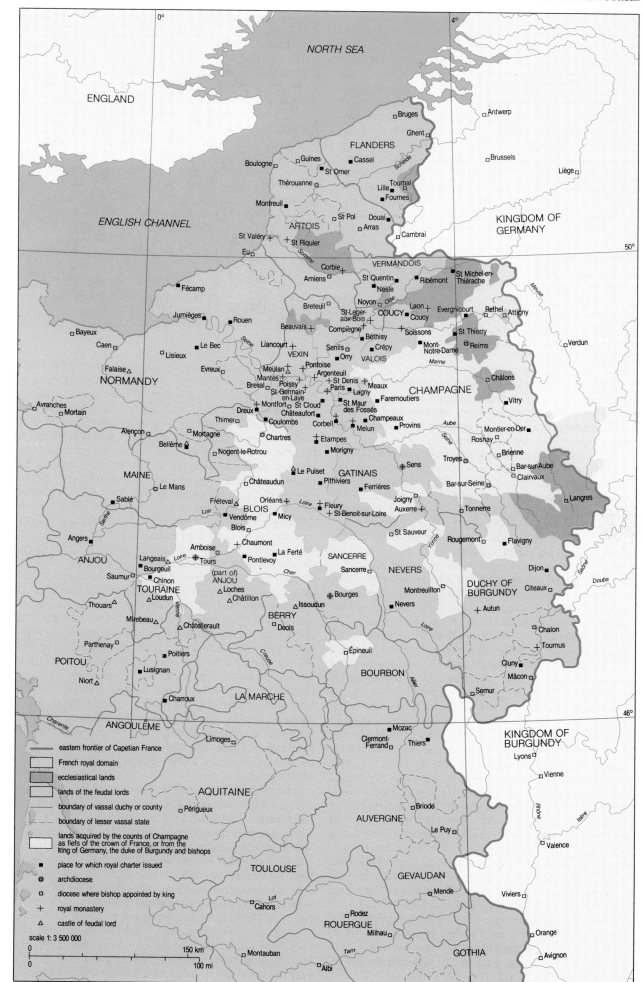

Feudal states of early Capetian France

Maps of territories are necessarily incapable of depicting the personal allegiances of lords and vassals. Even a map like this one that does show the mosaic of lordships, the continuity of inheritance and the permanence of such sites as bishops' sees and monasteries can only suggest the complexity of the situation. It shows lordships like Blois and Champagne capable of historical metamorphosis, and sites of castles that could have long-term strategic significance. The limits of the map are determined by the reach of the Capetian kings of France for two centuries after 987. In this period the Carolingian lands to the east formed part of the German kingdom. To the west the lands that were subsequently united in the Plantagenet dominion already eluded Capetian control. Occasional royal charters for places in the south cannot conceal the fact that in this period the most Romanized parts of Gaul once again lived on their heritage, including the vestiges of written law, dispensing with the feudal experiences of the north. Feudal France embraced the lordships that had to reckon with the existence, if not with the authority, of the kings. The royal lands were not originally so extensive or so subservient to their lords as some feudal states, notably Normandy. But in these lands the idea of France retained its fascination and inspired a new vernacular literature. These sentiments mattered greatly to the Capetian rulers when they tried to create a new political reality in the kingdom.

Legend:

— eastern frontier of Capetian France

French royal domain

ecclesiastical lands

lands of the feudal lords

— boundary of vassal duchy or county

--- boundary of lesser vassal state

lands acquired by the counts of Champagne as fiefs of the crown of France, or from the king of Germany, the duke of Burgundy and bishops

■ place for which royal charter issued

▣ archdiocese

□ diocese where bishop appointed by king

+ royal monastery

△ castle of feudal lord

scale 1 : 3 500 000

0 — 150 km

0 — 100 mi

(912–37) as his price for renouncing his claims to Italy. The original Burgundian kingdom with its base at St Maurice d'Agaune, on the Rhône and on the road from Langres to Italy across the Great St Bernard pass, was created by Rudolf I (888–912). He had initially hoped to make himself king of Lorraine (888) in lands that had been Lothar II's, before they were divided among the kings of Italy, France and Germany and reassembled in the hands first of Charles the Bald (died 877) and then of Charles the Fat. Rudolf seized the opportunity presented by the deaths of Boso and Charles the Fat (887 and 888) to proclaim himself king, but in a matter of months he had to give up his claims on Alsace and Lorraine and console himself with lands in eastern Switzerland and across the Jura. His son Rudolf II extended this kingdom, initially to the northeast by acquiring the counties of Aargau and Zurich. Drawn into northern Italy after 922, he allowed his claims there to be bought out in 923 in return for Hugh of Provence's surrender of the southern kingdom of Provence to him. The effectiveness of the Burgundian kingship in lands that had pursued such diverse histories for nearly a century was even feebler than that of the last Carolingians and early Capetians in France. But the kingdom, such as it was, passed undivided to Rudolf's son Conrad, albeit under the protection of Otto II of Germany, his brother-in-law, and then to Rudolf III (king 993–1032). His niece's husband, the German king Conrad II, finally added the kingdom to his own (1037).

The acquisition of the Burgundian kingdom was the last stage in German efforts to reverse the process of division in the Carolingian lands broken up in 843. The penultimate stage had been Otto I's assumption of the title king of Italy. This finally settled disputes about the kingship there, which had been recurrent since the death of the emperor Louis II in 875. Italy subsequently had no king other than the German king or emperor until the 19th century. Claimants for the crown usually came from the north: Carolingians included Berengar I (888), Arnulf (896) and Louis of Provence (900); others included Rudolf of Burgundy, Hugh of Provence, Berengar of Ivrea (950), all before Otto. Otto appeared in Italy in response to the appeal made to him by Adelaide, widow of King Lothar (946–50) and daughter of Rudolf II; when Otto married her he acquired with her such claims as the kings of Provence and Burgundy could make. He also brought to Italy the advantage of being in a position to block invasions from the German duchies of Swabia and Bavaria, ruled respectively by his son and brother.

Rule in the north of Italy had not so far brought royal rule to the whole peninsula, and Otto's power in north Italy did not at first seem any less precarious or more welcome than that of his ephemeral predecessors. The ruler of Rome, the patrician Alberic, refused to receive Otto there, but after Alberic's death (957) his son, Pope John XII (pope 955–64), found Berengar of Ivrea and his party such a menace to the papal state that Otto was invited to return to Italy. When Otto arrived at Rome he was crowned emperor (February 962). By that time Otto had also proved himself the great victor over the Magyars (955). However, John XII still wanted an ally rather than a master, and discovered too late that Otto was not content to help the papacy. Otto intended to be master of Italy and spent six years there to prove it (966–72).

The popes, who had brought the Carolingians to Italy in the first place, had sought northern protection against the local powers of the peninsula after the imperial support of Constantinople had been withdrawn. Disputes in the Carolingian family after Charlemagne's death had deprived them of this advantage. Only the emperor Louis II had properly discharged the imperial duties, fighting against the Muslims who were active in Italy from the early 9th century. He even recovered the Greek city of Bari from them before his death (871). Louis II had himself disposed of only the resources of the Italian kingdom, and his successors, whether they called themselves kings or emperors, showed none of his ability or devotion to duty. Hugh of Provence, who became king of Italy in 926, had aimed to extend his rule towards Rome. He reached the city, where he married Marozia widow of Alberic I in 932, but was chased out. Though he acquired Ravenna and the Pentapolis (938), his difficulties in Italy had only made it easier for the Magyars, whose raiding had proved the major scourge of the whole peninsula since 899. Breaking into Italy across Friuli, they three times raided as far south as Apulia and many times more in Lombardy, even wintering in central Italy (937–38). They sought booty and slaves, striking where they anticipated little resistance, avoiding mountains and cities where their cavalry was at a disadvantage. Against their unpredictable attacks the only protection was to build defensive points and encourage scattered populations to regroup and reorganize agriculture around these strongholds. The initiative for 50 years lay with local lords whose program of "castle"-building (incastellamento) shaped the development of Italian society for future generations.

Chaos in the southern Italian peninsula

The Saracen conquest of Sicily, which was achieved from North Africa during the 9th century, left the emperor of Constantinople in possession of Calabria and the heel of Italy, from which the Macedonian emperors eventually expected to restore their government over the whole of Italy. Before the loss of Syracuse (878) the Greeks had received possession of Bari (876) on the death of Louis II, and they had also taken under their protection the prince of Benevento (873). The affairs of southern Italy could not, however, be managed any longer by an imperial power. The Greek general Nicephorus Phocas was soon called back to the pressing needs of the Bulgarian and Cilician frontiers. The position of the Greeks in Italy was reinforced by the late 9th century, but it could not prevent the Muslim capture of Taormina, the last outpost of Sicily, in 902. The island, even under the Muslims, experienced a highly checkered history, in part because of the ascent of the schismatic Fatimid caliphate in North Africa to which Sicily belonged. After the Fatimid base was transferred to Cairo, Sicily became autonomous and isolated, and this, after a brief period of glory, encouraged disputes within the island which opened the way for Greek and later Norman intervention. Until the mid-10th century, however, Fatimid naval strength had deprived Italian coastal towns of all sense of security. The Muslims had taken advantage of political disputes

The church of St Angelo in Formis, belonging to Monte Cassino, was reconstructed by Abbot Desiderius (1057–87) whose work at Cassino itself has perished. This monument therefore is the best indication of his sumptuous schemes for beautifying his churches and is the finest piece of painting to survive from the 11th century in Campagna. The painter may have been Greek. The scene of the Last Supper shows the antique manner of reclining at table.

to intervene at Naples in 837; they appeared even in Venetian waters in the early years of Venetian autonomy. They sacked Rome outside the walls in 846 and John VIII paid them tribute 30 years later. They sacked Genoa as late as 934/5 and the base they established at Fraxinetum in Provence in 888 was not destroyed till 975.

The affairs of the area of central southern Italy between the Lombard kingdom and the Greek empire had been dominated by the great duchy of Benevento set up originally in 570/1. It had held together, expanding into Greek territory, and, unlike the other southern Lombard duchy of Spoleto, had eluded the clutches of the last Lombard kings. Under Charlemagne it had accepted imperial protection and called itself a principality (774). In the mid-9th century this principality was divided into two, Benevento and Salerno (849). Fifty years later Salerno lost control of Capua, which became a principality of its own. Gaeta, Naples and Amalfi, which had never accepted Beneventan lordship, were maritime republics and reckoned it was politic, as Venice did, to acknowledge the emperor at Constantinople, since the Carolingians had not made good their pretensions in the south.

In Rome, where popes had made emperors since 800, the chaos of the peninsula had as elsewhere brought local powers into prominence. With the collapse of the Carolingian imperial mission the popes too had lost their role as universal figures. This is reflected in a great series of papal biographies, which extends no further than 872. For the next two centuries the Roman official history records no more than the bare names of popes. John VIII (pope 872–82) was the last pontiff of the time to rise to his responsibilities for dealing politically with the Muslims. In the succeeding century only one pope reigned for more than nine years. There were 30 popes in this time which meant that the average pontificate was too short for effective government. Most popes were drawn from Rome,

and Rome was ruled by the aristocratic family of Theophylact, which itself provided three popes including John XII. In a post-Carolingian world the papacy could hardly avoid the common fate, particularly since the chief consequence of Carolingian rule on the papacy had been the acquisition of the lands of Peter. Thus the papacy, in law at least, made good the losses of church lands confiscated by the Lombards to the north and by the iconoclastic emperors to the south, but this state of the church required government as much as the king's domain lands. The adventurer Alberic I (died 925), who had fought successfully against the Muslims, and his son Alberic II provided what rule the popes themselves could not. In 962, when Otto I set himself to rule in Italy, there was much for an emperor to do.

The power of the western emperor was that much more necessary in Italy after 963 when the new eastern emperor Nicephorus Phocas signified his plans to reassert imperial authority in southern Italy. Otto therefore received the support of Pandulf of Benevento and attacked the city of Bari. But Otto also wanted recognition of his position in Italy from the ruler of Constantinople and so he negotiated. Eventually a marriage was arranged for his son Otto II with Theophano, niece of the new emperor John Tzimisces (972). Otto, content with this last success, returned to die in Germany (973).

The Saxon empire

The German kingdom had, like the Middle Kingdom and France, been divided into three (865) by its first king Louis the German, even before his death (876). But the divisions into southeast, southwest and northern territories had little time to establish themselves. After Charles the Fat was deposed in 887, Arnulf of Bavaria reunited the kingdom. Since 870 this had included Lorraine, acquired by Louis from the Middle Kingdom. When Arnulf died in 899 leaving a child to rule (Louis the Child, king 899–911), the kingship became a fiction; real power

Alpine Passes

The post-Augustan Roman empire transcended the Alps and Roman roads enabled the empire to dispatch armies to all the northern provinces across the mountains. Yet the empire itself also hindered the exploration and development of numerous passages through the mountains. It was therefore in the Middle Ages rather than in the ancient world that the Alpine passes became important. The English, due to the Gregorian mission, were among the earliest barbarian peoples to maintain constant relations with the church of Rome along as direct a route as possible. From the 8th century the progress of the English missionaries in Germany made this desire for good routes into Italy more widespread. The papacy itself began to appreciate how much support it could find in the north. The creation of diplomatic and political ties eventually brought the Franks into Italy as papal allies and revived the concept of Roman empire. For centuries to come the medieval empire, based on northern barbarian strength, was involved in Italian and Roman affairs.

The Alps had to be crossed frequently, often by considerable military forces. The inhabitants and rulers of the mountain regions could not elude the responsibilities and pressures put upon them. To provide for travelers, both official and private, tracks and passes were developed with various resources and amenities, guides, hospices, even entertainers, and the facilities both demanded the services of tradesmen and attracted merchants with valuable goods to sell. If the barrier had never been insurmountable, there can be no doubt of the tremendous development of the Alpine passes linking Italy to the north, once the entirely new pattern of political, economic and church affairs inaugurated by the Carolingian empire had gathered momentum.

At the beginning of this period, when the German kingdom itself did not extend far to the east, the passes to the west were still the most important, and lay for the most part through the lands of the kingdom of Burgundy. For much of the 10th

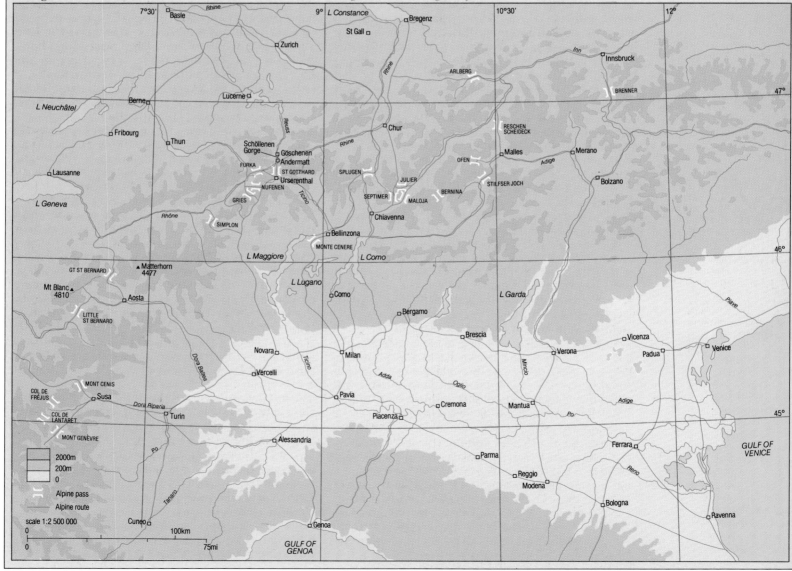

Above Though descriptions of travel are found in medieval writers, drawings which convey an impression of the hazards of the routes and the savagery of the landscape, like this one of Devil's Bridge, were not made before the 18th century. Artists who ventured to sketch had to feel secure enough of their own way and sufficiently inspired by their situation. Even drawings which accentuate the drama cannot demonstrate the real difficulties once experienced by travelers.

Left The riches of the Po valley drew men across the Alpine passes along the great arc from Austria to Dauphiné. The crucial passes were those in the central sector, of greatest importance for all the German kings of Italy down to the 14th century. With Milan as the magnet, travelers from Basle or Bregenz had difficult and complicated routes to follow, and their choice of pass depended on the season and the weather as much as on the urgency of their business and the size of their convoy.

century they were rendered hazardous by Saracens who used their base at La Garde Freinet for extensive raids throughout the Alps, but after they had been dislodged (972), merchants and pilgrims moved more freely. Politically the German king hoped to intervene more in the affairs of the kingdom of Burgundy. However, till the 13th century, there was no direct road across the Alps which linked the Rhine valley at Basle to Milan, so the road south took travelers towards the east; after Chur they had to decide whether they wished to proceed to Chiavenna and thence via Lake Como to Milan or to Bellinzona in the Ticino. The road to Chiavenna led either over the Julier pass (2287 meters), which required more climbing, or over the Septimer (2311 m), which was shorter but not easy and had a bad reputation for snow.

Neither of these approaches to Italy could however rival the St Gotthard pass when it was opened in the early 13th century for it established a direct link between Basle and Milan. The obstacle to the use of this route earlier had been the problem of negotiating the Schöllenen gorge between Andermatt and Göschenen. Only when some kind of road was cut in the cliff face and a bridge – the Devil's Bridge – constructed over the Reuss, were travelers coming north from the St Gotthard pass proper able to leave the Urserenthal and reach Göschenen without climbing up another considerable ridge. Thereafter the route was an easy one.

To the east the favored pass was obviously the Brenner (1370 m), but its importance really grew after the development of Austria and central Europe encouraged Venetian commerce to pass directly into south Germany. On the west the simplest route was that over the Mont Cenis (2100 m) which linked Italy to the heart of France. More famous was, however, the Great St Bernard pass (2472 m), and the hospice on the pass (2113 m) was patronized by travelers from all over Europe.

lay with the dukes of Bavaria, Swabia, Franconia, Saxony and Lorraine.

None of these duchies, apart from Bavaria, had any long history; none of the dukes in 911 was of the royal family. Arnulf of Bavaria had, however, managed to impose a relation of his as duke in Franconia and in 911 this duke Conrad was elected king of Germany (ruled 911–18). In Bavaria a new duke Arnulf attempted to maintain the preeminence of that duchy, even against Conrad's successor, Henry of Saxony, but the Saxons' affirmation of kingship prevailed over the aspirations of the dukes. Of all the kingdoms that appeared in the Carolingian empire it was the German that proved the most capable and merited the imperial crown. For this the Saxon kings themselves deserve the most credit, above all for sedulously resisting the pressure to divide royal lands between sons. The monarchy was thus lifted above the ordinary noble rules of inheritance. Instead, the royal brothers and sons were entrusted with the government of the duchies, left as meaningful divisions of the kingdom but retained under royal supervision. The duchies were far from being homogeneous, either in law or custom or in the cohesion of their leading families. The dukes tended also to be pulled in different directions by the plain facts of geography, or into rivalry, as between Swabia and Bavaria over Italy. Only in Saxony did the promotion of the duke of the most recently converted of the German peoples to the kingship, and then the empire, generate such pride as to sustain the Ottonian rulers into the 11th century. Unlike their Frankish predecessors, however, the Saxons were not to spread across the empire in the wake of their kings nor to establish a new imperial aristocracy, for they and their kings were committed to local and protracted warfare on their eastern frontier against the Slavs.

Both Henry I and his son Otto I eventually established unassailable reputations by their resolution and success in dealing with the Magyars. Henry I began modestly, imitating his English contemporary Edward the Elder by building fortress towns, such as Quedlinburg and Merseburg. He also tricked his Magyar enemies into making a truce for nine years, until his preparations should be complete. When war was resumed Henry was victorious (933) and his son Otto I repulsed them when they returned in 937. The brunt of their eruptions from their base in Hungary was borne by Bavaria; under Otto's brother Duke Henry the Germans pursued them for the first time into Magyar territory itself. Their return attack in south Germany was well timed to coincide with political upheaval there, but Otto resoundingly defeated them at the battle of the Lech in 955. Their leaders were captured and executed.

The Slavs were not so easily disposed of. They were settled peoples, cultivating lands beyond the river Elbe but still pagan. War on this very broad front persisted throughout the 10th century and beyond. The Saxon kings descended from a family with great lands in Eastphalia and were committed to extending German influence to the east. The Saxon pressure extended across the Elbe into Holstein and from there north through Schleswig towards the Danes or up the Elbe against the different Slav tribes, Abodrites, Ljutizes and Lausatians. Further south the Slavs, Serbs and

Czechs impinged on Franconia and Bavaria. Under Henry I Brandenburg, an important Slav center, had been captured and Meissen further out to the south established as a base, but Otto I, from the beginning of his reign, made a determined effort to colonize and convert the Slav lands, establishing two marcher districts, on the lower Elbe and in the Elbe-Saale region. By 947 Otto considered it safe enough to establish six new bishoprics, three north of Holstein dependent on the archbishop of Hamburg, three dependent on Mainz at Oldenburg, Havelberg and Brandenburg. Only after his victory at the Lech did Otto plan a new ecclesiastical province based at Magdeburg in Eastphalia, which had long been one of his favored places of residence, part of his first wife's dowry. It was already endowed with a new monastery (founded in 937) dedicated to St Maurice whose reputation as a warrior saint was at its height. This project, nursed by Otto I and brought to fruition only with papal support 13 years later against the wishes of the local diocesan bishop of Halberstadt and his metropolitan at Mainz, would

Left Christ receives Magdeburg, an Ottonian ivory of 950–1000. This plaque from an altar decoration was probably made in Milan or Reichenau and is typical of its date. The openwork pattern serving as background accentuates the artificiality of the representation. The strongly stylized figures and simple draperies suggest a very special kind of classicism, distinct from that of the Carolingian renaissance.

The German kingdom in the 10th century
A separate kingdom of Germany developed from the Carolingian partition of 843, but it was the Saxon kings after 919 who first succeeded in holding its component duchies together. Their most intractable problem was the continued pressure to expand into the Slav lands to the east which was to leave the definition of the German eastern frontier open for centuries. At the same time the pull of Italy on the duchies of Bavaria and Swabia brought the German kings south and saddled them with responsibilities for both Italy and the empire. The German kingdom itself comprised lands of very different historical traditions, and the ability of its kings to hold them all together until the 13th century remains remarkable. The authority wielded in this kingdom by its bishops was in the best late Roman imperial tradition. The importance of the duchies generally declined as the royal regime grew more confident. The prestige of its rulers opened Germany to contacts with Constantinople and Cordoba. For the first time Germany became a power in its own right.

have created a new province from which all the Slav peoples to the east could be converted. Magdeburg itself was to have a splendid establishment with cardinal priests, deacons and subdeacons: it was to be Otto's "New Rome" in the east, the rival of Aachen or Constantinople. By the time the project was realized, however, Mieszko the ruler of "Poland," even further east, had already entered into friendly relations with Otto. In consequence of this a distinct new political community emerged there, so limits to the spread of German influence to the east were to be foreseen. Further south the ruler of Bohemia, Wenceslas I, had also become a Christian. Before the still improbable conversion of the Hungarians, Otto I, following his victory in 955, protected Germany from further Hungarian attacks with the establishment of marcher border-districts in Austria and Carinthia. In effect, therefore, whatever Otto's ambitions to press further east, he sketched in the eastern boundaries of the German empire.

Well before his imperial coronation he had, like Charlemagne, become the most outstanding ruler of his day, and worthy of being emperor. He received from and sent embassies to the great ruler of Cordoba, Abd al-Rahman III. He traveled around his empire, showing himself to his subjects as far away as Calabria. But the effective government of his empire, more even than that of Charlemagne's, came to rest on the shoulders of the bishops, for the Ottonian rulers disposed of no Frankish-type aristocracy such as Charlemagne had been able to use for the government of his empire. The Ottonian empire therefore had more need to dazzle contemporaries, to emphasize the role of the king as specially consecrated by God, to exalt the parvenu Saxon dynasty above the dukes. In this respect the alliance with Constantinople enlarged the royal repertoire of forms and ceremonies. The clergy rose to the occasion, and their value to the monarchy at this stage is in contrast to their position in France where the whole ecclesiastical organization had been eclipsed by the aggressive show of warlike qualities among the territorial princes.

Otto I consciously modeled himself on Charlemagne but he never contemplated any conquest of the French kingdom to restore the unity of the western empire. Unlike Charlemagne, Otto had no Romance-speaking people in his lands until the conquest of Italy and it was only slowly that his dynasty discovered the obligations of their Roman title. Otto I tried to obtain imperial lands in southern Italy (967–70) and his son Otto II fought the Saracens there (982). It was however Otto III who first conceived of his government as a *renovatio imperii romani* (renewal of the Roman empire), drawing inspiration from both his Greek mother and his learned tutor Gerbert, whom he made pope (Sylvester II, 999–1003). Otto died too young to have accomplished much of what he dreamed, but in one respect his idealism had profound practical consequences. A Bohemian prince, Moytiech, on his confirmation as a Christian, took the name Adalbert and in due course became second bishop of Prague (982). He baptized the Magyar prince Stephen and eventually suffered martyrdom in Prussia (997). Otto III, who had known him at Rome, became devoted to his cult and went on pilgrimage in 1000 to his tomb at Gniezno. Here Otto set up a new

archbishopric with three suffragan bishops at Kolberg, Krakow and Wroclaw. This undermined his grandfather's expectations for Magdeburg and reflects the important change that had occurred, particularly since the Slav revolt of 983. Otto III, instead of trying to reverse the position, preferred to authorize the independence of the emerging Polish state, and so squeeze the other pagan Slavs between two Christian powers. He could also exalt his own empire in the process: his empire would have dependent kingdoms. At the same time Otto III's pope gave the ruler of Hungary both a crown and a metropolitan. It was these states of Poland and Hungary which, with papal blessings, marked the limits of German expansion.

The Magyars had first pushed themselves into the great plains around the bend in the Danube in 895 and until defeated on the Lech had shown no disposition to settle down and live at peace with their neighbors. Economically they were for the most part nomads. In the 12th century they were still practicing a pastoral life, living in tents in summer and taking winter shelter in primitive huts of reeds. It is hardly surprising that in the 10th century they preferred the profit and adventure of raiding their prosperous neighbors, particularly when there was scant resistance to be expected. After resigning themselves to stay at home they spread through the plain but the centers of their new state were along the Danube and in Pannonia.

Christianity crept up on the Magyars from four directions. At Constantinople two of their chiefs received baptism c. 950; from the west the Bavarian thrust was maintained for Christian reasons by Bishop Pilgrim of Passau; from the northwest came missionaries out of Bohemia; at the end of the 10th century others arrived from Italy. A crown was conceded by the pope to the Magyar prince who was baptized as Stephen and married the sister of Henry of Bavaria (later emperor). Under King Stephen (1000–38) the monarchy and the church were organized on Carolingian lines. Its religious center at Esztergom may have previously sheltered Slavonic Christians; its secular capital Székesfehérvár was a royal ceremonial center on the new pilgrim route to Jerusalem. The Hungarian bishoprics were particularly thickly clustered along the Danube and in Pannonia, the former Roman province. Much more slowly did the great plain between the Danube and the river Tisza become absorbed into the new political structure. But by the end of the 11th century the kingdom had edged across the rivers Drava and Sava into Croatia and to the east into Transylvania.

The Magyar conversion had, however, from the beginning turned the Danube into a Christian highway, and by 1020 the Greeks to the south, completing the conquest of "Bulgaria," had brought their northern frontier back to Belgrade. For the first time it then became possible for pilgrims to travel through Christian lands from the Rhineland to Constantinople. They began to do so in great numbers, to visit the Holy Places in Jerusalem. The church of the Holy Sepulcher, destroyed by order of the Fatimid caliph in 1009, was repaired at the expense of the Greek emperor by 1038. In one sense the conversion of the Magyars had stabilized Christendom; in another it enabled Christians as never before to set themselves in motion.

The Medieval Church

Not until the 12th century was there any possibility of creating a central direction for the western church. At that point the need to clarify and enforce church law gave the bishop of Rome a new authority in church affairs. At the same time the hope of promoting a higher level of monastic observance by aiming for greater uniformity and closer supervision of individual monasteries brought into being various organizations of monks, such as Cluny and Citeaux. These reforms reinforced the movement for centralization. From this time onwards the papacy worked for uniformity of law, doctrine, teaching, organization and indeed spiritual opportunity in the church. It acquired great influence with all monastic houses and became the patron and promoter of various new orders like the Franciscan. It summoned church councils, defined heresies, preached crusades, appointed and disciplined bishops. It aimed to set standards in the whole Latin church. For three centuries the efforts made by education and discipline did effect an unparalleled uniformity of belief and practice.

There were however many imperfections and the system, for which the papacy was held responsible, aroused much vocal discontent, by no means all well intentioned. Some of this dissatisfaction was due to the system, but much could also be blamed on the impossibility of imposing uniform conditions on western churches that had developed for centuries before the reform movements were thought of. The ideals of the new age also appealed more to the educated and the officials than to others. As the new religion had gained ground among the barbarians, the desire to establish local places of worship tended to diminish the importance of great monastic centers as the focus of religious devotions. Every inhabited locality thus acquired a resident priest to serve its sacramental needs, and parish churches were endowed according to local resources and munificence. This was not only highly variable; it was not necessarily even appropriate in later times. Attempts to supervise these parishes came up against all kinds of difficulty. Some bishops never counted for much in the organization of their dioceses. The papacy, which advocated uniformity, could not relinquish churches under its special protection to the bishops. Such bishops as did succeed in building up effective diocesan administrations, appointing assistant clergy like archdeacons to scrutinize smaller, more manageable districts than the diocese, found that every effort was made to frustrate their operations, not only by the sinful, but by monks, clergy, patrons and laity—all with claims and rights that could not be summarily dismissed. The power of Rome was never great enough to impose an entirely new order. Rather than push for radical solutions, it preferred to encourage new movements of religious zeal, provided their orthodoxy could be relied on, and allow older movements to linger on into decadence or decay. As a result the medieval church, though

superficially united under Rome, was in practice a highly complex affair, which harbored "abuses" of every kind in its bosom. Its history would be better written from the bottom up, rather than from the top down.

In a simple parish, the resident priest was often only a vicar, acting in the place of the legal incumbent, whose actual employment in the service of bishop, Roman curia, king or great nobleman kept him out of the parish. Parts of the church's tithes might be due to a distant monastery. The church's patron was not necessarily living in the settlement. The diocesan bishop, more likely himself engaged in public and "secular" business, would be represented by a deputy or an archdeacon. Thus, at the most local level, church government was far from simple. The religious enthusiasms of the medieval centuries piled up complications for ecclesiastical government which may explain why the papacy could not work wonders, why heretics could remain so long unchecked, even why persecutions of non-Christian peoples, like the Jews, occurred in spite of official disapproval. The west did not derive its Christianity exclusively from the ecclesiastical hierarchy and it would be historically erroneous to equate the church's organization with the body of Christian people. Historians have in the past been too ready to take clerical and educated criticisms at face value. Whatever its failings, the church provided for late medieval Christians the opportunities and encouragement for the development of the spiritual life in every place of Christendom and in every walk of life. The Protestant Reformation did not call to an unbelieving and indifferent generation, but one that already knew how to take its religion seriously.

Above St Dominic preaching at Recanati, from an altarpiece painted by Lorenzo Lotto in 1508 for the church of St Dominic, to commemorate the saint's preaching there three centuries before. Dominic is shown preaching from a wooden pulpit on the steps to his church in the piazza, painted as it was in 1508.

Left Urban VI (1378–89) receiving the keys from St Peter, from the pope's tomb in the Vatican. Executed after Urban's death, the image puts the pope and the saint on the same level and emphasizes that the pope received the keys from Peter himself.

Right Jean Fouquet's depiction (c. 1460) of the first great French theologian, St Hilary of Poitiers, presiding at a 4th-century council of bishops.

Far right The intense personal piety of many lay folk in the later Middle Ages can be judged at both the institutional and the private level. Many prayerbooks survive. Unusual is this 15th-century tapestry from south Germany which depicts scenes from one devout woman's religious life. Here she is seen kneeling beside the lily, symbol of purity, and receiving the host.

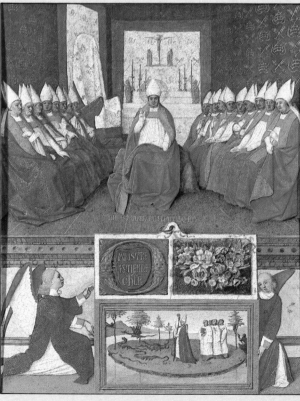

Right This 12th-century diagram of the water system of Christ Church, Canterbury, is drawn with such picturesque detail that it is not difficult to envisage from it the actual appearance of the cathedral and monastery in Becket's time. Each building is labeled and the diagram could be turned by hand at will, but it was evidently drawn to be read normally with south to the top.

Above At the end of this second Canterbury copy of the Utrecht Psalter, made in 1147, the copyist has proudly provided himself not only with a eulogy but this self-portrait, which is unique in 12th-century art for being a full-page picture showing the scribe like an evangelist from a Gospel book. Not intended to be a likeness in the modern sense, it remains a splendid affirmation of the artist in pictorial terms, with his massive figure squeezed into the frame. At this period Romanesque reached its apogee in England.

Above right This initial from a Cistercian manuscript is typical of the artist. He depicts monks at their physical labors with a strong sense of amusement at their awkwardness. This may reflect the attention given by choir monks to working ones, but the satire is so muted that it seems rather to reflect favorably on the Cistercians' humanity, which is often overlooked in accounts of their austerities.

Far right The life of Guthlac (667–714), the hermit saint of Crowland, is here shown in roundels, drawn in ink c. 1200, possibly intended as cartoons for painted glass. The style of draftsmanship proves the tenacity of the pre-Conquest English skill in line drawing. The pictures shown here illustrate three crucial episodes – his acceptance of the monastic rule, his death when angels receive his soul from his mouth, and the monastery's benefactors offering their charters while a small figure on the right, possessed of the devil, is cured at the shrine.

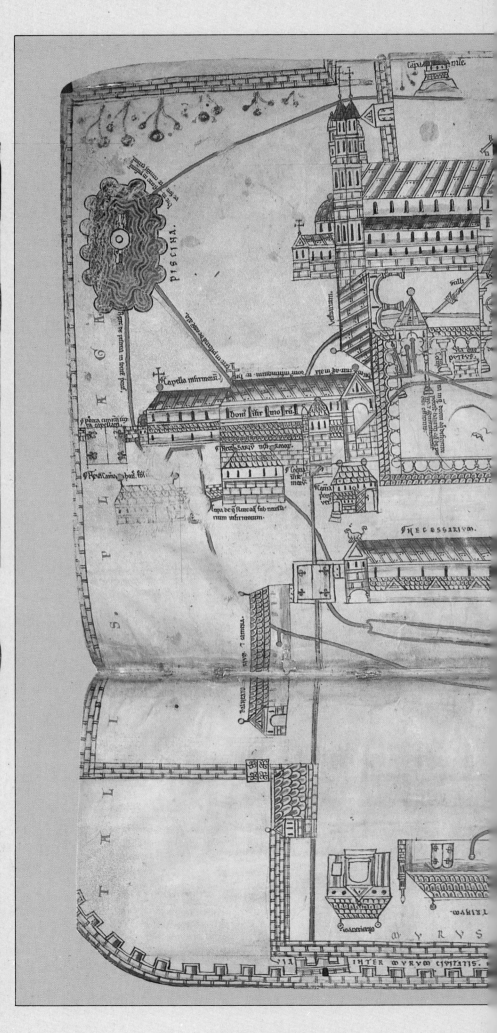

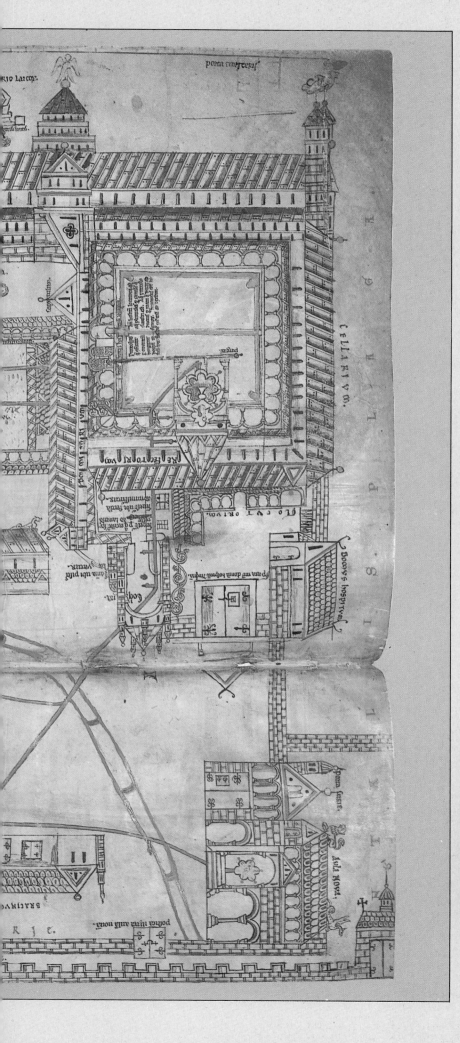

CHRISTENDOM ON THE MOVE

A new fervor in Christian Europe

Europe's Christian communities emerged from the 11th century with a deep sense of religious commitment and in a state of military vigor. These qualities were deployed over the succeeding centuries to extend western influence far beyond its homeland for the first time. The creative powers of the Middle Ages were shown at their best in the period that witnessed the crusades, the intellectual renaissance of the schools, Gothic aspiration in architecture. It is also a period of population growth, shown most strikingly in the revival of urban life. It is easier to illustrate this renewal of western energies than explain it, and enthusiasm for what was achieved can blind us to the complexity of the matters at issue. Very obviously, for example, the successes of organized and intellectual religion in dealing with unorthodox discontents, such as the Cathar heresy, tempt us to accept too readily the church's own analysis of its problems. If we could penetrate the nature of the discontents for ourselves we should see the quality of life actually experienced in the great "ages of faith" with fewer illusions. Similarly our attempts to understand the great movements of people of all sorts inspired to go to the east in the name of God have not been much helped by the historians' invention of the term "crusades" and their inclination to treat them like military campaigns with definable military objectives. The fervor of soldiers easily comes to seem in modern times either hypocritical or barbarous since religion and war are now normally placed in opposition. The whole modern attempt to divide life according to categories derives from the efforts made in the 12th century to understand ancient philosophy, but it took centuries for those lessons to be learned. The clear divisions of subject matters we regard as essential for our understanding of the past can themselves become a barrier to understanding when we divide what men then kept together. Our very concept of a civil society with professional armies properly committed to purely defensive operations runs counter to medieval experience and expectation of life. Even recent experience of emigration and colonization of parts of the globe across the seas has little to teach us about the manner of opening up the lands of Europe for cultivation by groups of peasants over centuries, working as opportunities occurred and usually unobserved by chroniclers.

The complexity of western affairs at this time is compounded by the impossibility of identifying one main political entity to carry the main burden of the story. The Carolingian empire disintegrated in the process of dealing with its barbarous enemies and with it disappeared the last possibility of describing European history in terms of its Roman predecessor. The new Europe was blatantly hydra-headed. Admittedly the German kings had achieved some preeminence by their acquisition of the imperial title, but they failed all the same to hamper the different monarchical styles of France or England or

prevent the appearance of a new monarchy in south Italy. Because Christendom was divided into monarchies it was united only at the religious level, but the zeal for the faith still took many different forms. With the conversion of the peoples of northern and eastern Europe to Christianity, through the agency of the barbarian kingdoms, the era of disorders that had rendered civil life so precarious for the latter came to an end. This enabled a fresh start to be made in their societies, most notably in the reforming of religious life to do away with "abuses." Not all of these were recent developments of disordered times, but all plans for reform assumed that the times were ripe for a general renewal of Christendom. Many clergy showed great self-confidence in proposing various schemes for monastic revival which came to a head in the program for not only restoring the reputation of the Roman church but for making it the promoter of reform all over Christendom. For more than a century there was a period of almost unbridled experiment, over which only the Roman papacy had any faint control and that was at best restricted to matters of more or less religious significance. Yet until the end of the 12th century such control was more theoretical than institutional. Such coherence as can be traced in the events of these years seems to derive from a subterranean source of energy and idealism that burst out once the immediate dangers from paganism were removed. This idealism was far from content to settle for limited or parochial improvements. It was universal by aspiration, aiming for the restoration of Christendom, and for a sustained onslaught on the main enemies – the Muslims. There was no planned program for renewal at home to be followed by defiance without. The whole Latin Christian world bubbled with excitement and boiled over in fury.

Only a few aspects of the whole can be sketched in here. At the religious level itself the most important development was the unparalleled expansion of monastic life – and the collapse of the long-established Benedictine monopoly over the religious inspiration of the west. Never had Christendom seen so many different programs for lives lived by religious rules or the number of houses founded been so high throughout every part of the west. The zeal for more and purer religion could not be more certainly proved to us. Since the church authorities began to enforce once again rules of celibacy for the ordinary clergy, Christendom was dominated by thousands of dedicated unmarried men and women at a time when there are nonetheless good grounds for believing that the population was generally growing. The enthusiasm for these houses of celibate life gave society an ascetic tone and influenced contemporary ideals of service and knighthood in particular, but its emphasis was on fighting the spiritual battles within the self rather than against the tangible enemies of Christendom. St Bernard of Clairvaux,

Left This simple bronze figure from the Rhineland expresses a new devotion to Christ crucified that both dignified and made more human the religious impulses of the 12th century.

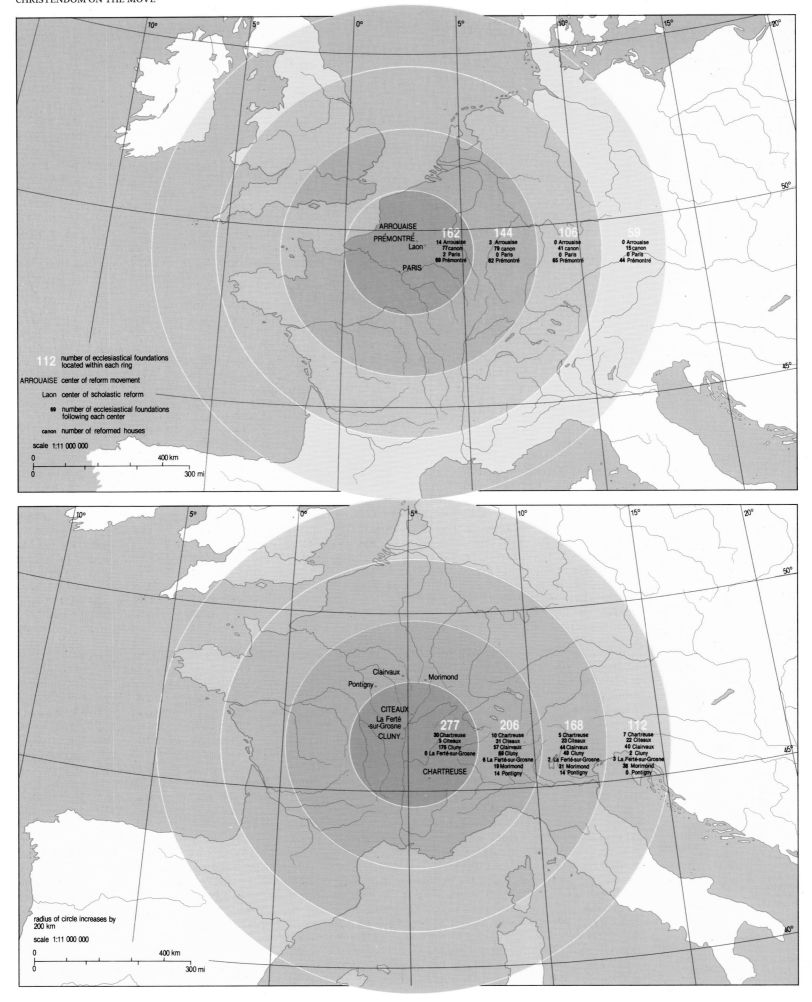

ARROUAISE
PRÉMONTRÉ
Laon

PARIS

162	144	106	59
14 Arrouaise	3 Arrouaise	0 Arrouaise	0 Arrouaise
77 canon	79 canon	41 canon	15 canon
2 Paris	0 Paris	0 Paris	0 Paris
69 Prémontré	62 Prémontré	65 Prémontré	44 Prémontré

112   number of ecclesiastical foundations
located within each ring

ARROUAISE   center of reform movement

Laon   center of scholastic reform

69   number of ecclesiastical foundations
following each center

canon   number of reformed houses

scale 1:11 000 000

0   400 km

0   300 mi

Clairvaux   Morimond
Pontigny

CITEAUX
La Ferté
-sur-Grosne
CLUNY

277	206	168	112
30 Chartreuse	10 Chartreuse	5 Chartreuse	7 Chartreuse
9 Cîteaux	31 Cîteaux	23 Cîteaux	22 Cîteaux
176 Cluny	57 Clairvaux	44 Clairvaux	40 Clairvaux
0 La Ferté-sur-Grosne	69 Cluny	49 Cluny	2 Cluny
	6 La Ferté-sur-Grosne	2 La Ferté-sur-Grosne	3 La Ferté-sur-Grosne
	19 Morimond	31 Morimond	38 Morimond
	14 Pontigny	14 Pontigny	0 Pontigny

CHARTREUSE

radius of circle increases by
200 km

scale 1:11 000 000

0   400 km

0   300 mi

Right Confirmation of the rule of St Francis in the upper church at Assisi by the Master of the St Francis cycle, c.1290. The great proliferation of monastic rules in the 12th century culminated with that of the Franciscans, the last new rule to be approved by the pope before the Lateran decree of 1216 against further innovations. The popularity of the Franciscans secured for them the attention of painters in 13th-century Italy, and it is therefore the picture of their endorsement by the pope which must convey the force of all those earlier efforts at reform approved as orthodox.

Ecclesiastical foundations of the 12th and 13th centuries
The great movement for the reform of the church blossomed in the 12th century. The sources of its inspiration, so sought after by historians, probably matter less than the circumstances which enabled idealists to capture attention and support. Three particular strands in the movement may, however, be isolated and mapped. The crusade preached at Clermont and Vézelay (1145) appears by its very nature to have inspired men to take the cross over a very wide area. Monastic reforms, on the other hand, needed to win enough support in a given locality before a new community could come into being. The success of the Cluniac, Cistercian and Carthusian movements in a band of territory in eastern France points decisively to the importance of that region in establishing the reform movement. More diffuse appears to be the effect of the new learning in philosophy, law and grammar found in the cathedral schools of northern France, and the new orders of canons, like those of St Victor. Together with the influence of the law school of Bologna, these were the centers from which radiated ideas that carried the church forward in this century. The religious enthusiasms that the authorities did not approve and labeled heresies show, however, that other regions were all the same exposed to intellectual and spiritual novelties.

the greatest spokesman of the new Cistercian order, himself persuaded a pilgrim bent for Jerusalem to join his monastery and to find there the "true" Jerusalem, for it was in the cloister, he claimed, that the spiritual ideal of Jerusalem was fully realized. Rather than believe that such an attitude positively hindered western support for the Holy Land, it is probably truer to see that those who were not called by God to the east could receive other spiritual calls. Christian idealism was not so much divided against itself as able to offer something to everyone, for it is certain that even the cultivators of the soil were attracted into the religious life and tempted to take priestly orders. The Cistercian order had grown so vast by Bernard's death in 1153 that efforts were made to arrest the process, but it continued and in eastern Europe its greatest extension came in the 13th century. By that time further west the orders of friars, Dominicans and Franciscans, had carried forward the ideal of religious reform into unpropitious areas where heresy and poverty had prevailed. As teachers and ministers, in contrast to the older monastic concern for the spiritual growth of the monastic community itself, they brought religion to those who did not seek it for themselves. From the late 11th century to the early 13th there was no fall in the spate of religious reform. Not all reforms were long-lived or approved, or indeed certainly orthodox, but the fervor for change, the faith in new rules (that is models of conduct) and the capacity of Christians to be swept up in these projects seem to us without limit. Only the papal decree that there should be no more new orders and the insistence that new projects adapt some existing rule actually succeeded in bringing all these movements under control.

Investigating each of these reforms brings to light a sense of the dissatisfaction felt with existing models for perfection and with the simple faith of earlier ages of perfection that had been corrupted by time and abuses. But it does little to explain what the real sources of inspiration were. For both the unorthodox lay preacher Waldo of Lyons and for St Francis of Assisi it is reported that they traced their religious inspiration back to vernacular stories with appeals to chivalrous values near their core. Until this period preaching to the laity had probably been rather intermittent. Preaching the crusade had first shown the power of preachers to excite popular response on a wide scale. Elsewhere, as in certain great towns, preachers had successfully stirred up popular protests against immoral clergy or suspected heretics, but the enthusiasm for religious reform on the whole cannot be traced back to clerical preaching as such. Nor did the ecclesiastical authorities themselves seriously contemplate a program of preaching for the laity until a late stage, when they recognized the need to deal with heresy by reasoned exposition. In the early stages power exercised to excite crowds by preaching, being often aimed at immoral clergy and other offenders against the Christian code, had usually carried heterodox implications. Not surprisingly the official Christian hierarchy tended to disapprove of both preachers and laymen for trying to enforce religion and morals on their own. This evidence for religious zeal demonstrates that it sprang up in the most unexpected quarters.

More accessible to us appears perhaps the new enthusiasm for learning from great teachers, shown by the willingness of thousands of young men (and perhaps also by some young women) to give themselves to study. Abelard, the most famous of Parisian teachers in the early 12th century, had himself been a student frequenting the schools of Paris, Laon and elsewhere. Disciplined study and

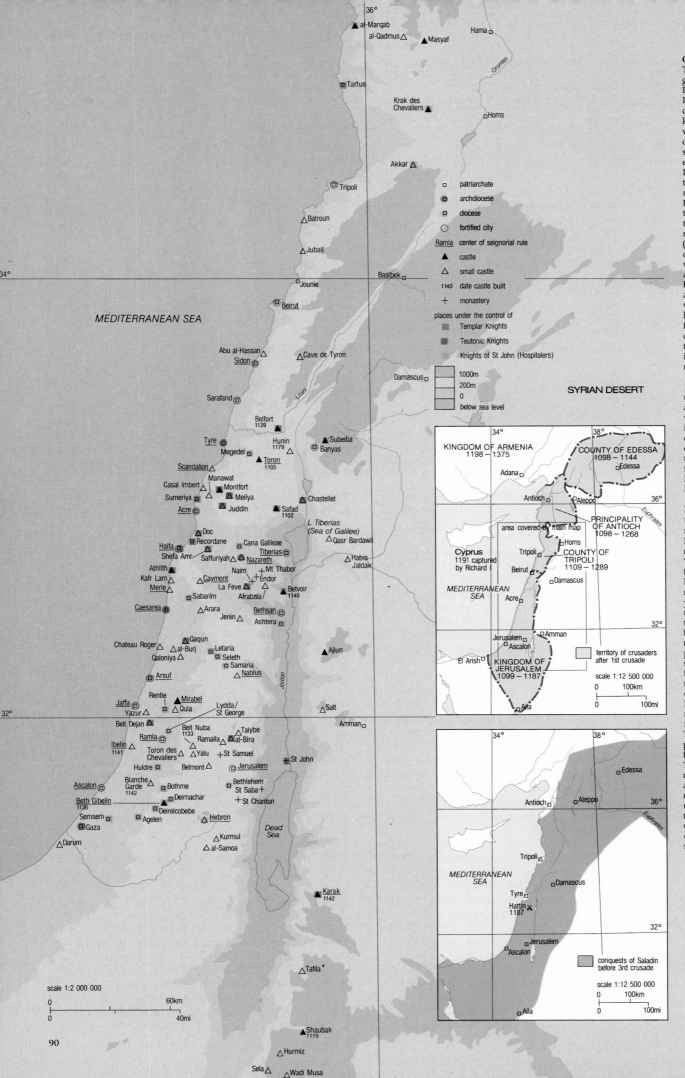

Crusader states

The kingdom of Jerusalem at its greatest extent established a Latin dominion over the Holy Land usually no more than 80 km deep from a coastline about 300 km long. The local inhabitants were inured to foreign occupations. Rarely and for only short periods has the land ever enjoyed political independence. Its fate was usually settled from the south by Egypt, from the northeast by the peoples of the Euphrates or from Anatolia. For their direct links with the west the kings of Jerusalem and the rulers of the other crusader states (see inset map, *above*) were dependent on Italian sailors, whose nearest Latin landfall was at Bari. Cyprus was acquired by Richard I on the Third Crusade as a valuable base (1191) but this was only after Jerusalem itself had already fallen (1187). The fate of the Latin kingdom depended therefore as much on the weaknesses and divisions of its enemies as on its own resources.

Saladin proved to be the only 12th-century Muslim able to unite Islamic forces in a holy war against the crusaders. His gains were swift and dramatic (see inset map, *below*) but because he did not manage to evict his enemies before his death in 1193 the kingdom was able to live on for another century; it lasted as long as its squabbling opponents lacked the will to destroy it.

In such circumstances the kings and their vassals may seem to have done wonders. Having rescued the future of the Latins in the Holy Land from the risks of rule by an eastern "pope" at Jerusalem, the kings, from Baldwin I (king 1100–18), built up a territory which had reached its limits after about 30 years. By dominating the trade routes of the region and holding their own in strongly constructed fortresses the kings mastered the main elements of policy. Their principal weakness was a shortage of reliable military forces. To remedy this the religious order dedicated to the care of the sick, the order of the Hospital, was entrusted with responsibilities for defending the infirm by force, and the Templars, founded to protect pilgrims on the road, acquired fortresses and military duties. The kingdom should be respected for learning how to adapt and meet its problems rather than be criticized for its ultimate failure. In the long term the idealistic scheme for Latin domination in the Holy Land could never be a practical success.

Legend

- □ patriarchate
- ⊡ archdiocese
- ◉ diocese
- ○ fortified city
- Ramla center of seignorial rule
- ▲ castle
- △ small castle
- 1140 date castle built
- + monastery

places under the control of
- Templar Knights
- Teutonic Knights
- Knights of St John (Hospitalers)

1000m
200m
0
below sea level

Map labels

MEDITERRANEAN SEA

SYRIAN DESERT

al-Marqab, al-Qadmus, Masyaf, Hama, Tartus, Krak des Chevaliers, Homs, Orontes, Akkar, Tripoli, Batroun, Jubail, Baalbek, Jounie, Beirut, Abu al-Hassan, Sidon, Cave de Tyron, Sarafand, Litani, Belfort 1139, Tyre, Hunin 1179, Subeiba, Megedel, Banyas, Toron 1105, Scandalion, Manawat, Casal Imbert, Montfort, Meilya, Chastellet, Sumeriya, Acre, Juddin, Safad 1102, L Tiberias (Sea of Galilee), Doc, Recordane, Cana Galileae, Qasr Bardawil, Haifa, Tiberias, Shefa Amr, Saffuriyah, Nazareth, Habis Jaldak, Athlith, Naim, Mt Thabor, Kafr Lam, Caymont, Endor, Merle, La Feve, Belvoir 1140, Sabarim, Afrabala, Caesarea, Arara, Bethsan, Jenin, Ashtera, Chateau Roger, Qaqun, al-Burj, Letaria, Ajlun, Qaloniya, Seleth, Samaria, Arsuf, Nablus, Jordan, Jaffa, Rentie, Mirabel, Salt, Yazur, Qula, Lydda/St George, Beit Dejan, Amman, Beit Nuba 1133, Taiybe, Ramla, Ramalla, al-Bira, Ibelin 1141, Toron des Chevaliers, Yalu, St Samuel, Huldre, Belmont, Jerusalem, St John, Ascalon, Blanche Garde 1142, Bothme, Bethlehem, Deirnachar, St Saba, St Chariton, Beth Gibelin 1136, Deirelcobebe, Semsem, Agelen, Hebron, Gaza, Dead Sea, Darum, Kurmul, al-Samoa, Karak 1142, Tafila, Shaubak 1115, Hurmiz, Sela, Wadi Musa

Inset map (above)

KINGDOM OF ARMENIA 1198–1375
COUNTY OF EDESSA 1098–1144
Adana, Edessa, Antioch, Aleppo, Euphrates
PRINCIPALITY OF ANTIOCH 1098–1268
area covered by main map
Cyprus 1191 captured by Richard I
Homs, Tripoli, COUNTY OF TRIPOLI 1109–1289
Beirut, Damascus
MEDITERRANEAN SEA
Acre
Jerusalem, Amman, Ascalon
El Arish, KINGDOM OF JERUSALEM 1099–1187, Aila

territory of crusaders after 1st crusade

scale 1:12 500 000
0   100km
0   100mi

Inset map (below)

MEDITERRANEAN SEA
Edessa, Antioch, Aleppo, Euphrates, Tripoli, Damascus, Tyre, Hattin 1187, Jerusalem, Ascalon, Aila

conquests of Saladin before 3rd crusade

scale 1:12 500 000
0   100km
0   100mi

scale 1:2 000 000
0   60km
0   40mi

Above The Winchester Bible, made for Bishop Henry of Blois (1192–71), is the finest of the three surviving 12th-century English illustrated Bibles. Several different artists worked on it. This initial (to the first Psalm), originally designed and gilded by the Master of the Leaping Figures, was completed by the Master of the Genesis initial. It shows Jesus driving out devils and the Harrowing of Hell.

examination with career prospects for graduates grew out of these 12th-century activities, but the universities were products of the revival of learning, they were not themselves promoters of it; indeed their medieval function was to preserve and defend accumulated bodies of doctrine rather than pioneer new courses of study.

In the law it is not difficult to point to the practical problems needing legal solutions that encouraged the study of Roman law and research into church law in the late 11th century. But such arguments have little relevance for the strides taken with the study of logic or of theology, though theology certainly owed much to the changes brought about in logic. At a time when the monasteries were themselves apparently being shaken to their foundations by the search for more spiritual perfection, there was obviously less agreement about the traditional role of book-learning for monastic communities, and perhaps for this reason the bishops' schools of northern France began to attract students with interests in learning, who were not attracted into the monastic revival. How and where such learned interest could originally have been stimulated we are at a loss to know. It is not difficult to show how the new intellectual disciplines requiring stricter use of words and an intellectual capacity to make clear distinctions could have practical implications and advantages for bishops recruiting staff for their administrations, but once again there is nothing about the studies themselves to suggest that practical considerations were originally important.

Even more worldly may appear the campaigns fought in the Holy Land by "crusaders," laymen exercising their military profession at the behest of the church in return for spiritual rewards; popes promised those prepared to rescue Jerusalem from the infidel remission of the penance due for their sins. But the great expeditions launched at papal initiative in 1095, 1145 and 1189 need to be set historically in the wider context of recurrent Christian aggression against infidels, both Muslim and pagan, at this time. Contemporary Norman attacks on Muslim government in Italy were in this sense as much a part of the proto-crusading movement as contemporary campaigns in Spain begun by the Christian kingdoms against the crumbling caliphate of Cordoba. On the other hand the crusading movement needs to be distinguished from both for its idealistic, even Quixotic, aspect. Both in Spain and in Italy the campaigns were waged for self-consciously acquisitive motives and were shaped by calculating political advantage. The crusaders, who had perforce to develop some political guile in the Holy Land, were placed in an impossible situation for want of political realism. The First Crusade was preached by Urban II in 1095, ostensibly taking up the call for western military aid made by the first emperor of the Comnenian dynasty at Constantinople, Alexius I, but turned by the pope into an enthusiastic program to recover Jerusalem from the infidel. In the process of making its way east the crusading army actually set up four Latin principalities as well as alarming the Greek emperor. The difficult situation of these crusading states – hundreds of miles from their real friends, at odds with their Levantine neighbors and frequently with one another, inspired by a religious rather than

a political ideal, yet forced to come to terms with local realities, dependent on western sympathies which were easily alienated by any apparent lack of idealistic fervor – has to be taken into account. These states were never devised or defended by men like the Normans of Italy who had watched and waited for their opportunity. The crusading states were created by the force of an army of zealots bursting into the unsuspecting Holy Land and were only preserved by the intermittent intervention of armies or the dispatch of well-connected rulers from the west. Eventually the regrouping of Muslim forces on the spot inevitably put a ragged end to these starry-eyed projects.

The very unworldliness of the crusading idea has given it a special appeal and this element cannot be eradicated in any analysis. Yet there is more to be said. For Alexius I himself, having restored the military reputation of Constantinople, had to recognize that the military forces of the west had become indispensable for his own wars against the infidel, and the pope, who transmitted his requests for aid, never imagined how many knights and others would leave their homes to make the incredible journey across Europe to conquer Jerusalem. The four crusading states in the Holy Land gave western peoples an obvious landed interest in the Middle East which they showed themselves eager to defend, as was shown by Eugenius III's call to rescue the county of Edessa taken by Zenghi in 1143 and by Urban III's still more panic-stricken plea to recapture Jerusalem after Saladin had taken it in 1187. By the 13th century there was even an established formula for the crusade: the papal appeal promised spiritual reward for military service undertaken and legal advantages for those who had once taken crusading vows. Idealistic soldiers even combined to achieve some temporary military effects in such expeditions down to the 15th century, even if the lost crusading states were never recovered from the Muslims; the last outpost of Christian government there, at Acre, was eliminated in 1291. The idealism of western soldiers in wanting to retain in Christian hands the government of the lands where Jesus had lived actually survived the succession of disappointments and the codification of crusading procedures. It also lived down the ill repute created by the papacy's own interpretation of war against the infidel to mean war against all active opponents of the church, heretical, schismatic and political. This had threatened to replace the idealistic notion with the idea that preaching a crusade was a device to raise a papal army and, by allowing commutation of vows for money, pay for it.

Throughout the period concerned, the attraction of the crusade was a complex, mysterious and wayward phenomenon. Alexius Comnenus presumably anticipated help in the disciplined form of bands of soldiers under their own leaders acting as imperial auxiliaries, but the crusading armies whenever they came in impressionable numbers inevitably brought with them men without political knowledge of the east and anyway disinclined to take their cue from the eastern emperor. Their leaders, if more restrained, were not necessarily more willing to see themselves merely as the emperor's allies. The creation of the Latin states in the Holy Land, which proved that the crusaders

could create their very own front against Islam, was not in fact the kind of military advantage that would help restore Greek control of Anatolia. The hostility between Greek and Latin Christians, and between one Latin state and another, gave local Muslims opportunities for political manipulation, and the intrusion of distant Christians into the divided Muslim world of the Middle East succeeded in stimulating a genuine revival of Muslim military vigor that did not stem from the caliph at Baghdad but from the great Muslim warriors like Nureddin and Saladin. The recrudescence of Muslim military might brought on by the crusades succeeded thus in recovering Egypt for Sunni orthodoxy. It was only a matter of time before the Latins were driven from the mainland and, indeed, before Constantinople without effective western help would fall to other Muslim warriors, the Ottomans. Judged by military standards, the crusades were neither glorious nor effective.

Judged by spiritual standards, it is of course impossible to say how many crusaders obtained the benefits for which they had ostensibly taken the cross, and it is indeed unlikely that those who took the cross seriously calculated the price of their spiritual benefits or long pondered their decision. The first three great crusades were launched in moods of tremendous enthusiasm, in which the selfless nobility of the few swept along the hesitant, and shamed others into acting as nobly as their peers. To all who went the crusade was a challenge to face the unknown. To none was it an adventure with the prospect of an earthly principality, not even to those who became rulers of the crusading states when they took shape. No great prince who took the cross could coerce or even encourage all his followers to do likewise, for immense responsibilities remained to devolve on those who had to stay behind in his absence. For those who went the decision to take the cross was personal and free.

Papal claims and the ideal of empire

The religious movements were patronized but not instigated by the Christian rulers of the 12th century, who were in general rather overshadowed by the religious idealists. But some developments in

The siege of Antioch, from the translation of William of Tyre, made at Acre in the late 13th century. This vigorous representation of an episode from the First Crusade, made in the Holy Land on the eve of Christian expulsion, is one of the earliest attempts to show military operations in pictures and does so with real knowledge of 13th-century warfare in Syria. The heraldic devices and the armor are not however realistic for the time of the First Crusade.

from German leadership and transfer attention from the empire to the universal city. Reforming bishops, in northern Italy and elsewhere, welcomed the resurgence of Rome and looked to its bishop for assertion of Christian order. Many individual monasteries also turned to Rome for protection of their independence against local nobles and bishops. A great monastic order, like Cluny, was naturally sympathetic to a movement that appeared to promote the cause of ecclesiastical discipline in the church as a whole since it ran parallel to its own efforts on behalf of monasticism. To Rome came therefore a stream of sympathy and a steady trickle of devoted workers for the new cause from the most high-minded clergy of all western Europe. With their help the papacy became a vastly different organization in the second half of the 11th century.

Inevitably such a reformed papacy itself eventually decided that the tutelage of the German kings was unacceptable. After Henry III's death (1056) his less idealistic son Henry IV became involved in a conflict with Pope Gregory VII (1073–85) in which the bishops of his empire found themselves in the disagreeable position of being made to choose between conflicting loyalties. The matters at issue were both complex and confused, and contemporaries who engaged in polemical arguments to persuade supporters only obscured the original issues and exacerbated ill-feeling about principles instead of seeking reconciliation. The particular problems of the pope and the king-emperor were submerged in argument about the nature of the spiritual and the secular powers and this caused the quarrel to spread to the remaining parts of Christendom as well, albeit with different implications. One part of the quarrel was patched up by pope and emperor in 1122, but real peace was conditional on the German king's playing only a nominal role in Italy. In 1159, when the cardinals of the church were divided about finding a successor to Pope Hadrian IV, yet another long dispute between pope and emperor began, which was not settled till 1177. For more than a century, therefore, without being permanently locked in conflict, the Roman empire and the Roman papacy were sufficiently often at odds with one another to destroy for ever the old Carolingian concept of Christendom. Both sides developed theories to justify their intransigence; both sides acquired habits of government, suspicions, partisans and traditions for dealing with their problems that caused them to develop independent institutions. Deprived of its ecclesiastical pretensions by the papal claims, the Roman empire of the German kings lost its moral claims on Christendom and more particularly on the loyalties of the Italian bishops. The papacy, on the other hand, forced to proclaim its spiritual ideals in general terms, found itself hailed in most parts of Christendom as the head of the universal church. The Roman ideal of universality was shown to have great powers of attraction at the spiritual level, whereas the old concept of Roman empire as the universal state entirely lost credit.

The relations of the German kings with the popes may seem to interest only part of Christendom, yet their importance must not be underestimated. Not only did they bring about the downfall of the empire as a concept and promote, from an early

the kingdoms of Europe call for attention. The German kings were indisputably the mightiest rulers in Europe, looking back to Rome for inspiration and across to Byzantium for alliances, but masterful also in dealing with the realities of the present. The course of western history was, however, diverted in the 12th century in consequence of the way religious idealism developed at an institutional level. The emperor Henry III who had tried to do his religious duty and make the bishops of his dominions in Germany and Italy into agents for the purification of Christendom had naturally wished Rome itself to play a full part in the work. But the papacy was in bondage to local Italian noble families and unprepared for its universal role. Successive German and Italian bishops were therefore installed in Rome after 1046 and they set about making the Roman church a respected reforming party in its own right.

Several different inspirations worked together to restore Roman leadership. The imperial revival had insisted on the idea of Rome. In the city itself there was an understandable desire to wrest this revival

The German empire in the Salian and Staufen periods

The German kingdom was united with that of Italy in 951 and with that of Burgundy in 1037. Not until the advent of a Staufen emperor in 1152, however, did the personal interests of the new ruler, Frederick I, encourage him to exploit his opportunities for giving the empire a new impetus after the disruption of the investiture controversy. The emperor's most conspicuous enemies were the Lombard communes, against whom he could muster little reliable support, and in effect this meant that the basis of the emperor's power remained dependent on his German resources. Here his own family had already shown what particular interests could effect. Their rivals, the Welfs, were hardly less powerful. In this period the powers of noble families and principalities began to take shape. The princes of Germany were confirmed in their existing privileges by Frederick II. Even before the emperor himself became an elected figurehead, the empire was already only united in a formal way. Thus its real structure began to show beneath the glamor from the time when Charlemagne's canonization (by Frederick I's antipope) in 1165 gave the empire its accolade.

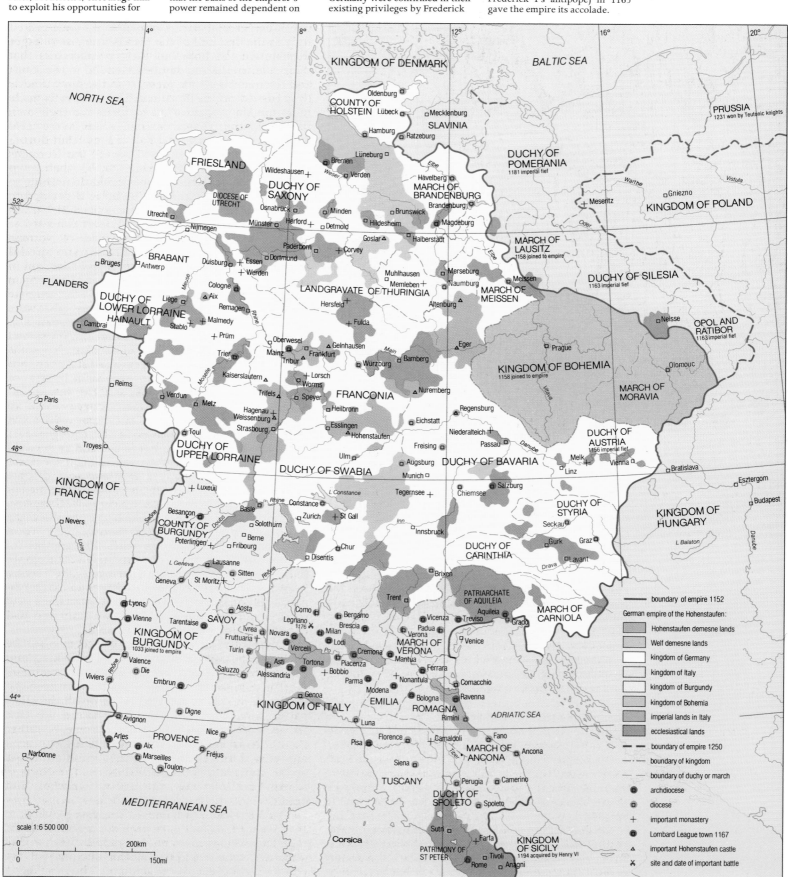

boundary of empire 1152

German empire of the Hohenstaufen:

- Hohenstaufen demesne lands
- Welf demesne lands
- kingdom of Germany
- kingdom of Italy
- kingdom of Burgundy
- kingdom of Bohemia
- imperial lands in Italy
- ecclesiastical lands

boundary of empire 1250
boundary of kingdom
boundary of duchy or march

- archdiocese
- diocese
- important monastery
- Lombard League town 1167
- important Hohenstaufen castle
- site and date of important battle

scale 1:6 500 000

0   200km

0   150mi

Scenes from the life of Gregory VII from Otto, bishop of Freising's, *World Chronicle*, a 12th-century copy of original illustrations in the manuscript presented by the author to his nephew, Frederick I, in 1157. The author passed as quickly as possible over the dispute between Pope Gregory VII and the emperor Henry IV for fear of stirring up old passions, but these four scenes present the pope's position with some sympathy and must express the author's own views. They also give an early example of how history could be tellingly depicted by pictures from this period.

11th century. Original Norman settlers are reported to have come to Italy in connection with religious devotions, but they stayed on to serve as soldiers. Gradually they built up a position of strength in south Italy by selling their services as professional soldiers to the quarrelsome local rulers. The Lombard inhabitants were disaffected under both their own princes and the nominal authority of the Greek emperor at Bari. German kings who visited Italy in the first half of the 11th century were eager to maintain the hopes of their predecessors that their rule would one day be extended to the south and remove the Greek pressure at the same time as they turned on the Muslims. The Lombards made what use they could of these visits for their own purposes and their Norman allies were also recognized and confirmed by the kings. But during the minority of Henry IV (1056–65) the Normans suddenly showed themselves to be their own masters, and the German popes could do nothing to diminish their power. Pope Nicholas II decided to come to terms with them and recognized Richard of Aversa as prince of Capua and Robert Guiscard as duke of Apulia in return for promise of Norman support (1059). Over the years Norman support did on occasion rescue popes from their enemies, but in practice papal recognition had helped the Norman leaders to coordinate their fellows and to dominate the Lombard principalities, for popes who were quarreling with the German kings could not also quarrel with the Normans to the south, still less find the means to contain their expansion. To some extent they could play Capua off against Apulia, but after Robert had acquired the principality of Salerno (1077) as well as Apulia the balance of power was upset. The popes proved adept at making the most of their limited opportunities and never reconciled themselves to the emergence of powerful Norman states, but in the end they could not prevent Roger II of Sicily gaining control of the whole of southern Italy as well and setting up a kingdom for himself (1130). Successive popes had to bow reluctantly to Roger's wishes. The kingdom against all odds was held together and the disparate traditions of its extensive lands, with their heterogeneous populations and mixture of religions, inevitably achieved coherence only through a government with an extremely secular emphasis. The kingdom of Sicily was an extraordinary creation of Roger II, but one that made a new sense of the geography of southern Italy and had therefore some considerable potential.

stage, a deliberate papal program for the leadership of the whole spiritual force of Christendom, they generated too a violent and unprecedented debate about the nature of power in Christian society and stimulated extensive research into the bases of Christian law. The papacy encouraged many men and women to break with earlier dependence on the idea of empire and ensured that medieval Europe was never again to be overawed by any one ruler with universal ambitions. In this struggle it was settled that the Carolingian dream of restoring the Roman empire as a basis for Christian Europe was dead.

Only one other medieval ruler, Frederick II, inspired popes with open dread at the extent of his power. But it was not in Germany but in his kingdom of Sicily that Frederick found the resources to challenge the popes in Italy. He owed his position there to the crafty schemes of his grandfather, Frederick I. Defeated as emperor by Pope Alexander III, Frederick hoped to annex to the empire the additional resources of that kingdom by marrying his son Henry VI to Constance, the heiress of Sicily. Sicily had become a coveted prize during the imperial–papal struggle.

The Norman achievement in Sicily

Less than a century before, Sicily itself had been laboriously conquered by Constance's grandfather, Count Roger, from various Muslim princes whose mutual jealousies gave him the occasion to set foot there in the first place (1060). While Roger was committed on the island over about 30 years, his brother Robert had been engaged in turning his position as duke of Apulia into one of mastery in the south of Italy. The two brothers and their kinsmen were only a small part of the body of Norman adventurers drawn out of Normandy from the early

The creation of the Norman kingdom of Sicily was accomplished while pope and German king (and Greek emperor too) had more immediate problems of their own to solve, but even while it was in the making it had considerable impact on all the other participants. What the Normans showed was that the south of Italy and Sicily had become, or rather that the Normans could make these lands, of crucial importance for Christendom: they were no longer on the periphery of Latin influence. The Norman rulers thus restored the Latin churches and organizations of their lands, built new monasteries and took the old Greek ones under their protection. The Muslims in Sicily, though not persecuted for their religion, became the first of their faith to live under Christian rule. The Normans also showed that they had no desire to stop there. They extended their conflict with the Greeks across the Adriatic into the Balkans and dared to set up a pretender to the throne of Constantinople itself against the "usurping" Alexius Comnenus. Likewise they challenged the Muslims living across the strait from Sicily in North Africa. The Norman challenge in the south was adventurist, prepared to go as far as audacity and opportunity permitted and not content with any "natural frontiers." The Normans were not themselves a particularly united army and had to be disciplined by their own rulers. Yet even a force like this took on all comers and found no consistent friends and supporters. They fought Greeks, Muslims, Lombards, Germans and popes too if necessary. It is hard in all this to discern strategy or to speak of an internal logic. The Norman success seems to be phenomenal and in its own day its first historian, the monk Amatus of Monte Cassino, described it in his *History of the Normans* as providential.

In detailed analysis the Norman achievement can be seen as more precarious and checkered than hero worship would like to believe. All the same, in general terms the Normans did succeed in effecting a major change in this area by their ruthless pursuit of their own advantage in troubled but treacherous

Right Christ crowns Roger II king of Sicily, a mosaic decoration from the church of Santa Maria del' Ammiraglio, Palermo. This church was originally founded in 1143 by the royal admiral George of Antioch for Greeks and decorated by Greek artists already working for King Roger in the city. Roger's title "Rogerius Rex" is written in Greek characters and he is presented like a Greek *basileus* in a long dalmatic and stole, wearing the crown with jeweled pendants presented by Christ directly.

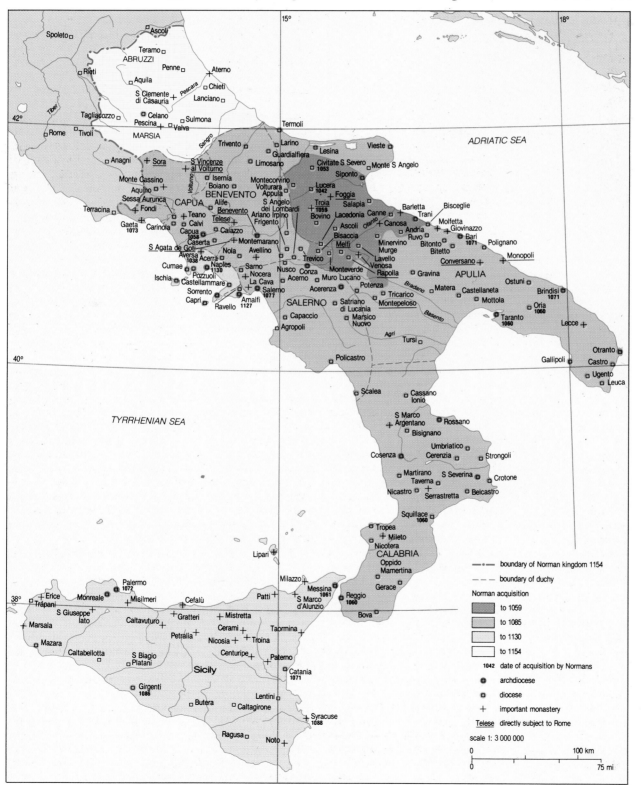

Left: The Norman states of southern Italy
Before the arrival of the Normans in south Italy, there were many local lordships and rival claims to jurisdiction. It took nearly a century for the various Norman conquests to be absorbed into a single kingdom set up by the ruler of Sicily, Roger II. After his death the independent kingdom lasted barely 40 years before it was obtained for the empire by his son-in-law, Henry VI. But the kingdom, even after it was divided into the two parts of Sicily and Naples (1282), never broke up again into tiny fragments. That part of the Normans' work survived them. The formerly semi-independent city republics, like Naples and Amalfi, never shared in the later communal movement. The old principalities of Capua and Salerno were replaced administratively by the Norman kings' own officials. The many small bishoprics and nominal archbishoprics gave the king no trouble; the many monasteries, mostly of ancient foundation, frequently in or near towns, welcomed the stability of the new regime. A feudal nobility, recently introduced, often resisted royal direction, but, until the later Middle Ages gave them opportunities for political activity, they played a less prominent part in government than the royal servants operating from Palermo. In the 12th century it was one of the biggest and most active cities of Christendom, in regular contact with Muslims who respected Roger II's power.

Norman acquisition
— · — boundary of Norman kingdom 1154
— — — boundary of duchy

▓	to 1059
▒	to 1085
░	to 1130
□	to 1154

1042 date of acquisition by Normans
⊡ archdiocese
▫ diocese
+ important monastery
T̲e̲l̲e̲s̲e̲ directly subject to Rome

scale 1: 3 000 000

0 — 100 km
0 — 75 mi

Above right The Bayeux tapestry is more properly a stitchwork which measures 50 cm in height and over 70 meters in length and shows a narrative of the events leading to the Norman conquest of England. It was made probably by English needlewomen before 1082 for Bayeux cathedral, whose bishop, Odo, half-brother to King William I, figures prominently in it.

seas. Their leaders had no training or tradition to fall back on, yet they defeated popes, emperors and princes. Small wonder that they seem like a force of nature, sweeping all before them and bringing into being a state of affairs prophetic for the future. Their wars against the Muslims predate the crusade; to the Greeks they gave a foretaste of what western military might could do; to the popes they proved that though papal allies and vassals they could all the same exact papal recognition on their own terms and that the pope might humble the emperor of the west but could not dislodge the Normans at his gate. Baffling though the Normans may be, they are there as positive proof of the kind of energy that could be thrown up in one part of Christendom to be put to full use in another.

One of the most powerful states of Christendom
The effective independence of Normandy and its honorary membership of the Scandinavian world gave it an influential role in the history of England in the 11th century. Edward the Confessor, king of England 1042–66, nominated Duke William as his heir and it was only the resistance put up by the Godwinson family that turned William's proposed peaceful accession into a Norman conquest. This gave the duke of Normandy a royal estate for the best part of 150 years. It was in this respect different from the Norman conquests in Italy, but historians, and indeed contemporaries, were eager to see in both enterprises common elements of martial dash and political finesse. As in the south, the initial achievement was quickly followed by a willingness to extend influence outward from the base wherever it could realistically be done. Where warfare proved inadequate, marriage, inheritance and alliances could be tried. Not without setbacks, but nonetheless with some sense of continuous momentum, the English monarchy had by the late 12th century acquired lands in France more extensive than those of the king of France himself and had

established links with every major ruler in Christendom. Before 1066 the English kings had played a distinguished role on the fringes of Christendom. After 1066 their successors became rulers of continental importance. Not until the 1190s did the king of France succeed in chipping away at some of the French frontiers of their dominion, and only in 1203–04 did the collapse of the whole arrangement suddenly seem unavoidable. Thereafter it has seemed easy to think of it as having been unnatural and necessarily precarious. However, contemporaries of its great days – and there were many who chronicled its fortunes – never doubted its viability. While it lasted it was one of the most powerful states of Christendom, and during its days Englishmen probably played their most ambitious roles ever in European affairs. Not by chance one of them actually became pope, the only Englishman ever to do so: Hadrian IV (pope 1154–59). How was this extraordinary government maintained?

In the past it was customary to attribute much of the success of this to the Normans themselves and to the mysterious quality of their "feudalism," which enabled them to create a powerful state out of institutions that everywhere else were held to be incompatible with good government. The Normans did indeed contribute certain qualities of vigor and vision and, because of the peculiar circumstances of the ducal conquest of England, they created their state in practically one blow: the Norman lords of the land formed a notably homogeneous and disciplined group, in sharp contrast, for example, to the "Norman" lords in Italy. But Normandy on its own was never remarkable for good government and in recent times historians have traced the origins of this powerful monarchy well back into preconquest England. The Normans certainly knew how to take charge of, and improve on, what they found. More important still they had a more urgent motive than their English predecessors for driving forward a manageable system, since their commit-

8°   4°   4°   0°   4°

△ Linlithgow

△ Edinburgh   Berwick

△ Ayr   Kelso
△ Roxburgh
SCOTLAND
1174 becomes English fief

△ Dumfries   Newcastle

Carlisle   Durham

54°   **NORTHERN COUNTIES**
1157 Henry II recovers land from
Malcolm IV of Scotland

ULSTER   ◻ Richmond

△ Armagh

NORTH SEA

CONNAUGHT   △ Lancaster

△ Granard   △ York

MEATH   ◻ Pontefract

△ Tuam

IRELAND   ◻ Conisbrough
1171 overlordship of   Rhuddlan
Henry II recognized   Deganwy   ◻ Lincoln

△ Athlone   Beaumaris   + △ Chester
△ Dublin   Caernarvon △ Conway + Hawarden
◻ Birr   St Asaph   ◻ Nottingham
△ Timahoe   Athy   Shrewsbury   ◻ Leicester   + Norwich

△ Limerick   **LEINSTER**   Aberystwyth   Lichfield   ◻ Ely   + Bury St Edmunds
△ Leighlin   **ENGLAND**
△ Ardfinnan   Cashel ◻   △ Builth   Coventry
Lismore   △ Cardigan   Worcester   Colchester
△   + Evesham
MUNSTER   Cork ◻   St Davids ◻   Hereford   Gloucester   Oxford +
Pembroke △   Llandaff   + St Albans   London ◻
△ Bath   Rochester ◻   Canterbury ◻
Thames   Dover +
50°   △ Wells   Salisbury
Exeter   Southampton   Winchester   **FLANDERS**
◻ Chichester   Boulogne ◻

ATLANTIC OCEAN   *ENGLISH CHANNEL*   **HAINAULT**

BRABANT
◻ Tournai
Meuse

Cherbourg ◻   △ Barfleur   ◻ Amiens   **VERMANDOIS**
St Pol de Léon ◻   ◻ Rouen   *Oise*   ◻ Reims
△ Château Gaillard
Bayeux ◻   Bec +   *Marne*
△ Tréguier   Mt St Michel   Caen +   Lisieux ◻   Évreux ◻
St Malo   + Avranches   **NORMANDY**   *Seine*   Paris ◻   **CHAMPAGNE**
PENTHIÈVRE   St Brieuc ◻   Dol   Tinchebrai   Troyes ◻
△ Sées
BRITTANY   **MAINE**   **GATINAIS**
came under Henry II's control in 1171 by   Le Mans   Orléans ◻
marriage of his son Geoffrey to
Constance of Brittany   △ Rennes   *Loire*   Blois ◻
Quimper ◻   Angers   Tours   **NIVERNAIS**
Loire   Fontevrault +   Chinon   △ Bourges
Vannes ◻   **ANJOU**   Loudun   **TOURAINE**
Nantes ◻   Issoudun   **BURGUNDY**
Mirebeau   **BOURBONNAIS**
The Plantagenet empire   **POITOU**
Already a powerful figure within   Poitiers   + St Savin
his own kingdom before 1066,   *Allier*
the English king from that date   **LA MARCHE**
played a prominent role in   La Rochelle ◻   *Saône*
continental affairs as well, by
virtue first of his lands in   46°   Saintes ◻   Clermont-
Normandy and Maine, and, after   Limoges ◻   Ferrand ◻
1154, through his possessions in   *BAY OF BISCAY*   Angoulême ◻   **LIMOUSIN**   **AUVERGNE**
western France from the Loire to   **SAINTONGE**   *Charente*
the Pyrenees. His lordship was   **AQUITAINE**   **VELAY**
sought by, or imposed upon,   **VENTADOUR**   Le Puy ◻
rulers in the outer fringes of   **TURENNE**   *Rhône*
Christendom from Scotland to   Périgueux ◻   + Souillac
Brittany. The king of France,   Bordeaux ◻   **PÉRIGORD**   *Dordogne*   + Conques   ◻ Mende
who clawed back control of the   Bazas ◻   **QUERCY**   Rodez ◻   **GEVAUDAN**
sweep of lands from Normandy   *Garonne*   Cahors ◻   ◻ Viviers
to Poitou (1202–26), did not   **AGENAIS**   + Moissac   Uzès ◻
thereby drive the Plantagenets   *Lot*   Agen ◻   △ Albi   Nîmes ◻
back across the Channel. For   **GASCONY**   **ARMAGNAC**   Lodève ◻   ◻ Montpellier
another two and a half centuries   Dax ◻   Aire ◻   Auch ◻   Toulouse ◻   **TOULOUSE**   Maguelone ◻
the English king played an   Bayonne ◻   Béziers ◻
independent role in French   **BÉARN**   **BIGORRE**   Carcassonne ◻   *MEDITERRANEAN*
affairs. This map illustrates only   Oloron ◻   Tarbes ◻   Conserans ◻   Narbonne ◻   *SEA*
the earlier part of that   Lescar ◻   Elne ◻
involvement, but already   **CASTILE**   Commingnes ◻   Agde ◻
encapsulates a complicated   **NAVARRE**   **BIGORRE**   **FOIX**   **ROUSSILLON**
history of more than 200 years.   **ARAGON**

Legend:
— boundary of Plantagenet empire in France 1154
◻ lands ruled by Stephen to 1154
◻ lands ruled by Henry of Anjou before 1151
◻ lands acquired by Henry II on father's death
◻ lands acquired by Henry II by marriage to Eleanor of Aquitaine 1152
◻ extensions to the domain under Henry II 1154–1189
▨ territory disputed between Henry II of England and Louis VII of France
-- boundary of Plantagenet empire in France 1226
◻ county of Toulouse 1154
⊡ archdiocese
◻ diocese
+ important monastery
△ castle

scale 1:5 000 000
0 ———— 150km
0 ———— 100mi

Above Domesday Book I, open, described the tenures and estates of all England south of the Tees–Ribble line except the three East Anglian counties; the latter were recorded in Domesday Book II, closed, which was slightly smaller and written by other scribes, following an inquiry without parallel ordered in 1086. The books have been stored in this wardrobe chest since the 17th century, but it was once fitted with three locks like Treasury chests and may have been used for storing Henry VI's regalia.

Right Orford castle, Suffolk, England. This castle, built in 1165–73 on a new coastal site selected by Henry II, can be shown from surviving records to have cost the king more than £1400 over eight to nine building seasons – the most costly of his fortifications to date. Timber was brought for the construction from Scarborough and stone from Caen. The design was also very unusual – an octagonal keep with three buttress towers and a forebuilding; a series of rectangular flanking towers was erected about the curtain wall.

institutions but with the capacity of some French princes to consolidate their hold on the affections and loyalties of soldierly forces. The successes of such rulers however depended on knowing how to profit from their opportunities. The greatest of them, Henry II of England, had both Norman and Angevin blood to inspire him to great deeds, yet the sudden extension of his power into the vast duchy of Aquitaine, by marrying its queen, Eleanor, in 1152, proves his basic opportunism. The nature of his government there is not as well known in detail as the nature of his government of England, but it was certainly more successful and durable than that of his predecessor, Louis VII, Eleanor's first husband. Henry II was soon able to deploy on the continent the resources of the English kingdom, and Aquitaine, or at least Gascony, proved to be more attached to the English kingdom than ever Normandy had been. Somehow or other the political links were maintained for three centuries. In Henry II's time certainly the continental domain of the king absorbed most of his attention, but England was never treated shabbily by him. He attended to its affairs when required, though its own orderly administration made it much less turbulent than other parts of his domain. The duty it showed to the king made it the obvious source of his reserves. It is hardly possible to prove that English money was poured into the continent, but it is easy to see how Englishmen in the royal service were introduced into Henry's affairs wherever required, serving the administration and his churches all over the "empire" and going on regular embassies beyond its frontiers, to Spain, Sicily, Rome and Germany, quite apart from fostering contacts in Ireland and Scotland. It is no wonder that the English chroniclers of this age have a wider horizon than their contemporaries elsewhere.

The historical records of the literate, like the need for professional scribes within the royal service, point to the inevitable involvement of the English monarchy with the learned and therefore the religious communities of Christendom. In particular the development of new schools and studies in northern France during the 12th century both attracted many English students and equipped them to serve a society like England's constantly in need of methodical, dedicated and even public-spirited servants. English bishops certainly maintained staffs of trained clergy, perhaps the more so because many bishops in England were set up with monastic chapters ill-equipped to deal with the bishops' special business. The bishops' staff in such dioceses had perforce to be independent of their chapters. Lay lords also valued the services of men trained in the schools. Learning was not a clerical monopoly. The king above all required their services. Henry II's first chancellor, Thomas Becket, was trained in the school at Bologna and, as archdeacon of Canterbury, was responsible for managing the archbishop's legal interests in his diocese. His services to Henry II were apparently more like those of a factotum. Two royal servants, wherever they received their formal education, were certainly accomplished enough to apply their learning in writing unique accounts of how the king's exchequer and law courts actually functioned: the *Dialogue of the Exchequer* by Richard Fitznigel and the *Treatise on the Laws and Customs of the Kingdom*

ments on the continent made it impossible for them to give their whole time to watching English affairs in person: their ambitions forced English institutions to develop more rapidly to meet the challenge of the royal responsibilities on the continent. The strength of the old English system lay with its local institutions. By enlarging the scope of royal supervision the monarchy devised a way of creating a coherent political society under its own leadership, knitting together local societies, feudal lords, the church and the royal administration. No other monarchs of the 12th century came near to doing what Henry I (king 1100–35) or still more Henry II (king 1154–89) of England could do to be the real masters of all the peoples of their lands. It was the combination of elements from both English and Frankish society that created this unique realization of royal power.

Given the real strengths of England, it is inconceivable that without French rulers these developments would have come about. The real strengths of French society lay not with local *of England* formerly attributed to the justiciar Ranulf Glanvill. They prove that in England contemporary developments in learning could be quickly adapted for practical purposes. The clergy as such played an important part in royal administration, but without changing its basically secular function. It would be unfair to scoff at their claims to serve a higher purpose than the king's alone. They were loyal to ecclesiastical rules but generally thought that the king too had a role to play in God's purposes and did not hesitate to promote royal interests accordingly. If their attitudes sometimes seem to us rather secular, their lay colleagues could be equally sanctimonious. Our categories hardly fit their times.

Of Henry II's contemporaries, Frederick I in Germany, Louis VII in France and Roger II in Sicily, all attracted to their courts distinguished men of talent as well as persons of birth and enjoyed the company of the witty and the conversation of the learned. But the service Henry II obtained from his courtiers was important to his government and the routines of administration. The dominions of the German kingdom were certainly more extensive than Henry's, but the king was required to do more by his subjects than King Frederick I was and his administrative procedures touched his subjects in every locality, so far as our evidence goes. This meant that the king was better informed and more active in intervening, but he also needed a constant supply of information, which in turn kept clerks, messengers and officials busy bringing the king up-to-date. Henry II was constantly on the move, always alert and active, and thus so incapable of sitting still that his major recreation was the chase. He was a man of action rather than an intellectual, but he had a fine mind, was himself well educated according to the standards of the day, and none of those learned men who knew him ever hinted that he was caught napping by persons of superior wit. His special skills as a ruler seem to have been in the law. He was an accredited arbiter of international disputes, and he devised ways of resolving legal problems that did not overtly undermine existing institutions. This is no place to spell out all the virtues and weaknesses of his government. Here, rather than dwell on his personal qualities, we should see him as exemplifying some of the features of his own times. The combination of the traditional English monarchy involved on the continent and using every up-to-date improvement then available enabled the Norman and Angevin rulers to make of their lands the most powerful state of the 12th century – a state with the mark of secular ambition stamped upon it, but one that could only function (and indeed only be known to us) by the multiplicity of its written records. Before the end of the 12th century the English government had so recognized the importance of this that it began to enroll its letters, that is, in modern words, to keep file copies of its own paperwork. The only other European government to act comparably at the time was, needless to say, the papacy itself. Such different ''states'' and programs had nonetheless this in common that they were self-consciously directing their own communities of faithful adherents and they showed the way to others who in due course discovered the same need to remain coherent and consistent.

Mirabilia Urbis Romae

The number of visitors, pilgrims and tourists who came to Rome in the 12th century made unprecedented demands upon the resources of the city. The strangers were often disappointed in their expectations and complained about the Romans and their avarice. They were not however deterrred from coming and took advantage of what facilities they could including, it would seem, the guidebook on the marvels of Rome, written c. 1140 probably by Benedetto, canon of St Peter's, who showed an intense feeling of respect for the ancient city. Outsiders were certainly struck by its strangeness, so Benedict seeks to explain the marvels of Rome for their benefit. The work itself is, however, better explained as another example of how 12th-century Romans themselves had recovered a pride in the whole of the city's heritage. There is no sense of shame or regret for its pagan past; and no special pleading for its Christian present; only a sense that the greatness of the past underlays the present and is properly completed in it. Thus after ten brief sections listing the dimensions of the city walls, the number of the gates, triumphal arches, hills, baths, palaces, theaters, bridges and cemeteries, the first anecdote given by Benedetto is an account of the vision accorded to Augustus Caesar in which the emperor, declining the divine honors proposed for him by the senate, consults the Tiburtine Sybil. She reveals to him the vision of the Virgin holding the infant Jesus – which vision, Benedetto writes, was granted to him in the room of his palace where now stands the church of Sta Maria in Capitolio, that is Sta Maria Ara Coeli. No more powerful story could have been told to the visitor to impress him with the special place of Rome in the Christian dispensation and the recognition of its Christian destiny by the pagan emperor who ruled the world. The story is told with supporting evidence derived from the reading of inscriptions, and in the guide the visitor is exhorted to pay due attention to the inscriptions, as the buildings are then described.

Not only are the buildings themselves explained. Benedetto also deals with the conspicuous sculptures and provides stories to explain them – like the statue of the Dioscuri with the horses or the equestrian statue of Marcus Aurelius. Legends had certainly developed by this time, as reported here, in the story of the national statues on the Capitol hill, each with a bell that tinkled when it was rebellious against Rome. The guide also tells the stories of how the month of August got its name and how the feast of the chains of Sts Peter and Paul was celebrated in August at the church of St Peter ad Vincula. Confusion over names mars the effect for modern writers, but Benedetto's concern to show how pagan customs were transformed in Christian practice shows a surprising wish to explain change in historical terms, as with his account of how Pope Boniface IV obtained the Pantheon from the emperor Phocas and rededicated it to the Virgin and all martyrs.

Right The seal of Louis the Bavarian, crowned emperor in 1328. Designed in 1328 for seals in gold, this seal concentrates in one image the remarkable buildings of the emperor's city: ROMA CAPUT MUNDI REGIT ORBIS FRENA ROTUNDI. Comparison with the map shows that the buildings are laid out in order as they would appear to travelers entering by the Porta Flaminia.

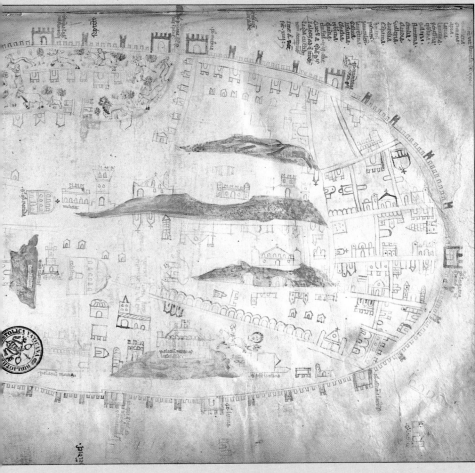

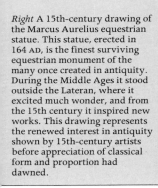

Right A 15th-century drawing of the Marcus Aurelius equestrian statue. This statue, erected in 164 AD, is the finest surviving equestrian monument of the many once created in antiquity. During the Middle Ages it stood outside the Lateran, where it excited much wonder, and from the 15th century it inspired new works. This drawing represents the renewed interest in antiquity shown by 15th-century artists before appreciation of classical form and proportion had dawned.

The interaction of the Roman past and the present makes it difficult to say whether the author was more interested in what became of Roman antiquities or in explaining how the churches acquired their ornaments. When dealing with Hadrian's tomb (Castel Sant' Angelo) he says that the original porphyry sepulcher was in his day at the Lateran *ante folloniam* and the *coopterium* was in the paradiso of St Peter over the tomb of the prefect Ginzio. But his interest in the imperial past for its own sake is clear in the account of Augustus' mausoleum; again he reads inscriptions; and he says of a temple of Gnaeus Pompeius that it was of wonderful size and beauty; this admiration of the past appears to be extended to its institutions, as when he describes the temple of Mars where the consuls were elected on 1 July and where they remained for six months; if the elected consuls were pure of crime, their consulates were confirmed. It was in this mid-12th-century Rome that Arnold of Brescia proposed the restitution of the senate. Not surprisingly therefore Benedetto gives a totally appreciative chapter on the Capitol hill, which is almost without Christian reference at all.

Benedetto's scholarship may not be impressive by modern standards, but his concern for the past, his precision in identifying ancient sites in the location of the monuments of his day, his references to the institutions and customs (the games and the public libraries) of the past suggest a predominantly educated readership for his book. He is not dealing with mere gossip to amuse sightseers. Nonetheless the book does appear to indicate that the reader will be traveling around Rome with a coherent itinerary. Beginning at the Vatican, the book takes in the Castel Sant' Angelo and the Campus Martius before going to the Campidoglio. Then the tour goes down into the Forum. From the Palatine it proceeds to the Colosseum, the Circus Maximus and to the hills, the Celio, the Lateran, the Esquiline and the Aventine before returning to Trastevere. The author concludes by saying that he has done his best to put in writing for the benefit of posterity how much beauty there was in silver, gold, bronze, ivory and precious stones and how many temples and palaces of emperors, consuls, senators and prefects of the pagan period there were in Rome, as he had read in earlier annals and had seen with his own eyes and heard about from the ancients. From this book even Petrarch, in the 14th century, like many before him, drew both inspiration and information. From its pages it is now possible for us to appreciate how Rome was able to exercise its fascination once again on the peoples of the west: not by empire, nor by the name of government, nor even by ecclesiastical discipline alone, but by a blend of pagan and Christian not to be paralleled elsewhere. Paganism had become quite harmless for 12th-century Christians, as is shown too by the poets and scholars of the period who had no fears that pagan authors or allusions would corrupt their religious purity.

Pilgrimage to Compostela

In two ways pilgrimages to the shrines of the saints can be seen as paradoxical: individual saints were treasured in particular places but attracted visitors from all over Christendom; pilgrimages presupposed an international situation sufficiently stable to guarantee peaceful travel yet assumed that pilgrims themselves were not so rooted in their localities that they would not embark on long journeys.

In the 4th-century Roman empire the pull of the Holy Places was powerful. Rome attracted pilgrims to the shrines of St Peter and St Paul, especially after the Muslim conquest of Jerusalem (638) made the journey there hazardous. By now churchmen had begun to impose pilgrimage as a penance. Irish monks cultivated the idea of the Christian life itself being a pilgrimage, to be lived in permanent exile. The long journeys of pilgrims to the shrines of the saints therefore seemed to be a mild form of self-denial. As long-distance travel itself was subject to unpredictable difficulties because of unstable political conditions, so the departure on pilgrimage remained an unusual decision, undertaken only with due solemnity. From the 11th century, however, it is clear that parties of pilgrims were deliberately organized to make the rigors of the journey less daunting for individuals.

No text earlier than c. 700 makes any mention of St James in Spain and not until c. 900 was a cult established at the place in the diocese of Iria where what was believed to be the apostle's tomb had been discovered c. 830. Though a church was built there, at Compostela, before the end of the 9th century, not until William Firebrace, count of Aquitaine (970–1029), made a pilgrimage is there evidence that the cult had spread beyond Spain. By the end of the 11th century the cult was so well established that the pope authorized the bishop of Iria to transfer his see to Compostela, where a new basilica in honor of St James had been started in 1076. By this time the pilgrimage had won international recognition and almost immediately became one of the major cults of western Christendom, where only Rome itself could also claim to have the corporal relics of an apostle.

The promoters of the cult saw sense in elaborating the story of how St James came to be at Compostela, in filling gaps in existing accounts to tell a more elevating story, and perhaps in dispelling any doubts. Our principal source of information is a compilation, *Liber Sancti Jacobi* (The Book of St James), made for Compostela probably in the time of Archbishop Diego Gelmirez (1101–39), an active supporter of the cult. It brought together a number of texts, including a legendary history of Charlemagne which became the best-known part of the text. When this was written is uncertain, but it points to the importance of pilgrim traffic from Charlemagne's native lands. It is followed by a pilgrim's guide written by a native of France, designed to point out to pilgrims the various stages of their journey across northern Spain from Puente

la Reina. The author refers to four routes across France which reach this Spanish point of departure. It is therefore clear that by the mid-12th century substantial numbers of pilgrims would set out for Compostela from places beyond St Gilles, Le Puy, Vézelay or Tours, from as far afield as Italy, the empire, the Low Countries and Normandy. Other pilgrims came by ship from the Christian lands to the north. But it is the importance of the French for the overland routes that is most obvious, particularly the influence of Cluny which was so marked in 11th- and 12th-century Christian Spain.

Although pilgrims may have been coming along these routes for several generations, everything points to a promotion of the cult in the late 11th century when Cluniac influence in northern Spain was at its height. Sancho the Great of Navarre (king 1010–30) had first reoccupied the Nájera-Logroño region and made the old pilgrimage routes, which 10th-century Saracen raids had interrupted, safe again for travelers. The wars against the Muslims attracted Christian soldiers to Spain, as much as they did to Sicily or later to the Holy Land, and they were encouraged by tales of Charlemagne and his peers having fought in the peninsula in earlier times. The success of Christian arms, which reached Toledo by 1085, put new heart into the Christian kingdoms of northern Spain, where new churches were built. One by one the stages along the route were adorned with new buildings, in styles that blended elements from France and Mozarabic Spain. The great routes extending back through France thus offered the pilgrims an almost unrivaled succession of distinguished posting-stages which sustained their religious fervor on the long march.

The Guide served the organizers or managers of pilgrim groups. About one third is devoted to a detailed description of the town of Compostela, its churches and the basilica, and more to an account of the saints whose shrines lay on the French side of the Pyrenees. Nevertheless the space devoted to the different regions of Spain traversed by the pilgrims, to their peoples, the stops on the journey, the hospices, the rivers to be crossed and the quality of their drinking water does give plain and specific information of use to travelers. The author assumes that his readers will share his impression of the uncouth peoples to be met *en route*. Travelers obliged to cross the wide rivers near Bayonne were made to pay extravagant sums to the ferrymen, against whom the author of the Guide rails in frustrated fury. Claiming that only merchants were liable for toll duties, not pilgrims, he reveals that the ferrymen actually paid over these fees to the king of Aragon and other lords, while the local clergy not only exonerated these predators but received them at the holy altars. In effect he makes it clear that the whole region had conspired to fleece the pilgrims. The author thinks desperately that only public excommunication of such malefactors at St James itself could halt the practice but the pilgrims'

Above The late appearance of legends about St James, seen here dressed as a pilgrim, does not inspire confidence in them. But a desire to believe that Christendom in its darkest days possessed the wonder-working bodies of the greatest saints transformed everywhere the character of popular devotions, revealing a desperate need to find religious backing for friendship and kinship and to make the saints accessible in feudal religious worship.

Right The Benedictine monastery at Silos stands off the pilgrim route but flourished nonetheless. Its church was rebuilt in the mid-11th century. Soon afterwards the First Master sculpted Christ as a pilgrim, pushing ahead with determination but being urged by the disciples at Emmaus to turn aside and sup with them. His figure conveys the magisterial resolution of the dedicated pilgrim.

Far right The west doorway of St James described in the Guide as surpassing all others was replaced (1168–88) by this doorway built by Master Matthew, whose name appears on the lintel. On the tympanum the impassivity of the massive triumphant Christ dominates the blessed above and the prophets and apostles on the door jamb. St James stands immediately below.

enthusiasm for the saint inevitably exposed them to cynical exploitation. The Spanish mountain men saw no good reason why all the profits of the pilgrim trade should be taken by the pedlars of cockleshell badges, wine, sandals, leather bags, purses, belts or herbal remedies, who waylaid the pilgrims before the great church of Compostela. The pilgrim who desired to squander his money on knickknacks touted in the holy city resented paying for the unavoidable expenses of the journey itself.

Fortunately, the author is able to assure his readers that in Galicia itself the travelers will find an agreeable land, with pure water and abundant fruit, rye bread, cider, milk, honey, fish, sheep and pack animals, together with gold, silver, cloth, furs and the riches of the Saracens. They will find that the Galicians, despite their choleric and argumentative natures, are in their ways closer to "our French people" than any of the other uncouth peoples of Spain. Nobody could be tempted by the Guide to embark on the journey to Compostela in expectation of a spree, or for the pleasure of ambling through novel and attractive lands. If travelers were beguiled on their journeys by anything other than the landmarks of the saints they have left no record of it. The journey was so long and hazardous that some willingness to mortify the flesh for spiritual blessings was indispensable. From the pilgrims' tribulations, however, there now survive only the monuments of the buildings erected along the way, in part at their expense. The road to St James was literally paved for their benefit and the maintenance of the pilgrimage to this remote Galician place throughout the Middle Ages represents the thankfulness of later generations that they could enter into the benefits made for them by pioneers in the 11th and early 12th centuries.

Pilgrim routes across France converged at Ostabat, now a quiet village (*below*). Over the Pyrenees they came to Estella where fine 11th-century capitals survive in San Pedro de la Rua (*bottom right*). The finest Romanesque monument of the region is the collegiate church at Santillana (*bottom left*).

BAY OF BISCAY

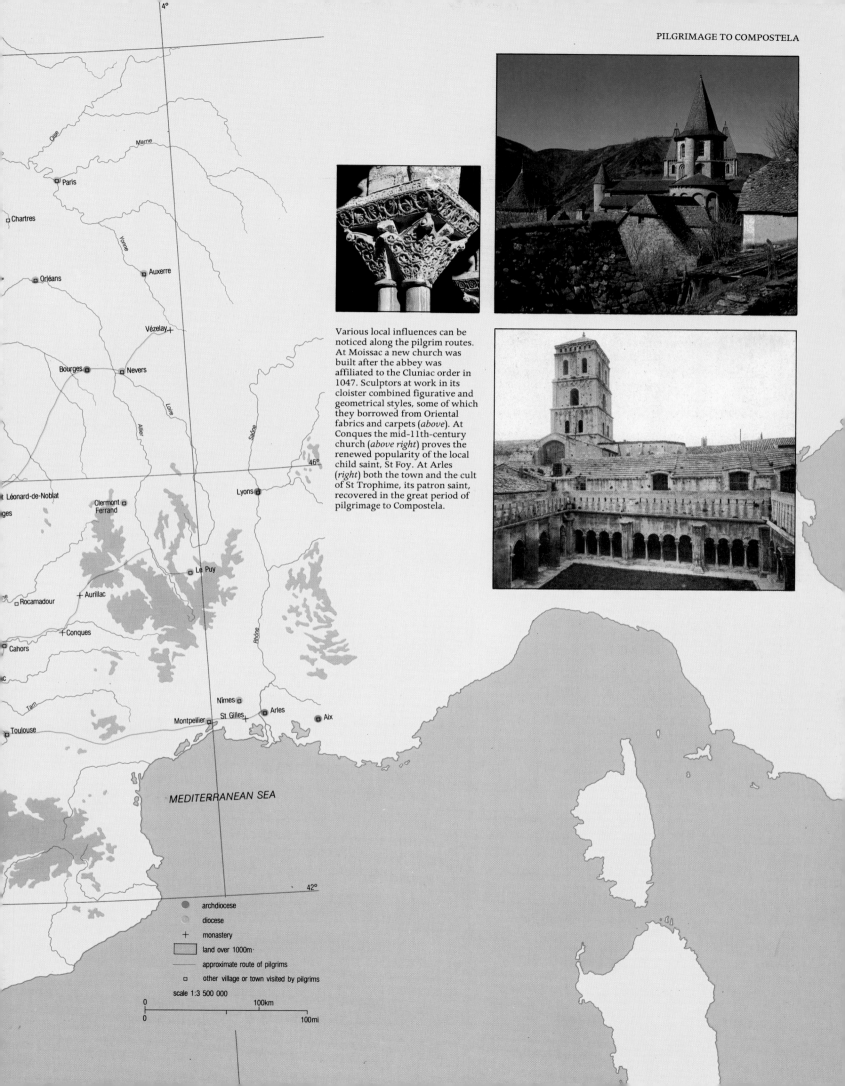

Various local influences can be noticed along the pilgrim routes. At Moissac a new church was built after the abbey was affiliated to the Cluniac order in 1047. Sculptors at work in its cloister combined figurative and geometrical styles, some of which they borrowed from Oriental fabrics and carpets (*above*). At Conques the mid-11th-century church (*above right*) proves the renewed popularity of the local child saint, St Foy. At Arles (*right*) both the town and the cult of St Trophime, its patron saint, recovered in the great period of pilgrimage to Compostela.

MEDITERRANEAN SEA

● archdiocese
○ diocese
+ monastery
▭ land over 1000m
— approximate route of pilgrims
□ other village or town visited by pilgrims

scale 1:3 500 000

0   100km
0   100mi

Paris
Chartres
Orléans
Auxerre
Vézelay
Bourges
Nevers
Léonard-de-Noblat
Clermont Ferrand
Lyons
Rocamadour
Aurillac
Le Puy
Conques
Cahors
Toulouse
Nîmes
Montpellier
St Gilles
Arles
Aix

Oise
Marne
Yonne
Loire
Allier
Saône
Rhône
Tarn

4°
46°
42°

Castles

Below left Abinger motte, Surrey, reconstructed from posthole evidence. Until the mid-12th century most Anglo-Norman castles were originally built in wood, with a palisade erected on an earthen mound, and a central tower. Such defenses could be put up rapidly with the help of forced labor.

Below Bodiam, Sussex. Permission to fortify this castle 16 kilometers from the sea was given in 1385. Its isolation in the moat, only crossed by the bridge to the north, certainly makes this four-range house look fearful for its safety. The 13th-century style of the fortification, with its round angle-towers and its

Not until the 9th century did the new centers of population discover the use of town defenses. The Vikings who besieged Paris in 886–88 were held up by the walls; Alfred in England about the same time devised means of enclosing towns with walls and arranging for them to be manned by forces from the local countryside. To erect and defend fortresses of this kind it was necessary for the public authorities to coerce men into paying for, building and manning these strongholds. If the exercise of public authority fell into other hands than those of the kings, as it did, particularly in France during the 10th century, such men had the power, and often the motive, to raise fortresses of their own.

Castles as strongpoints to be held permanently were built of stone, which from the beginning would require the use of skilled masons and take time to construct. To establish some defense work promptly, earth mounds with a stout wooden palisade on top were sufficient to provide a refuge for a small body of soldiers. An invading force probably took with it specialized workmen to provide for the rapid erection of such castles, but it also seems likely that the labor force for raising the earth mound would have been rounded up locally. Not even the smallest castle could be put up by any lord who was without considerable powers, however temporary, over the local area and over a body of soldiers. The castles, once built, had to be entrusted to their own castellans and such men discovered that the stronghold could become the base for their own independent political action. The castle, if adequately supplied with water and stores, turned out to be capable of giving quite minor local lords the power to maintain their own effective independence.

Kings with great military resources and some political determination, such as Henry II of England, were apparently able to deal with castellans who threatened their own security, to dismantle the superfluous castles and find loyal castellans for the rest, but there were few rulers of this kind, and many castles continued in effect to be the centers of autonomous states. The basic function of the castle was always defensive. The site was chosen primarily for the advantages offered by the terrain for defense: a neck of land with only one possible approach, steep sides, even a rocky crag. All over Europe the ruins of such castles, some perched in astonishing places, are still visible, now more picturesque than menacing. Gunpowder has wrecked their defense works, but only after political and economic conditions had already undermined their security. By the 13th century the renewed importance of towns made access to them, if not control of them, indispensable for pre-eminence in public life. Towns were from the first provided with defensive walls of their own and these walls needed to be permanent and substantial. The techniques of building defenses of this kind had implications for castle building itself. Edward I of

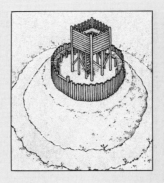

Below Krak des Chevaliers in Syria. This was the greatest fortress raised by the crusaders in the Holy Land and it was held by the knights of St John of the Hospital from 1142 to 1271 when it was captured by the Mamluk Sultan Baybars. An earlier Muslim stronghold had occupied the commanding site, but the position was reinforced by the crusaders with two concentric walls set with towers and separated by a wide moat.

outmoded chapel windows on the east side, suggests that the basic buildings were older.

The plan of the castle (*below*) shows how the separate apartments were ranged around the open square courtyard to provide a two-storied house with three stories in the towers. The hall was at the SE end of the building and the water tank in the SW tower.

Below Curemonte in Brive la Gaillarde, Corrèze. These two castles, restored in the 16th century when they were still linked together, had in the later Middle Ages become the property of several copossessors. One of the families left its name – Plas – to the castle built between two square keeps. St Hilaire was the name of the castle with round towers. The castles are surrounded by an enclosing wall with round turrets. In the 12th century the site was occupied by the lords of Curemonte who probably built the original fortification, but the present structures, like most of the castles of this region, date from the period of the Anglo-French wars.

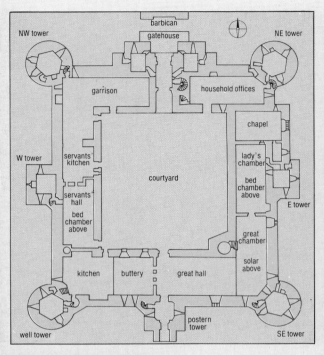

England, the greatest English builder of castles in Wales and Scotland, made use of an architect from Savoy, James of St George, who showed at Caernarvon how the castle and the town were to be defended together. Only castle building of this quality could in effect resist the assaults of medieval enemies. And only castellans in isolated and improbable places could thereafter preserve their independence. Elsewhere the castle had lost its significance for local politics.

In the two or three centuries of its preeminence the castle had a profound effect upon the lives and mentality of lords, vassals, soldiers and local inhabitants. A castle's main purpose was to enable a beleaguered garrison to hold out longer than any enemies were prepared to sustain a siege. No castellan had any vested interest in antagonizing the local population or in depriving himself of food supplies and labor from the immediate vicinity. The castle offered a refuge from intermittent but recurring raiding parties from afar, not from the local population; when their enemies appeared, the castle became the refuge for the men and animals of the neighborhood and was provisioned accordingly. The castle, if it continued to be maintained for more than temporary purposes and became a stout stone structure, acquired a special role as the strong point of its district or of its political society. Always garrisoned with a minimum force capable of holding it under siege, it could also on occasion accommodate a large number of persons, not necessarily assembled there in wartime. When its lord arrived with his attendants, he could hold court, entertain his vassals and neighbors in the great hall, giving lavish display of his wealth, his munificence and, if necessary, of his justice. He could call his local bailiffs to give account of their charges, meet new tenants, issue new regulations and settle old disputes. His castle was his country house, his treasury, his palace, his temporary home, the permanent symbol of his power and dignity. There are castles enough still extant in the British Isles, some still in use like Windsor or Warwick or Alnwick, to suggest their purpose. Later repairs have not altogether obliterated their original aspect, though it is more difficult to imagine their interiors. Later improvements on the 13th-century framework suggest that only belatedly did the lord acquire quarters more specially intimate and comfortable. For the most part it was a public place where men who trusted one another lived, ate and slept in company, with only the ladies of rank specially secluded. Castles, like monasteries, were austere places with proper recognition of the importance of sanitation, as their construction proves. Of the soft furnishings, the wall hangings or tapestries, the comfort of the beds and bowers, only the romances give the faintest hints. Their castellated profiles were intended to strike awe and respect into those who approached them; but once admitted to the castle yard, the visitor became part of the lord's extended family and lived within its fellowship.

SETTING UP A NEW ORDER

Authority, discipline, law and logic

The sheer vitality of the 12th century created new problems for Christendom that could only be resolved by new methods. For example, the momentum of monastic invention had enormously extended the range and influence of monks, but in the process the plethora of rules undermined the basis for belief in the simple monastic profession as the only ideal for Christians. The monks themselves had shown it to be capable of too many diverse interpretations. Disputes about the ideal and rivalries between orders made it imperative to impose discipline upon the monks from above. Pope Innocent III (1198–1216) therefore decreed that the Benedictine houses should be grouped in congregations and hold regular assemblies, an idea inspired by the Cistercians, and he also decreed that no new rules for religious life should be devised. Future monastic reformers would have to make one of the many existing rules suit their purposes. Authority, discipline and law were used to control the luxurious growth of the earlier ages, to make an ordered garden for Christendom.

Something comparable occurred in the crusading movement. Though its conquering period was over well before Saladin recaptured Jerusalem in 1187, crusaders had already perceived the need to think seriously about their strategy. Enthusiasm and valor were not enough. Throughout the 13th century the crusading ideal remained powerful, and Christendom, in spite of its disappointments, kept hopes alive. In fact however it seemed as though the Holy Land would have to be taken on the flank rather than by direct assault. The Fourth Crusaders were caught up in the affairs of the Greeks and diverted into capturing Constantinople (1204), with the forlorn hope that this would prove to be an advantage for the movement; the Fifth Crusade was launched against Egypt, the main enemy (1218–21). Louis IX's crusades were also directed against Egypt (1248–54) and Tunis (1270). Only Frederick II, characteristically, tackled Jerusalem head on, but alienated Christian sympathy by his negotiations with al-Kamil, sultan of Egypt, although these did result in the occupation of part of Jerusalem (1228). Many kings traveled to the east in the 13th century and the movement was ever on their minds, but careful preparation of the forces and assessment of the political realities necessarily had a sobering effect on soldiers. The old blind enthusiasm was seen to be dangerous.

In these and other ways therefore the outcome of 12th-century innovations was that by the 13th century men realized the importance of taking thought about their problems and trusting to rulers to act with responsibility. As a result the political units of Europe began to crystallize. There were no more newcomers like Norman Sicily. The old powers emerged to assume the new tasks of government, giving certainty and making peace between rival factions. Symbolic perhaps of the new position was the organization of the university of Paris in the early 13th century with its guild of teachers and its system of examination and graduation, which developed out of the much more spontaneous type of teaching known in the 12th century. The men who succeeded in organizations of this new kind had to be clear-minded, certain of their fundamental objectives, and to have confidence in themselves. These characteristics also emerged in contemporary Gothic architecture and painting, in which proportion, order and clarity prevail.

The direct source of this self-confidence among 13th-century leaders was their belief in God and the work of the church. Throughout the 13th century a succession of popes, mostly from Roman families, gave Christendom energetic and capable leaders, who tried to make a reality of the unity of Christendom that their position symbolized. The primacy of the Roman see in the west had never really been in doubt, but the popes had claimed in the past to be the vicars of St Peter: from the 13th century they monopolized the title "vicar of Christ," with all that this implied about their supreme spiritual power and with more than a hint of their rights to deal with temporal rulers as well. As Roman nobles by origin they were in a position to deal with local problems, to recruit staff for their own extensive administration and therefore to master the lands of St Peter in central Italy, as well as to deal with the affairs of all Christendom. As Romans they understood something of the universality of the Roman ideals but they were also hard-headed realists, convinced of the importance of having a territorial basis for the church if their work was to become effective. The popes of this period had the gift of being able to deal with Italian affairs and with those of the whole of Christendom as though these interests were compatible. Their wars with the Staufen emperors were paid for in part by levies on other parts of Christendom, which were unpopular, and resisted. Nevertheless some money was paid and allegiance to Rome, however critical, was not undermined. The popes were not always as long-suffering or as wise as their position required, but for all their mistakes they did not alienate important sections of Christendom.

In their spiritual task the popes recognized the importance of obtaining effective fellow workers and did not aim to achieve their objectives by mere bureaucratic manipulation. Innocent III hoped to decrease the burden put on the Roman curia by getting his fellow bishops to accept their own responsibilities. To judge from the abundant registers left by the English bishops, the bishops' senses of zeal and duty could do much to provide oversight and spot defects in the system, but they could not eliminate abuses and did not reduce the burden of business sent to Rome for adjudication. They brought to light more matters for papal attention. In the 13th century the pope and the

Right: The development of the papal state
Early in its history the Roman church had been generously endowed with lands. Much of this estate was lost by Lombard aggression and, in the south, by the hostility of the iconoclastic emperors and then by Muslim conquests. To compensate them for these losses, the popes obtained the concession of lands in Italy from the Frankish rulers. After Charlemagne later emperors frequently confirmed and augmented these grants. Effective control of the lands ceded was not so easy to obtain as their charters. This proved also to be the case with the lands bequeathed to the Roman church by the pious Countess Mathilda of Tuscany, who died in 1115. The longest-reigning pope, Alexander III, spent much time in exile or in papal Benevento. Not until the late 12th century were popes able to bring their nominal lands in Italy under their own control. The benevolence of the German emperor was necessary for the continuation of this state of affairs. The papacy's concern for the real independence of its territorial interests in Italy eventually caused the fatal breach with Frederick II. This broke the empire and confirmed the papacy's Italian territory, which was held for six more centuries.

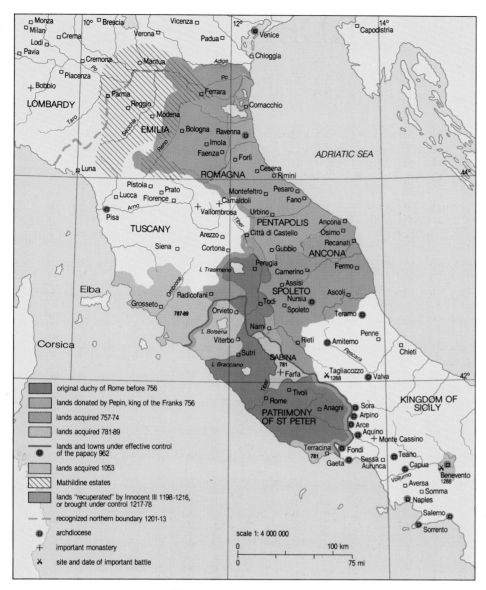

Monza
Milan   10°   Brescia   Vicenza   12°   14°   Capodistria
Lodi   Crema   Verona   Padua   Venice
Pavia   Cremona   Mantua   Chioggia
            Piacenza   Adige   Po
Bobbio   Parma   Ferrara
LOMBARDY Reggio Modena   Comacchio
         Secchia
         EMILIA   Bologna Ravenna
         Reno   Imola
Luna   Faenza   Forlì   ADRIATIC SEA   44°
              ROMAGNA   Cesena Rimini
Pistoia Prato   Montefeltro Pesaro
Lucca Florence   Camaldoli   Fano
Arno   Vallombrosa Urbino
Pisa   PENTAPOLIS Ancona
TUSCANY   Arezzo   Città di Castello Osimo
         Siena   Cortona   Recanati
Elba   L Trasimeno Gubbio ANCONA
              Perugia   Camerino Fermo
         Radicofani   Assisi
         Ombrone   SPOLETO Ascoli
Grosseto   787-89   Orvieto Nursia
              Todi Spoleto
Corsica   Narni Teramo
              L Bolsena   Penne
         Viterbo Rieti Amiterno
         Sutri   Chieti
         SABINA   Pescara
         L Bracciano 781   Tagliacozzo Valva   42°
              Farfa   1268
              Tivoli
              Rome   KINGDOM OF
         PATRIMONY Anagni Sora   SICILY
         OF ST PETER   Arpino
                   Arce
                   Aquino
              Terracina Fondi Monte Cassino
              781   Sessa Teano
         Gaeta   Aurunca Capua
                   Volturno Benevento
                   Aversa   1266
                   Somma
                   Naples
                        Salerno
                        Sorrento

original duchy of Rome before 756

lands donated by Pepin, king of the Franks 756

lands acquired 757-74

lands acquired 781-89

lands and towns under effective control of the papacy 962

lands acquired 1053

Mathildine estates

lands "recuperated" by Innocent III 1198-1216, or brought under control 1217-78

recognized northern boundary 1201-13

archdiocese

important monastery

site and date of important battle

scale 1: 4 000 000

0   100 km
0   75 mi

bishops tended to believe that a better-educated parochial clergy might in the end be an indispensable, if not sufficient, means to deal with the weakness of the ministers and the ignorance of the laity. Here bishops' schools and eventually the universities would have to help. In the 13th century, however, the universities were places for educating the upper clergy rather than the parish priest. Only at the end of it did Boniface VIII take steps to make it possible for parish clergy to obtain a few years' study by granting permission for them to use the revenues of their benefices while absent from their parishes. Most 13th-century students were therefore dependent on their own families or on patrons during their studies. In the meantime, before well-educated clergy could become available in every parish, the pope and the bishops were aided in their task of instructing the laity by the new orders of friars, Dominicans and Franciscans, both directly under papal protection. Both orders made a special point of preaching, an activity formerly reserved for bishops and abbots, and of accepting poverty – that is, refusing endowments for their convents and therefore needing to live in town communities and beg daily for their needs. This self-denial itself shows how much the former monastic way of acquiring endowments to serve religious needs had generated hostility and the suspicion that the religious themselves had benefited more than God. The new religious tried to disarm suspicions by proposing to live on the charity of others, thus reversing the role of the monks in earlier centuries. Though these orders proved to be extremely popular all over 13th-century Christendom and even beyond it, both orders had at an early stage become committed to the task of combating the influence of heresy in particular parts of southern France and central Italy. The Dominicans intended to confute Albigensian heretics by polemical debating on doctrine;

Left Innocent III in a mosaic from the apse of old St Peter's and now in the Vatican. When the Constantinian mosaics of St Peter's were restored in the time of Innocent III (1198–1216) two insertions were made, including this fine head of the young mustachioed pope. The workmanship with fine tesserae and the highlighting of the cheek suggest Greek workmanship, and the style of his headgear is notable. The papacy stood then at its apogee, but it had not yet adopted the triple crown to symbolize its sovereignty.

Right The cathedral of Ste Cécile, Albi, begun in 1282, completed in the 14th century. Built of rosered brick in the southern French style, with a spacious interior, the outside view demonstrates the severe grandeur of the conception. Counterforts buttress the vault and accommodate side chapels. The south door was added later. This is the finest monument of Gothic art erected in southern France, where the heretics had once flourished.

Left This pulpit from the baptistery in Pisa was executed in 1259 by Nicola "Pisano," who was born and raised in Apulia, where a strong tradition of figure sculpture had been maintained since the 11th century. Everything about it, shape, large-scale reliefs, the way of showing draperies and its style of figure sculpture, would have contrasted with the prevailing Gothic styles of Tuscany at that date.

Far left San Stefano, the Church of the Crucifixion, is one of a group of nine churches in Bologna which attained their present form in the 11th and 12th centuries and symbolized the stages of Christ's earthly life. On the facade facing the piazza an outside pulpit provides a suitable rostrum for a preacher – an early indication of the new importance attached to public exhortation in one of the greatest intellectual centers of Christendom before churches, like those of the friars, were specially designed as great auditoriums.

Below left The *ambone*, or desk from which the Epistle and Gospel were sung, in San Lorenzo fuori le Mure, Rome. In the 12th and 13th centuries, when the Roman churches were reformed and renovated, they were equipped with new fittings in majestic and magnificent style. The "Cosmati" style of decoration, using slabs of marble or porphyry framed in mosaic, was particularly esteemed, and this is the finest example of a Cosmati *ambone*.

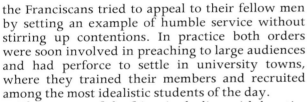

the Franciscans tried to appeal to their fellow men by setting an example of humble service without stirring up contentions. In practice both orders were soon involved in preaching to large audiences and had perforce to settle in university towns, where they trained their members and recruited among the most idealistic students of the day.

The success of the friars in dealing with heretics in this period undoubtedly helped to sustain general confidence in Christianity. The Albigensian heretics in particular had resisted all attempts to win them over by preaching in the 12th century. Their recalcitrance had finally provoked even Innocent III to preach the crusade against them (1209). It was by military means that their force was broken and the danger reduced (in the 1240s). By the time the Dominicans were entrusted with the duties of preaching and then of rooting out heretics through the Inquisition, the psychological reactions of the Albigensian region can be imagined. Heresy was not stamped out by the intellectual superiority of the Dominicans, but contemporaries nonetheless believed that the church had been able to deal with heresy, because it was intellectually confident of its position.

The friars also played an important part in the universities in building up intellectual confidence in the truths of religion. The most famous teachers of scholastic theology were all friars – Albert the Great (Albertus Magnus), Thomas Aquinas, Duns Scotus and William of Occam. When the university of Paris was first organized in the early 13th century the main intellectual influence on studies there was Aristotle. The rediscovery of his logical works had excited interest during the 12th century and his reputation among logicians secured at least a

respectful attitude to his scientific works. However when the latter became generally known in the early 13th century some teachers were at first hostile to their patently un-Christian teaching, for example about creation or the nature of man. A further reason for their hostility was that Aristotle's scientific works were too difficult to be understood without reference to commentaries and the only ones available in the early 13th century were translated from Arabic, written by Muslims. Suspicion of Aristotle was therefore reinforced by hostility to his advocates. Christian admirers of Aristotle were not however discouraged. They saw that they had much to learn from these difficult works and did not allow themselves to be deterred by their objectionable features. Some bolder

Below: The Mongol empire
The history of the Mongols does not properly form part of European medieval history, but the existence of the empire had a profound effect on Europe. Despite their destructive activities in eastern Europe (1237–41), they were immediately recognized as potential allies against the ancient Muslim enemy. Pope Innocent IV and King Louis IX of France both sent embassies proposing this, and the reports of their intrepid messengers, who reached the Khan's court at Karakorum, still stir amazement, though they are not so famous as the more fanciful reminiscences of Marco Polo. Merchants and missionaries certainly maintained steady contact across Mongol Asia till the mid-14th century. The Mongol empire also had a more direct and lasting influence on the Russians, changing the course of their history and for long impeding their development. The Islamic Middle East was, however, certainly shattered by the Mongols in a way that Christianity was spared. The caliphate at Baghdad was broken for ever and the caliph came to rest under the wing of the Mamluk sultans of Egypt. As late as the early 15th century the Mongols under Timur broke up the burgeoning Ottoman state. The Christians had therefore good grounds for welcoming the Mongols as potential friends, even though their hopes of converting them came to nothing.

thinkers went further and tried to reinterpret his doctrines and show that they could be acceptable to Christians. Others bolder still began to think that there might be two truths, one for religion and one for science. Thirteenth-century universities remained highly argumentative places and, though scholasticism has become a word that suggests rather sterile intellects, in fact the issues were important and very stimulating in the intellectual development of Christendom. Above all, Christian teachers in this period took the measure of the problems presented by the pagan rationalism of antiquity and of the intellectual giants of Islam and, overcoming their initial awe of both, struck out on their own. The west for the first time acquired intellectual self-confidence. As an indication of this change of mood, consider Aquinas's *Summa contra Gentiles* (''Summa'' against the Gentiles), said to have been commissioned to help train Dominican missionaries in the newly conquered Balearic Islands. It is conceived as a rational exposition of Christian theology and on the assumption that Muslims could be led from their own monotheistic position to acceptance of Christianity. But, whatever its merits for any immediate proselytizing purpose, as an intellectual achievement it is a *tour de force*.

Missions to the Mongols
The new religious orders, unlike the old, went out to influence and convert those who stood beyond the range of the church. Their most striking successes came in the now flourishing towns where they were able to erect enormous churches ideal for preaching – in many places still extant. But their

most startling achievement must surely be the astonishing missions they established outside Christendom itself. The Dominicans had reached lands east of the middle Volga before 1239. Ten years later Andrew of Longjumeau had reached Tabriz. For about a hundred years Dominicans were to be found in central Asia, in India and at Samarkand; in the same period Franciscans reached as far as Peking itself, the capital of the Mongol empire, where they established a bishopric. These missionaries, so far from their base, had extraordinary faith and courage. They were certainly not the only Christians to be found so far east or to take their lives in their own hands. They found Nestorian Christians in China itself and unknown numbers of Christians had been drawn into Asia by the Mongol rulers after their raids in Europe. The visit of Venetian merchants, the Polo brothers, to the court of the Great Khan (1275) shows that other intrepid Europeans could make the long journey for motives other than saving Christian souls. The times, however uncertain, were seen to be propitious in the west. And the Mongol presence throughout Asia was one of the factors that helped to make them so.

The Mongols had first entered Christendom in 1237 when, raiding beyond the central Asian steppe, they had fallen upon Kievan Russia and destroyed its great trading cities. They had continued to advance into Europe under their leader Batu, grandson of Genghis Khan, and were met by a great force at Legnica in Silesia in 1241 which they defeated. Only the death of the Great Khan Ogedei in central Asia distracted Batu from

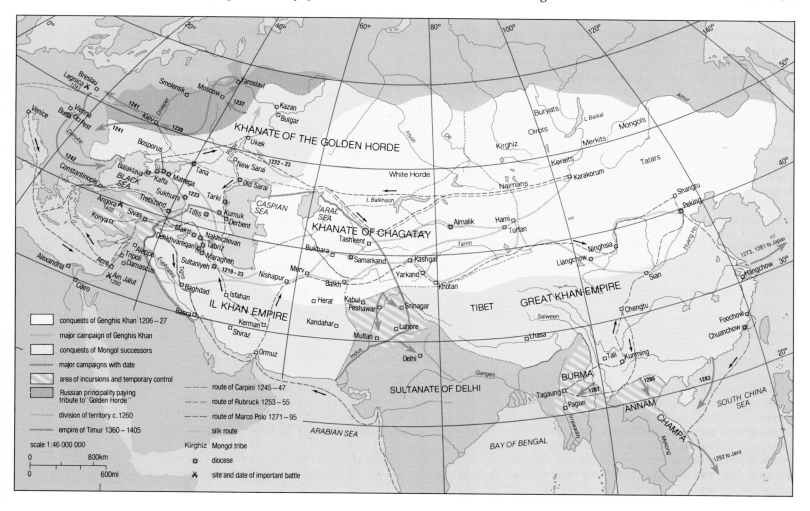

any further advance. He withdrew to settle the problems of the succession to the khanate and, as it happened, never returned. But Pope Innocent IV was so impressed by the arrival of such a powerful force, as yet uncommitted to Islam, that he sent Giovanni Carpini after the Mongols deep into Asia to propose an alliance (1245–47). This initiative was renewed a few years later by Louis IX who, from his vantage point in the Holy Land, saw the sense of cultivating the Mongols. His messenger, William of Rubruck, like his predecessor Carpini, eventually reported back and their accounts of the Mongols thus encouraged many others to make the journey across to the Crimean ports of the Genoese colony and thereafter across the steppe, as far as Peking if necessary. For more than two generations, until the khan of Persia accepted Islam in 1300, the Mongol power of central Asia seemed to Christians like a further reason for hope, particularly after the Mongols had destroyed the caliphate of Baghdad in 1258 and provoked the fury of the Mamluk leader Baybars, who actually defeated them in Syria in 1260.

This defeat might have convinced Christians that as potential allies the Mongols were not likely to be very valuable. By the end of the century the Mongols most accessible to the west had in effect come to terms with Islam. By accepting that religion they were able to preserve their dominance in central Asia but the unity of their empire did not survive the death of the Great Khan Möngke in 1259. The Mongols in China (the Yüan dynasty) and in Persia (the Il Khan dynasty) had at least the native traditions of government to assist them. In the khanates of Chagatay and the Golden Horde the Mongols retained their style of nomadic life, though they were able to keep neighboring peoples like the Russians in a state of subjection by their own capacity to inspire fear. Since they did not however take the opportunity to develop a more stable kind of society for themselves, it could only be a matter of time before the tables were turned. For while they persisted in their traditions some of their neighbors were obliged to develop in order to protect their own values. In the last third of the 14th century the leader of Il Khan, Timur, raided and conquered all over western Asia – including the empire put together by the Ottoman Turks – in the destructive manner of his predecessors a century and a half earlier. But unlike them his empire was not able to survive even one generation after his death in 1405. The Ottomans, for example, were quick to recover their position and were bold enough to open an attack on Constantinople itself in 1422. But the negative qualities of the Mongols cannot be allowed to obscure their historical importance. Everywhere they blazed like a forest fire; but renewal of growth, when it came, brought new vigor.

Christendom and Islam: losses and gains

The cautious and respectful attitude of the Russian princes towards the Golden Horde down to the 15th century fittingly indicates the realities of Islamic power as experienced by Christian Europe. The Latin crusaders had challenged Islam in its heartland and little by little it had reassembled and redistributed its forces to eliminate this alien element in its midst. Christians beyond their influence had remained surprisingly optimistic

about their chances of making a counterattack in their turn. The faith of St Louis, defeated in Egypt yet lingering for four more years in Syria to put heart into resistance there, not only represents Latin fervor at its best but itself obviously contributed to strengthen the faith of others. Only at the end of the 13th century were their hopes obviously dashed when the Mamluks of Egypt cleared out the last Christian strongholds in the Holy Land (1291) and, about the same time, the Mongols of western Asia accepted the embrace of Islam. Islam had recovered its hold on Asia and North Africa. The advance of the Ottomans into the Balkans in the second half of the 14th century was, from the Islamic point of view, only a resumption of a long-interrupted duty to spread the faith; the old religion was resurgent with new confidence. It is the period of some

Right The great complex of buildings erected in 1284–85 by Sultan Qalawun, hospital, madrasa and mausoleum, constituted an architectural achievement without parallel in the already built-up city of Cairo. The unity of the scheme combined with the architect's varied treatment of the facade, with its window tracery and battlements, to create Muslim architecture that was attractive and interesting from the outside. The influence of Christian building in the east seems to be detectable.

Far right Marco Polo leaving Venice for China, from *Li Livres du graunt Caam* by Marco Polo, c. 1400.

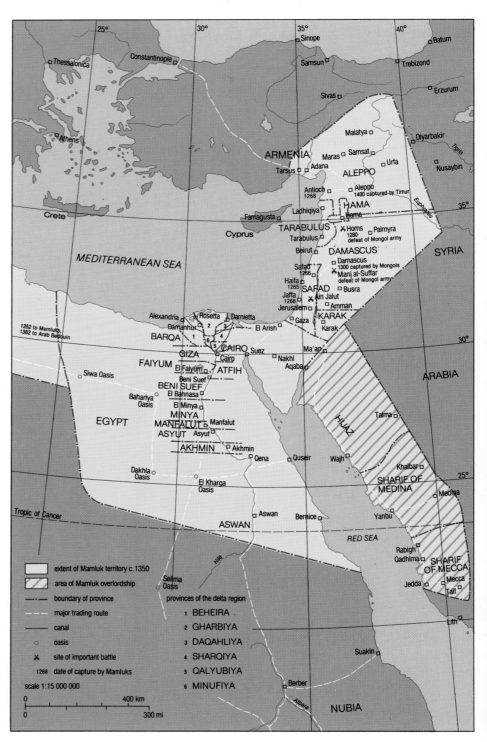

Egypt under the Mamluks
Mamluk Egypt was the greatest
Muslim power known to late
medieval Christians, who left
accounts of what they saw,
admired and feared there. Cairo
was their greatest bazaar and
must have impressed all the
merchants and pilgrims who
went there, as one of the great
cities of the world. After the
disintegration of Islamic unity
Egypt had become an important
political power again, but its
religious unorthodoxy had
denied it the position of
leadership in the Islamic world
which its wealth, population and
strategic position justified. After
its conquest by the orthodox
Saladin in 1171 it rapidly took
the lead in Islamic affairs. Its
military elite, the Turkish slave
army of Mamluks, provided a
regime that lasted for more than
two and a half centuries. By
name it might seem disreputable,
but in fact it eliminated the
Christian outposts in Palestine,
held the Mongols to a frontier in
Syria and extended its hegemony
over the Holy Places of Arabia. It
maintained an effective
provincial organization in the
Nile delta and up the Nile,
conquering south in Nubia as far
as Ethiopia. Christian and
Muslim merchants benefited
from its presence on the coast of
the Red Sea, which kept open
Muslim access to the Horn of
Africa and India. Its monuments
and artifacts prove that the
Mamluk state surpassed all its
medieval predecessors in making
Egypt rich, independent and
respected.

famous Muslim scholars, like the historian and
philosopher ibn-Khaldun (1332–1406). It is also the
period when the capital of Christendom,
Constantinople, the old enemy of Islam, was finally
taken by the Ottomans. The traveler ibn-Battuta,
who visited the whole world, as he saw it, from one
end of Islam to the other, was not surprisingly
indifferent to the unimportant peoples of western
Europe who lived on the fringe of his civilization:
he could not have imagined that they too in their
turn would have their day.

The greatest of the Islamic states facing Christendom in the late 13th century was certainly Egypt.
Saladin had restored the country to Sunni orthodoxy in 1171 and it became the real base of the
movement to eliminate the crusading states in the
13th century. Louis IX's campaign against Egypt
was the occasion not only of his own defeat but of
the installation of the Mamluk dynasty which gave
power to the Turkish "slave" army. From this
period Egypt was able to pull its weight again in the
Islamic world. It was rich in corn, had a large
population and played a vital role in trade with its
contacts in the Indian Ocean and the interior of
Africa, whence it obtained silver and slaves. Sultan
Baybars (1260–77) extended his dominion not only
in Syria but in Numidia and over the Berbers. He
promoted the economic well-being of his country
and played the part of a pious Muslim by building
mosques and schools and encouraging orthodoxy.
His successor Qalawun (1279–90) continued in the
same style and is famous for building the oldest
surviving Muslim hospital in Cairo. Sultan al-Nasir
(1298–1340) was equally vigorous, though the
troubles later in his reign presaged the decline of the
system. A second Mamluk dynasty (1382–1517) has
a less distinguished history but held out till it was
finally ousted in the Ottoman conquest, by which
time the Portuguese had already arrived in the Red
Sea. The power of Egypt in the 14th and 15th

centuries was not underestimated by Christians,
and many travelers there were impressed enough to
carry back favorable reports. Islam could not fail to
command respect in Europe.

The consolidation of these great Islamic states,
which put an end to the petty principalities of the
11th and 12th centuries, did not however serve to
reinstate Islamic frontiers in the west. One of the
decisive differences between this high point of
Islamic civilization and the earlier ones was the fact
that the western Mediterranean was not recovered.
The Norman conquest of Sicily for Christendom was
not even challenged. On the contrary, from Sicily
itself irritating reminders of its hostility were shown
by intermittent raids against neighboring Tunis.
The Balearic Islands were also taken from the
Muslims in the mid-13th century, while both
Aragonese and Castilian kings pushed south in the
Spanish mainland. By 1300 only the truncated
kingdom of Granada remained to the Muslims of
Spain, left for nearly two centuries as a vassal state
of Castile, but as resplendent as its contemporary
Muslim courts for its culture. The Castile of Pedro
the Cruel (Pedro I, king 1350–69) was much in the
debt of its Muslim vassals for the refinements of
daily life, for architecture, domestic decoration,
craftsmanship in wood and textiles. But it showed
neither the political nor the religious will to destroy
Muslims or Islam. The cultural eminence of Islam
earned it the reluctant respect of Christians. The
Christian kingdoms of the north – small, poor and
thinly populated – were only drawn deeply into the
affairs of the Muslim kingdoms further south by the
collapse of the Cordoban caliphate (1038), the
rivalries of the successor kingdoms (the *taifas*) and
the resurgent Muslim forces from North Africa (first
the Almoravides, then the Almohades). The initial
burst of activity that culminated in the Christians'
capture of Toledo in 1085 was followed up by a
great religious crusade, as might have been

expected, in the 12th century. This great contest between representatives of Christianity and Islam did not result in a clear-cut victory for either side and not until the early 13th century did Christian forces recover the initiative. It was to meet the Almohades' challenge that the Christian forces had regrouped to win the battle of Las Navas de Tolosa in 1212. In one generation the main work of reconquest was accomplished with the capture first of Cordoba (1235) and then of Seville (1248) by the Castilian forces under Ferdinand III (canonized in 1671). The king of Castile found himself therefore master of an extensive domain, and one that was

heavily depopulated after the Muslims had fled. The new king of Castile, Alfonso X the Wise, tried to tempt people from the north to settle in Andalusia. Great tracts of land were entrusted to the churches, the military orders and the nobility in order to encourage as many Castilians as possible to make the most of these new-won lands. The assimilation of these territories which had been under Muslim control for five centuries absorbed the energies of the government. Proposals to complete the reconquest by capturing the kingdom of Granada never came to much until 1492. The Spanish kingdoms for two centuries ceased to think mainly

Spain in 1300
The most dramatic changes recordable on maps of medieval Spain occurred either in the second half of the 11th or in the first half of the 13th century. As a result of these Muslim power in Spain was reduced to the kingdom of Granada. Even this acknowledged Castilian overlordship, though it was not finally eliminated for more than two centuries. During this period the peninsula was divided into five kingdoms, Portugal, Castile, Navarre, Aragon and Granada, each of which cultivated its own interests and alliances.

Right This copy of Frederick II's treatise on birds and falconry, made for his son Manfred, king of Sicily (1258–66), is the best evidence available about Frederick's own text, which must have included pictures, presumably reproduced here faithfully. Illustrations for only the first two of the six books were completed.

Christian reconquest

	to 1080
	to 1130
	to 1210
	to 1250
	area of Muslim domination
●	archdiocese
□	diocese
+	important monastery
—	boundary of states c.1300
- - -	ecclesiastical boundary
	cañada route (Sheepwalk)
•	royal toll point
Soria	Mesta capital
○	Christian capital
✕	site and date of important battle

scale 1:4 500 000

0   120km

0   100 mi

of hostilities against the Muslims and indeed tolerated the presence of Muslims and Jews to a surprising extent, until the end of the 14th century when a new intolerance manifested itself in a great pogrom.

Sicily and European power

While Castile had overrun southern Spain, the crusading zeal of King James I of Aragon was channeled down the east coast and across the sea to the Balearic Islands. As a result, by the end of his reign the states of the crown of Aragon had rather taken the form of a maritime empire with Barcelona at its heart — more like the state of 13th-century Venice than any other kingdom of the day. Aragon itself was the least important part of the king's possessions. He and his successors turned their faces to the sea, as firmly as the kings of Castile likewise turned their backs on the Asturian origins of their dynasty. The Spanish kings of the 13th century, having overcome their pressing problems at home, were also ready to take prominent roles in the affairs of Christendom. In the past the king of Aragon had had dealings with the empire through his estates in Provence. The disintegration of Staufen power, particularly after the death of Frederick II, inevitably concerned later kings as well. More surprising perhaps is the eagerness of Alfonso X of Castile himself to get drawn into imperial affairs. As a grandson of the great emperor he accepted election to the German throne in 1257 and only relinquished the title in 1274. Castile was too remote to sustain a connection that even Carlos I (the emperor Charles V) three centuries later found a burden. But the king of Aragon's involvement in Sicily was a more serious commitment. Peter II married a granddaughter of Frederick II and accepted in 1282 an invitation from the Sicilians to take over the kingdom and help them drive out the French king Charles of Anjou. From that date Sicily was ruled by the Spanish royal house until 1860.

In the 12th century Sicily had been the base of the Norman kingdom; in the first half of the 13th century it became the foundation of Frederick II's power in the empire. From 1282 it became either a province of the crown of Aragon or a semiautonomous kingdom that made little stir in the world. The repeated failures of its rulers since the 11th century to extend their sway into North Africa around Tunis meant that Sicily was at the end of the line and not a main junction. The rulers of Naples failed to recover the island and no Aragonese king before Alfonso V (1416–58) conquered Naples from Sicily. Sicily was therefore, for more than two centuries after 1282, relegated to a subordinate position. Sicily had naturally prospered when its rulers were able to draw resources from the central Mediterranean into Palermo. Once North Africa became of interest to Christians for trading purposes only, Sicily reverted to its role as a mere appendage to Italy or the crown of Aragon. Even under Frederick II Sicily had been left very much to itself, for, though Frederick had spent 15 years there from the age of three, he only visited it on five occasions thereafter and only once for as long as two years, and never set foot in the island after 1233. When free to attend to the kingdom rather than the empire, Frederick appears to have actually preferred the mainland.

Historians have looked back on the history of the empire in the 13th century without high expectations for its prospects. Contemporaries do not seem to have shared their skepticism. The papacy obviously remained extremely wary of its power well into the 14th century. Kings of Castile and France, the king of England's brother, were candidates for the imperial title. Germany was a land rapidly expanding its demographic and cultural frontiers in that period. The greatest state of Christendom might seem to historians to be in a state of advanced decay and ready for dismemberment. To the poet Dante the emperor Henry VII, when he arrived in Italy (1310), still represented the force of the one universal state — the monarchy of Christendom.

The western empire

Historians who salute St Louis as the founder of the later French monarchy have been nonplussed by his brilliant contemporary and ally Frederick II. Frederick appears to stand on his own and not in any sequence. He inherited no policies and bequeathed none to his successors. At first the faithful papal vassal, he soon became an execrated enemy. Incredible stories were repeated about him, mainly by pro-papal clergy. But invective did not inspire any effusive biographies. In later times the emperor's urbane dealings with his Muslim fellow rulers, his patronage of science and culture, his own ornithological observations as reported in his treatise on hunting birds, have commended him and won him the reputation of being born before his time. All books about him betray bewilderment. He still fascinates and eludes our understanding.

The position from which he began was the wished-for consequence of the marriage between the emperor Henry VI and the heiress of Sicily, Constance, in 1186. When his father died prematurely, before the union of the two states had proceeded very far, the German princes were not ready to accept Frederick, then aged two, as their ruler. His mother then renounced Germany and the

empire, making Frederick her heir for Sicily and entrusting his upbringing to the pope. When Frederick was still in his teens, however, he was drawn into imperial affairs by virtue of his ancestry and by papal pressure upon him. His son Henry was crowned king of Sicily in 1212 before Frederick himself was recognized as king in Germany, but Frederick had no intention of allowing his own joint inheritances to be divided and Pope Honorius III gave in to his insistent pressure allowing Henry to be elected king in Germany and Frederick to retain Sicily. Frederick is often thought to have neglected the interests of Germany. Though he spent eight busy years there as a young man, he only returned for two shorter visits in the years 1235–37.

Constitutionally he is famous for two important confirmations of princely privilege: the first to the ecclesiastical princes in 1220 as their price for electing his son Henry of Sicily as king of the Romans, and the second to the secular princes in 1231/2. The use of these privileges by later princes when there was no effective emperor proves nothing about their political significance in Frederick's own day. More to the point is that Frederick II retained his hold on Germany and drew military support from there for campaigns in Lombardy in 1235, and at the end of his life papal plans to set up an anti-king were not very well supported there. The power of the Staufen in Germany outlived Frederick II. His success in securing recognition of his sons Henry and then Conrad as his successors would certainly have led in due course to a hereditary rule in the empire as well as France; what destroyed the Staufen was not

errors in Germany but the implacable hostility of a series of popes, beginning with Gregory IX.

Frederick may not have been as devout as Louis IX or Henry III but he was certainly no avowed skeptic, and not hostile to the papacy as such. It was an institution he knew he had to live with. But he had difficulties with the popes both about his control of the bishops of Sicily and over the pope's claims to the papal state. In his youth he had been forced by Innocent III to confirm concessions previously made by the Welf emperor Otto IV, but in time, with his maturity, the political situation of Germany, of the pope in Italy and the crusading program all prevented Innocent's successors from feeling they could treat the emperor as though he

Top left Sculptures from the western choir of Naumburg cathedral, 1250–70. Formerly an important commercial center on crossroads in central Germany, Naumburg was architecturally renewed in the late 13th century, when the cathedral was rebuilt in the mature Gothic style. There are two choirs; in the west, 12 statues of founder and benefactors were raised to complete the architectural scheme, but the individuality of expression achieved in the faces and figures proves that the sculptors were more than mere servants of the architect, and were doing more than make anonymous tribute to the dead.

were no more than the papal vassal for Sicily. After making peace and arranging for the smooth government of Germany, Frederick II felt free to devote himself to the affairs of the Sicilian kingdom and showed no eagerness for the crusade. It was this that first provoked the ire of Gregory IX, and it was as an excommunicate that Frederick II was finally driven to the Holy Land (1228–29). His negotiation of a settlement for Jerusalem added insult to injury. The pope was cornered into absolving him on his return, but after 1236 his hostility came out into the open again.

The virulence of abuse hurled by pro-papal publicists against Frederick suggests that they exaggerated to hide their own doubts. Louis IX

never seems to have been persuaded that Frederick was the enemy of Christendom. Despite some reverses Frederick was far from defeated by the papacy at the time of his death in 1250, and later popes continued to be alarmed by his Staufen successors. Their position still seemed formidable. If in the end the determination shown by several pontiffs thwarted the ambitions of the imperial family and effectively destroyed them, the fundamental reason was that the papal direction of Christendom by the mid-13th century allowed no role for the Roman emperor. The papacy preferred to have a number of kings to turn to when it needed the help of the secular arm.

It is quite possible that in his own way Frederick

117

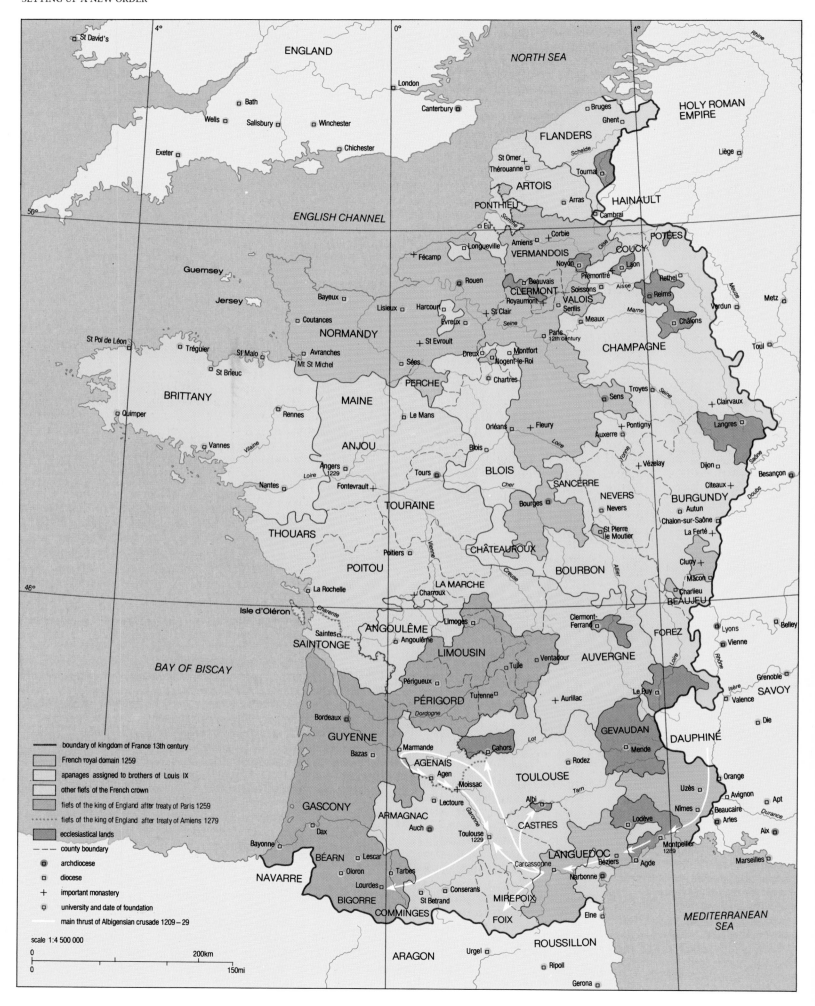

St David's

ENGLAND

London

Bath
Wells   Salisbury   Winchester
Canterbury
Exeter   Chichester

NORTH SEA

HOLY ROMAN
EMPIRE

Bruges
Ghent
Liège

FLANDERS

St Omer
Thérouanne
Tournai

ARTOIS

Cambrai

Arras   HAINAULT

PONTHIEU

ENGLISH CHANNEL

Eu   Somme
Longueville   Amiens   Corbie   POTÉES

Fécamp   VERMANDOIS   COUCY

Guernsey   Noyon   Laon
Prémontré   Rethel
Rouen   Beauvais   Reims
Bayeux   CLERMONT   Soissons   Châlons
Jersey   Royaumont   VALOIS   Aisne
Lisieux   Harcourt   Senlis
Coutances   Évreux   Meaux   Marne

St Pol de Léon   St Clair
Tréguier   St Evroult   Paris   Verdun   Metz
St Malo   Avranches   12th century   Toul
St Brieuc   Mt St Michel   NORMANDY   Dreux   Montfort   CHAMPAGNE
Sées   Nogent-le-Roi

Quimper   PERCHE   Chartres   Troyes   Clairvaux
Sens
MAINE   Langres
Rennes   Le Mans   Orléans   Fleury   Pontigny   Citeaux
Vannes   BRITTANY   Auxerre   Vézelay   Dijon   Besançon
Vilaine   ANJOU   Blois   Yonne
Angers   Tours   BLOIS   SANCERRE   NEVERS   BURGUNDY
Nantes   1229   Loire   Cher   Bourges   Nevers   Autun
Fontevrault   St Pierre   Chalon-sur-Saône
le Moutier   La Ferté
TOURAINE   Doubs
THOUARS   Cluny
Poitiers   CHÂTEAUROUX   Mâcon
Vienne   BOURBON   Charlieu
POITOU   Allier   BEAUJEU
La Marche
La Rochelle   Charroux   LA MARCHE   Lyons   Belley
Isle d'Oléron   Charente   Limoges   Clermont-   FOREZ
Saintes   ANGOULÊME   Ferrand   Vienne
SAINTONGE   Angoulême   LIMOUSIN   AUVERGNE   Grenoble
Tulle   Ventadour   SAVOY
BAY OF BISCAY   Périgueux   Isère   Valence
PÉRIGORD   Turenne   Le Puy
Aurillac   Die
Bordeaux   Dordogne   GEVAUDAN
Marmande   Lot   Mende   DAUPHINÉ
GUYENNE   Cahors   Rodez   Orange
Bazas   Uzès   Avignon
AGENAIS   Agen   TOULOUSE   Nîmes   Apt
Moissac   Tarn   Lodève   Beaucaire
GASCONY   Lectoure   Albi   LANGUEDOC   Durance
ARMAGNAC   Castres   Montpellier   Arles
Dax   Auch   Toulouse   CASTRES   1289   Aix
Bayonne   1229   Béziers
BÉARN   Lescar   Carcassonne   Agde   Marseilles
Oloron   Tarbes   Narbonne
NAVARRE   Lourdes   Conserans   MIREPOIX   Elne
BIGORRE   St Betrand   LANGUEDOC
COMMINGES   FOIX
Urgel   ROUSSILLON   MEDITERRANEAN
ARAGON   SEA
Ripoll
Gerona

Rhine
Schelde
Oise
Meuse
Seine
Saône
Loire
Rhône

Legend:

— boundary of kingdom of France 13th century

▓ French royal domain 1259

☐ apanages assigned to brothers of Louis IX

☐ other fiefs of the French crown

▓ fiefs of the king of England after treaty of Paris 1259

⋯ fiefs of the king of England after treaty of Amiens 1279

▓ ecclesiastical lands

--- county boundary

◉ archdiocese

☐ diocese

+ important monastery

☐ university and date of foundation

━ main thrust of Albigensian crusade 1209–29

scale 1:4 500 000

0 _____ 200km
0 _____ 150mi

II also preferred his role as king of Sicily, to which he gave special attention, particularly in issuing the administrative constitutions of Melfi in 1231. He even founded a university at Naples in 1224 for the specific purpose of training officials for his kingdom. But as emperor, as a Staufen, he could hardly be expected to become subservient to the pope as his feudal lord. Not even his Norman predecessors had treated the papacy with more than formal deference. Nor could Frederick II avoid the consequences of uniting the lands of the Norman kingdom to those of the kingdom of Italy in the north. Frederick was the first ruler of most of Italy since Theodoric. This in itself disquieted not only the pope but the Italian towns, who feared that the new emperor would reopen the question of imperial rights there, which had been grudgingly conceded to them by his grandfather, Barbarossa, in 1183.

Frederick II's own position was probably a very conservative one: to preserve his family rights. He was not interested in institutional innovations, like the French king's court of appeal for example. He did not have Louis's problem of having to win the loyalty of new subjects. But the eclipse of his dynasty deprived him of posthumous panegyrics. To this day he retains the fascination of the enigma.

New constitutional life in France

The most famous Christian champion against Islam in the 13th century was Frederick's ally Louis IX of France (king 1226–70), who served Christ in the Levant for six years of his reign (1248–54) and, back in France, spent much of his energy planning a further expedition. When launched (in 1270) it was diverted to Tunis, against the Muslim enemies of his brother Charles, king of Sicily, not as a subsidiary campaign but as part of the challenge to the Muslims of North Africa. The first of Louis's campaigns had been fought naturally against Egypt. The king himself was captured, but released for a ransom, and he spent four more years in the Holy Land infusing the beleaguered Christians there with his own faith and spending his resources on improving their defenses. By the end of the century it could be argued that the king of France and his vassals had more pressing Christian duties to their subjects at home than to the Christians of the east or for recovery of Christ's own homeland, but in Louis's own lifetime it is probable that the king's concern for the crusade was not criticized. It could certainly not be argued that he neglected his obligations in the kingdom itself and it would be mistaken to suppose that his physical presence was constantly required for its affairs. On his long absence (1248–54) general supervision was provided by his mother, Blanche of Castile, who had managed to govern the kingdom with equal ability in his own minority. St Louis, canonized in 1295, became the model for all his successors in the dynasty, and the later kingship of France, if not inspired by his spirit, grew naturally out of the institutional life he had launched.

The problems of Louis's government in France originated in the unexpected results of his grandfather's reign. Philip II (1180–1223) had transformed the nature of Capetian rule. After two centuries of torpor the kingship suddenly became a powerful leading force in France. To the initial successes in recovering the land of Vermandois (which earned him the soubriquet "Augustus" from the chronicler Rigord), Philip added the much more substantial conquests from King John of England. These rich and well-governed provinces, from Anjou to the English Channel, gave the king of France enormous advantages in men with experience in government on whose expertise he could draw for new projects. Philip's reign had also seen the successful expansion of northern French barons into southern lands that had not been ruled directly by Franks since the 9th century, and whose culture, law, speech and even religious attitudes differed greatly from those of their conquerors. The latter had provided the justification for the crusade against the Albigensian heretics. Though King Philip had nothing to do with this, the effective elimination of the king of Aragon from most of the region by the defeat of Miret in 1212 opened the way for a French royal presence in the south, and after Louis VIII had rather ungallantly conquered Poitou from the young Henry III of England, the direct involvement of the French king there became inevitable. Louis IX was the first king of France to accept the new responsibilities thrust upon him by the changes of the early 13th century. He had no ambitions to add to his kingdom, only to reconcile his new subjects to his rule and to find ways of making their relations with one another more harmonious and just. His crusading ideals probably helped to bring many men to accept his leadership more willingly, though it would be false to see crusading used by him as the means to some political end. Louis had very firm ideas about the duties of kingship and about his rights. He had no hesitation in defending his position in the French church, for example, against papal encroachments. But Louis was not pugnacious. He saw his royal role as one of reconciliation and he chose to implement it by inquiry into the abuses of administration and by offering to adjudicate disputes in reorganized courts of law. Before leaving on his first crusade he ordered an inquiry into the royal administration throughout the kingdom, in order to clear up outstanding grievances. But it was on his return in 1254 that he embarked upon a series of measures designed to rectify administrative abuses that had occurred in his absence and to initiate more general reforms in the law courts. Louis did not enjoy general powers to change the laws of the kingdom, but he did succeed in suppressing trial by battle in his own domain lands. His most important legal reform was to use in his own royal courts the procedure of the *enquête* or inquest as used in the ecclesiastical courts. The king's *parlement* at Paris developed from his time into a powerful tribunal of first resort for his own lands and for appeals from his vassals. Among these Louis included his many brothers, for whom their father had arranged the assignment of extensive lands in apanage, and Henry III of England, who became his vassal for the duchy of Aquitaine by the treaty of Paris in 1259. This brought to an end the hostility between the two kingdoms that had begun when Philip II had confiscated John's French lands. For a period it successfully achieved Louis's own expectations but in due course the terms of the treaty itself gave rise to further problems, when both kings began to think less in terms of mutual commitments than of their positions as sovereign rulers.

THE GROWTH OF TOWNS

The significance of towns

Just as for classical scholars the revival of Latin studies signifies the end of the Middle Ages and the renaissance of learning, so for economic and social historians the reappearance of town life seems to indicate the collapse of the feudal order. Middle-class observers who identify progress with towns do not need the Marxist dialectic to persuade them of the "obvious" facts that the rise of towns, the growth of town populations and the promotion of trade and industry are the means to prosperity and progress. Born themselves into moneyed industrial and urban societies, they take for granted their superiority over stagnant rusticity. These same prejudices came just as naturally to medieval clerks, who derided the countrymen on whose labors all

prosperity then necessarily depended. Until the countryside yielded any marketable surpluses, the medieval economy, like that of all peasant societies, aimed no higher than local self-sufficiency for each community. Rare luxuries were secured at fairs, or dispensed with. The greatest expense of Roman imperial government, the army, ceased to burden the economy after the collapse of the empire, which left defense to each locality and to the freemen who bore arms. In due course the countryside, relieved of the burdens of government, began to prosper. As the population grew, fresh lands were brought into cultivation. Communities, as they clustered together, discovered the advantages of specialization. Self-sufficiency took second place to exchange. Local authorities, such as they were, had to extend

Ambrogio Lorenzetti's *The Art of Good Government* in Siena town hall, 1338–40. The frescoes in this council chamber presented allegories of good and bad government with their consequences for the instruction of the Sienese authorities. Those of good government are better preserved than the others. Lorenzetti achieved a pleasing illustration of the happiness and prosperity brought by good government to both city and countryside by depicting a cavalcade leaving the cheerful city to cross the landscape.

protection over wider areas. From them had to be obtained the formal authority for setting up fortified trading posts, where exchanges could be safely concluded and to which merchants could travel without impediment. Towns came to play their part in the economy of the west. As time passed these urban conglomerations adapted to the prevailing conditions of their regions. A few might be so fortunately placed as to draw supplies from great distances by water; most of them could not dispense with a livelihood based on local supplies of food, labor and raw materials. Outside Italy few towns ever succeeded in subjecting their immediate localities to urban political control. Whereas the ancient colonies of the Mediterranean had begun as small towns and from their security had proceeded to cultivate the lands around, in the Middle Ages the cultivation of the land came first: in this sense medieval towns were parasitic. The town was not the acorn from which a new civilization would spring: it was the demonstration that societies were already flourishing well enough to allow specialized traders to live in artificial conditions.

Even before the end of the western empire the old social and economic function of the city as the nucleus of new settlements had possibly lost its savor. Once the empire itself could guarantee civil peace, smaller units no longer needed to fend for themselves, and were discouraged from doing so. The coastal districts first reached by immigrants had by then been colonized. Penetrating ever deeper into the countryside involved the setting up of individual estates to clear waste land. Citizens of the empire, except perhaps those in the most flourishing of the great cities, also began to appreciate the social amenities of their own estates more than those of the smaller cities. If the cities of the empire began to "decline," it was because late Roman society had less use for them. The barbarian invaders of the west, who might initially have been dazzled by the novelties of Roman cities, had still less reason than the Romans to keep them flourishing and almost no idea about how to do so. Roman cities that survived into the Middle Ages had the Christian bishops to thank. They valued the cities as the administrative centers of their jurisdictions, for which the imperial term "diocese" (an administered region) was appropriated. Like the empire, the church divided

its responsibilities geographically. Bishops' sees were spread out fairly evenly across Christendom, with a notably higher density in Italy, though uneven within the peninsula. Few of these sees changed location in the later period. In Britain, where city life was not sustained into the English period, and in Germany and further east, sees had perforce to be established in new sites anyway. The resulting distribution of episcopal cities was less even than under the empire, for the new sees served existing Christian communities rather than being, in the ancient manner, nuclei of new settlements as such. These new towns might well be laid out systematically at first, but medieval towns, if successful, soon spilled over and developed their own idiosyncrasies. A basic plan was overlaid with new districts and rebuilding. No imperial government controlled its development or prescribed an ideal.

The episcopal towns in medieval Europe corresponded most closely to the ancient cities, with their administrative and cultural functions. In the old imperial lands they maintained, at a modest level, some continuity from imperial times, and in due course, once the episcopate had embarked on a program of Christian renewal, its towns became still more active. Cathedrals were rebuilt with episcopal palaces, buildings for canons or monks, shrines and churches for saints and relics, accommodation for pilgrims, houses, booths and workshops for the tradesmen needed in such towns. But the civil, as distinct from the religious, management of medieval Europe continued to operate independently of towns, for its manner was fundamentally different from that of the Roman empire.

Of the northern peoples the English and the French were the first to develop royal seats of government. By the 13th century their clerical staffs, their judges and accountants settled down together in administrative capitals like Westminster or Paris. However, as long as kings themselves continued to move around their dominions to attend to their estates, meet their people and urge forward important business, even such great assemblies as their "parliaments" could as frequently be summoned outside the capital cities. Though some parts of government business could be dealt with in fixed offices, the more exacting task of managing powerful, potentially independent lords had to be dealt with by kings moving about in person. On its travels a royal party was as often lodged in the great fortresses as in the towns. In Italy a few city governments obtained authority over surrounding country districts from the 13th century onwards and a handful of these became powerful enough to subject princes and country landowners to their municipal councils. But most medieval city-states had very limited territories and responsibilities. Medieval Europe was more often governed by princes with great landed estates who thought of government less in terms of administering a territory than as a matter of relationships between individuals at various "social" levels, from that of personal dependence on the lord's estate, through leases and vassaldom, to such matters as the duty owed to king or emperor.

Princes who had no particular concern with towns as administrative centers might have appreciated their possibilities for helping with the development of their estates. As the effective powers in the region, their charters and benevolence were indispensable if towns were to thrive. The north German plain was a region opened up in the medieval period. In the 10th century fortified outposts had to be constructed to defend the frontier against northern and eastern invaders. This helped to stabilize the frontier itself. These became towns and centers of new bishoprics; special privileges encouraged settlement and attracted commercial business by the setting up of special courts to protect merchants; towns obtained exemptions from economically restrictive dues such as toll payments. Without the benevolence of the great military and political powers, such towns would have been swept away by the incursions of still-pagan peoples beyond the frontier.

The reappearance of sizable urban settlements, at least by the 12th century, may seem like the return of "civilization" after centuries of barbarism, but too much can be made of superficial resemblances between medieval and ancient towns and of the odd cases where "continuity" seems plausible. By Roman standards the medieval town was no more civilized than the countryside. The most powerful men of the age did not consider themselves as "citizens," they did not resort to towns for the necessities and amenities of city life, the law courts, the theaters or the baths. The towns were not essential to contemporary government. They came into prominence mainly as units of the new kind of medieval economy, as dense settlements of limited size (as small as possible to make defense easier) dedicated to manufacture and exchange. They represented therefore a new kind of division of labor in society. They were on the one hand a necessary complement to the improvements of the agricultural sector, which produced surpluses enough for marketing and feeding nonagricultural populations and expected to find certain tools or products, like cloth or wine, that it was not able to provide at all, or so well, for itself. On the other they were nodal points on a commercial network that grew up in a medieval world no longer homogenous as the Roman world had been. Europe now was composed of different regions with different specialties. To this world the Carolingian empire, despite its plunderers, had first brought economic conditions in which regional specialization was possible. Towns strung out along the great routes, including the main rivers that traversed Europe, enabled all products to move short distances, and some prized articles of commerce to travel vast distances, to and from Muslim Spain, Constantinople or the far north. Towns remained integral parts of this world. They did not constitute civilized islands in barbary. A town might contain very wealthy, powerful men, but until they moved out of the town their influence was circumscribed by the limits of its territorial extension. However wealthy or important, townsmen, unlike princes, were businessmen, active about their own affairs, not born to public responsibilities. The countryside looked to the towns not for direction but for economic purposes, not least as places for sending boys to acquire special skills to serve the whole economy, such as training in craft industries. In this respect modern towns obviously owe more to the medieval than to the ancient legacy.

As integral parts of the medieval world, towns also experienced the effects of local political conditions. In England, for example, monarchs from Alfred onwards played an influential role in building burhs or defense points, and then by legislating for them as sites for markets. Kings satisfied the commercial demand for sound money by striking reliable coins according to a national standard in mint towns all over the country. They granted charters that secured nationwide recognition of a town's freedoms. Much later, under Edward I (king of England 1272–1307), similar fortified towns were established in Wales to consolidate his conquest. In royal England there was very little scope for towns to act independently. Only London succeeded in obtaining the privileges of a commune. In the kingdom of Aragon the position was comparable to that in England, though Barcelona for a time at least claimed privileges greater than those of London and against royal opposition. Towns could not singly or in league persist in defiance of royal authority. In each kingdom the histories of individual towns were more important than any common characteristics.

Towns and the empire

The position in the (German) empire deserves special notice, for emperors working within a "federal" kind of government designated certain imperial free cities, subject directly to the emperor, to save them from the heavy hand of local princes. When the emperors lost effective authority such cities strove to defend their autonomy. In Italy, especially, the chronic weakness of the emperors after 1122 left the ancient cities under the nominal rule of the bishops. This made it easier for townsmen to force concessions from them. Favorable conditions for urban independence did not blind all towns to the advantages of retaining the protection of great lords, or enable all the ambitious ones to emancipate themselves.

Among the most flourishing cities of 11th-century Italy must be counted the maritime republics of the south, such as Amalfi, which enjoyed the nominal overlordship of Constantinople. From the 1130s all the independent cities of the south had to come to terms with the new Norman monarchy. At that stage the cities further north had already experienced pangs of growth, due to the new position of the peninsula after the crusades which brought northern peoples regularly to the Mediterranean. Some fierce local opposition to the authority of the German kings as kings of Italy had not then become a general movement to establish practical autonomy for the towns. This came in the next generation in the struggles of the Lombard league with Frederick I, whose concessions were ratified in 1183. This did nothing to revive the older maritime republics of the south, where, as in England, the effectiveness of royal government stifled real urban independence. The different development of northern Italy was due to the inadequacies of royal government and the determination of some towns to make good its defects from their own municipal institutions.

Frederick I himself precipitated the struggle with the cities by trying to reverse the decline in imperial effectiveness in Italy. He did so by appeal to his rights by law, as contemporary teachers of Roman jurisprudence were proving them to be. The towns successfully resisted, confident of their superior claims based upon recent customs. The emperor, rather than the towns, here broke with tradition. Not all cities proved to be irrevocably hostile to him. Fear of aggressive Milan drove its rivals into the imperial camp. There was no class struggle between princes and merchants. Had the German position in Italy been more secure Frederick might well have obtained even more support and provided the sort of overall protection offered by his fellow kings in England and Sicily. Although the main interest of the dispute lies in the constitutional nature of the contrast between the theory of the law and the power of custom, the victory of the towns indicates that they could already muster adequate military, diplomatic and political support, quite apart from economic resources. The towns wanted the right to appoint their own magistrates. They had no political plan for the government of northern Italy and no hope of perpetuating their wartime alliances. When the emperor Frederick II in the next century appeared to promise a more coherent government for northern Italy the contest was resumed. This time, though the emperor was unsuccessful in the long term, many towns in the aftermath succumbed to the rule of military captains, who assumed the powers of local despots. Individual cities thus preserved their independence but lost their republican freedoms. These despots were also eager to enlarge their dominions and hand on their offices to their families. One by one the smaller independent cities were absorbed into city-states. Only the greatest cities were able to retain any measure of public control over such men. In a matter of generations therefore most of the urban republics of northern Italy had become the patrimonies of many "princely" families, able and willing to marry into the noble families of northern Europe, and no less aristocratic. These towns ceased to be nurseries of a distinctive style of urban life. Their renaissance culture was easily absorbed by northern Europeans from quite different cultural traditions in the 16th century.

New towns in the region of the Rhine

The distribution of medieval towns across Europe, not being a planned response to the needs of central government, necessarily reflects the superimposition on the ecclesiastical framework of many new, and mainly economic, pressures. The concentration of towns in the region of the old Middle Kingdom basically indicates that the Carolingians could guarantee security for all traffic from the Mediterranean. It came by the shortest route, direct from northern Italy, across the Alps and down the Seine and especially through the Rhineland, which was, after Charlemagne, not a frontier but a corridor opening to east and west the rich regions of Christian Germans and others. In the Roman empire, by contrast, the routes north had passed by sea to Provence and then up the Rhône. At the Italian end of these routes it was hardly necessary to found new towns, for it was already well supplied with them and they had survived the invasion periods remarkably well. The Ottonian emperors had used the bishops as royal officials there and the episcopal administrations had been permeated by citizens able to elbow their way into power. The eastern

CHARTR
1568

Above The siege of Chartres in 1568. Paintings of towns, as they might be viewed from a panoramic vantage point or by imagination from the air, began to appear in Europe from the end of the 15th century and had become a well-established art form, also much appreciated by politicians and soldiers, by 1568. These views, reproduced by engravings for the most part, give the best evidence available for the appearance of towns as they had been in the Middle Ages, allowing for the additional fortifications subsequently added to the old town walls.

emperors also retained the overlordship of several maritime cities, including Venice, the most famous of all medieval Italian cities. Its isolation in the lagoon, which guaranteed its early independence, also symbolized the exceptional character of commercial activity with the eastern Mediterranean in a predominantly rustic world. To the north, along the Rhine, the great cities were bishops' sees installed in Roman sites. In the Rhine delta, however, the old Roman organization had been submerged by the Frisian and Frankish settlements. Not until the Carolingian period was the region even converted to Christianity and this was not so much

through the routine efforts of established bishops as by missionaries, monastic, English, Irish and Aquitainian, obliged to start up the church from scratch. The 4th-century see of Tongres in these unsettled conditions migrated to Maastricht before reaching Liège in the early 8th century. North of the Rhine the Roman city of Utrecht had a little earlier than this been provided with a bishopric, but few other towns in the region occupied Roman sites. The raids of Northmen in the 9th century also affected development there; they caused less damage in the smaller centers which recovered more quickly and took the lead. In the 11th century the way towns

Ghent and Ypres, did not owe their importance to any Roman origin. Their early development occurred in the 9th and 10th centuries, when records are sparse. The name Bruges is of Norse origin. It had become a *portus*, a trading center, by 1000 and the seat of power of the count of Flanders.

As long as the Rhine marked the frontier of civilization this whole region's development was retarded. Only under the Carolingians had the settlement and conversion of northern Germany offered a chance for the Rhine delta to enjoy its geographical advantage as the terminus of the greatest waterway of western Europe. From Flanders the multiplication of town centers was extended into Brabant, Holland and Zutphen. From bases on the North Sea it crept along the shores to the Baltic. The organization of the Hanse league in the 13th century proved that the commercial towns of the north, though they valued their independence, perceived also the benefits of association. Of the many towns in this northern region Bruges became the central depot of trade and finance. From the early 14th century Venice and Genoa, the leading ports of the Levantine trade, sent regular fleets around via Gibraltar and Biscay to do business in Flanders. By that stage the rich men of the northern towns had themselves abandoned seagoing. They received foreign merchants in their own towns and pushed ahead with ambitious manufactures, particularly in cloth. In these places the peculiar features of medieval towns probably attained their fullest realization.

The Hanse league and the Baltic

Further north the Vikings from the 10th century had themselves established fortified trading posts and promoted active trading, but it is difficult to trace any continuity from this early phase of northern development into the 13th century. By that time trade in the north was in the hands of various German towns. There were few Scandinavian bases involved, except as depots. Wisby, which had once been central to the Novgorod trade, had declined. Trade disputes were transferred from there to the courts at Lübeck, which in the second half of the 13th century assumed the leadership of the league of towns called the Hanse. *Hanse* is Middle High German for fellowship, used as a term for associations or guilds, particularly for merchants in foreign ports. By 1300 the law of Lübeck was enforced in some 19 towns, otherwise autonomous, but clearly in league with one another. Lübeck itself had been founded in 1143 and had received an imperial privilege in 1226. It did not aspire to political dominance over other towns, but the adoption of its laws at ancient Hamburg in 1232 put a seal on its position of primacy. At this period the movement for German penetration into eastern Europe had gained momentum. The order of Teutonic knights was installed in Mazovia. The Lübeck code reached the towns of Livonia in 1254 and Riga in 1270. The merchants of the leading towns in the Baltic, as well as other towns, began to cooperate in enforcing common codes of commercial law, acting together against piracy and other enemies of commerce. One of the reasons for this political cooperation was the absence in this region of any effective princely ruler in whose name laws could otherwise be issued.

Overleaf Carpaccio's *Miracle of the Relic of the True Cross* in the Accademia, Venice, 1494–95. This painting, from the school of S. Giovanni Evangelista, is most notable for the blending of several scenes to create an impression of Venice as it was in the late 15th century. Already elegant and ceremonious, Venice was still a center of business, with a Rialto bridge of no more than practical utility. It was at this date that Venice commanded more fear than affection in the rest of Italy.

grew in the Rhine delta reflected the impact of several different factors. West of Liège the Low Countries formed part of the ecclesiastical province of Reims. The Roman city of Tournai was devastated by the barbarians in 406 and from the 6th century the bishopric there was tied to Noyon, 120 kilometers to the south. These two sees were not separated until 1146. Similarly the see at Arras was transferred to Cambrai and not revived until 1093. The see of Boulogne was established at Thérouanne. The Roman past contributed little therefore even to the ecclesiastical organization of the Low Countries. The most famous towns of the region, like Bruges,

After the death of Frederick II (1250) the emperor could not be invoked. Trade and commerce were on the increase, as the lands of eastern Europe were opened up for colonization or exploitation. Polish Christian princes were still fighting pagan Prussians and welcoming assistance from the west. Produce from the hinterland, floated down eastern rivers to the Baltic ports, could be at the mercy of different political authorities. The coasts of these northern seas were also under the jurisdiction of several small princes. Cities like Hamburg and Lübeck were able to hold their own and the merchants discovered that they had adequate resources to police their own coastal waters,. In this way the members of the Hanse league embarked on political activities in cooperation with one another, for which no parallel can be found elsewhere in Europe.

The main opponent of the league was the king of Denmark, for he represented the best chance of providing an alternative form of government for the region. Denmark had continued since the Viking period to have mainly maritime interests. Its authority was continually asserted in Scania (now part of southern Sweden) so it had potentially the power to close the Baltic or filter trade into the North Sea at will. For Baltic traders, like Lübeck, easy access to the ports of Flanders was indispensable for their successful activities. Despite the obvious advantages of a regular dynastic succession for continuity in policy, the kings of Denmark made little progress in curbing the confidence of the proud Hanse towns. Eric VI (king 1286–1319) dominated all the Wend towns, except Stralsund; Waldemar IV (king 1340–75) seized Scania and sacked Wisby. His aggression provoked the Hanse into making an alliance with the Swedes. The allies managed to impose on Waldemar the humiliating peace of Stralsund (1367) which gave the Hanse the monopoly of the Scania herring industry, liberties for the confederation of Cologne merchants and powers of political interference over Denmark itself. To deal with the Hanse the Danes had to win over the Swedes. Waldemar's daughter, Margaret, was the architect of a scheme to unite the Scandinavian crowns and thus confront the Hanse with a more formidable enemy.

In the 13th century the Scandinavian peoples did not form any naturally coherent group. In Sweden the great nobles who ruled the country were pulled in different directions according to regional interests. The strongest pull was the possibility of expansion into west Finland. The frontier with the Russians remained fluid until 1323. By that time the Swedes and the Norwegians were ruled jointly by Magnus Ericson (king 1319–55), for the Norwegians were anchored to Scandinavia after they ceded Hebrides and Man to the Scots in 1266. Of their formerly extensive maritime dominion the Norwegians retained only Greenland. Magnus's united monarchy worked well enough to point a way forward, but it was not until 1397 that Eric of Pomerania actually succeeded in bringing all three Scandinavian kingdoms under one scepter. Each kept its own laws and the unity proved precarious, particularly after the death of Queen Margaret in 1412. Nevertheless, the threat of political unification alarmed the Hanse towns sufficiently to provoke a reorganization of their own association, to strengthen themselves and coordinate their

political response. New regulations were agreed that established a clearer role for Lübeck (1418). A supreme assembly or *Hansetage*, which met at Lübeck when required, represented nearly 100 members of the league. This new organization enabled the towns to blockade Eric in Denmark in 1426. The Swedish mining areas were particularly hard hit and this stimulated a movement for Swedish independence. Though the blockade was successfully pursued against Denmark, the Hanse did not recover its old position. In the meantime the king of Poland recovered control of the Polish littoral from the German knights and their towns, while the duke of Burgundy in the Low Countries had fostered Dutch maritime enterprise to the point where the Dutch had been emboldened to challenge the Hanse in the Baltic, where of course they also found Danish allies. The greatest days of the Hanse were over.

Urban influence in the late Middle Ages

The political involvement and initiatives of the Hanse indicate that sooner or later economic and social units with legal autonomy would be obliged to pay the military cost of independence. In a predominantly rural society, on which towns were mostly dependent for their resources, they were heavily outnumbered and could only preserve independence by becoming small states with their own territories and rural populations, changing the characters of their urban governments to deal with their new "imperial" responsibilities. In Germany many imperial free cities managed to survive on small territories because many small lordships in the empire delayed the emergence of a few powerful states. In the Low Countries the aspirations of Bruges or Ghent to the status of city-republics were stifled by the jealousy of many smaller neighbors, by the highly urbanized nature of the region (which left them no potential hinterland) and by the determination of the counts of Flanders and dukes of Burgundy to win back political dominance over townsmen. Only in Italy did a few towns – Milan, Venice, Florence and some smaller ones – succeed in creating viable states from city nuclei. To the north, similarly, Berne built up an impressive state whereas the ambitions of Zurich to do the same were thwarted. The duchy of Milan absorbed many smaller towns which became "provincial" without necessarily losing much more than their civic pride. The new political organization did not mean the collapse of town life as such. But it had to change its character, adapting to the circumstances of the 15th century, as it had in the 10th and 12th centuries. The new order of things invariably represented the installation of governments with fixed seats, in capital cities, deriving from towns many of their most characteristic features, such as corporatism in government and literacy as well as cultural styles in ceremonial trappings and religious disputations. From this time on towns did set the pace in the transformation of European values. They had ceased to shut themselves off psychologically from the countryside. Their citizens acquired rural estates and began to turn them into orchards, gardens and parks.

These changes in medieval town life reflect the many different changes over the centuries experienced in various parts of the continent.

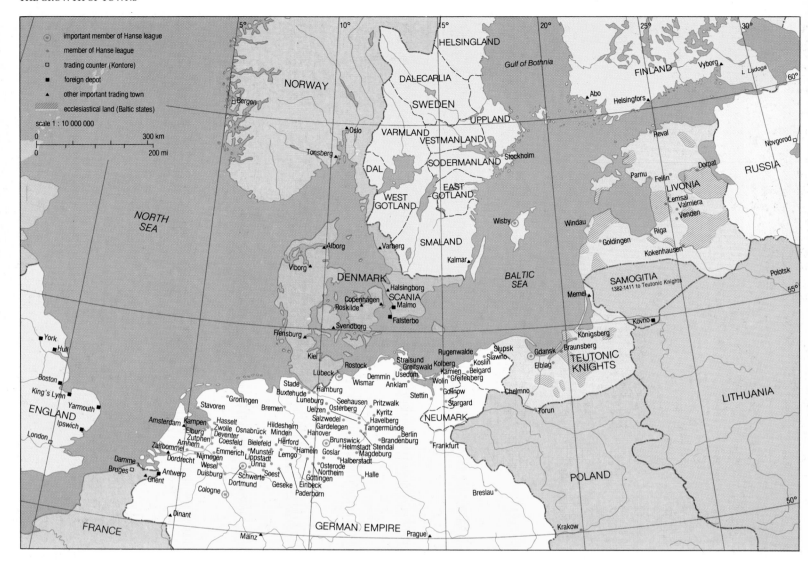

Towns had originally grown rapidly by drawing from a vigorous rural society its most adventurous spirits. By the end of the 13th century the process of expansion was slowing down, for reasons that are not easy to define. Europe had probably reached saturation point as far as having enough towns for its economic needs. Hopeful town foundations in excess of requirements inevitably failed to take root. When there was no longer an unsated demand for manufactures and raw materials to be supplied by merchants, towns began to compete with one another, with increasing desperation, to hold their own markets. To these difficulties must be added the consequences of waves of pestilence, which hit towns particularly hard, given that towns tended to be more favorable environments for breeding infections. Town populations were certainly reduced, but as certainly recovered as soon as rural numbers went up, for towns tried desperately to attract immigrants, especially men with certain skills. It is even possible that after the shake up a more stable economic order emerged, in which the towns as a whole improved their position relative to the countryside. There was obviously nothing comparable to the consequences of the barbarian migrations a thousand years before to blight the possibilities of urban recovery. In this respect, the exaggeration of some recent historians about the effects of plague on town life can be very

misleading. Town governments themselves regarded the problem of numbers as only one of their difficulties and it is the modern obsession with numbers that has made this aspect seem primary.

The appearance of medieval towns is more difficult to describe than might be supposed. Surviving buildings from earlier than the 13th century are few: mainly churches, themselves added to and rebuilt since and now often preserved as "historic sites" – isolated and mollycoddled to save them from modern vandalism. It is difficult to remember that even such churches would not in the Middle Ages have constituted "Gothic" features among more recent buildings. Though undoubtedly the most carefully wrought of the buildings in a town, they would nonetheless have dominated an urban environment comparatively homogeneous in architectural character. Not until the late 15th century did artists begin to draw towns in such a way as to convey some impression of their physical appearance. Only with imagination is it possible to recapture the manner of urban living and even then it is necessary to remember how much towns were constantly changing throughout their greatest days. The concerns of the 12th century were different from those of the 15th, as much in Florence as in England. Under the historical microscope the dot that signifies "town" on the map becomes transformed into a heaving mass of changing individuals.

Northern waters
The area of northern Europe mapped here is actually very large, though much of it is sea, and most of the land lightly populated. Settlement beside coasts and rivers provided access to the major trade routes, which were essential for local prosperity. No single political power could extend its authority across the area, but the importance of the sea for all the populations enabled the Hanse towns to enjoy a special consideration everywhere. Their trading counters from Novgorod to London and from Dortmund to Bergen made them indispensable middlemen that not even kings could browbeat. At the heart of the region the kings of Denmark, who resented them most, nurtured a scheme to unite the Scandinavian kingdoms which was realized in 1397. Even so, this created as many problems as it solved. But the slow decline of the Hanse that did ensue owed more to the enterprise of Dutch merchants fishing in Hanse waters than to the people of Scandinavia themselves. By that time Baltic affairs had become a normal part of the European shipping world and ceased to maintain their own closed system.

PART THREE
FRUITS OF CIVILIZATION

URBAN SOCIETY

Towns that flourished, even if they started as datable foundations, soon began to adapt to the conditions of life, in which it would be rare for even a town council to exercise planning control over development. Within the limited space of the town every plot of land had a high potential value, and the closer to its market center, the more desirable the plot. Rather than tear down the walls, every effort would be made to make the maximum use of land within a town. To think of starting new walls a town would have had to exhaust every other possibility, and to have already acquired surreptitious suburbs built up along the main streets outside the gates. Only at this point would the town authorities, aware of the need to enlarge the area of their protection, agree to a new perimeter lavish enough to allow for estimated continued growth. Within these new walls provision for open spaces, new convents, market places, market gardens and orchards reflected the ambitions of a flourishing town to equip itself with amenities. Some of the best-known towns appear to have exceeded even these limits and been constrained to fix a second line of walls in the 13th century. Florence began building new walls, c. 1290, which were not completed until 1334. Shortly after this a series of misfortunes appears to have drastically reduced the population, or at least to have prevented it rising to meet the new levels expected when the walls were replanned. Not until the mid-19th century did Florence grow up to and beyond those walls. Renaissance Florence was therefore a much more open and spacious environment than its modern appearance would suggest at first sight. Moreover what are now its historic buildings were then its towering novelties: the new town hall, aggressive and domineering; the new cathedral, capped with the triumph of the most modern engineering. Any new layout of a street plan involved demolition of earlier work and a break with the old pattern.

The prominent buildings of towns, both civil and ecclesiastical, expressed the defiant individuality of each place and it was the spiritual tradition of a town that inspired townsmen rather than any affection for particular buildings in it. For this reason the main concern of any town government was to secure control of its own affairs so that the town's business would not be hampered by outsiders: this was the real embodiment of civic pride. In a sense it was a pompous bluff, for though urban autonomy and town walls proclaimed a self-sufficient community, no town in contemporary conditions could be sufficient unto itself. The town walls shut in a population and shut out the rustics beyond the walls in their fields, but the walls attempted to render insoluble problems manageable; they did not separate two exclusive worlds.

Within, the town populations steadily absorbed immigrants from the countryside but denied the force of social bonds familiar there: lordship, kin, cooperative agricultural work according to the seasons. Towns contained traders and craftsmen, rich and poor, living in close proximity, potential competitors, rivals, even enemies. To keep the social peace, special efforts by the clergy, directly in parishes or from friaries, indirectly through fraternities and guilds, appeared to offer the only hope of civic harmony. Towns could not, unlike the countryside, police the activities of strangers. Their trade and industry made it desirable to attract traveling merchants, customers and skilled men. Town populations were by nature multifarious and difficult to govern.

If the main problems of towns were social and economic, in this period they were articulated in religious rather than ideological terms. In some towns resident bishops had to bear the brunt of any criticisms about the ecclesiastical establishment. From the 12th century poor weavers were considered as likely fomenters of unorthodox religious opinions. In the 13th century Dominican preachers, the Franciscans and other friars swarmed through all the major towns of Europe to counter heresy and fraternize with the poor by their own espousal of poverty. Most towns were already divided into several ecclesiastical parishes. The complexity of religious life in the towns imposed modification of the church's pattern of rural ministry. The sacramental rituals at least needed supplementing with instruction, exhortation, prayer meetings, communal devotions and the multiplication of words, spoken and written. Towns fostered religious excitements that could boil over into disturbances. The most famous of these occurred in Renaissance Florence under the friar Savonarola (executed 1498). The reason for such ferment is most likely to have been social: the life in an enclosed space for men of different status, wealth, length of residence, trades and skills with their fluctuating numbers of unemployed, unemployable and parasites. The unruly passions of townsmen, so unlike the bourgeoisie of social theory, struck the earliest medieval chroniclers who took note of townsmen. Such writers, from the outside, hardly offered sympathy or understanding of the urban predicament and not until the 13th century do town chronicles and customaries begin to shed more light on town development from the inside. They tend to confirm the narrowness of the urban vision and sense of loyalties.

Outside the walls, the towns confronted problems over which their governments necessarily had even less control, and from the consequences of which their town walls could not protect them. At first the growth of the town population depended on the securing of new immigrants from smaller towns and particularly from the fecund countryside. When towns stopped growing, the stability of the population demanded regular topping up from elsewhere. But towns that reached a certain optimum size became that much more vulnerable to shortages of food supplies and raw materials, without which their relatively huge populations could not operate. From within the walls therefore town governments had to contemplate their relations with those outside. Towns might try to induce immigration by offering favorable terms for settlement, particularly the advantage of emancipation from servile dues. The countryside, where productivity depended upon servile obligations, could therefore suffer from excessive departures. Landlords might themselves be caught in a dilemma, wishing to retain adequate labor in the fields and yet encourage towns as markets for their goods. Countrymen tempted to escape rural servitude anyway needed reassurance that town privileges for immigrants would be respected by local princes. Princes might need persuading if they were to recognize the towns' rights to receive fugitive serfs. Yet there was no inherent incompatibility or contradiction between towns and lords. Towns provided markets for the surpluses of princely estates and tempted princes to spend their profits on the many articles of commerce they displayed. These men were their best customers and the indispensable forces of order in the countryside, which merchants had to traverse on their way to market.

Communications, transport and trade

Towns well spaced out drew upon predictable resources. Medieval towns in the Low Countries especially had developed in fairly close proximity to one another mainly because their geographical location made it reasonable to rely on supplies coming from some distance away. As the towns prospered, so those supplies had to be sought ever further off. The further the source of supply, the feebler the power of the town to guarantee those supplies. No single political order prevailed, as in the Roman empire, to protect the transport of goods. The towns' own merchants had to acquire supplies and bring them from afar. Thus the development of many towns in a restricted area implied the prior existence of a commercial network and adjacent reserves of productive lands, to be exploited for the towns' benefit. In Italy only the great plain of the Po could be cultivated well enough to feed many urban mouths. In the north the towns of Flanders came to depend on the granaries of eastern Europe.

The main motor of medieval commerce was the Mediterranean traffic, which the Italian towns were the first to exploit. During the crusading period Christians had challenged Muslims and won a considerable share of the trade. The two Italian towns that dominated in the Levant were Venice and Genoa, both of which had benefited particularly from the Latin usurpation of the empire at Constantinople in 1204. One quarter of the empire was immediately assigned to Venice. The islands provided Venice with harbors, sailors and produce for centuries. The great island of Crete remained a Venetian "colony" until 1669. The Genoese did not obtain so much, nor so quickly, but by offering their naval services to the Greeks they did secure a foothold in the Aegean. In a series of wars with the Venetians in the 14th century they proved themselves to be formidable challengers. For both, the control of commerce through Constantinople and access to the Black Sea trade were the basis of their

prosperity and their leading positions in the commerce of western Europe. The significance of the Black Sea trade in the 13th century was enhanced by the security for commerce offered by the political power of the Mongol empire. This enabled merchants, as well as travelers and missionaries, to cross from the Crimea to China, a journey frequently made until the mid-14th century when the Mongol dynasty was supplanted by the Ming (in 1368).

Until the late 13th century the international commerce of western Europe appears to have focused on the great fairs of Champagne, on which Italian merchants had converged across the Alps to meet traders from the north. Apart from the risks from robbers, the convoys of pack animals used in the Alps limited the volume of goods that could be sent to market. As the towns of the northern coastal waters began to enter into leagues that protected the movements of shipping, so the sense of trying to bring the Mediterranean traffic into contact with the north became more obvious. Even Venice, the Italian city best placed geographically to deal with the lands of the north across the eastern Alps and down to the waters of the Rhine and Danube, did not hesitate, in spite of the longer sea journey with which it was presented as compared with Genoa. The main hazard of the long journey was the open sea beyond the English Channel. Piracy in these waters was, however, hampered from the 13th century by the king of England's new interest in his ports for access to France, along the Biscay coast. Alliance between the duke of Gascony and the king of Castile gave a new stability in that region which Italian traders could take advantage of.

When transport by pack animals was normal, merchants inevitably concentrated on trade in small and valuable objects. By the 14th century trade by sea made it possible to think in terms of bulk goods such as grain or wool being shifted considerable distances. Town populations came to count on regular shipments. In the famine year 1315–16 Flanders was even supplied with grain, exceptionally, from Sicily, thanks to the enterprise of some Florentine merchants. Wine too was shipped from specialized regions like the Bordelais to England or Flanders. The English gave up making wine altogether, once they could be sure of supplies from the Rhineland or from Gascony. Other essential foods that moved considerable distances were salt from the Bay of Biscay and salted fish from the North Sea. As for manufactured goods, growing towns needed to import raw materials and to find customers or markets for their products. Competition for shrinking markets encouraged some centers to specialize, for better-quality goods kept their price. The woolen-cloth industry had become established in Flanders at an early stage. By the 12th century the industry there needed English wool to function to capacity. In the 14th century quantities of wool were obtained from Castile. Not all this northern cloth was sold in a finished state. Italian merchants bought cloth of fine quality to be embellished in the workshops of their own cities. The Genoese exported Flemish cloth to the Levant. Without extensive use of shipping lanes, medieval industry on this scale is inconceivable. Industry was developed in expectation of a steady demand. It served the market, rather than specific customers.

Commerce in the 14th century
The great trade routes of maps, like major rivers, depend on the contributions made by countless small streams of traffic, which by the 14th century had left almost no European settlement isolated in self-sufficiency. The process of bringing all these minor streams into one great interconnecting system may have been going on for many generations. The proof that all Europe was involved comes most forcefully from the decision of the Venetian and Genoese governments in the early 14th century to provide for regular sailings from the Mediterranean to Bruges. This brought into normal contact the maritime commerce of the north, where the Hanse were dominant, and that of the Mediterranean. There many western European peoples were involved in trade, with North Africa, Egypt, the Black Sea and with one another. The Catholic occupation of the crusading states, then of Cyprus and other parts of the Greek empire, gave merchants a valuable sense of security, only disturbed by the progress of Ottoman armies in the 15th century. These waterways enabled the precious goods of both ends of Europe to travel in contrary directions to satisfy eager purchasers, at a time when the old routes across Russia were abandoned. It is more difficult to show all the land routes beaten by merchants in this period. Fairs were important to them, but more significant is probably the specialization of regions in products like salt or wine or precious metals. Men became dependent on trade with distant places. More remarkable still is the specialization of industry, particularly in cloth manufacture, for here markets were won not by natural endowment but by enterprise, competition and specialization in superior-quality goods.

Previous page The town of Cordes (Tarn) was founded in 1222 by Count Raymond of Toulouse to foster the recovery of the region devastated by the Albigensian wars. It was planted on top of the hill with two circuits of defense walls. The population so prospered and multiplied in commerce and industry that by the early 14th century a new circuit lower down had to be built, with a barbican to the least steep, eastern side. Beyond this a new suburb promptly grew up. But later extensions to these fortifications overextended the perimeter and the town could no longer resist capture. However in the 13th and 14th centuries Cordes admirably fulfilled the expectations of its population who had known how to take advantage of both its site and its artificial reinforcement.

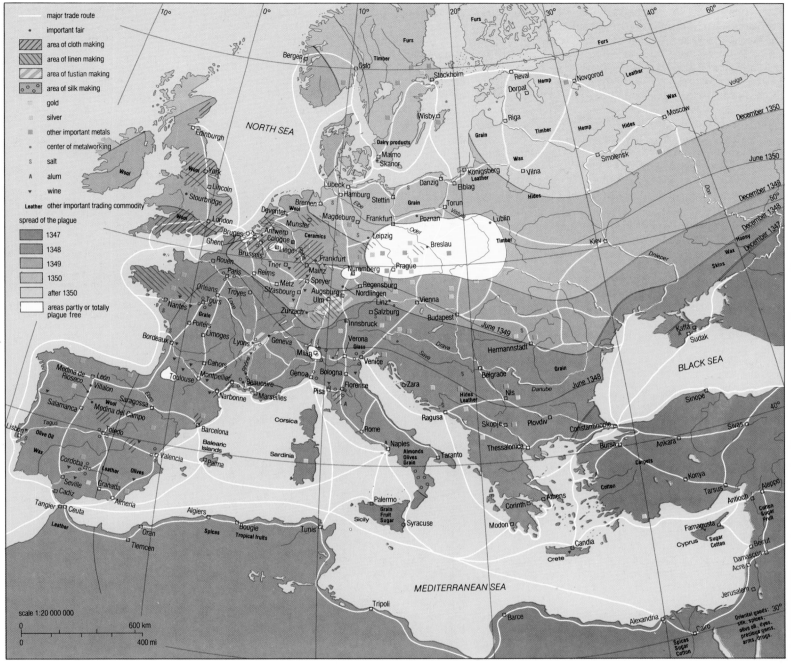

This market comprised an astonishing complexity of interests. Many things could go wrong and business remained risky. Some entrepreneurs made fortunes. The soundest companies of traders could be ruined by a run of bankruptcies. Merchants devised ways of cushioning themselves from the worst hazards. The Hanse trading association is one sign of the times. Italian businesses depended more on partnerships, including investment by sleeping partners. They borrowed and obtained credits. They devised insurance schemes. Diversification of business was often a sensible precaution, but required close supervision of numerous subordinate businesses. The successful often retired. Their families might acquire country estates and higher social status outside the town. New men took their place. The urban aristocracies tended to be less stable than in the country. It was the continuous activity of a certain kind, rather than persistence of particular family interests, that brought all Europe within the scope of commercial activity.

Never before, certainly not in the Roman empire,

had there been trade on this scale, trade which both encouraged specialization of produce and product, and constantly forced up the standard of quality demanded on the international market. By the 14th century no region of Christendom was not linked in some way to the network of international commerce. To that extent all regions were liable to suffer or benefit by the consequences of events in remote places over which they had no influence. Products reaching the west from far away in the east found their way thanks to the activities of many different merchants, operating a system they alone understood and which politically they could not protect. The survival of such a system says much for the sense of contemporaries who valued the enterprise of their merchants. And townsmen only too well exemplified some of the most typical "medieval" attitudes, sharpening their weapons, exaggerating their devotions and cultivating their wits with no less enthusiasm and ingenuity than their fellows beyond the walls, without whose aid their own enterprises would have come to nothing.

Bottom The stone bridge at Regensburg, more than 300 meters long, was built in 1135–46 to replace an earlier bridge of boats. The bridgeable character of the Danube here explains the early importance of the town. The cathedral, begun in 1275, is a rare example of Bavarian Gothic.

Below center The aerial view of Rothenburg spreadeagled across the hillside shows how closely the line of the town walls is affected by the contour lines and how securely the town was defended by such natural advantages.

Below Rothenburg from the church tower. The substantial town houses in the foreground with plain and stepped gables indicate both the wealth and the taste of late medieval Germany.

Below Toplerschlösschen im Rosenthal near Rothenburg. This outlying fort was built by Bürgermeister Topler in 1388 to assist with the protection of the town's mills and the supervision of the approach road and was itself originally surrounded by water and reached only across a bridge.

Rothenburg

Part of this town was wrecked by an earthquake in 1356. Its prosperity in the 14th century permitted a total rebuilding at one time so that a uniform and harmonious impression could be created which has been preserved. The ruined Staufen castle shows that the importance of the site was appreciated at an earlier time. The town grew on the terrace above the steep valley of the Tauber from the 10th century, providing a market center for the rich agricultural zone round about. The 14th-century walls and towers were embellished with new gateways in the 17th century.

Below This gateway in the 15th-century walls of Dinkelsbühl contains an upper gallery to conceal its defenders and is further protected by water.
Bottom This view of Segringergasse, Dinkelsbühl, with the Three Negroes inn shows the broad street and steep roofs of a well-laid-out town.

Regensburg

This great city owes its importance to its site on the Danube at its most northerly point where it can be easily bridged. Its bishopric was founded by St Boniface in 739; it was the favored place of residence for Bavarian rulers till the 13th century when its status as an imperial city encouraged the citizens to resist episcopal and noble pressures. Its merchants traded across the whole of Europe. Its famous churches and monasteries helped to create a city of exceptional character which increased its perimeter by building new walls in the 14th century.

Dinkelsbühl

The prosperity of this town on the river Wörnitz grew out of its patronage by the Staufen rulers, who founded it c. 1180. It became an imperial city in 1273 and it continued to expand in the next century when the rebuilding of its walls was begun. At that time it was geographically well placed for trading, though mainly as a local market. There was industry both in cloth making and in the making of tools such as scythes and sickles. Not till 1387 did the craftsmen gain admission to the town government.

Below The Guildhall, Lavenham, originally the hall of the Corpus Christi guild, was probably not built before 1529. The timber-framed building is richly decorated with carving.
Below center The late 15th-century wooden door to Little Hall, Lavenham, shows Perpendicular influence.

La Couvertoirade

This fortified village is itself built on a rock in the Dourbie valley and overlooked by a castle on the summit of St Guiral (1349 meters). When the Templars acquired it in 1182, they built a castle there in the early 13th century; after the dissolution of the order in 1312, the village passed to the Hospitalers. The present rampart was built in 1439 to provide an enclosure where travelers and their beasts could be sheltered from the mercenary companies of soldiers who prowled about the Causses. The new wall reduced the importance of the original Templar castle which became a barn and place of final refuge. The elaborate defense work served its purpose, and age rather than human enemies is responsible for its decay.

Below The Shambles is the most famous old street of York with timber-framed houses whose overhangs almost touch. Modern restoration has eliminated both the bustle and the casual neglect and made it a picturesque corner for tourists.

Overleaf La Couvertoirade lay on the Compostela road between Millau and Lodève on the Causse de Larzac and is first heard of in 1142. Apart from its importance to pilgrims, the site was valued by the military orders on account of the neighboring pastures where they bred war horses.

Lavenham

Lavenham is a market town on a tributary of the Stour in west Suffolk. It was important among many other towns of the region for its share in the wool trade and reached the height of its prosperity in the late 15th century when its church was rebuilt. Whereas comparable towns have since lost their medieval appearance, Lavenham has retained its former character, partly by consequence of its own decline and more recently by determined efforts of restoration and conservation.

York

The site of York made it till recent times the principal city of northern Britain, where the Romans established a base used at an early date by the English settlers and then by the Danes. It became the see of the northern ecclesiastical primate in 735, though it never succeeded in rivaling the power of Canterbury. The importance of Danish York suggests its potential, but after the definitive establishment of the united English monarchy on a southern foundation, real prosperity only developed in the north from the 12th century. The extensive pasturing of sheep in the Yorkshire dales provided raw materials for wool export and cloth making and stimulated commerce. The settlement of the border with Scotland at first gave a new security, and when the wars began again, York once more became an important base for military action. Its walls, 4 kilometers round, were rebuilt in the 14th century at the same time as the cathedral when the town reached its most prosperous phase.

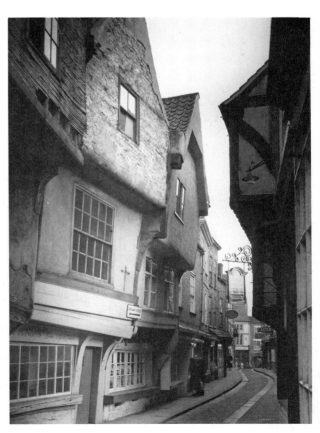

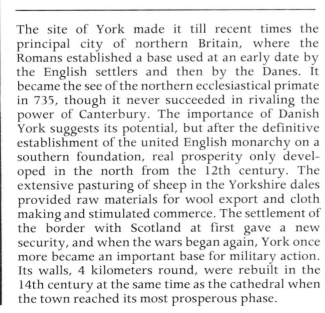

Right The siting of most medieval Tuscan towns on hilltops creates a very aggressive impression from afar. This was deliberate and San Gimignano was no exception: the town itself was a great castle, with its fields all around under its protection.

San Gimignano

San Gimignano lost its self-government to Florence in 1354. Its subsequent decline explains why its medieval buildings have been better conserved than in many Italian towns, though only 15 towers survive of the 72 known. The towers suggest a violent domestic history but these disputes did not in the 12th century prevent the town claiming autonomy and dominating the Valle d'Elsa. Its special economic importance was due to the local cultivation of saffron, a valuable source of drugs and dyes. It was also a region favored for its grain and wine.

Right The Palazzo del Popolo at San Gimignano was begun in 1280 and enlarged in 1323 as the headquarters of the Podestà, the town's chief magistrate. By an early ordinance, no other tower in the town was ever to be built higher than the tower of this palace, from which not only the courtyard, but also the surrounding country, could be surveyed.

Below At street level the height of the towers is not often as obtrusive as here. The narrowness of the building and their entries blend easily with later reconstructions.

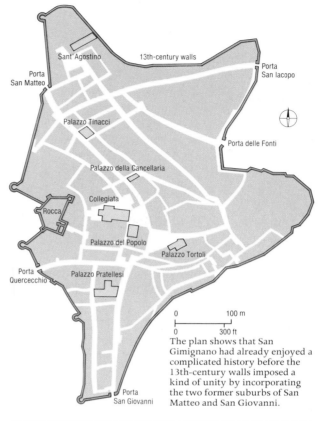

The plan shows that San Gimignano had already enjoyed a complicated history before the 13th-century walls imposed a kind of unity by incorporating the two former suburbs of San Matteo and San Giovanni.

Florence

Florence is unusual among the medieval towns of Tuscany for being built in the plain. Its subsequent fame obscured its origins even in the Middle Ages. Its history was in no way exceptional until the mid-13th century. At this point its economic importance prompted it to strike its own silver and gold coinage and its reputation for maintaining their value guaranteed its financial importance throughout the period. Linked by road to France, where it nursed valuable markets, Florence had no seaport and owed its prosperity to its industries rather than to commerce. Its merchants and cloth makers with other guildsmen took charge of the town government after 1282 and preserved this "republican" constitution even after real power passed into the hands of an oligarchy and then of the Medici family (1434). Florentines enjoyed debating the nature of political life and their intellectual bent was encouraged by the many schools of the town. Education in the vernacular produced an exceptionally high level of literacy and the quality of Tuscan literature from Dante onwards gave Florentines high expectations of their citizens. These intellectual attainments were more than equaled by the craftsmen, painters, goldsmiths, sculptors and architects that enhanced the physical beauty of the town.

Below The Porta Soprana, Genoa. This massive gateway with its two towers, eloquent of the wealth of medieval Genoa, formed part of the city's defense system when the walls were first extended in the mid-12th century.

Genoa

The natural advantages of the harbor at Genoa meant that the site was inhabited from an early date, but the greatest days of the city's independent history began with the success of the First Crusade which brought Genoese to the Levant. The city flourished as the Mediterranean port closest to the trade with northwest Europe, successively defeating its nearest rival Pisa in 1284 and holding its own against Venice. The city's first expansion from its 10th-century confines came with the new walls built in 1155, but by the 14th century another perimeter had become necessary. Genoa, unlike Venice, had developed no strong constitutional forms and the rivalry between noble families remained a source of weakness even after the dogeship was introduced in 1339. Despite its modern importance Genoa retains many buildings of its medieval past.

Far left The Ponte Vecchio, Florence. A bridge at this point, where the Arno is at its narrowest, has existed since the late 10th century. The present bridge, built in 1345, replaced the one swept away in the destructive floods of 1333. The erection of shops along both sides of the road preserved the commercial character of the streets for this obligatory passage of the river.

Left The impressive height of the campanile, the dome and the cathedral as a whole, towering above the even level of medieval building in the city, have since the mid-15th century given Florence a new image.

Avila

Avila is an ancient town with Christian traditions antedating Constantine and became the seat of a bishopric after the reconquest of the land from the Muslims. The site of the town above the river Adaja at 1131 meters above sea level makes it very cold in winter, but attractively cool in summer for Castile; it was therefore a popular place of residence for Castilian kings in their youth, and there were also many noble residences there. These connections brought the new French ''Gothic'' building style early to Avila and it remained an important city until the 17th century. Its later decline preserved its medieval appearance from the usual consequences of prosperity.

Alquézar

This town, perched on the mountains around the river Vero, was originally established by the Muslims on a strategic site pointed at the Sobrarbe region in the Pyrenees. The fortress was first constructed by them. It was captured by King Sancho Ramirez in 1067 who used it as a base for his

further campaigns in the valleys of the Cinca and Alcanadre. The importance of the town in the late 11th and early 12th centuries for these military purposes explains the special efforts made to recruit Christian settlers and to build town walls and an important church beside the castle. The present church, built in the 16th century, has a cloister with sculptures dating from its first Christian resettlement. With the consolidation of the Aragonese conquests, however, the town lost its special attractions for the kings, which explains the preservation of its earlier aspect despite subsequent rebuildings.

Left The little town of Alquézar clinging to its rock is itself visibly dominated by its 11th-century castle and has retained its medieval aspect.

Below The walls of Avila were built by Casandro and Florin de Pituenga after the town was captured from the Muslims at the end of the 11th century. They are 12 meters high and 3 meters thick. Every 20 meters there are round towers, and there are eight gates. The cathedral at the top of the town is attached by its apse to the defenses. Roman materials were used in the construction and it has been frequently restored, but it remains one of the finest examples of medieval town fortification, though the walls had ceased to contain the town at least by the 13th century.

Town Government

The 14th century saw the heyday of European municipalities. The town halls built from the last years of the 13th century, robust and castlelike with watchtowers and battlements, affirm the independence of the town and its preparedness to ward off outsiders. The Florentine call for "liberty" appears confusing and misleading to those who have read J. J. Rousseau. The independence of the town never implied enfranchisement of all the citizens. This did not necessarily provoke discontent. Pressure from outside the ranks of those eligible for admission to office was rarely successful for long. Governments were run by those with the leisure, the ambition, the connections and, above all, with sufficient stake in the town's property or prosperity to take an interest in its well-being. The majority of the inhabitants had particular occupations of their own which demanded their attention. The insistent claims of family, work, guild, fraternity, parish or city district gave most citizens more than enough share in management at the level where they knew most about affairs. Only those who achieved influence in these obscure local politics sought eminence in the town halls. Here the liberty of the whole town required political negotiations with great lords, kings, even popes, and therefore great political experience, patience and wealth. Few individuals, or indeed towns, could support the burdens of such independence for very long. Most municipal authorities had asserted their independence only by suppressing dissident groups and no towns were spared internal disturbances. Unenfranchised citizens bore arms in the city militia and could therefore flex their muscles when roused. The city's finances depended either upon loans made by rich citizens at guaranteed interest rates or upon indirect taxation on wine or salt or goods coming into the town for market, all comparatively easy ways to collect revenue. Medieval town life was no more ideal or forward-looking than life in the country. Its institutions, though more broadly based than feudal ones, proved to be no more popular or durable. Cities like Venice that survived to become capitals of states were already aristocractic. In the 15th century generally the great cities such as Bruges or Barcelona had to come to a new understanding with the princes, for conditions were no longer propitious for municipal independence.

Left At the instance of the mayor, Robert Ricart became town clerk of Bristol in 1479 and probably served for nearly 30 years. This illustration from the record book in which he wrote down the local customs shows the making of the new mayor, probably his patron, on 29 September 1479 in the Guildhall. The old mayor proffers a book on which to take the oath in the presence of the officers in particolored livery, the aldermen and citizens. The mayor's hat and sword, the objects on the table and the town arms in the window should be noted.

Below Ambrogio Lorenzetti's *Allegory of Good Government* (1338–40) from the town hall in Siena. This allegory was painted on the wall of the council chamber facing the window and is therefore the centerpiece of the decorative scheme. On the right a group of townsmen is dominated by a figure in black and white symbolizing the comune of Siena watched over by the three theological virtues and attended by the four cardinal virtues with Magnanimity and Peace. On the left Justice sits beneath Wisdom, dispensing on the one hand punishment and rewards, and on the other responsibility and charity, in accordance with Aristotelian teaching. Below Justice sits Concord, from whom a cord literally passes through the hands of the citizens, who turn towards the comune. This cord links both parts of the picture and completes the allegory.

Trade

Most of the great medieval towns owed their importance to their role as trading depots rather than to their industries. They were situated in protected sites with easy access to the sea-lanes of Europe: Venice, Genoa, Bristol, London, Bruges, Lübeck. Their trading role tended to diminish the former importance of great international fairs because it became possible to ship goods in greater bulk. Up country, however, such fairs continued to attract trade for more local purposes. At a third level the holding of weekly markets by authority of the local government lifted a number of privileged settlements into the modest rank of market towns. In a country like England, where markets were carefully spaced out, this system must have placed most villagers at a convenient day's journey from a market. This made it possible to dispose of their surplus produce very easily. At least from the 13th century visits to towns ensured the rapid diffusion of information across the country and this promoted a sense of a community larger than that of the basic settlement. In other parts of Europe similar developments worked for regions rather than whole kingdoms. The setting up of markets, the protection of roads of access, policing the market and supervising traders' weights and measures, all imply the intervention of authorities able to enforce rules beyond the market's own territorial limits. These conditions were obtained at different times in different parts of Europe, but under the same pressures. On the one hand, international trade was itself fed by the country streams that filtered the more esteemed goods to the sea and brought others back into the shops; on the other, the protection of small trading posts inland relied on the goodwill, even positive encouragement, of monasteries, bishops or other landlords, who saw the advantages, financial and otherwise, of setting up markets.

Right The establishment of guild customs became very common from the 13th century as the advantages of corporate organizations over individual enterprise loomed larger. The control of buying and selling was particularly important and the setting up of stalls or businesses in a particular street enabled all the tradesmen to keep an eye on one another. This street scene of drapers is dominated by the altar shrine at the top. Down each side of the street may be seen the counters and trestles on which the goods are examined, while the merchandise hangs from lines suspended across the booths.

Below Genoa was one of the earliest cities of Europe known for its money changers, or bankers, whose activities are revealed in notarial deeds of the 12th century. In this scene the accountants are counting out the coins, prior to assigning payment to the widows and children, of whose interests the text in the upper left wall, to which the figure of Jesus points, bids them be mindful. The great chest appears to contain the treasure. Early banking was bound up with the problem of exchanging coins of the many denominations struck by various authorities all over Europe.

Left The crowded harborside of the great European ports is not frequently depicted by painters, and even in this picture of Hamburg the particular occupations of the figures in the foreground are dwarfed by the great ships on the water, three-masted cogs of the 15th century. Unloading them involves the use of lighters and a great crane on the quayside. In the middle the clerks await delivery of the goods. To the right, merchants or investors discuss the success of the enterprise, decked out in their finery and Russian fur hats. Inside the office the harbor authorities or the shipowners sit with greater assurance. The picture thus concentrates in one image the many activities characteristic of the ports.

Left Blessing the Lendit (June) fair at St Denis. The religious blessing on commerce was central to the conduct of this famous fair, which was opened by announcing the religious festival. This illustration comes from the liturgical order of proceedings. It is notable for the great number of inns shown, with their signposts, in one of which a repast is already being served. A shepherd has also led his flock into the market place, for the fair took place throughout the plain of St Denis.

Industry

The earliest medieval guilds were those of the merchants in the towns, but by the 13th century specific craftsmen's guilds began to appear alongside corporations of doctors and lawyers. When Louis IX of France ordered a book of the customs of different trades to be compiled, the inquiry revealed that effective regulations not previously put into writing had depended on oral transmission through respected tradesmen. Guild regulations written down in 13th-century towns not surprisingly placed much emphasis on the religious duties of members to attend collective devotions or their moral commitment to the welfare of deceased members' families, as well as more directly professional matters. Religious obligations gave a divine sanction to the association, where members felt the passions of competitive rivalry more quickly than fraternity. But guilds also defined such matters as fair practice over apprenticeships, offered a tribunal for the adjudication of disputes and insisted on quality of production.

The guilds played an important part in the town. Which trades formed guilds, became subsidiary members of guilds run by more powerful trades, or were denied group organization altogether, varied from town to town. In Florence membership of certain guilds was required for election to civic office. In London attempts to replace the wards (a territorial division) as units of local government by forms of representation through guilds came to nothing. In all towns, however, the organization of guilds indicated that the meaning of the professional classes was not confined to such "educated" groups as lawyers or students. Craftsmen too had their powerful organizations (*universitates*), and their members sat on city councils alongside bankers and international shippers.

Most craft activity was carried on in small workshops under masters who knew their work force personally, some of whom would in favorable circumstances start their own businesses. The system did not guarantee that every day-worker (journeymen) would become a master himself. Workers in unorganized trades were dispersed among too many enterprises for the organization of their grievances to offer any substantial improvement in conditions. The cloth industry was probably the one where the many different trades involved were most susceptible to factory-type conditions, though the use of waterpower in the process of mechanizing the industry eventually forced it into the countryside, beyond the reach of guild regulations. The medieval interest in mechanical gadgetry stemmed from the acute shortage of manpower at every level in a society that took no slaves in warfare and had to supplement human labor wherever ingenuity suggested a way.

For the early period, the main changes came about in agriculture: water mills are mentioned in barbarian laws from the 8th century. By the 12th century horse collars and harness had subjected the

Below Most tradesmen paying for painted glass in churches dedicated panels to their patron saints. At Semur in 1465 the drapers unusually chose to have the processes of cloth finishing depicted to commemorate their profession. The scenes shown include sorting, carding, raising the nap and shaving; some of the tools of the trade are clearly visible. Several stages of the process have been omitted, but the number of trades linked together in cloth manufacture is obvious and their importance for employment of the drapers could not have been more forcefully presented.

Left This picture of the architect supervising the construction of a building shows a number of workmen with different tools and the manner of wooden construction in the early 15th century. The architect's luxurious appearance is notable, though the lavish character of the manuscript may be responsible. It is one of four full-page illustrations to the Book of Genesis in the Bedford Hours and purports to show Noah building an ark, the animals for which are being rounded up behind the site.

noble steed to direction by the plowman. The use of waterpower for ever more ingenious purposes, driving saws, fulling, making paper, shows that its possibilities were constantly exploited. It took much longer to use wind power in comparable ways. Windmills appear in the 12th century. They were raised on a base and could be carried about. In the 14th-century Low Countries they were used for systematic drainage operations. The Dutch built windmills for Frisia and the Rhineland. Not till the 15th century did mechanical contrivances become an ordinary part of human experience. In addition to the use of clocks to measure out time, jacks for raising heavy burdens by the use of cranks and connecting rods or cranes on swivels had become familiar, at least in towns.

The desire for military superiority was also a constant incentive to innovation. The invention of gunpowder, frequently mentioned from the latter half of the 13th century, naturally had a new impact. The casters of cannon persisted with their efforts to make these weapons more dangerous to the enemy than to themselves. Metalworkers more consistently perfected the defensive armor of the knights, though improvements in steel making were not mentioned by writers. The notable improvements of the mining industries in 15th-century Germany were not described until Bauer published his book on metallurgy in 1556.

Individual industries responded to other pressures when introducing new machinery. The mechanization of fulling in the cloth industry may suggest that men could not be easily found for such work. But the desire to speed up the processes also contributed. The invention of cardage in the 14th century was quickly followed by mechanization. The spinning wheel supplanted the distaff. Candle making was improved by the substitution of animal fats for wax. Distilling was a new industry based on Arabic learning and first known in 12th-century Salerno. The importance of this to sailors needs no emphasis. Navigation was also being improved by the use of the compass before 1200, the introduction of the stern rudder, astrolabes and charts, not to speak of the constant changes in the building of ships. Like clocks, spectacles were a medieval invention made possible by medieval learning.

By the end of the medieval period acknowledged experts of the new technology did not hesitate to offer their services to the greatest rulers. Leonardo da Vinci was by no means the first of his type. Mariano di Jacopo, Il Taccola, a Sienese, has left an illustrated description of his achievements in three handsome volumes. He was a notary and bursar of a student hostel, as well as designer, wood-carver and miniature painter. He designed bridges and harbor installations and offered to look after the emperor Sigismund's waterworks. Germany also produced many men of this type. Their activities grew from the work of their predecessors and were not inspired by any spirit of renaissance.

Everyday Life

Misericords allowed weary clergy the indulgence of support while ostensibly standing for singing the divine office. As such they are evidence of decadence, or compassion, in the late medieval church, the oldest surviving examples dating from the 13th century. At first very simple, they were later frequently decorated with elaborate carvings. Half-hidden and unobtrusive, as bum props they could inspire a mischievous humor. Biblical scenes are rare; a high proportion of the subjects depicted are scenes of everyday life, sometimes coarse, often humorous, particularly at women's expense. Here some unusual examples of the genre are given.

Emptying a shoe.

Picking nits from a girl's hair.

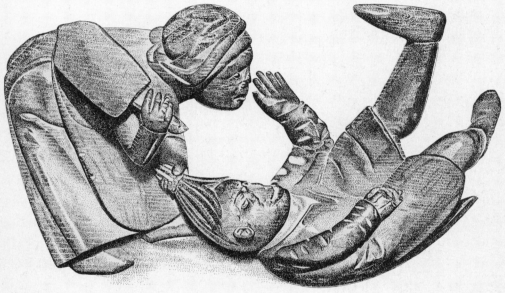

The battered husband.

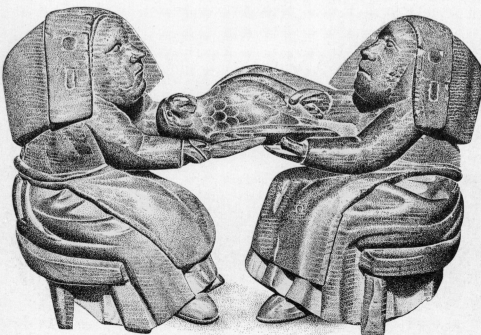

Two women preparing a bird.

The alewife.

At the fireside.

Mother and child.

A girl dressing.

Travel

Bottom left This early 16th-century Flemish painting of May Day celebrations by road and river shows that, though mounted individuals could travel faster, more could travel together by water. One man in the stern paddles; another in the bow fends off the arches of the bridge and the musicians remain unperturbed.

Below center Musician mummers, with their droll appearance and their noisy exuberance, were themselves among the most constant travelers of the period, entertaining fellow travelers and their hosts wherever they could find lodging and audiences. The figures here illustrate the satirical novel by Gervais du Bus and represent the rough music inflicted upon errant neighbors.

Despite conditions of work that tied men to their own localities, they could in some respects prove more robust travelers than might be supposed, for it was less of a wrench to leave behind their earthly possessions. The period began with mass migrations from one homeland to another and ended as Europeans were preparing to colonize the Americas. In the meantime medieval rulers traveled constantly on their estates, or to meet other rulers and visit the Holy Places. Christian pilgrims from every rank journeyed to the Holy Land, Compostela and Rome. If they were less insistent than Muslims on the duty of the pilgrimage, they probably went with more passion and certainly to more different places and with a mixture of motives. That they traveled is certain. The difficulties begin as we try to visualize the conditions of movement. Much of western Europe was paved with Roman roads, but the barbarians had certainly been capable of moving in great numbers where roads had not been built. No imperial government kept the roads in repair, but they might have survived for centuries the trudge of many feet and the clatter of horses moving at slow speeds. It was the wear and tear of wheeled vehicles that finally disposed of the roads. If maintenance work was attempted, it had to be at the local level, where new roads, if any, bridges and fords certainly did receive attention. Road building at this time has not yet been studied with care. Bridges were paid for by local benefactors and toll charges helped to lighten the burdens. Whenever possible, travelers took to the water, frequently using the great rivers, but avoiding the sea by preference. Merchants moved produce by mule train and by water. Political disturbances could of course interrupt the flow more easily by land, but even at times of greatest disruption movement from one part of Europe to another was never paralyzed.

Much travel was to some degree involuntary, for even pilgrimages could be imposed as penalties, and travelers can never have expected comforts or conveniences, as tourists do. Throughout the period it was assumed that there would be a regular obligation to supply hospitality on an unpredictable scale, and it naturally fell to monasteries to show charity. There were therefore no hostelries spaced out along the way at regular intervals. Travelers on foot took refuge when darkness fell in whatever house they could find. There was no system of post-horses or stagecoaches to encourage innkeepers. As certain routes could begin to predict the traffic by seasons, this state of affairs probably changed. In any numbers, however, bands of pilgrims, like armed crusaders, could hardly expect to find food and accommodation on demand; they had to be prepared to provide their own.

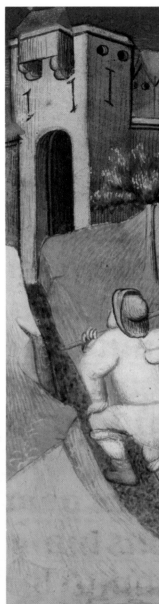

Left William of Normandy's flotilla for the conquest of England, illustrated here in the Bayeux tapestry, was prepared in less than six months. Special ships were used for transporting horses. The duke was dependent on the wind. His ships had no oars, only a steering rudder.

Right This representation from a choir stall in Amiens of an elaborate cart drawn by two horses shows that by the end of the Middle Ages little progress had been made with regard to comfort or speed, even if the vehicle was stoutly constructed and handsomely decorated.

Below Travelers before the walls of Peking from the *Livre de merveilles* by Odoric de Pordenone. This book was made up of various travel records about the east and decorators of it were often hard put to depict the strange marvels of the world described there. Inevitably they fell back on what was familiar wherever possible. The appearance of the Mongol capital, though known to the author, had to be imagined by the painter, whose fantasy has supplied the rocky landscape and the dormer windows on the town walls. This splendid manuscript was made for John duke of Burgundy in the early 15th century by Jacques Coëne, a Fleming.

Education

School education is the only form of training for young people known about in any detail for this period. Its scope was restricted to the teaching of reading and writing, and originally only in Latin, as required for boys destined for the religious life. Its unpopularity with schoolboys must be assumed from the evident expectation of the need to beat attention and learning into the young. Though medieval adults may have had less indulgence for even young children than would now be considered proper, the main reason for harshness is likely to have been that children could have no inkling of what pleasure and advantage they would reap in later life from mastering their letters in a foreign tongue. These boys came from non-clerical families and were not following in the footsteps of any respected elder. Their brothers, on the contrary, were being brought up to imitate their older kinsmen, seeing their way to achieve parity quickly. Learning to ride or to plow would have seemed more interesting certainly than grammar.

Schooling in Italy and southern France opened the way for laymen to a few esteemed professions, like law and medicine, but everywhere else in medieval Europe it was left to bishops and monks to maintain schools, principally to provide recruits to their establishments. Only in the late 11th century did ecclesiastical studies have to aspire to more than mastering older learning. Discussion of controversial points of church law forced the clergy to study the formal law of the Roman empire; they also found that training in formal logic and argument had both academic and practical advantages. These studies helped to form young minds and encouraged them to believe in the power of words to resolve problems. A few great centers for these advanced studies began to emerge. The teachers in Paris and the (older) students at Bologna organized societies to protect their interests (in Latin, *universitates*), and these became the models of comparable institutions all over Europe. North of the Alps, however, it was mainly religious encouragement of learning that led to the endowment of schools. The clergy also stimulated the desire for basic literacy by providing suitable religious books in the vernacular tongues, which otherwise had little or no written literature worth reading. As a literate audience for vernacular works came into being, the cultural environment favored the composition of notable works. Without this development the writing of Dante's *Divina Commedia* in early 14th-century Tuscany or Chaucer's poetry in England at the end of that century would have failed to command attention.

Right The warden, fellows and scholars of Winchester College from the *Brevis Chronica*, written in 1463 and now at New College, Oxford. This drawing shows the warden and company of the school, with the buildings in the background, including the original belfry taken down in 1474. While the company is assembled, two commoners practice tilting in the school yard, symbolizing the formal parade of respect and the irrepressible sporting spirit behind.

Right Hugh of St Victor teaching. Hugh was born and educated in Germany. He entered the important reforming college of canons at St Victor, Paris, in 1116 and became prior in 1133. His works had a profound influence on the development of scholastic thought, and he was in his lifetime a great teacher before the establishment of the university. This St Alban's picture of him at his cathedra suitably indicates how the monasteries were still in the forefront of learning in the 12th century.

Left Nicholas of Lyra (1270–1349), a Franciscan from Normandy who taught at Paris, was the most authoritative biblical scholar of the later Middle Ages. This 15th-century illumination presents him conventionally lecturing from his cathedra in a university *aula*.

Medieval masters
The medieval educated world
formally acknowledged four
Latin doctors of the church:
Ambrose, Jerome, Augustine and
Pope Gregory I. Of these,
Augustine (*above*), bishop of
Hippo Regius, had far and away
the most powerful and critical
intelligence. The range of his
learning in every branch of it in
Latin, religious and profane,
together with the rationality of
his thought and the eloquence of
his writing, secured respect and
gratitude throughout the west.
The profundity of his meditation
on the Christian revelation in the
light of the most sophisticated
learning of the ancient world
opened a new intellectual era.
The medieval enthusiasm for his
teaching was not the result of
declining intellectual standards,
but the modest continuation of
the approval he had secured in
his own lifetime. No other person
of antiquity wrote more vividly
about the human predicament;
for no previous writer had his
own ''personality'' been such a
matter of interest; no medieval
teacher could hope to equal his
achievement.

With the revival of interest in
logic, however, came the
realization of the great intellect
of Aristotle (*top*). This was a new
discovery, because in the ancient
world his reputation had been
constantly overshadowed by
that of Plato. Unlike Augustine,
Aristotle won no disciples by his
religious insights. He conquered
by purely intellectual brilliance.
The fascination he then began to
exercise over western minds has
not faltered since the 12th
century. Most of his writings
were not even easily accessible.
They had to be hunted down and
then translated from Greek or
Arabic, together with the Arabic
commentaries, without which he
seemed unintelligible. The
difficulties of assimilating his
strange ideas, from such a
contaminated source as Islam,
must reinforce our amazement
that Aristotle, not merely as
logician, but as scientist and
metaphysician, became the
teacher of those who know.

151

Science and Medicine

The scientific and medical knowledge of the ancient world was preserved at Constantinople and other cities of the east, from where it was acquired by the Muslims. Islam stretched from Spain to India and Muslim science was patronized in the courts of great rulers and cultivated in the cities between Seville and Khwarizm. The mathematical knowledge of India was brought into contact with the culture of the Mediterranean and the diversity of the lands of Islam played some part in stimulating inquiry. Islam, unlike the Greek empire, was normally without one dominant cultural capital. It was important for its vitality at a cultural level that men of learning flourished in many cities. Muslim contributions to the advances of scientific learning notably improved on the details of observation and characteristically concentrated on the acquisition of comprehensive, even encyclopedic, information rather than on theory. After the first great phase of assimilating non-Islamic knowledge under the Abbasid caliphs in the 9th century, pious Muslims were soon inevitably engaged in exploring the philosophical implications for their religion of all this alien information. This encouraged on the one hand a religious revival and on the other a new philosophical attitude and neither helped to encourage fresh scientific thought. Muslims, like their contemporaries in the Christian world, found the answers to their most difficult questions in holy books or from the cogitations of the wise; they did not believe that probing further the curiosities of nature would yield more than entertaining but meaningless anecdotes.

The ancient world had worked out enough knowledge of the natural world for it to conduct daily life with sufficient technical accomplishments and its major preoccupations had become political and spiritual. Its technical knowledge was deposited in some great libraries, like that of Alexandria, and in some special "schools," but it never became part of the ordinary school curriculum. After the fall of the Roman empire such knowledge was transmitted to subsequent generations by handbooks like those written by Boethius and in such schools as survived, like those of the monasteries. The breakdown of the Roman political organization of the west enormously simplified the process of administration, so that formal education for men in ruling positions became unnecessary. Only churchmen cared for exact knowledge of measurement and astronomy, not for scientific purposes, but to know when to celebrate liturgical feasts at the proper time. With the passing of the centuries, a new educational pattern acquired status and changing it became difficult. A few isolated scholars in the west, figures who acquired the reputation of magicians, like Gerbert, took pains to learn long-neglected subjects. In the 12th century more contact with Muslims, particularly in Spain and Sicily, enabled a greater number of enterprising scholars to go there and learn, and sometimes to translate what they found. Not before the 13th century did the west too begin to measure the full effects of all this knowledge for traditionally received truths. The new interest in the natural world probably brought certain practical advantages rather quickly – the use of the magnetic needle for navigation, the invention of spectacles from the new learning about optics – but for the most part the new learning appeared to be mainly a challenge to the established truths of revelation. Attempts to reconcile them, like that of Thomas

Right Astrolabes are instruments for making observations of the heavenly bodies, for measuring distances or heights, as of buildings, for ascertaining latitudes and determining time. The instrument was described by a 6th-century Greek from Alexandria, but the required knowledge probably came from Babylonian astronomy. Muslim scholars had access to the whole learning of the east and the oldest surviving astrolabes were made in 10th-century Islam. The Muslims made larger and better instruments than before but effected no real improvements on the methods of observation. Each instrument had to be designed for use in the latitudes of a particular place on the assumption that the vernal equinox occurs at a particular time. Such instruments were used for astronomical (and astrological) purposes and not applied in navigation before the late 15th century. This one was made in Toledo in 1068.

This book, the *Tacuinum Sanitatis*, offering tables of health, was devised by the Christian physician of Baghdad, Abul Hasan al-Mukhtar ibn-Butlan (died 1063), whose name was latinized as Elluchasem Elimithar. Several illustrated Latin versions were made of it in Italy in the 14th century when the recurrence of plague had stirred interest in preventative medicine. This 11th-century summary of medical knowledge appeared to offer precise, systematic, dependable and intelligible information for laymen concerned about their health. The method of the handbook may be judged from its captions for the squash (*left*): "Its nature is cold and wet; it is at its best when fresh and green; it is suitable for quenching thirst; the disadvantage is to act as a strong purgative; this can be counteracted by applying salt water and mustard; thus it provides a moderate cold refreshment, particularly suited for choleric temperaments, for the young, in summer, in all regions, especially in the south."

Aquinas, did not then command respect, still less wide acceptance. Some improvements were made in observations; some individuals persevered with these new studies. As a whole, however, they did not commend themselves, and the "scientific revolution" did not occur until the 17th century.

The ancient interest in astronomy was the basis of understanding the nature of the earth and its place in the universe, but at a less theoretical level it had practical advantages for sailors and farmers who were without formal education. Such knowledge was passed to other generations without schooling, even among the barbarian peoples of the north, who were less favored than the peoples of the Mediterranean for observing the heavens. Mingled with this information there went a fair amount of popular lore, not subjected to the intellectual scrutiny of teachers but accepted like other superstitions for a variety of reasons good and bad. The ancients had also accepted spurious learning as part of their natural science and men in the Middle Ages were no less capable than earlier generations of carrying on familiar occupations. They could, for example, cross the North Sea and colonize new lands without formal education, unhampered by superstitions. The simplicity of their conditions of life should not mislead us into thinking of them as primitive peoples confined to the only habitat that they knew how to cope with.

The folklore of the Middle Ages is an elusive subject, because the main evidence for it comes from books which are necessarily written by those who have at least the smatterings of an education based on quite different foundations. Thus the medical lore of the English before the conquest, as found in manuscripts, comprises not only herbal recipes,

The illustrations to the *Tacuinum Sanitatis* may have been sometimes intended, as in the manner of herbals, to help with the identification of plants. For the most part, however, they are as vapid as the text itself. As evidence of popular taste, both scientific and artistic, they remain invaluable, despite their weaknesses. The dull domestic scenes, like the one (*far left*) illustrating the properties of hot water, and the conventional personifications, for example of the west wind (*left*), show that artists worked from exemplars without enthusiasm for adding personal touches. The butcher's shop (*right*), which illustrates the virtues of veal, looks like a tableau from a stage show. Such scenes amount to medieval genre painting. As such they extend our perception of daily life in the Middle Ages.

Below The surgeon's clinic, from a 15th-century illustrated text of Guy de Chauliac's *Chirurgia*. Guy was one of the most famous 14th-century surgeons and this version of his work suggests that it was being edited to make it more useful for general practitioners. The doctor is shown with his textbook propped up in front of him, dealing with a queue of patients with different ulcers, of the arm, eye and crotch. The sufferers point towards their afflictions and anticipate relief.

Bottom This drawing from a manuscript of the Pseudo-Dioscorides herbal, made in the 12th century, is in a recognizably animated English style and shows summary treatment of cataract of the eye. Such drawings give a vivid, but rather misleading, impression of contemporary medical practice, since they appear to have been originally designed as light relief to this text.

drawing upon a knowledge of Mediterranean plants found in monastic gardens, but also charms combining references to deities of different religions. This tissue of nonsense, as we see it, makes early medieval medicine more alien to us than pure ignorance of it would do. It is necessary to realize that medicine itself was then a different kind of art and not to compare the chemistry and the patter of the leeches with their modern counterparts.

It is of course also possible that the sicknesses needing the services of leeches were also different, for the strains put on men's physical strength could be greater than those of modern societies and the moral and psychic efforts of medieval "athletes" would have created general assumptions about sanity and health very different from our own. The fact that the majority of the population lived in the country, that towns were small and communications between them much reduced meant that there must have been much less opportunity for the epidemic spread of contagious diseases, like that which struck Constantinople and the places in touch with it in 542. Even in the country men suffer illnesses and accidents; on a frugal diet they might suffer from nutritional deficiencies. How these troubles were cured we do not know, but there is every reason to believe that the more familiar afflictions were alleviated with tolerable success and the rest endured. Infant mortality was no doubt high, but not necessarily as high as that found in later industrial populations. Calamities, as they struck, were accepted as divine punishments. Since cures could not therefore be expected from leeches, there was no point in anyone studying diseases, observing symptoms or even describing the malady in any detail. The imprecise language employed by medieval chroniclers when referring to ailments shows that no special attention was given to medical description and this makes it difficult for writers to be very precise now about the nature of the problems. Popular medicine still uses the term "influenza," derived from a time when the influences of the atmosphere could be considered the cause of infections and medical history is often still content to speak of the Black Death in quasi-apocalyptic terms, instead of soberly assessing the plague scientifically.

The plague arrived in Europe from Asia in the autumn of 1347 and spread over the continent, most rapidly disseminated, it would seem, by contacts effected initially through shipping. The plague is clinically known to be incidentally transmitted to humans by fleas normally parasitic on the black rat, an animal itself normally found nesting in the roofs of timber houses. These facts now known were not observed by men in the 14th century who had no idea how the disease spread or how it could be averted. But from what they did report, some account of the epidemic is now possible. Its origin in Asia, where it was endemic, emphasizes how much contact western Europe had established there by

1347. A century earlier no western Europeans had penetrated beyond the Muslim Fertile Crescent; even 50 years before, Marco Polo had barely returned to Venice from fabulous Cathay. Second, the disease, transmitted presumably by infected rats on Genoese galleys from the Crimea, could only have spread by the fleas infecting the rats of the coastal shipping of Europe, and then the rats of the towns and the barges or wagons that led off into the countryside, where little by little its effects petered out. By 1347–50 there were few parts of Europe not plugged in somewhere to the commercial network of towns and shipping. A century earlier no epidemic of this kind could have been spread in this way.

It is also true that a century earlier there would not have been enough medical knowledge available to describe the disease closely. Experts could do nothing to cure or explain the plague, but they could observe it, they tried to provide theories

Below This 13th-century manuscript contains 96 medical illustrations. Those shown here relate to the text of Roger of Salerno's *Chirurgia* (c. 1170) which diffused the medical learning of Salerno through western Europe. The surgeon, consistently shown in a long sleeveless outer robe and coif to emphasize his professional status, examines diseased patients displaying their afflictions. These appear to be disorders of the bowel, the thigh, the groin, the knee, the feet and the leg. Such pictures were probably copied from one manuscript to another; their practical function is limited, providing a crude indication of the book's subject matter; and since they have no captions, they need to be explained by reference to the text. Their chief historical value is their evidence for the growing authority of doctors as worthy of respect for their learning in every aspect of health.

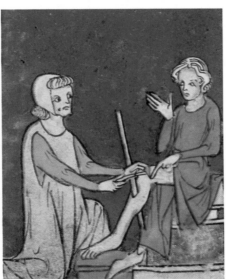

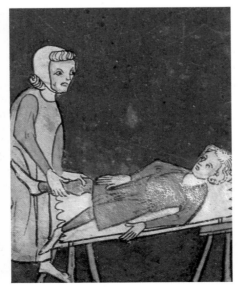

about it, and, above all, the public authorities in some places at least tried to deal with it as a matter of public order. It is the first evidence we have of a new public awareness of disease. The high mortality rate and the apparently indiscriminate way it affected rich and poor, old and young, good and bad, also shook some men's confidence in the theory that it was a divine scourge. In many ways therefore the plague of the mid-14th century opened up a new period. Until the 12th century the study of medicine had been confined in western Europe to the schools of Salerno. Then it began to establish itself in the university towns and, from there, graduates (doctors) were taken on as personal advisers to rulers about health, as their counterparts in Islam served patrons there. Others began to form guilds of association for their art.

Independently of medicine, the provision of hospitals for the care of the sick had also multiplied in Europe since the 12th century. Earlier the monasteries had maintained infirmaries for their brethren. Not until the 12th century do towns appear to have been sufficiently large to need special hospices for the care of the sick, though the foundation of houses for lepers goes back long before. When King Louis VIII of France issued regulations for leper hospitals in 1226, there were assumed to be about 2000 of them in the kingdom. However, given ignorance of the nature of the disease and imprecision about observations and indeed of definitions, contemporaries probably used leprosy quite unconsciously to cover a variety of ailments. For several centuries it appears to have been a considerable scourge and to have died away mysteriously in the 14th century. But the provision of hospitals for special purposes did not disappear. Louis IX of France, for example, founded a hospital for the blind; another for orphans was founded in 1326. Another probable improvement in public hygiene was also provided by the public bath-houses, which were popular from the 13th century. There were also famous spas and it was the uninhibited indulgence in the pleasures of mixed bathing and its concomitants that eventually caused the authorities to close down these institutions.

On a more gruesome note, it should perhaps be also emphasized that, with the new academic interest in medicine and anatomy, there came also the practice of human dissection, perhaps encouraged initially by the interest shown by lawyers in autopsies and their encouragement of it by their university colleagues. Though the practice was maintained from the 14th century, it was not obvious that any great improvements in anatomical knowledge could automatically flow from it, since the dissector did no more than identify parts described in the medical books. There was no systematic attempt made to compile information for the purpose of providing alternative explanations to those offered by the standard authorities.

RURAL SOCIETY

Rural history over the extent of Europe for more than a thousand years is concerned with the exploitation of each locality by a settled population. Since this everywhere grew at least as well as local resources permitted, given the contemporary level of technical skill, in general terms it is a history of success in dominating the environment. The primary importance of each individual unit of settlement in achieving this result was accentuated by three factors operating over most of the period: (1) the absence of any single political authority capable of imposing economic policies, or even a single monetary system, not merely at the continental level, but even over what are now territories the size of nations; (2) the fact that the rural economy was not burdened with a tax system for the support of civil government and military expenditure – the burden of tax, when it fell at all (as it did with church tithes), was local, usually indirect and frequently administered laxly; (3) the lack of international commerce in the necessities of life before the 13th century, so that each locality had to be more or less self-sufficient. Some favored sites lived well; others eked out a precarious existence. In these conditions the rural economy did not have to suffer more than the disasters of nature and the disorder brought by invaders. It was not set high standards of productivity by government or great luxury-loving landlords. Over the centuries it encroached upon the uncultivated lands of Europe, woodland, marsh and mountain, bringing them into cultivation, developing regional specializations of products that in turn made possible the resumption of trade in such basic supplies as wine, wool, salt and even grain. Many modern historians, alerted by the demographic problems of the contemporary world, suspect that the populations of medieval Europe in some places even exceeded the limits of local resources. By the early 14th century the long period of expansion appears to have been abruptly checked by famines and disease and followed by one of economic depression lasting for more than a century. This theory seems excessively pessimistic. The difficulties encountered in the few mainly urban regions can more plausibly be explained in terms of the unprecedented and unpredictable impact of revived commerce on both towns and countryside. The rural economy had to adapt to new conditions, both by supplying the large towns with food and raw materials and at the same time by accepting new industries.

The undoubted importance of the separate localities in this study makes the patchy nature of the historical records for each place an insurmountable difficulty for understanding the economy. Knowledge depends to a great extent on the records of the great owners of estates, especially monasteries and cathedrals, kings and great lords, whose households comprised stewards able to supervise record keeping, often in their own interest. Little is known about the many small lordships or about the conditions of work in the field, except in terms of their legal obligations to their lords, where they existed. The closer we get to the actual problems of cultivating the land, the fewer the records become. Rather than emphasize the burdens described in 13th-century texts, it is desirable to remember that in many parts of Europe settlers were being attracted to the cultivation of new lands taken from the Muslims or in eastern Europe by the offer of favorable terms; this inevitably had implications elsewhere. How far immigrants traveled it is impossible to say, but no region constituted an isolated unit. Conditions and definitions of agricultural labor differed widely from one region to another and considerable social distinctions operated within a single settlement. There was no uniformity about medieval serfdom, except that it was not comparable to ancient slavery. In some parts of Europe, particularly on the poorer soils, the land was enclosed and cultivated by individual families. To a great extent, however, agriculture required the cooperation of a large work force, if the better lands were to be brought under the plow. This involved village settlements, open fields cultivated in strips, regularly assigned through village communities; the latter had also to protect the fields and animals from thieves, marauders and scoundrels. These communities were not made up of social equals. From the first they often had lords, including churches, in whose name their courts were managed. But to what extent could lords or their stewards actually direct the village economy? The probability is that local management prevailed. Lords disposed of no superior technical resources or knowledge and were not prepared to invest more capital or create new outlets for produce, as later agrarian reformers could do. At best, lords hoped to improve their position by better account keeping or stricter enforcement of labor dues. Such devices appeared late and were not effective or long lasting. The English evidence is among the best for Europe and shows that in the 14th century many lords gave up direct management in return for leasing land to farmers. The actual working conditions in agriculture and village life left the cultivators with a great deal of initiative. Their tenures were protected by custom and they could not easily be turned out. Evicting one tenant to replace him with another on the same terms served no purpose. Some laborers were paid by the day, but since such landless men could seek better terms in the towns if they were dissatisfied, money payments prove only that the country had become involved in the new money economy. The crucial fact is that throughout the Middle Ages there was a chronic shortage of labor.

Left The month of March in *Les Très Riches Heures du duc de Berry*, painted by the Limburg brothers, 1411–16. Country pursuits not infrequently appear in medieval drawings, particularly in representations of the labors of the month. Not until the 15th century did artists become interested in showing a number of people working simultaneously at the principal medieval industry – agriculture.

The Social Structure

Bottom This remarkable manuscript illustrates the magnificent displays put on at 15th-century tournaments for the *bon roi René*, one of the great French patrons of the mid-15th century. The artists were employed both for staging the ceremonies and for recording them. The display of arms is sufficiently spectacular to attract even a feminine audience. The picture incidentally enables us to appreciate the lavishness of contemporary fashions, in civil and military dress. The officials of the tournament, in the center, appropriately wear dignified dress of slightly old-fashioned appearance.

Until the 12th century the political framework of medieval Europe was still derived from the Roman empire. Effective power was exercised on the extremities of the continent by kings in the barbarian manner and everywhere locally by the greatest landowners, who disposed of what military strength there was. Some of these were privileged monasteries or bishops; others were laymen. If they were clergy, they acquired, by formal education and zeal for their calling, other values than those of the military aristocracies they were born into, but all of them shared certain characteristics by virtue of their families. Lay nobles received no formal education, so they owed to their background and their early upbringing the development of their basic outlook. Their indifference to books makes it difficult to study this elusive but important topic. In the 12th century, when an aristocratic vernacular literature did appear, it influenced this upbringing by encouraging the adoption of a new courtly behavior. Apart from this, however, it probably also perpetuated other, traditional values that elude historical scrutiny at any earlier phase.

Barbarian society seems from the first to have been divided into distinct social grades, fixing different values for individual men in each grade, presumably according to their estimated importance in war. A nobleman was many times more valuable than a mere freeman. Slaves, who had no right to bear arms, had still less value. The significance of a man's status in battle proves the importance of warfare in these early societies. During the medieval period there were rapid and radical changes in the manner of fighting, first to deploy cavalry forces, and then at the end to exploit the possibilities of cannon and pikemen. Adjustments were made in the social order, but belief in the importance of social rank was not itself shaken.

The nobility were committed to life in the country, on their own estates or on those of their connections. By inheritance, marriage or patronage they added to their estates and then moved from one to another across the lands of their neighbors, to meet their dependants, consume their produce and enjoy the amenities. The contacts they made with their peers brought them favorable marriages. They held their estates of many different lords. The exclusive ties of kingship and nationhood they resented as curbs on their rights.

By the 12th century the nobles of Europe had to learn how to command more than purely local respect. They had to cope with clerical ideals that demanded autonomy for clergy. Towns sought legal independence. Kings were learning about their rights and duties from educated clerks. The nobility had perforce to formulate their own code of chivalry in an idealistic way. They took a new pride in the display of their noble ancestries by heraldic devices. From the educated they learned how to formulate their beliefs in vernacular poetry; from the merchants they acquired domestic luxuries and

Below Chess was known in western Europe at least from the 11th century, but in the later Middle Ages less cerebral indoor games became popular. On this backgammon board the player is reminded during the winter months of more energetic sports, fighting with swords and staves. No social distinction is implied by these panels and the fine quality of the board permits us to assume that the nobility appreciated these sports without prejudice.

Below right This enamel was made to commemorate a great 12th-century soldier, Geoffrey of Anjou. He is said to have applied his study of the Roman text of war by Vegetius to the capture of castles. The ceremony of his own entry into knighthood in 1128 is one of the earliest known in detail. Geoffrey, who died about 40 years of age, is hailed here as the prince whose sword dispersed brigands and gave peace to the churches.

clothing that marked their social eminence. If anything, education and the multiplication of chattels accentuated the distinction of their class. Individuals might move up the social ladder, but the respect due to nobility did not waver. The clergy stressed that moral worth should count for more than noble birth, but they had little success in undermining the belief that some men were socially superior to others. The clerical emphasis on the equality of all men as sinners ought also to have had implications for the afterlife, but the nobility used their advantages in this one to build themselves lavish tombs and endow chantries where priests said masses for the repose of their noble souls. Modern industrial society has made it almost impossible to realize to what degree social gradations once seemed natural and indeed indispensable for social order. Society in this period suffered not so much from social distinctions as from the intense parochialism of life. In this context lordship was not resented. It represented the preservation of decent order in men's affairs, an effective means of securing patronage and support for every kind of local enterprise, from the decoration of churches to the education of a promising lad in the village. Employment in the lord's service gave advantages unknown in modern commerce and industry. Those who disputed his role were not admired as fighters for freedom but rejected as social outcasts.

Hunting
and Fishing

Restricting access to game, designating reserved areas, protecting valued beasts from indiscriminate slaughter already in the Middle Ages signaled the extent to which human settlements had encroached on the wild. Access was only limited in countries of dense settlement and little unproductive land, such as England. It was not a problem in underpopulated lands like Spain or eastern Europe. Beyond the cultivated zone lay the primeval woodlands of northern Europe, offering apparently inexhaustible supplies of many raw materials including timber itself. Pigs were driven there to fatten up in the summer. Villagers collected such food as berries and honey there. They killed beasts and found the materials for industries like tanning, ironworks,

soap and glass making. Deep within were the haunts of charcoal burners and hermits. The woods harbored wild and dangerous animals, like wolves and bears. Medieval villagers did not buy meat from the butcher: hunting was the principal source. When kings reserved the noble deer for their own sport and table, other animals and birds fell to the arrows and snares of humbler folk. Fish were no less at the mercy of the rising populations. At sea, merchant fortunes were made by the catching of herring and the preparation of salted and smoked fish. Towards the Arctic, sailors hunted for sealskins and walrus ivory. Inland, fish were taken in rivers and fishponds specially stocked on great estates. Gradually the measureless reserves began to show signs of depletion. Efforts had to be made to reorganize the economy, raise animals for meat, use stone instead of timber and price hunting out of everyman's reach. So hunting became more discriminating, more a sport reserved for those who cultivated its rituals and a new kind of relationship between men and beasts. It ceased to be the normal counterpart to rural society.

Left Birds from the Pepys sketchbook of c. 1380/90. This manuscript is the only surviving patternbook from an English medieval artist's workshop. A great many subjects (though not buildings) are found in it, but it is most remarkable for eight pages crowded with bird pictures, some of them labeled, as here the bullfinch. More species are shown than in any earlier manuscript, but they are not drawn from life, since identical poses, such as the central image of the hawk awkwardly catching a drake shown here, can be traced in earlier English manuscripts. This comprehensive collection of designs proves not scientific awareness, but the variety of subjects needed by designers, particularly of embroideries and wood carving, in the late Middle Ages.

Gaston Fébus, count of Foix (1343–91), began his *Livre de la chasse* in 1387, writing it in French for his friend Philip, duke of Burgundy. It is the finest and most technical treatise on hunting composed in the Middle Ages, written at a time when aristocratic appreciation of the refinements of hunting was reaching its apogee. The text reveals the author's systematic organization of his lifelong experience of hunting and his care for his different hunting dogs. His preferences are for stag and boar hunts (*above and far left*) (green and gray liveries respectively), but he condescends to deal even with traps and the taking of hares and foxes (*near left*). The matter of refreshment is not forgotten (*center left*), but the final pleasures of the day were the sluice down and retiring to a comfortable bed.

161

THE ARTS

Until the Italian Renaissance no distinction was drawn between fine and applied arts, or indeed between arts and crafts, or arts and sciences. The skills involved in making shoes or carving wood or building churches were all acquired by "crafty" men without reference to book learning, so the "educated" confined themselves to matters intellectual and barely referred in writing to the artifacts around them. The useful and ornamental objects that furnished their lives and enhanced their visual pleasures changed according to fashion and no objects were treasured in museums or collections for their intrinsic value. As late as 1508 Julius II swept away the paintings recently made in the Vatican *stanze* to have them redecorated by Raphael. After his time Raphael's work has been jealously preserved as Art.

To do justice to medieval art should not mean creating an imaginary museum to house treasured objects, but restoring them in imagination to their proper habitat — statuary to cathedral niches, triptychs to their altars, reliquaries to their shrines — to treat them, that is, not as works of art at all. Their makers worked to commissions and none of them that we know of preferred to live in poverty for art's sake. There was then no glamor about art, and craftsmen expected to please, working for the best money and the noblest patrons who crossed their paths. The criteria of expertise and ingenuity were clearly defined and patrons were therefore not deceived by charlatans. When conditions of life generally were restricted, the talents of craftsmen might win them only local renown, but by the 12th century architects, sculptors and even painters could certainly travel far on business.

However ingenious the craftsman, he owed his savoir faire to his teachers in the craft, and the more cunning the learning, the more canny the craft to reserve its secrets for members of the fraternity. Artists were not loners, but clubbable men. If the fame of one man won him commissions, the larger projects were expected to provide work for his whole workshop, whether it were building a cathedral or painting its interior. The master mason had to be entrepreneur as well as architect. To modern connoisseurs it may come naturally to contemplate painting, sculpture and buildings as separate art forms. In the Middle Ages the discrete art unit was the church itself, enriched by all three, and for most men the church in their own place was the only "museum of art" they ever saw. They did not compare one painting with another but saw each one in relation to the other cult objects, not assessing them as the products of human skills, but rather valuing them as visible representations of the holy mysteries they could not themselves imagine.

The *Maestà*, painted by Duccio for Siena cathedral in 1308–10, was rapturously received by the citizens who installed it and has in this century won growing appreciation, particularly since its restoration. Both sides of the altarpiece were painted. Among scenes relating to the Resurrection, Christ here shows himself to Mary in the garden.

Architecture

When Constantine renewed the empire, in a typically antique manner he provided it with a new capital city, Constantinople, built to outshine Rome. For more than a thousand years this city gloriously demonstrated the meaning of Roman civilization. No city in the west ever came near to rivaling it. Barbarian rulers there, even if they made use of Roman cities, never planned or built on the grand scale. New forts and fortresses were often outposts on the margins of their power, erected to secure slices of territory, not to radiate splendor. Once they had given up migration and "settled down," the rulers and great men of the barbarians remained peripatetic, moving across their lands, from one estate to another, rarely resident for long in one place. The more enterprising spent the summer season campaigning and knew their tents better than their palaces. Henry III is the first English king known to have concerned himself with the comfort and decoration of his castles; his successors, however, continued to be more active in the field and therefore less concerned about acquiring beautiful fixed residences. At the other end of the social scale there was a comparable indifference to building durable habitations. Building in timber, or more cheaply still with half-timber frames filled with wattle and daub, medieval villagers, living close together, must have frequently experienced the destructive force of fire. Rebuilding, whatever use was made of professional craftsmen, also certainly involved the cooperation of neighbors. Housing had to be simple and easily constructed. It was more than a house. It had to provide protection against marauders, store the householder's valuables, including his supplies of grain and food, and harbor his animals in winter. For centuries ordinary housing must have been rudimentary by modern expectations and architecture seems hardly an appropriate term in this context. When in the 13th century great castles were built of stone in western Europe, military engineers became responsible for leveling a site and planning the construction of these permanent camps. Engineering had likewise been the skill required by Justinian for his church of Holy Wisdom in Constantinople, the most beautiful building of the whole Middle Ages.

Building to last was more properly the response to the human encounter with eternity. Christian buildings in the Middle Ages served at least three different religious purposes. Before Constantine the needs of worshipers had been met by communities from their own resources and conformed therefore to no model. With the emperor's conversion the public authority itself began to provide magnificent basilicas for general assembly and appropriate ceremony. The Lateran basilica in Rome was capable of accommodating thousands of Christians together. Such churches were bound to influence later generations when they came to build congregational churches of smaller dimensions. Churches, not intended for regular use in the same way, were also,

however, erected over the shrines of the saints or "holy places." Some of these remained small, while others, if the cult became famous, had to be enlarged. If such places became the seats of bishops or monks, regular liturgical worship made fresh demands on the building. The churches of Rome and the Holy Land tended to be adopted as models for western churches looking for distinguished precedents. Barbarians of the north, without native skills in stone building, had anyway to look south initially for the craftsmen themselves, once the art of monumental building had been lost in the north.

With the Carolingian renaissance a great effort may have been made to construct again on an imperial scale for the richer churches of the empire. Modeled on those of Rome, the term "Romanesque" has come into use to describe them. The major technical problem was the dressing of the stone. Their massive structures reveal the anxiety of the masons to build securely; the heaviness was relieved by decorating friezes and capitals. As they acquired confidence, the masons began to modify the construction, aiming to build higher and lighter and yet with enough strength for the pillars to bear the weight of stone vaults. In the north the churches desired greater windows to admit more light to God's house. A new architectural style, "Gothic," was devised to meet these demands. Stone masons, who succeeded in solving the technical problems involved, took the style from its original home in France to other parts of Latin Christendom, where it acquired local "national" characteristics.

Left The church of Holy Wisdom (St Sophia), Constantinople, built by Justinian and engineered by Anthemius of Tralles and Isidore of Miletus, replaced an earlier church on the same site and was completed in five years (532–37). Massive but rather unimpressive from the outside, the church has since its completion aroused admiration and wonder in everyone who enters it. The harmony of its proportions and the dazzling beauty of its ornamentation are completed by the marvel of its dome, 31 meters across. In the medieval period this church was the most impressive in the whole of Christendom.

The distribution of Gothic architecture and universities
More blatantly than the other maps, such a presentation of late medieval culture in map form betrays the bias of modern aesthetic judgments. Cathedral churches erected all over Europe to embody the ideal of the age for every Christian community were not then judged primarily as works of art but as public buildings dedicated to God. To highlight Gothic masterpieces and pass over other churches serving the same ideals reflects a novel modern interest, not a contemporary concern. Masons built where they received commissions. The religious life in older buildings could have been no less ardent than in new ones. The map should not be interpreted to signify the strength of religious conviction in the Gothic age.

With intellectual centers the criteria used are slightly more acceptable. The international reputations of such schools as Paris or Bologna attracted students from all over Europe. When the number of universities was increased, this did not completely change, for some smaller universities had very local reputations. In 15th-century Italy intellectual activity was far from being a monopoly of universities. Princely courts and republican officials attracted scholars, artists and inventors. The courts of all great medieval rulers from the time of Charlemagne should be included among centers of contemporary intellectual inquiry. The limitations of a map in illustrating places of cultural activity must be allowed for. To dispense with all allusion to such matters would create even greater misapprehension. No map of Europe could ever be drawn on a sufficiently large scale to show every place where medieval men left evidence of their mental and spiritual achievements.

Cathedral Building

The Gothic builders of the 12th century were the first men to discover how to construct great buildings whose stability depended not upon the thickness of their walls, but upon knowing how to transmit the thrust through localized parts of the structure, the ribs and buttresses that formed its skeleton. The result was a dynamically stable architecture capable of building to unprecedented heights, yet giving an impression of wonderful grace and luminosity. The craftsmen who knew the secrets of construction were much sought after. For about a century, beginning in the heart of the French kingdom, the masons explored the possibilities of their discovery and moved from place to place on demand as enthusiasm for this new "style" captured the imagination. Then the skills became sufficiently familiar and teachable for every part of Latin Christendom to have its resident masons. But until then the advance of any one building appears to have been in the hands of itinerant workmen. A master mason with about 30 senior workmen took over responsibility for a building season when the necessary funds were available. The master mason designed the templates for the stone masons. Locals were used for the rough jobs including cartage. The slow-setting mortar eventually imposed a necessary cessation of building, particularly on arches and vaults, before the centering could be removed and new loads placed. At this point the mason was free to take his team elsewhere. The peculiar technical circumstances and the economically favorable moments must have had unsettling social effects on these sites, alternately busy and static. The excitements they generated have been shared by later generations but the devotions of historians to these wonderful buildings have left many mysteries unresolved.

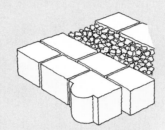

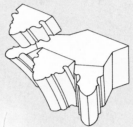

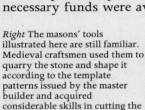

Right The masons' tools illustrated here are still familiar. Medieval craftsmen used them to quarry the stone and shape it according to the template patterns issued by the master builder and acquired considerable skills in cutting the hardest stone with the greatest precision.

Above Romanesque concern for stability required the construction of massive walls, with an inner core of rubble. In Gothic, the weight of the building rests not on the walls but on the piers and buttresses. These had to be constructed of precisely cut strokes, exactly joined. The illustration shows the intricate cuts required for the stones that bore all the stresses as they were transmitted to the columns of the nave.

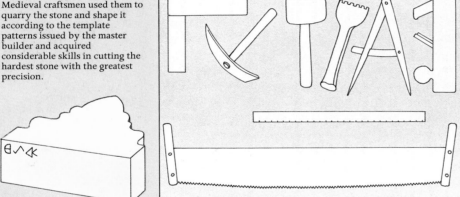

Above Masons' marks to indicate which mason cut the stones, though of ancient origin, occur frequently in late medieval times. They appear to have been cut in connection with the payment of piecework; for the best-dressed stones, cut by masons with regular contracts, often lack them.

Below The great blocks of stone, when cut, had to be transported and then hoisted from the site into their precise position. Without the use of machinery this feat would have been impossible even for gangs of slave labor, which were anyway not available. This machinery, of which two of the most important pieces were the winch and the tread wheel, appears to be new in the 12th century and is frequently shown in illustrated manuscripts.

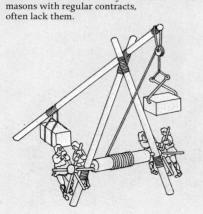

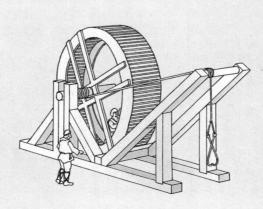

Left Flying buttresses first appeared in Paris and Reims about 1175 and Chartres was the first building wholly designed after that (1194) which could take their potential into account. If they were to be used to bear the thrust of the high vault, the galleries could be eliminated, the aisles roofed immediately over their vaults and great clerestory windows inserted at a lower level to flood the building with light. The weight of the masonry having been transferred to the buttresses outside, the interior was thus transformed into the luminous house of God, and the whole resembled a tremendous tent (*tabernaculum*) pegged firmly to the ground.

Below This cutaway drawing has been devised to give an idea of the structural scheme of a great Gothic church. Men with various degrees and kinds of skill were involved in a common enterprise which gave the master mason and carpenter charge of one of the largest industrial enterprises then known.

Below The combined talents of carpenter and mason were required for the vaulting operation, though the dismantling of the carpenter's contribution leaves the glory to the masons alone. The vault, as seen from below, was in construction masked by the wooden structure called centering which provided a frame for setting the rib stones. They were locked together by the keystone as it was lowered exactly into place at the highest point of the arch. When the mortar was fully set, the supports could be removed, and the vault revealed for general admiration below.

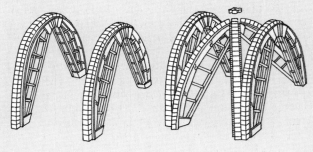

Below When the new cathedral at Chartres was planned, towers at the transept portals, flanking the choir and over the crossing were intended to complement the two surviving at the west end. This would have given the cathedral nine in all, a mystic number known to have been important at Chartres. More than a quarter of a century later the plan was step by step abandoned. The result is the dramatic form known today.

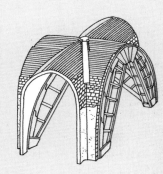

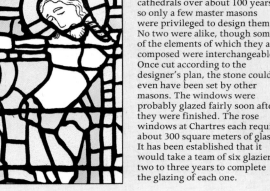

Left About 20 rose windows were installed in French cathedrals over about 100 years, so only a few master masons were privileged to design them. No two were alike, though some of the elements of which they are composed were interchangeable. Once cut according to the designer's plan, the stone could even have been set by other masons. The windows were probably glazed fairly soon after they were finished. The rose windows at Chartres each require about 300 square meters of glass. It has been established that it would take a team of six glaziers two to three years to complete the glazing of each one.

167

Orvieto

The decision to build a new cathedral at Orvieto was made in 1284 and work began in 1290. Two large drawings survive to show the preliminary designs, which is without precedent in medieval Italy. If extra care had been taken, nevertheless by 1309 there was anxiety about the fate of the construction when the first roof beam was put up. Recourse was had to the Sienese architect Lorenzo Maitani and for the next 20 years he was in charge of the building and of the execution of the lower west front sculptural decoration. To his period belongs the building of the choir. Later the transepts were built out beyond the originally proposed rectangular form, to make a cruciform plan. The conception of the building involved the combination and reconciliation of contrasting ideas, most blatantly obvious in the use of striped travertine and basalt stonework throughout. The facade is particularly intricate with its four horizontal bands, its arched doors, its pointed gables, its sculptures, mosaics and rose window.

Right Apart from the obtrusive transepts, the exterior view shows that the cathedral was built in accordance with the plans shown on the original drawings. The dramatic contrasts of color and rhythm express the excitements generated in Italy at the time of its construction in art, as in politics.

Inset left The harmonious impression created by the interior is the result of balancing a number of different features apparently set in contrast. The great pillars, 2 meters in diameter, have their contrasting feature in the concave aisle apses. The horizontal moldings are held in check by the bays of the nave with their matching lancets in the upper story set plain in the wall.

Inset right This detail gives some idea of the varied decoration applied to the facade on the flanks of the portals, the different kinds of materials used and skills called for to create a rich and glittering effect. The twisted columns of Cosmati work are derived from Roman techniques, here combined with the newer French style of the west door.

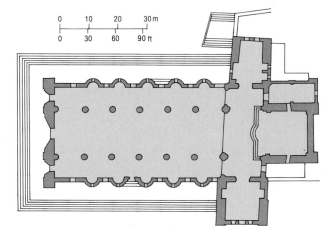

Below This creation of Eve, from the lower part of the west front, is attributed to Maitani. Analysis has revealed that these sculptures were roughed out and worked on in stages. Only some details were fully completed. Different sculptors may have been involved in the work to finish the foliage or the hair of the subjects. Two angel figures have been finished to perfection and reveal what the master's skills could do.

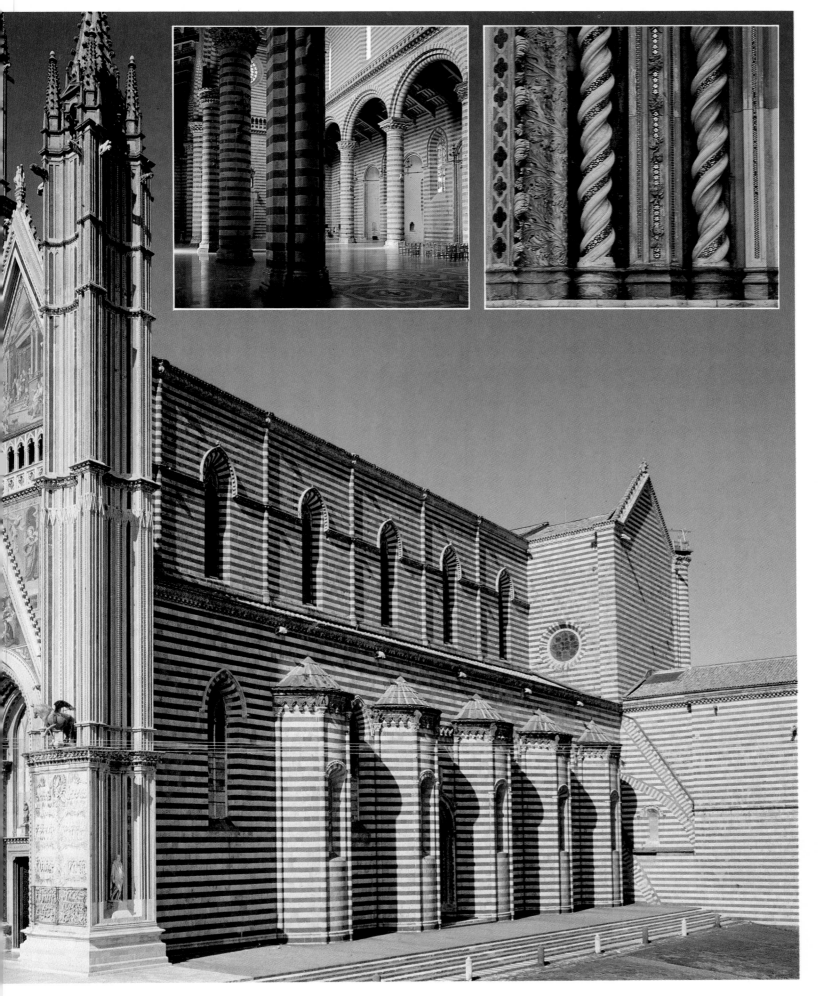

Stone Sculpture

Figure sculpture in the ancient world found its chief inspiration in the anthropomorphic religion of the Greeks. The barbarians of the west caught a glimpse of this tradition through the Christian dispensation. Such evidence of barbarian art as we have suggests that they had no original interest in representing the human figure, either in the round or in relief. By the time they encountered Christianity, the freestanding sculptures of antiquity had become limited to the public effigies of emperors. Representations of Christ and his saints are known in mosaic and carving, as in ivories, but not as figure sculpture. The Roman preference for building in brick rather than marble also reduced the scope of sculptors as decorators of buildings, though magnificent door frames prove that at least in Italy the craft of stone cutting did not disappear with the barbarian invasions. If the barbarians already had skill in carving wood, they did not quickly transfer their attentions to stone and the decrease in demand for dressed stones for building purposes probably caused a serious decline in knowledge of how to carve stone at all.

The Carolingian and Ottonian revival of interest in ancient Roman culture eventually led to a renewal of interest in stone carving. At this point there seems to have been a lead given by metal-workers, for whom modeling in wax was a necessary stage in their operations. In parts of Italy and southern France medieval sculptors studied the numerous examples of ancient sculpture lying around in their cities in order to improve their techniques. The main stimulus on the masons was, however, the extensive church-building program that by the 11th century began to provide worthy places of worship and gave masons an assured, esteemed and lucrative trade for the first time since antiquity. The organization of the craft, which gave the master mason the direction of the building sites, involved the training of young men in the mysteries of the lodge. Increasing specialization duly encouraged the most skilled to do more than cut stones and pillars. In the Romanesque period already they fashioned arcades, corbels, friezes and capitals and in some churches executed elaborate tympana that became the centerpieces of huge western portals. Massive churches originally benefited decoratively from the sculptural reliefs. By the time sculptors were ready to decorate the whole west fronts of churches, the masons had found alternative ways of building to make them light and lofty. Sculpture ceased to be an ornament. The building itself became a vast three-dimensional construction. All around outside it the stone masons installed decorative stonework, erecting niches where full-scale figure sculpture in the round was once more required. The Gothic fashion, duly exported to Italy, there provoked a renewed study of ancient Roman work, as revealed in the work of the Pisano family. From the 13th century sculptors never lacked for inspiration or commissions.

Above left Roman Augusti of the 3rd century. Each figure is in military dress, carries a globe in one hand and embraces his partner with the other. These odd dwarflike creatures give no impression of majesty, but the strength of the design conveys a message of power shared and harmony.

Above St Peter from the south door to the abbey church at Moissac, c. 1115. This figure of St Peter may be compared to an earlier one in the Moissac cloister, which proves how capable sculpture had become of suggesting tension and energy in the figure. Peter with the keys is seen trampling on the lion of the devil, but turning his head towards the Christ above him with poignant glance. The posture is strained but the force of the composition electrifying.

Left The prior's door to the cloister at Ely, 1130/40. This doorway is conceived in an ambitious manner, with arabesques of foliage, birds and beasts. In the tympanum is a beardless Christ in an aureole flanked by supporting angels. The design is derived from English manuscript drawing but its grandeur was not matched by the sculptor's technical resources.

Below The Easter candelabra of c. 1170 in San Paolo fuori le Mure, Rome. This unique candlestick, 6 meters high, is signed by its makers Nicolo d'Angelo and Pietro Vassalletto. Its base is composed of half-human and half-animal figures. At the summit a classical vase is held by a group of fantastic creatures. The column itself is divided into zones, the lower half recording scenes from the story of Christ's death and resurrection. The artists drew upon classical sarcophagi and Lombard designs for the disparate elements in the composition.

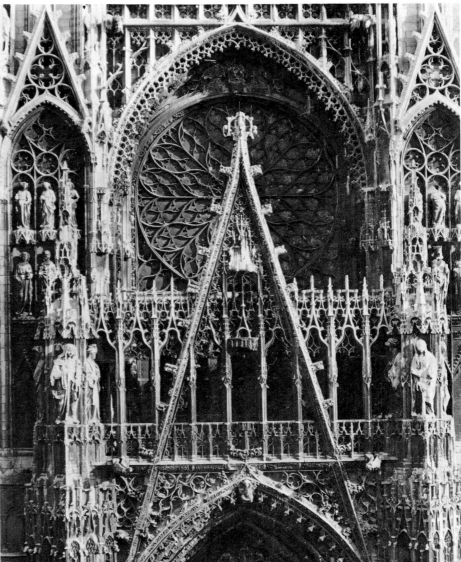

Above The west front of Rouen cathedral. The splendor of this facade, composite and unfinished though it was, has been spoiled by the last war. Even so its conception and execution are amazing. The Flamboyant tracery cannot be dated precisely but probably belongs to the period when Charles VIII and Louis XI of France were fighting in Italy.

Left The new cathedral at Reims was designed in 1210. These figures from the inside middle door show Melchisedek, prefiguring Christ, offering the host to Abraham, dressed like a 13th-century warrior, as he is also in the St Louis Psalter. The quality of the sculpture, the magnificent presence of Melchisedek and the translation of biblical scenes into contemporary dress all give grounds for amazement and admiration.

Woodwork

Bottom left The carving of this 5th-century door in Sta Sabina, Rome, was probably the work of Syrian craftsmen who illustrated 18 scenes from the Old and New Testaments. Here Peter is caught betraying his Lord at cockcrow. The execution is crude but the classical manner is still unmistakable in proportion, gesture, space, raiment and architecture.

Below A wooden Virgin from the church at Griske, Sunnøre, Norway. The devotion to our Lady developed from the 12th century as part of the new emotional response to the human life and suffering of Christ.

Medieval craftsmen executed works in the material of their skill – metal, stone or wood. They did not aspire to realize some artistic idea; nor did they strive to arouse aesthetic appreciation in the patron. The skills of a metalworker might be deployed in a number of different ways, but gave him no advantages in sculpting stone. His figure-making arose as part of his work in making fonts or altarpieces and not as "sculpture." The barbarians did not originally work in stone, but in metal or wood. Wooden artifacts have been more vulnerable to the effects of time and the nature of the material has not made it a popular subject of study.

The availability of timber, at least until the 12th century, meant that most buildings were more easily and cheaply built of wood. Fires made frequent rebuilding necessary and buildings must have been designed as only short-term structures. Early barbarian buildings prove that large halls could be constructed and roofed for great lords. Down to the 12th century castles continued to be constructed of wooden palisades mounted on great earth mounds. The new stone architecture did not deprive the carpenter of his employment. Early stone churches usually had timber roofs, and when Gothic masons learned how to build stone vaults, the services of carpenters were no less essential for providing the necessary centering and scaffolding, quite apart from the roof itself. The massive woodwork required may still be admired in many cathedrals, the other side of the vault. Examples of the structures supplied for great halls in full view of the public give a formidable impression of their assurance and mastery.

Wood carvings of the medieval period are more easily overlooked. Some of the most charming examples, the misericords, were not even designed for display. Only a fraction of the decorated work once provided for the furnishings of church and hall survive to indicate how important they once were. Yet the earliest surviving examples of wood carving bear comparison with sculpture of any date and show that craftsmen had already acquired great expressive power.

Below Borgund church, Søgne, Norway, c. 1150. All the wooden churches of Norway were built in the period 1000–1300; 25 are still standing; 700 buildings are known to have once existed. The basilica stone churches had some influence on the plan of building, but the craftsmen improved their building techniques in wood over the centuries to provide better weather resistance.

Bottom left The roofing of this country church at Garway, Herefordshire (tie beams, collar beams and two tiers of pointed trefoiled windbraces), demonstrates the skills of local artisans. The more elaborate and decorated wooden roofs of larger buildings depended on the existence of long-established and highly professional workmen throughout the Middle Ages, though only a fraction of their work survives.

Below This attractive figure of a thatcher with a thatcher's rake forms a bench end in the church at Ixworth Thorpe, Suffolk, England, and is a tribute by one craftsman to another. Despite the clumsiness of the execution the face and figure are expressive and the slightly jaunty posture is properly reminiscent of the thatcher astride the roof.

Bottom right Limewood angel by Tilman Riemenschneider (1460–1531). This Thuringian sculptor is the most admired and best-documented of the many German craftsmen working in wood in his day. Several splendid altarpieces survive to demonstrate the power and delicacy of his technique.

Stories in Painted Glass

Church windows of painted glass stir in us the most powerful impressions of the Middle Ages. Emmanuel Viollet-le-Duc (1814–79) wrote of a childhood experience in Notre Dame de Paris that when the sun shone through the rose window of the south transept and the organ began to play he was convinced that the window was singing. However, seven centuries earlier Abbot Suger of St Denis had stressed that painted glass windows were installed in his monastery church to show simple people unable to read the Bible what they had to believe. Powerfully though the windows may strike our sensibilities, in their own day they were intended to be equally instructive and like modern billboards they caught the eye for a purpose.

Churches of the early Middle Ages certainly had painted glass windows, but from surviving fragments it is not possible to speak convincingly about the nature or extent of their decoration. A head of Christ from Wissembourg in Alsace survives from the second half of the 11th century, but despite its technical accomplishment does not suggest that artists had pushed very far the art of presenting narrative scenes in painted glass. Yet in the early 12th century craftsmen had advanced their skills so far that Suger could require them to illustrate biblical and allegorical scenes in six windows, of which only 16 panels, all restored, survive. Suger chose the themes and was inspired by the biblical scholarship of Rupert of Deutz (c. 1075–1129/30), which probably means that there were no existing pictures to be copied by his workmen. One of the windows, a Tree of Jesse, a subject known to have been painted in earlier manuscripts but not in glass, was almost immediately copied at Chartres cathedral. Three other windows of the same period also survive at Chartres. Elsewhere in northern France, notably at Le Mans and at Poitiers, windows illustrating biblical scenes and extending over the whole window (at Poitiers the crucifixion scene is over 8 meters high) show that the art of painting glass, if only recently developed, had already achieved mastery of form.

From the 12th century to the 16th the art flourished throughout northern Europe in conjunction with the use of Gothic techniques in building. Gothic architects deliberately set out to build tall churches that were flooded with light in honor of God's houses, and it might seem that great windows fitted with plain or, as in early Cistercian churches, with very simple patterned glass would have better served the architects' purpose. Though colored glass admitted light less well, it did, however, have other advantages. The glittering effect of many colors, like that of precious stones on a metal reliquary, probably did have the emotional effect of heightening the worshipers' sense of God's holy mystery, but the combination of pieces of colored glass to tell stories from the Bible and the lives of saints, however difficult it must have been in some parts of the building to read them, shows that

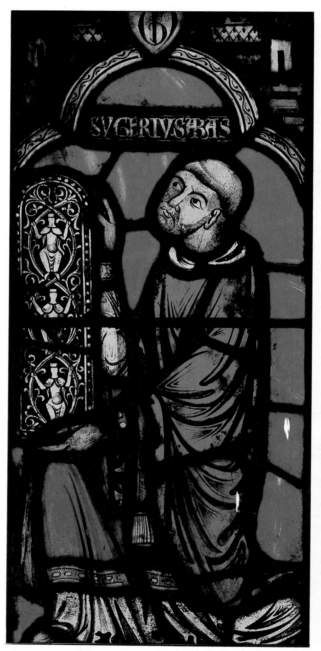

Above Suger, abbot of St Denis 1122–51, was devoted to his monastery. In his account of his administration he describes the care he took in rebuilding and beautifying his church and calls attention to the painting of many new windows. He comments on the power of painting to elevate the mind from the material to the immaterial and quotes verses that may have inspired his own choice of subjects. He also realized the value of the windows for the skill involved in making them and for the cost of materials, and appointed an official master craftsman to protect and repair them. By having himself represented he could, as it were, keep an eye on posterity. His windows, however, were wantonly destroyed in 1793 so the present disposition of the glass results from the mid-19th-century restoration by Emmanuel Viollet-le-Duc. Despite his admiration for painted glass his restoration now seems very heavy-handed.

Right The 11th-century head of Christ from the abbey church of Wissembourg (Alsace) gives an idea of the marvelous expressive power that had been quickly attained in the medium even if the art of telling stories had not by then been perfected.

Below Moses and the Golden Calf, one of the 16 panels to survive from Suger's scheme of stories capable of being depicted in the medium of which he was the earliest significant exponent. The composition is remarkable given the apparent absence of any earlier examples to develop.

patrons desired to translate the pictures of the books, as formerly found on church walls, into the new medium. As a result new skills were developed and the windows became one of the most carefully studied parts of a Gothic building. Glass painters were, like masons, commissioned and moved around from place to place as soon as sections of buildings were complete.

After a disastrous fire at Chartres in 1194 it became necessary to rebuild the cathedral, and it was in this new church that the glass painters accomplished the first fairly complete scheme known and visible to us. Between 1200 and 1235 more than 100 windows were glazed, covering an area of 2000 square meters. Many glass painters collaborated on the site and the work was paid for by a great number of donors, from the king, Louis IX, and his mother, Blanche of Castile, down through the count of Brittany to the many traders, masons, merchants, craftsmen and even water-carriers who wished to be commemorated in glass raised in honor of the Virgin's principal French shrine. Their desire to bring their own saintly patrons into the scheme may also explain why the program of scenes at Chartres presents special windows to a motley of saints, Nicholas of Myra, Thomas Becket, and the local saint, Bishop Lubin, whereas later, at Bourges or Reims, though schemes were fired by the example of Chartres, their authorities obtained more coherent systematic presentations. The great cathedrals put up at this time drew on the experience of their neighbors without ever becoming mere imitators. It is hardly possible at this stage to identify individual masters or trace them as they moved about; like the masons, they too must have been learning all the time from their own experiences.

The culmination of the painters' art was reached in Louis IX's Sainte Chapelle at Paris, built to receive

Left 12th-century glass at Chartres shows the medium's possibilities for telling stories. Cycles in the west end depict the genealogy of Christ in the Jesse window, his life in the center lancet, and the Passion, beginning with the Transfiguration at the bottom and concluding with the

Resurrection appearances. They prove how the workmen achieved subtle variation of color, but the main effect depends on the play of light. The western rose, showing Christ in Judgment, was inserted above the evidence of his earthly life in the 13th-century rebuilding.

Below In the 14th century stained glass was positioned at a more visible level in accordance with more popular religious devotions. This depiction of St Catherine, holding her wheel and wearing crown and stole, is in Regensburg cathedral and dates from 1343.

Above These panels of the Resurrection window from the mid-14th-century chapel of St Lawrence in Strasbourg cathedral show the medium of painted glass adapting to Gothic taste with its architectural canopies and elegant figures. The scenes were probably modeled on contemporary illustrated books.

Right This rose window in Notre Dame de Paris was built by Jean de Chelles and Pierre de Montreuil c. 1270, about 40 years later than the rose windows of Chartres. The pattern is now purely geometrical, allowing light to sparkle through colored glass without regard to the need for representational forms.

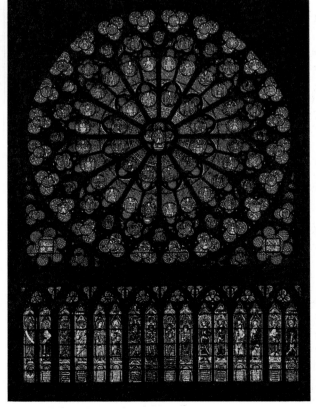

the relics of the Cross of Thorns and a piece of the Crucifix brought to the king from Constantinople, and glazed between 1244 and 1248. The upper chapel is effectively a glass house, with 15 large windows and a western rose, showing 1134 scenes mostly from the Bible but including a window depicting the story of Christ's cross down to the arrival of its fragment at Paris itself. As at Chartres the contributions of several workshops and even more glass painters are evident but without spoiling the harmonious effect. The completion of the great cathedrals and the reduced scale of building in the 14th century probably encouraged the emergence of local workshops to deal with the smaller-scale requirements of new chapels and restoration. The glass painters continued to improve on their techniques, to adapt their styles to innovations in the other arts and to explore the possibilities of the medium into the 16th century. But changes in taste and the revival of classical styles caused even Catholic countries to reject glass painting, whereas in countries of the reformed religion it was destroyed as easily as sculpture in wood and stone.

The techniques of the glass painters are first described in the early 12th-century handbook of Theophilus (*On the Various Arts*). Glass had first to be made. Originally the simplest glass came in a rather greenish color and was opaque. To color glass it was necessary to add iron and copper oxides in powder form to the materials used for making colorless glass. The English made no colored glass of their own and imported it either from Germany or from France, probably because cobalt, the source of metal oxides, could only be obtained in Bohemia or Saxony. It also suggests that by the time this type of glass painting was introduced into England, probably to Canterbury after 1174, the profession was already well established on the continent. Improvements in preparing the glass and the pigments continued to be made, particularly by the discovery in the 14th century of a technique for painting plain glass with a liquid containing silver which would turn various shades of yellow when baked in a hot oven.

The glass painters who designed and executed the windows did not make their own glass. They drew upon the skills of the designer, probably using manuscript illustrations for their images, and perhaps too upon the techniques of cloisonné enamelers. It is thought that these were introduced into France by Venetians before 1000. Here too strips of metal had to be shaped and soldered onto a surface in a design then fitted with different colored glasses, fired in a kiln. As in other highly esteemed craft-trades of the time, however, specialization was soon needed to meet the needs of the new kind of architecture. For painted glass belongs to Gothic building styles and became an integral part of its aesthetic scheme. Without the form and the structure of the Gothic window it failed to retain its place and became a lost art.

Music

In the present generation medieval music has once again been performed and appreciated, so that it is no longer an esoteric interest reserved for scholars. In some ways, however, this complicates the problem of understanding the topic: nothing could be less attuned to the nature of medieval music than its performance in the concert hall or on disc, for the original performers did not expect a restrained response from their audience. Apart from the vexed question of how to produce performable editions of old music, the main historical problem is to assess the role of music in such societies, for without this it is difficult to establish a context for the very limited amount of annotated music that has come down to us.

In the case of church music we know enough to realize that the plain chants of the monks, as codified in the time of Pope Gregory I, were not harmonically enriched until the 11th century. It was the development of harmony by the composition of additional lines of melody to be sung by other voices, while the "tenor" held to the basic tune, that led in due course to the composition of entirely original works of polyphony. Music for the church naturally benefited from the clergy's knowledge of ancient theoretical writings on music, such as those of Augustine and Boethius, where music's links with both mathematics and the muses were understood. But did such musical learning affect secular music too? We know from the other side that certain songs in the 13th century were so popular that the Franciscans had to compose more seemly words to fit their tunes. Secular music as such can only be known from what was written down, and since writing music was only necessary for works written in several parts, the single melodic lines of lyrics or dances are almost

unknowable. In performance, the virtuosity of the singer or instrumentalist had free play: it was this that established his reputation. We do not know whether the medieval equivalent of the Irish fiddler was ubiquitous or rare, nor whether choral singing in unison was more popular than solo singing. Did communities expect to find professional entertainers in their vicinity, or were they occasional visitors? Did the communities improvise music for themselves, or do without it most of the time? Singing was probably more cultivated than instrumental music. Women sang at the spinning wheel and weavers at the loom; plowmen presumably whistled to their oxen, and reapers sang in the fields. Did the Vikings sing at their oars? We know at least that in battle the minstrels sang to inspire soldiers to emulate ancient heroes and that drummers and pipers played to stir martial passions, if not to drown screams and frighten the enemy. Of all the medieval arts music is the one which most eludes our understanding.

Above A trumpeter from the Luttrell Psalter. This Psalter was written c. 1340 for Sir Geoffrey Luttrell of Irnham in Lincolnshire and is generally held to indicate that the high level of English decoration in manuscripts could no longer be maintained. The expressionless features of the figures and the jumble of colors mean that the main attraction of the decoration lies with its evidence for everyday life and with its grotesque blend of human and animal figures.

Above left An early drawing of a harp from an anthology of Anglo-Saxon poetry, c. 1000.

Literature

In the early Middle Ages literature and letters in the ancient manner could have only been cultivated by the clergy, who, like St Jerome, tended to feel uncomfortable about appreciating pagan poets such as Virgil. As classical paganism itself ceased to appear a challenge to Christianity, this attitude changed. The better-educated clergy of the great schools, particularly in the 12th century, achieved an expressive fluency in writing Latin prose and verse. Their interest in ancient literature had a decisive influence on the writing of a new French and German literature, intended for the courtly circles and to be heard rather than read. Some barbarian languages of Europe had been used before this in writing, mainly for scriptural translations. In England there was a long-standing tradition of using the English language in the writing of both poetry and laws. By the 10th century this had already reached a high level of accomplishment. Similar precocity was shown in both Wales and Ireland. Probably throughout barbarian Europe the vernaculars had been used for entertaining un-Latined peoples with heroic poetry and tales. Such compositions were not written down and have not been preserved, except in *Beowulf*, an English poem that gives a glimpse of the world as these peoples saw it. Heroic poetry, praising the skills and qualities of warriors, is now best exemplified by the *Song of Roland*, a French poem relating the story of an episode of Carolingian intervention in Spain in 778. The oldest manuscript of this poem was written more than three centuries later. Just when the poem was composed in the modern sense, even whether it had one (anonymous) author at all, are questions that excite lively discussion. The poem bears such obvious signs of Christian ideas about fighting Muslims and feudal ideas about lordship that it cannot be taken as representative of "heroic" times. The redaction of all vernacular compositions is inescapably Christian, for non-Christian barbarians did not value writing. If they had literature, it is unknowable in a pre-Christian form.

Medieval literature in the various vernaculars of Europe grew from the romances in which Latin stories from the classical and Celtic past were retold by educated poets. They adapted the literary devices of their sources for the benefit of those not able to read the originals. Their verse stories about Charlemagne, and Arthur's knights with their adventures and their loves, found their way into even more accessible prose forms. The romantic interest in the emotions of love, the claims of duty and the resulting conflicts had a stimulating effect on the lyrical talents of writers, particularly in Provence, Italy and Germany. Such poetry was more frequently recited aloud than read silently from books, but the audience at such recitals was probably more restricted socially than had been the case with heroic poems declaimed at public feastings. Increasingly literature came to be reserved for refined company; it endorsed courtly values; it encouraged personal responsibility and decision. Other poems, songs and stories for coarser tastes, animal fables, like the tales of the wily Renard the Fox, and humorous anecdotes show the variety of medieval literatures, not to speak of the sermons, educational and devotional works abounding in all the languages of Europe.

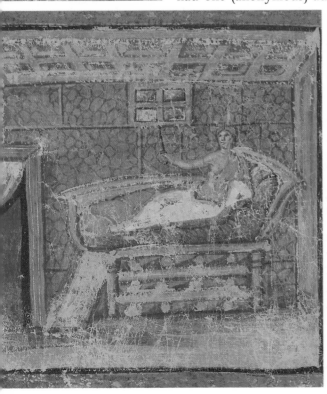

Manuscript Illumination

Illustrated manuscripts are more easily destroyed and defaced than other artistic objects but, despite the losses, many thousands survive in public and private libraries to give a remarkably comprehensive idea of the genre. As a result we can probably form a better understanding of this than of any other known medieval artistic activity. Unlike architecture and sculpture, illustrated books did not go on public display at the time, and even now only scholars with privileged access to manuscript collections ever have the chance to examine these books at leisure. Books illustrated and decorated for however restricted a readership were of many different kinds. Those laid on the altar for the church's liturgy could be solemnly and magnificently adorned as for God's own eyes. Individual prayerbooks, such as those books of hours made for the use of the later medieval nobility, might try to blend uplifting pictures with droll scenes which could only encourage the mind to wander. Once university students and pious Christians were numerous enough to guarantee a market for books, professional artists, particularly in Paris, began to work in an organized manner, being apprenticed to accredited masters and producing books of high quality to meet the demand. In earlier periods, however, when books had much more restricted circulation, their writing and decoration were more likely completed in the same church or monastery, though the scribes and painters were not always the same person. Some texts were illustrated by their authors, as was the case with Matthew Paris, who drew both formal pictures and marginal sketches in his histories. Some works, like herbals, needed illustration to be useful to readers. Medical and astronomical treatises commonly carried pictures to elucidate the meaning of the texts. From the very beginning of the Middle Ages extensive illustrations to the Bible challenged artists with an enormous range of subject matter.

Below The *Codex Augusteus* Vatican Library Ms. Lat. 3256. This 4th-century Italian manuscript of Virgil's *Georgics* is written in square capitals, bold and regular, without punctuation, but with wide margins and ornamental colored initials – a de luxe manuscript of the late empire. Here the initials

have not acquired any special decorative treatment.

Below The St Omer Psalter, British Library, London, Ms. Yates Thompson 14. This manuscript, painted in East Anglia c. 1330, indicates the extremes to which the purely decorative treatment of the initial

could be carried by English artists at the high point of Gothic illumination. The first Psalm is illustrated with a tree of Jesse and the borders are alive with little human and animal figures.

Left The Book of Kells, c. 800, Trinity College, Dublin, Ms. 58. This famous page is the ultimate in the purely decorative treatment of initials. It celebrates Chi Rho, the Greek letters used for Christ's name, in a manner that is related to the patterning art of the goldsmith.

Below left Pierpont Morgan Library, New York, Gospels. This is a beautiful example of the clarity pursued and achieved by the revivers of learning and letters in the 9th century. Letters are clearly modeled on ancient imperial inscriptions and the decoration does not compromise the legibility of the writing.

Below center A Benedictine Bible of c. 1070, Bibliothèque Nationale, Paris, Ms. Lat. 254. The clarity of the writing achieved in the Carolingian period was not lost in later centuries, but initials often attracted the attention of decorators.

Below right Pliny's *Natural History*, copied in Siena c. 1460. The bold letter form divides the illustration into three scenes, where the painter takes his cue from the subject matter of the text itself, metals and minerals, including the painter's own material.

PART FOUR
CONSOLIDATION OF THE LAND

SEPARATE IDENTITIES

European states in the melting pot

The clear objectives of 13th-century rulers and their vigorous pursuit of their interests had by the end of that century created unforeseen difficulties for them. The papacy had become an office difficult to fill and a former hermit, Celestine V, had to be replaced after his unique abdication by a Roman noble and canon lawyer, Boniface VIII. His troubles with his cardinals and with the kings of France and England precipitated a sequence of events that brought the papacy in the 14th century to the haven of Avignon in Provence and a reputation for subservience to French influence. The king of France, however, came to appreciate what moral support the papacy could give, for Philip IV's high-handed policies had provoked a sharp reaction in Flanders and his army was routed by townsmen in the battle of Courtrai (1302). Succeeded by sons who died after brief reigns leaving only daughters, Philip and his line appeared to pay God's price for insulting his vicar the pope. The new line of Valois kings of France fought for over a hundred years to vindicate their rights to the throne against challengers like the king of England. In Spain the great campaigns against the Muslims of the 13th century lapsed and Christians fought one another, even in civil wars. In England itself the king Edward I took on the Scots and failed to master them even by victories and conquest. Two of his successors in the kingship were deposed and murdered. Not surprisingly the 14th century has a reputation for disorder, disaster and dismay.

If the king of France was outraged at being thwarted in Flanders by mere townsmen, and the king of England by rebellious Scots, historians should however be careful not to echo royal regrets but to adjust their focus to take account of groups that had not hitherto forced themselves on public notice. When the Scots showed that without a king of their own they did not cease to consider themselves members of a kingdom and that kings would have to be found somewhere or other, and that the kingdom itself would survive, they indicate that a historical preoccupation with kings and their archives can sadly misrepresent reality. Neither in Scotland nor in Flanders did kings have their own way. In Flanders the "French" cities of Bruges and Ghent, which Philip IV had taken over as sovereign lord of the country, have, by their resistance to his lordship, permanently eluded control from Paris.

Not all such bids for independence in the 14th century have been similarly vindicated by time. The state of the Teutonic Order of knights on the Baltic littoral enjoyed practical sovereignty for a century and a half before being absorbed back into the kingdom of Poland-Lithuania. The independent principalities of Latin Christians in the Levant succumbed to the Ottomans in the late 15th century. The autonomous duchy of Brittany was brought back into the fold of the French monarchy at the end of the 15th century. In this period, however, great

rulers failed to dominate events in the way they had tried in the 13th century. Political control everywhere had to become more relaxed and more local, which meant that more political communities were able to win recognition of their independence. The empire in particular benefited by this arrangement to allow the great Italian and German cities to become autonomous. The French monarchy had to acquiesce in the emergence of separate provincial legal institutions. In Spain the overwhelming strength of Castile was balanced by the emergence of firmer political institutions in the neighboring kingdoms of Aragon, Navarre, Portugal and Granada, as well as by dissensions among its own aristocrats. To describe all the political entities of the time would take much space; the complications of the complex relationships between them can only be fully accounted for by detailed description. To explain individual changes in terms of general factors would falsify the truth of their variety and take too much for granted.

The earlier period had been able to assume a comparatively simple structure for Christendom that events quite simply proved to be unjustified. Originally, as it were, there had been the one Roman empire, firmly seated at Constantinople; one pope at Rome; and a restored western empire under the control of Charlemagne and his German successors. The bid to restore the idea of order that Rome stood for had affirmed papal power, but had cut the Germans down to size. Other kingdoms had come into their own. The number of kings in western Christendom tended to increase. By 1273 there was papal recognition that a German and an Italian kingdom might be created out of the empire, though Dante was still thinking of a universal monarchy in 1311–12. There was therefore a certain reluctance to accept the fissiparous character of Christendom. The old mold of empire was unsuitable for Europe, but could not easily be replaced with another. Kingship, of barbarian origin, was easily assumed by dictators or upstarts: how durable would it everywhere prove to be? The model of empire owed more to the example of Constantinople than to any theory of politics and it was the disintegration of the system at Constantinople that probably did most to plunge western Christendom too back into the melting pot. In the west men became aware of their own strength compared to that of the east, so they had perforce to discover how to harness the real sources of that strength in original political forms; to do this meant shedding their vestigial respect for the Roman empire.

Latin (or western) involvement in the affairs of the eastern empire during the crusades came to a head with the capture of Constantinople in 1204 and the setting up of a Latin emperor there. In fact the Latin empire did not strengthen the position of Constantinople, for western concepts of power were not imperial but princely and assumed the virtue of dividing the territory among the Latin allies. The

Above right The papal palace at Avignon was begun by the former Cistercian pope Benedict XII (1333–42) in the style of a severe fortress to defend the court of the church against the military companies (free-lance soldiers). It was added to in more sumptuous style by Clement VI and finished by Innocent VI (1352–62). The range of buildings provided a setting for the most illustrious court of 14th-century Europe, but it is only since the end of its military occupation (1791–1906) that its artistic merits have emerged from centuries of ignorant disparagement.

Below right The castle at Karitaina in central southern Greece was built by the Franks in 1254. The bridge, which crosses the river Alpheios below the town, probably dates from the same time. According to an inscription it was renovated in 1439 by a Turk in the service of the Palaeologi at Mistra. In two centuries central Greece owed much to people of several different races.

Latin emperor was himself driven out by Michael Palaeologus in 1261, but the revived Greek empire was not able to recover all the territories taken by the other Latin rulers, still less to restore the imperial authority. By the end of the 13th century, therefore, both the eastern and the western empires had only nominal existence. Power was in both states a matter of local strength alone. Yet the offices themselves continued to be prestigious and to attract pretenders, even those with some real power. So Stephen Dushan, ruler of Serbia, aspired to the role of emperor and, foiled at Constantinople, consoled himself with coronation as emperor of the Serbs at Skopje (1346). Likewise in Germany the failure of the Staufen emperors did not daunt men of lesser family and the emperorship passed from one family to another before the Luxembourgers and their lineal heirs, the Hapsburgs, succeeded in making it a family property. And while these empires continued their shadow plays, between them to the southwest and to the northeast and beyond them in France more substantial rewards were sought by the local princes, struggling without fear of intervention from powerful neighbors. There were no prefects left and small boys played war games without fear.

The languishing of the eastern empire

The Greeks in their heyday, and later the Ottomans, maintained enduring empires by allowing no place except the imperial court itself for dissensions within and by keeping standing armies and their own fleets for defense. Between the 13th century and the 15th, however, no power was able to muster adequate armies, let alone combine military with naval strength, sufficient to establish a united empire. The reasons for this must be complex and remain controversial. The signs that the Greeks were losing control of the empire were already clear by the late 12th century. The Comnenian dynasty that had restored a sense of political purpose to the empire had not been able to dislodge the Turks (who had settled in Anatolia after the battle of Manzikert in 1071) and had accepted that their strength was at sea through their control of the littoral. But already there were signs of the growing strength of Italian maritime forces, particularly through the crusading movement. After the death of Manuel Comnenus (1180), rival families struggled for the succession to the empire and crusaders from the west were inevitably drawn into these conflicts both in 1191 and in 1204. The Latin occupation of Constantinople itself, which dismembered the empire for the benefit of the Latins, obviously did nothing to bring the Greeks together; on the contrary they fought among themselves for the nominal glory of empire. The Greek emperors, restored after 1261, found the territories of the empire shared out among numerous potentates Greek, Latin and Slav. For the Slavs too had taken advantage of the breakdown of imperial government to build new principalities of their own. It is not necessary to assume that these were proto-nationalist movements. In the absence of the normal source of government, some kind of authority had to be improvised. To some extent these "native" states bequeathed a valuable legacy for later times, but without exception they proved to be unequal to the burdens of government when the latter duly appeared.

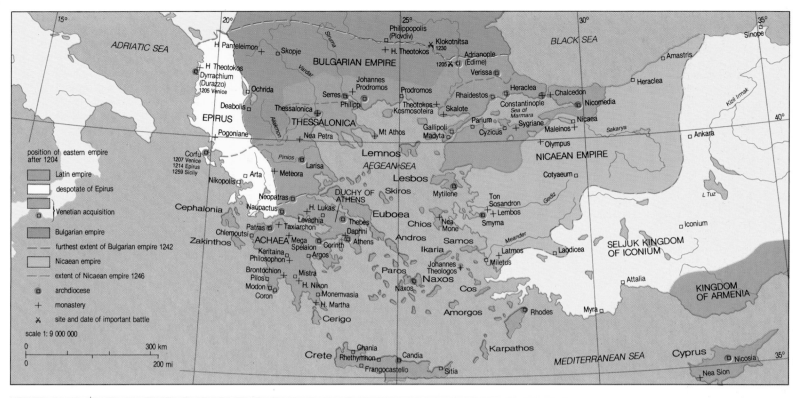

position of eastern empire after 1204

- Latin empire
- despotate of Epirus
- Venetian acquisition
- Bulgarian empire
- --- furthest extent of Bulgarian empire 1242
- Nicaean empire
- --- extent of Nicaean empire 1246
- archdiocese
- + monastery
- ✕ site and date of important battle

scale 1: 9 000 000

0 _____ 300 km
0 _____ 200 mi

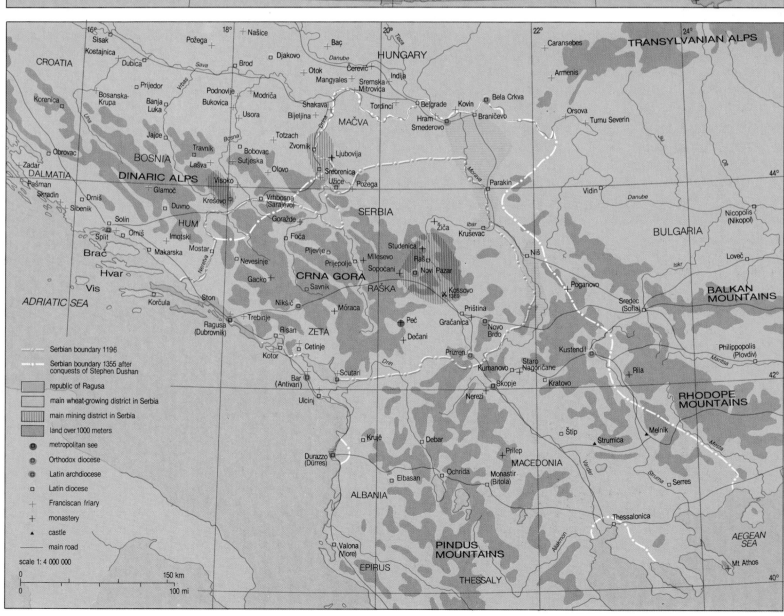

- Serbian boundary 1196
- Serbian boundary 1355 after conquests of Stephen Dushan
- republic of Ragusa
- main wheat-growing district in Serbia
- main mining district in Serbia
- land over 1000 meters
- metropolitan see
- Orthodox diocese
- Latin archdiocese
- Latin diocese
- + Franciscan friary
- + monastery
- ▲ castle
- main road

scale 1: 4 000 000

0 _____ 150 km
0 _____ 100 mi

Left: Greece and the Balkans
Modern nationalists of southeastern Europe draw upon the history of the Middle Ages for their claim to autonomy. Sandwiched between the old Byzantine and the new Ottoman empires, the medieval states of this area enjoyed ephemeral, precarious and protean independence. The intrusion of adventurers from near and far, together with the assertion of economic powers such as Venice, hampered the smooth development of local states.

Below: The Ottoman empire
For four centuries the Ottoman empire established a Roman-type stability in lands that had previously been subject to many fluctuations, lands of both Christian and Muslim traditions. When it collapsed, fluctuations of a different kind again occurred. This map, by contrast to the one opposite, gives therefore an impression of simplicity as the Ottomans extended their empire outwards from a secure base across the Sea of Marmara.

The eastern empire was not comparable to any modern national state and had no homogeneous character except what was provided by religion. The infiltration of the Latins brought to light the differences between their religious practices and those of the Greeks. Deprived of the firm control of the Greek emperor, the Orthodox church itself exacerbated the problem by allowing autocephalous metropolitans to appear, as in Cyprus. The Bulgars and the Serbs were quick to follow suit. As religious discipline became more local, so heretics, like the Bogomils in Bosnia, found it easier to defy authority. The history of this area for more than two centuries defies any attempt to emphasize any one thread at the expense of the others. Of importance in their own principalities, local affairs were drawn into no pattern by the magnetic effects of cause or leader. Historians can focus on the fortunes of the Ottoman dynasty which was already installed in Bithynia by 1329. They used the Greek civil war between John V and John VI Cantacuzene to insinuate themselves into the heart of Greek politics and they had mastered Serbia by 1389. Contemporaries seem nonetheless to have been obtuse about

the Ottoman danger, apparently hoping that the Ottomans would prove as ephemeral as other military powers, like the Catalans installed at Athens (1311–88) or the Navarrese in the Morea. Being Muslim, the Ottomans were probably less well known or understood than their Christian counterparts and their role in Asia Minor was quite unsuspected. Nevertheless the facts of Ottoman power by the 1380s (the full effects of which for Constantinople were only delayed to 1453 by the quite fortuitous setback caused by their defeat at the hands of Timur the Lame in 1402) mean that in practice there was only about a century during which the usual certainties of the area were completely set aside. The Christians were also given a remarkably long period of grace to prepare the salvation of the Christian empire. Some rulers were even aware of how much desperate action was required. The real problem was that no Christian ruler or state could be found to take on the Ottomans or rival them in strength, purposefulness or indeed acceptability. To the diverse Christian peoples of the area the Muslim Ottomans could at least offer the familiar attractions of toleration when

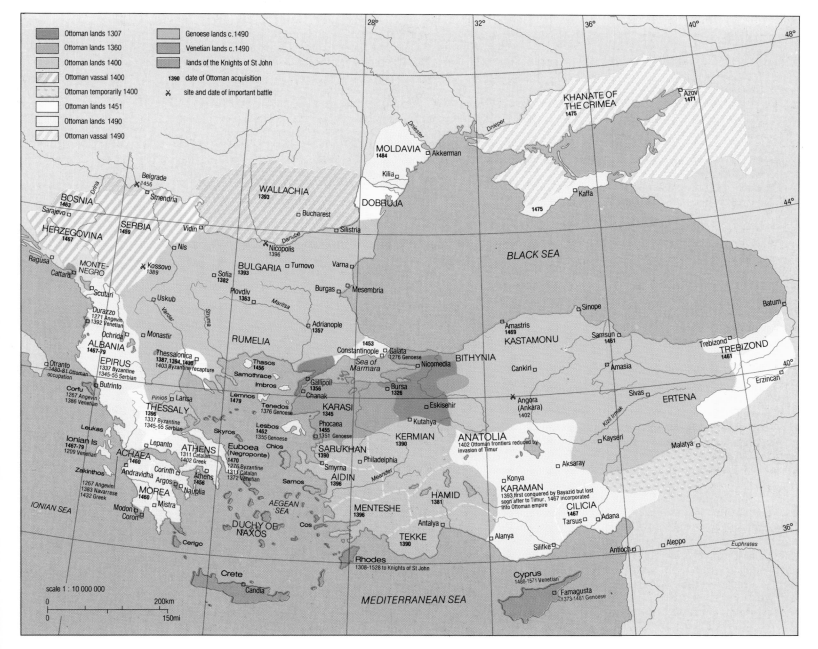

Ottoman lands 1307	Genoese lands c.1490
Ottoman lands 1360	Venetian lands c.1490
Ottoman lands 1400	lands of the Knights of St John
Ottoman vassal 1400	**1390** date of Ottoman acquisition
Ottoman temporarily 1400	✕ site and date of important battle
Ottoman lands 1451	
Ottoman lands 1490	
Ottoman vassal 1490	

scale 1 : 10 000 000

0   200km
0   150mi

threatened with the tyranny of one enforced Christian tradition. The Latin powers that held their own in the Aegean were basically dependent on their strength at sea, and lacked the capacity to raise and maintain large armies able to match the Ottomans. The Balkan states, Serbia and Hungary, were for various reasons unable to field sufficient troops and anyway Constantinople was much more difficult for them to succor by land. They were able to slow up the Ottoman advance into central Europe, but not to push it back into Asia Minor.

The Ottomans were a dynasty of soldiers operating in an area given up to the rule of many princelings dreaming of empire. The most determined and consistent political interests were probably demonstrated by such groups as the Knights of the Hospital on Rhodes, who were committed to perpetual crusading but who were not calculating politically how to achieve the defeat of the Ottomans, or by the Venetians, whose main concern however was commerce rather than empire. Throughout the 14th century the Venetians' main enemy remained the Genoese, their commercial rivals. For both, their Aegean interests were mere colonies to be exploited for domestic gain. For all their share in the later struggles with the Ottomans, neither of these Italian city-states could propose itself for succession at Constantinople itself. Their political commitment was to that extent halfhearted. By directing the profits of trade and industry from Constantinople, which had previously enjoyed the monopoly, to Italy, which was enriched beyond measure, Latin interests acted in effect like leeches. Their hold was inevitably ephemeral.

Most of the western rulers with resources equal to imperial responsibilities were situated too far from Constantinople to aspire to the succession there. In the crisis period after the battle of Manzikert (1071) the Normans of south Italy had at least been interested in extending their power into the Balkans, and in the 13th century Charles of Anjou, having acquired the Norman kingdom (1260s), showed himself willing to follow up earlier Norman interests in the old Greek empire. These ambitions led to Angevin lordships in Greece, up the Dalmatian coast and into Hungary, and a kind of Angevin maritime empire rivaled and challenged that of the Venetians, though it had political rather than commercial objectives. Their thrust against Constantinople was however turned aside by the Palaeologus emperor Michael VIII (emperor 1261–82) who allied with Charles's enemies at home, as a result of which Sicily passed into the hands of the king of Aragon and Frederick II's powerful kingdom was divided into two. The kingdoms of Naples and Sicily weakened one another by recurrent war and a separation which lasted for two centuries before the Spaniards finally acquired Naples (1499), but they drew some strength from the new empires to which they belonged. The Angevin dominion straddled the Adriatic, but its Italian capital at Naples was geographically ill-placed to take advantage of its maritime situation. The Angevin rulers themselves, unlike their Norman predecessors, appear to have had scant appreciation of the possibilities of sea power. For commercial purposes both Genoa and Venice were better placed geographically, especi-

ally for supplying hungry markets in the north. In the kingdom of Naples itself financial affairs came to be managed by the Angevins' Guelf allies from Tuscany.

More advantage came to the Spaniards from their acquisition of Sicily in 1282. The kings of Aragon, who were also counts of Barcelona with possessions along the Mediterranean shore as far as Montpellier, had in the previous generation conquered the Balearic Islands and down the coast in Valencia. From Barcelona in particular a commercial empire in the western Mediterranean had been effectively built up and sustained with royal approval, despite the hostility of the barons of the Aragonese kingdom. They, like their peers in Naples, were more concerned about their own estates than about commerce or imperial expansion. . The kings of Aragon held onto Sicily however and also tried to annex the other islands of Corsica and Sardinia. Merchants from Barcelona even ventured into the Aegean and a company of mercenary soldiers acquired the duchy of Athens by conquest and held it as a fief of the king of Aragon for much of the 14th century. Such activities indicate how fluid the situation remained in the Mediterranean as long as there was no masterful hand at Constantinople, but also demonstrate that from the west there was no chance of creating more than a superficial presence by sea. The western Europeans could always find a refuge back home across the water; they could not hold important landmasses by the means at their disposal. The tradition of empire that had lingered in the east for so long had lost its strength and found no Christians to take on its responsibilities. The Ottoman conquest, which restored political realities, belonged nevertheless not to a Roman but to a Muslim cultural tradition. The Roman empire was in its terminal phase.

Bohemian domination in the German empire

The western empire had no rationale or tradition comparable to that in the east, but the value of the concept did not quickly lose its appeal. In practice the empire ceased to have any real impact on Italy after the death of Frederick II in 1250 and only the

Right This Venetian fortress at Frangocastello on the south coast of Crete, built in 1371, is a reminder that these quiet beaches were for several centuries in need of military supervision, when many powers were in rivalry for control of the Aegean.

Below right: The lands of the crown of Aragon
The lands of the crown of Argon had been vastly increased by the rulers of the house of Barcelona, whose interests stretched along the northwestern shore of the Mediterranean from Provence to Murcia, and to the islands – the Balearics, Sicily, Sardinia and even beyond. The Aragonese nobility remained aloof from these more distant enterprises, but they were more congenial to the Catalans and Valencians. The Angevins who took over Provence (1246–1482) and Naples (1266–1435) became the Catalans' normal enemies and rivals. This conflict prefigured the later wars between the kings of France and Spain, when Italy was the chief prize at stake. In the Middle Ages the disputes reached as far as Greece. The range of the king of Aragon's concerns in the 14th century was thus exceptionally extensive. His involvements in Spain made Barcelona a city of political as well as commercial importance.

Below The castle of the Knights of St John, Rhodes, 1310–1522. For more than two centuries the Knights of St John, driven from Acre, defended their occupation of Rhodes against Muslim opposition. Their control of this port so near the mainland, backed up by the island's natural fecundity, was reinforced by the powerful defenses they constructed, using local labor over a number of years. The buildings comprise the palace of the Grand Master, the cathedral and the hotels of the seven (later eight) nations of the order. The influence of French and Spanish military architecture not surprisingly prevailed.

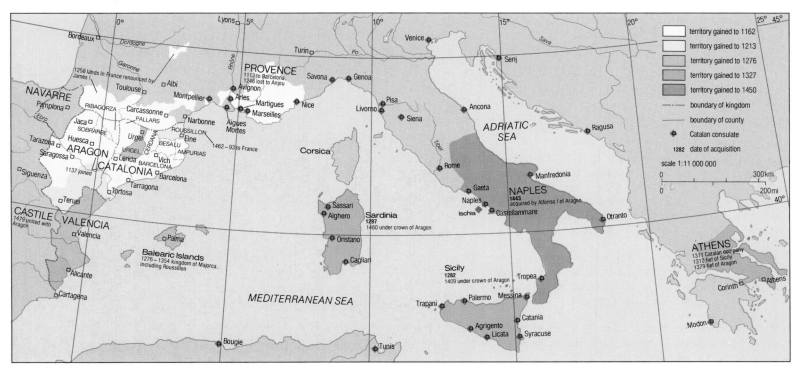

Bohemia

The Czechs were the first Slavs to be drawn into the affairs of western Catholic Europe. By the 14th century the king of Bohemia had become the most important political figure in central Europe, with a key role in the affairs of the empire. By then the kings of Bohemia had ceased to be native Czech princes. Bohemian prominence derived not only from its strategic position and its mineral wealth but also from the ambition of its rulers to show their muscle. At various times they sought to extend their rule into Austria, Silesia, Poland, Hungary and Brandenburg. This involvement in the great affairs of Europe had the effect of stirring Bohemia's economic activities and intellectual awareness. The first university of the empire was founded at Prague in 1348. Religious enthusiasms were also roused and in the absence of firm directions in church and state during the schism after 1378 overflowed into heretical activities. This unfortunately led to the isolation of Bohemia as a land of heretics. Its neighbors in the 15th century treated it like a leper in their midst. The map, which illustrates the reach of Bohemian political involvement, reveals at its heart the associations of towns and peasants implicated in the Hussite wars. In the century before the German reformation these heretics struck fear into the rest of Christendom. They revealed great diversities of opinions and a gamut of religious practices in a land where Catholic and Orthodox traditions met.

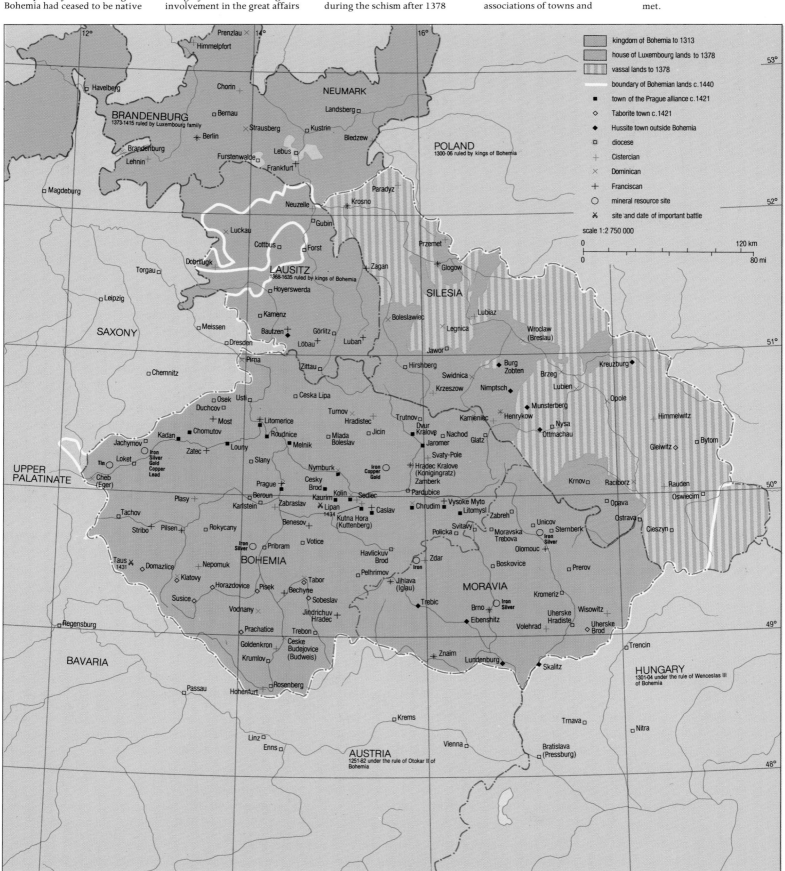

Germans persisted in keeping the notion alive, showing little interest in projects to adapt it for a more limited national purpose. The king of the Romans was elected by princes of the empire, and called emperor only after coronation with papal approval; from 1338 he was formally considered to be sovereign from the time of his election. The electors were the king of Bohemia and six German princes, three ecclesiastical and three lay, deemed to represent all the princes of the empire. Though the electoral college could not be called representative in the modern sense, it demonstrated that the empire comprised very divergent interests and peoples, all nonetheless consenting to continued membership of the *Reich* (which in German means rulerdom, rather than kingdom or empire in particular). To spell out the specific duties of the ruler would mean listing a miscellany of powers, none particularly impressive, but the role was not merely ornamental and honorific. Against the Staufen family, 13th-century popes had encouraged the election of minor figures but the princes came to realize that only men of some real standing were suitable for the office. By the mid-14th century only members of the most distinguished German families had any chance of winning recognition, and their eminence, for example as king of Bohemia, reinforced their position as king of the Romans. This crystallization of the structure of the German empire did mean however that other territories of the old empire which ceased to participate in the new structure tended to fall away and acquire alternative political loyalties of their own: Italy, for example, which received perfunctory visits from a few emperors but learned to cope without reference to their nominal powers. In the Low Countries Brabant and Holland actually obtained imperial authority to act like sovereign states; others acted likewise without authority. To the west, fragments of the empire made their own terms with the kings of France. Only to the east did the revival of Polish power discourage fragmentation. The princes of the east valued too much their membership of the empire to risk independence for themselves.

The failure of the empire to develop along centralist lines, as it was believed other western European states, notably France, did at this time, has for long discouraged sympathetic historical study of this period, which remains comparatively neglected and despised by students of both history and literature. Although a few great princely families or towns have secured attention, they never succeeded in dominating their times, and to do them justice it is necessary to consider the dozens of small states, principalities, bishoprics, monasteries, towns, lordships and knightly estates all directly dependent on the emperor and effectively sovereign. Only the Italian and Swiss sovereign states within the empire are recognized as such; yet in practice the German states, often small, and even sometimes comprising territorially scattered fragments, were no less important. Their buildings and ideals have not stirred the imaginations of other Europeans as those of late medieval and Renaissance Italy did, but they have left as enduring an impression of the local vitality of those times. Merely to list their names would be unhelpful. Even to map them induces confusion. In its own way the empire remained a microcosm of Europe as a whole.

Under the aegis of basically local, unambitious authorities the benefits of civilization in medieval terms were made available to the communities of the 14th and 15th centuries. The artifacts of that age witness to the high level attained in domestic life, not just by princes, but by townsmen and villagers. There can be no measure of the affluence of the majority, but painted scenes of popular life certainly suggest an unparalleled comfort and well-being with children playing and peasants drinking and feasting. The somber reminders of death, disease and poverty spring not from the people but from the deliberate efforts of the clergy to restore a sense of proportion. And it is above all from the empire that this evidence is abundant. The small principalities appear to have served the political needs of the people well.

The striking feature of the German empire in this period was however the dominant position enjoyed in it by the kings of Bohemia. King Ottokar II of Bohemia in the 13th century had already aimed for the imperial crown, but had been defeated in battle by King Rudolf of Hapsburg (1276). But Ottokar's granddaughter's son, Charles IV of Luxembourg, used the same power base in Bohemia to arrange the affairs of the empire in his family's interest, and perhaps by not being overtly Czech himself, reduced German resentment of Bohemia's role. It is interesting to consider how central Europe might have developed had these auspicious beginnings been maintained. Unfortunately in the early 15th century Bohemia was convulsed by religious dissensions that not only isolated that kingdom from the rest of the empire but deprived the empire itself of its effective center. The empire fell to the Hapsburgs of Austria with fateful consequences.

Bohemia was however, for more than a century, one of the most dynamic and prosperous states within the empire. In its mountains were mined the gold and silver that gave Europe much of its basic supply of precious metals. Its mining towns grew rapidly in this period — they lay across the important network of roads linking Italy to the Baltic. Prague, the chief city of Bohemia, was no mere place of royal residence but a powerful urban center in its own right. Its population appears to have been growing. When Charles decided to establish a university for the empire it was founded at Prague in 1348. The religious devotions of the people were intense and proselytizing, but there were latent hostilities between Czechs and Germans, easily aroused. The development of deviant religious ideas was probably intensified by the outbreak of the great schism in the church (1378) and by the political circumstances that led to the deposition of the king of Bohemia, Wenceslas IV, from the empire itself (1400). But in a sense the tremendous enthusiasm shown throughout Bohemia for these religious ideas, particularly after their condemnation from outsiders, as at the Council of Constance (1414–18), was only the fitting conclusion to the great period of Bohemian resurgence itself. If King Charles IV had planned a Bohemian hegemony of the empire, the Czechs themselves turned that movement towards goals thought more appropriate by their own spiritual leaders. The course of events followed a logic of its own, irrespective of the intentions of king or reformers. When the emperor Sigismund died in 1437 it was not only the

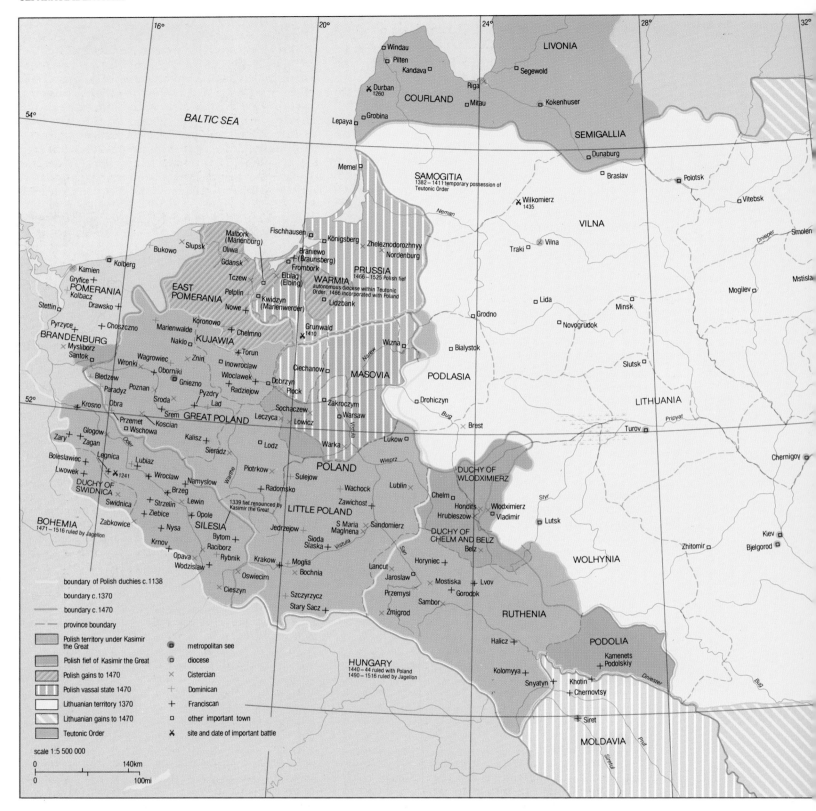

Map legend:

— boundary of Polish duchies c.1138
— boundary c.1370
— boundary c.1470
-- province boundary

Polish territory under Kasimir the Great
Polish fief of Kasimir the Great
Polish gains to 1470
Polish vassal state 1470
Lithuanian territory 1370
Lithuanian gains to 1470
Teutonic Order

- metropolitan see
□ diocese
× Cistercian
+ Dominican
✚ Franciscan
□ other important town
✗ site and date of important battle

scale 1:5 500 000

0 — 140km
0 — 100mi

Luxembourg dynasty that came to an end: a scheme of empire and the prospects for central Europe had totally collapsed. Even the Bohemians, who had beaten off foreign armies, found that it was difficult to maintain an ecclesiastical discipline and a separate kingship of their own. These events had done nothing to help forward reforms for the empire as a whole, proposals for which had ominously fallen to theorists. Meanwhile the empire itself had begun to contract, with imperial blessings. The Swiss had begun to show how to establish their real autonomy by using the emperor against their

Hapsburg lords; the ruler of Milan had blatantly bought the nominal title of duke of the empire from the emperor, and made himself the single most powerful ruler of Italy.

After Ottokar II's death the kings of Bohemia, shut out of the empire by the Hapsburgs, had for a time sought to extend their interests into Poland; their attempt to install themselves as kings there, by coronation at Krakow, had been one of the factors that induced the Poles to work for the reunification of the fractured Piast kingdom (see page 191). The king of Bohemia remained a persistent enemy of the

Poland and Lithuania
The map lays bare the intractable problem of Poland's territory, sprawling in all directions from a heartland itself divided into distinct regions. Its original interest in expansion to the west was frustrated by the persistence of German efforts to push east, particularly along the Baltic coast. This directed Polish energies rather to the south and eventually into an improbable association with the Orthodox Lithuanians. The auguries for cooperation were not good, but for a time the Jagellon dynasty succeeded in holding together a gigantic state in eastern Europe whose influence was extended even further by their dynastic links with other kingdoms. It was this great state that was dismembered in the first of the 18th-century partitions. The Catholic bishops of Poland played an important part in preserving the traditions of the Catholic and Polish part of the Jagellon state, but not even the ecclesiastical boundaries could define Poland in any effective way. Modern questions about Poland must refer to the medieval experience, but answers to some of them remain unattainable.

Above right Krakow has played a central role in Poland's cultural life since the early days of the kingdom. It became the seat of a bishop in 1000 and the Piast capital in 1038. The cathedral, shown here, was built c. 1018, rebuilt in the 14th century and restored in the Gothic style in 1712.

new monarchy of the Piast kings and actually succeeded in obtaining the principalities of Silesia for his own kingdom, but failed in the end to frustrate the attempts of other princes to bring about a reunification of the Piast lands. After a century and a half of disruption Poland reappeared. It was the first of the several Polish historical resurrections.

Establishing Poland

Poland (from Slavonic *pole*, a field or plain) first appears as a political community in the Baltic region between the Oder and Vistula rivers under Mieszko I (963–92) who paid tribute to the German king Otto I for the lands he held to the west of the Oder (Stettin, Pomerania and Lubusz). The beginnings of ecclesiastical organization date from the setting up of an archdiocese at Gniezno by Otto III in 1000, with bishoprics at Kolberg, Wroclaw and Krakow, though a bishopric at Poznan, formed earlier, remained dependent on Magdeburg. The rulers of the Polish Piast dynasty were however less interested in consolidating their hold than in extending their influence wherever they could force back their neighbors. In the absence of clearly definable frontiers, characteristic of their part of eastern Europe, they were therefore at different times drawn both deeper into Germany itself and more adventurously to the east towards Ruthenia. Their capital was however established at Krakow by Kasimir I (1038–58), whose son Boleslav II was crowned king (1076) after reaching Kiev (1061). The pressure of German rulers on Polish lands in the west tended to be more persistent, particularly after the mid-12th century, so that Piast rulers began to concentrate more in the east. After the death of Boleslav III (king 1107–38) his territories were divided between his sons and for nearly two centuries the Poles developed within several distinct ducal territories; even the title of king was dropped until 1294. The period of division had permanent consequences for the Poles. The princes of Silesia, who aspired at the end of the period to reestablish the kingship for themselves, nevertheless preferred to accept membership of the Bohemian kingdom under the Luxembourg kings rather than recognize any other Piast as king of Poland. Bohemian ambitions on Krakow were not maintained so successfully, for Krakow continued to be drawn into the affairs of Ruthenia. The concerns of "little" Poland mattered little to the peoples of the Polish heartland, who were faced in the late 13th century with a renewed burst of German pressure. The arrival of German colonists, the ambitions of Brandenburg, the settlement of the Teutonic Order, all served to separate Pomerania from other Poles and to divide that duchy into east and west parts. In the lake district of Mazovia yet another Polish duchy with its own interests tended to concentrate on its own difficulties with the pagan Prussians to the north and used the Teutonic Order for the purposes of defeating them. The various attempts made by the Bohemians and the rulers of "great" Poland to revive the Piast monarchy came to nothing until Ladislas the Short managed to obtain coronation at Krakow in 1320. The revived kingdom of Ladislas lacked both Silesia and Pomorze and even his son Kasimir III made no more than minor adjustments to the western frontier.

Kasimir had no son to succeed him and the kingdom passed first to his nephew Lewis king of Hungary (1370–82) and then to Lewis's younger daughter Jadwiga, who was married by the Poles to Jagellon, duke of Lithuania. Under the Jagellon dynasty Poland became the most powerful state of eastern Europe, but the disadvantages of linking Polish interests to those of other peoples like the Hungarians and Lithuanians were considerable. Admittedly the union with Lithuania enabled the Poles to defeat the Teutonic Order and recover control of Pomerania, giving access to the Baltic ports and the advantages of the urban settlements fostered by the Order in Prussia in its heyday. The temporary extension of Jagellon influence into Hungary and Bohemia put an end to the pressure formerly exerted on the Poles from those regions, though Silesia was not recovered. The union with Lithuania helped also to define the eastern limits of Polish influence, for the Lithuanians remained Orthodox and the Poles had to abandon their infiltration to the east. The beginnings of the rivalry with the rulers of Moscow were regarded as a more specifically Lithuanian problem.

The concerns of the Jagellon dynasty for their farflung territorial interests and their war against the Turks certainly distracted them from more specifically Polish problems or from concerns to develop the political apparatus of the monarchy. Lewis of Hungary had in effect bought recognition of his kingship in Poland by conceding privileges to the great landowners who could have given him problems. By their control over taxation and their growing ability to develop their own estates for supplying the grain markets from the Baltic ports, these landowners came to be a power in the land, with more concern for their own property than for the kingdom as a whole. This nebulous responsibility they left to their rulers. The cultural life of the Poles became a particular concern of the Latin clergy, who remained hostile to the Orthodox Lithuanians and somewhat suspicious of the Jagellon kings because of their origins. The university founded at Krakow in 1364 began to play its part in educating the clergy and strengthening their ties with the church in the west, particularly in Italy. Italian merchants also began to establish themselves in Poland from the same period. The cult of native Polish saints like St Stanislas combined with the cultivation of Polish history in Latin and popular religious literature in the vernacular to promote a strong feeling for Polish identity, through their religious rather than their royal allegiance. The papal chancery itself consistently used the term "Polonia" to define a region that otherwise appeared, characteristically, to be indefinite; when the earlier fluctuating frontiers of the kingdom were stabilized by the Jagellons, the spread of their dynastic mantle in eastern Europe made secular definition as elusive as ever.

The development of the Poles in these five centuries, though shaped by political events,

amounted to more than politics. The process of taking root in a definable space, of accepting conversion to Christianity and of opening up new lands for cultivation required the cooperation of many groups. Penetration by German settlers along the Baltic littoral was not always contested by Poles. Colonists were attracted by the offer of favorable terms. New towns or at least some town craftsmen were established with the privileges of their homelands. A great extension of Cistercian influence in the countryside came in the 13th century and overlapped therefore with the arrival of the friars, particularly the Dominicans. Their earliest settlements were in the established towns, Gdansk, Wroclaw and Krakow, as might have been expected. Their later extension to the towns along the Silesian Oder and the Vistula indicate how urban centers were growing at that time.

Hungary
Medieval Hungary, when it became a settled Christian kingdom, succeeded in doubling the size of its territory in its first two centuries. In the later Middle Ages its rulers stretched their frontiers even further afield. Only the Ottoman advance in the Balkans placed firm limits on Hungarian ambitions. For its first three centuries it enjoyed the advantages of a native royal dynasty, despite the feuding common among its members. After 1301 most of its kings were foreigners with international interests that demanded much attention, most notably in the end responsibility for dealing with the Ottomans in the Balkans. Royal wealth was considerable from control of the mining industries.

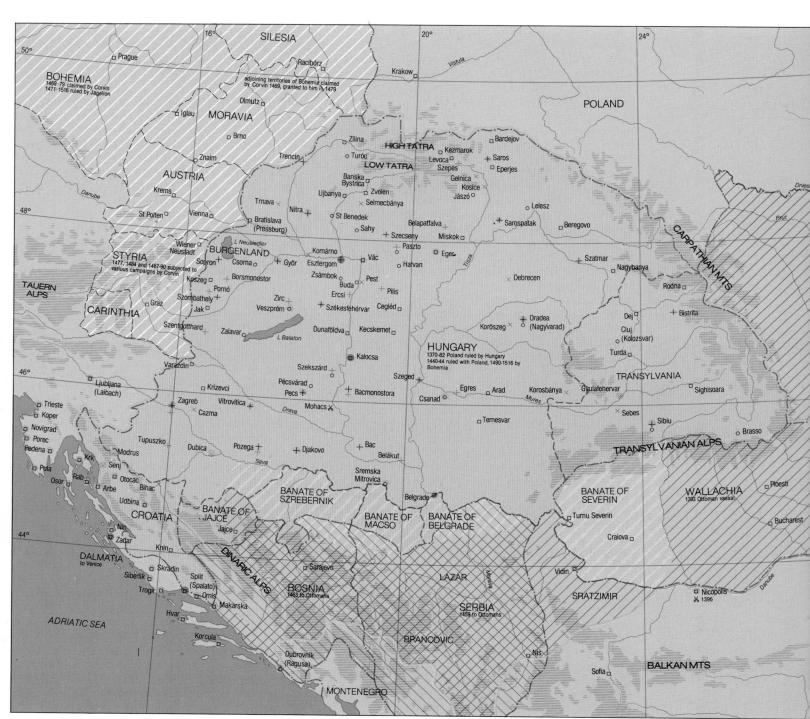

boundary of Hungary under Lewis the Great c.1380

vassal lands c.1380

banate lands c.1380

extent of Hungary under Matthew Corvin c.1470

vassal lands c.1470

area of temporary Hungarian control c.1470

archdiocese

diocese

royal monastery

Cistercian

Dominican

Franciscan

site of important battle

land over 1000 meters

1:5 000 000

150 km

100 mi

MOLDAVIA
Hungarian suzerainty until 1365, in-dependent until 1397 when under tem-porary Polish control. 1504 Ottoman vassal.

BLACK SEA

Hungary and European dynasties

The revival of Poland in the 14th century was one of the most lasting achievements of the period and in this respect may be favorably compared with the position of its neighbor Hungary, with which it shared a ruler for one brief period, Lewis the Great (1370–82). By that time, however, Hungary had itself become part of the great Angevin dominions that had developed after the Angevin conquest of southern Italy, so that to some degree Hungarian rulers already tended to view their own interests in dynastic rather than national terms. This means that a dichotomy between the outlook of the rulers and their subjects, similar to that found in Jagellon Poland, had already developed in Hungary. The basic reasons for this are also related: the absence of any clearly defined boundaries for the kingdom or, in contemporary terms, the lack of effective resistance put up by neighbors to Hungarian expansion, even under the native Arpad dynasty.

Until the Magyars accepted Christianity and with it a settled way of life, there had been no organized settlement in the region, where nomads and raiders had roamed at will. The acceptance of Christianity from the west and a royal crown for Stephen (king 1000–38) from the pope stretched Latin Christianity to the point where it impinged on areas of Orthodox mission and gave the Hungarian state an abiding Catholic characteristic. In the east, Transylvania was conquered by Stephen himself; later Croatia and Ragusa were brought within the kingdom (1189–1204). Zeal for religion inspired campaigns to extinguish the Bogomil heresy in Bosnia and Herzegovina (1237–84), which were also annexed. A marriage alliance with a French princess in the late 12th century established political relations that were reinforced a century later when the Angevins became kings of Naples. Thwarted of their ambitions on Constantinople by the Sicilian Vespers (1282), the Angevins turned to Hungary, easily reached across the Adriatic. Charles Robert was crowned king of Hungary at Zagreb in 1290, and was accepted throughout the kingdom after the death of Andrew III, the last representative of the native Arpad dynasty, in 1301. An Angevin empire embracing the Adriatic naturally made Venice its principal opponent and Lewis the Great, at the end of a reign of active intervention for control of the Dalmatian coast, obtained Venetian Dalmatia by cession in 1381 as well as recovering Herzegovina as far as the Neretva river. After Lewis's death in 1382 disputes over the succession enabled the Bosnians and the Venetians to reassert themselves, leaving Hungary without an important maritime base. Lewis's daughter Mary was married to Sigismund of Luxembourg, whose brother was emperor, and for the first time Hungary became more involved in German affairs. Sigismund was well aware of his responsibilities as a Christian ruler against the Ottomans in the Balkans. Great hopes were placed in a crusading campaign of 1396 and its defeat at Nicopolis in the same year was humiliating. Sigismund himself was soon deeply involved in the affairs of his brother's kingdom of Bohemia, with the schism of the Latin church, the Hussite heretics and the affairs of the German kingdom after his election as king there in 1411. Hungary inevitably bore the brunt of the renewed Ottoman advances from the 1450s, particularly after the failure of

Sigismund's nephew Ladislas III in his crusade at Varna in 1444. The Hungarians' main glory was the defense of Belgrade in 1456 under John Hunyadi, whose son Matthew Corvin became king of Hungary (1450–90), the last native king.

Hungary was far from being a united land by the 15th century. It comprised many peoples and even contained Orthodox Bulgars as well as important numbers of Bogomil heretics whom the zealous Catholic clergy failed to repress. The long period of foreign rulers that brought Hungary into the limelight of international politics did not witness any institutional development of the monarchy. The crown's estates and mining monopolies made it wealthy enough not to force its subjects to share in its schemes, so the great landowners could manage their own interests without royal interference. Foreign merchants, particularly Italians, and clergy played no part in building up the educated or enterprising classes. The Ottoman advance from the south meant that the kingdom had already contracted to modest proportions before Belgrade fell in

193

1521; the defeat at Mohacs put an end to its precarious independence, even if half the kingdom survived in Hapsburg hands.

Both Poland and Hungary as Catholic kingdoms became hopelessly involved with the Orthodox peoples on their frontiers, who in this period found themselves everywhere on the defensive. The collapse of the Greek empire (1204) and the Mongol overlordship of Russia (1237) meant that Orthodoxy had lost its traditional secular protectors without hope of finding another. It is hardly surprising that the authority of the patriarch of Constantinople was challenged by the appearance of several autonomous archbishops, or that pious Christians turned to a renewal of the monastic tradition, or that these fostered the devotions of the mystical Hesychasts. In the monastic republic of Mount Athos Orthodox men from all over eastern Europe began to cultivate traditional pieties that would inspire the Orthodox world to live through the centuries of political eclipse. Such men made no difficulties about accepting the nominal overlordship of Muslims and Mount Athos itself easily made its peace with the Ottomans.

The transformation of Russia

During this period, almost unknown to the Latins, the Russians were also engaged in reorganizing both their ecclesiastical and their secular life after the great shock of the Mongol invasions. The earliest organization of the Russians as a distinct political group dates from the 10th century when the cities linked to Kiev and converted by the Orthodox to Christianity were ruled by the descendants of Scandinavian merchant-soldiers. At that time colonization into the adjacent forests had barely begun and as elsewhere in eastern Europe the vastness of the land and the paucity of settlers made progress slow and unhurried. To a considerable degree it also passed comparatively unrecorded. No doubt the political disturbances of the Kievan cities in the 12th century encouraged emigrants to move into the forests and develop new settlements. There was as yet no demand for grain exports so that colonization at the most represented demographic expansion or political dissatisfaction. Peasants moved freely and did not need to be tempted or coerced to work the land. For centuries the peasants were their own masters and managed new settlements through their own organizations. How far these settlements had already developed when the Mongols overran Kievan Russia in 1237 is incalculable. The initial response was of course to scatter the remaining urban populations into the forest. The Mongol domination of the southern steppe and the Volga kept the Russians under pressure, and they remained predominantly rural peoples for more than two centuries.

The most lasting consequence of the Mongol overlordship was not so much the burden of paying tribute-money as the division of the Russian peoples themselves. Kiev, both princely capital and the religious base of the Orthodox metropolitan, acquired a ruler who, after the Mongol raids, received support from the pope in the west. After his death the territory was occupied by the Mongols and the Orthodox metropolitan felt sufficiently uncomfortable to leave for Moscow in 1308. The Little Russians or Ukrainians remained Orthodox,

Left The Russian town of Suzdal was replanned in the mid-12th century and the present cathedral, inside the kremlin (citadel), was rebuilt in 1222. Only its lower parts survived the devastations caused by the Mongol invasion of 1238, from which the town recovered slowly. The five domes were added in the late 14th century and the present building was completed in 1528.

Right: Russia
Modern Russia has developed directly from the principalities living in the shadow of the Mongol presence after the mid-13th century. The Mongols were generally content to levy tribute through the princes, but they did not hesitate to intervene directly on occasions. The old Russian metropolis of Kiev ceased to play an active role in Russian affairs. The Orthodox metropolitan archbishop moved to the north and eventually settled at Moscow, in a region where religious idealism was infectious. But the Russians were now isolated from other peoples and Christians. They were even divided among themselves. In this period the linguistic frontier between Great and Little Russians indicated the separate political experience of the Ukraine. Looking back, the period seems to be focused on the inexorable rise of Moscow as the leading power of the Great Russians. At the time the endless rivalry with other northern principalities proved the continuing vitality of local traditions and Russian indifference to any concern for holding together a political unity against the Mongols. The resilience of the Russians depended on those who were steadily encroaching on the forests to enlarge the areas of human settlement, which included monks, whose communities became more numerous at this time. In this way medieval Russia, formerly a land of associated trading republics, passed into the hands of the countrymen whose main concern was cultivation. The bishops were less prominent than the monks. Only in the mid-15th century did the outlines of the future czarist regime emerge under the grandduke of Moscow and the Russian metropolitan. The Russians repudiated the union of Catholics and Orthodox agreed at Florence in 1439 and after 1453 saw themselves as the true heirs of the Byzantine empire.

but after the Mongols began to cede ground to the Poles and Lithuanians, the Ukraine was brought for centuries into close contact with the west. Under Lithuanian leadership they attempted to recover their leading role in Russian affairs, but significantly they were already unequal to beating the Great Russians to the north. The White Russians (Belorussians), along the Dnieper, were also under pressure from the Lithuanians; they too came to constitute at the same time a distinctive group.

The Great Russians who emerged as the leading peoples of Russia in the 13th and 14th centuries had perhaps been growing more numerous and powerful long before the Mongol invasions, but the Mongol government itself helped their rise to power, both by smashing Kievan Russia and because the Great Russians were somewhat cushioned against the full force of Mongol power by the forests of their northern homes. Novgorod was the only Kievan city of importance to survive the Mongol attack, but it did not itself become the focus of Great Russian revival. The new Russia, as befitted a community based on agriculture rather than trade, was led by princes, the earliest of whom to achieve prominence was Alexander Yaroslavski, prince of Vladimir (1246–63), who became the great hero Nevski. He owed this name to his defeat of Novgorod on the river Neva in 1240; this was followed by his victory over the Teutonic knights on Lake Peipus in 1242. Novgorod did not lose its independence altogether till the latter part of the 15th century, but it accepted the lordship of princes from Vladimir who thereafter set the pace in Russia. Nevski himself took a very cautious line with his Mongol neighbors and by not exciting notice or arousing alarm his successors were able to build up the reputation of his family among the Russian peoples.

At the time of his death his sons shared out his lands, the youngest taking Moscow as his part, a proof that Moscow did not yet rank high among them. Yet within half a century the Russian metropolitan had come to settle in Moscow and he made it the religious focus of all Russians. This was anyway important, but the nature of the Russian predicament in the 14th century certainly con-

Far right A 14th-century icon depicting the divine fatherhood, from the school of Novgorod. The anthropomorphic representation of the Trinity probably derived from the Balkans. The merchant city of Novgorod gave medieval Russia a window on the west.

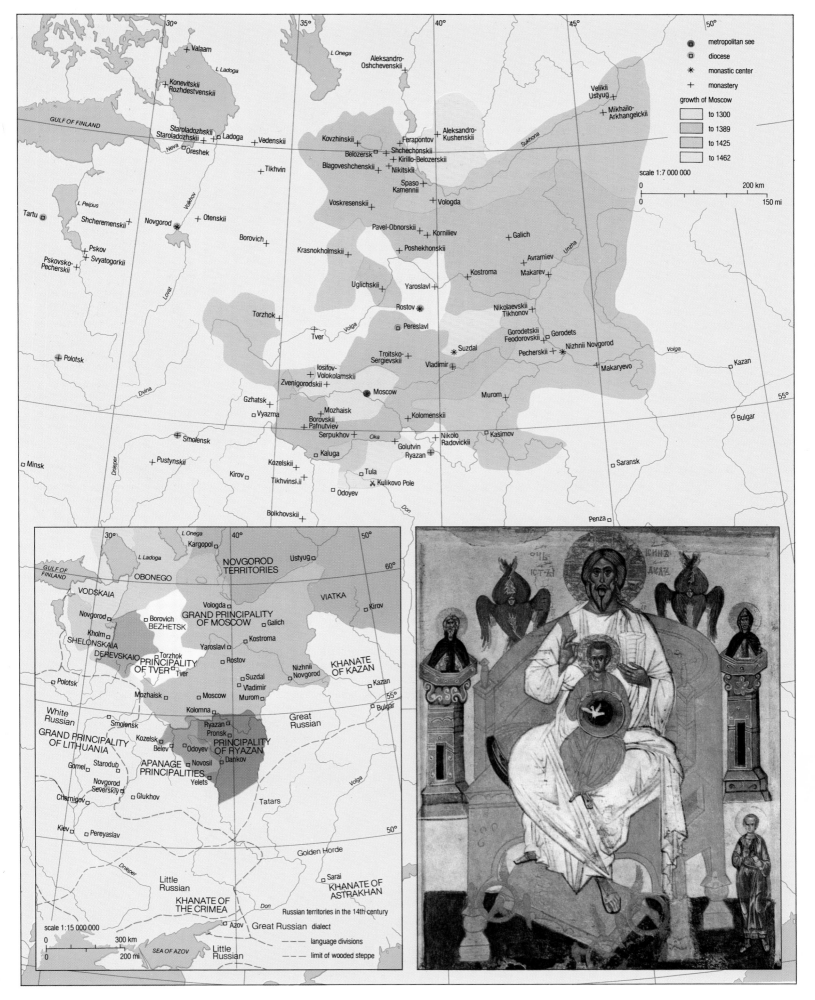

Main map labels (top):

metropolitan see
diocese
monastic center
monastery

growth of Moscow
to 1300
to 1389
to 1425
to 1462

scale 1:7 000 000

0 — 200 km
0 — 150 mi

Valaam
L Onega
Aleksandro-
Oshchevenskii
Velikii
Ustyug
Konevitskii
Rozhdestvenskii
L Ladoga
Mikhailo-
Arkhangelckii
GULF OF FINLAND
Staroladozhskii
Staroladozhskii
Ladoga
Vedenskii
Kovzhinskii
Ferapontov
Aleksandro-
Kushenskii
Neva
Oreshek
Tikhvin
Belozersk
Shchechonskii
Kirillo-Belozerskii
Sukhona
Blagoveshchenskii
Nikitskii
L Peipus
Shcheremenskii
Novgorod
Otenskii
Spaso-
Kamennii
Vologda
Tartu
Voskresenskii
Borovich
Pavel-Obnorskii
Korniliev
Galich
Pskov
Svyatogorkii
Krasnokholmskii
Poshekhonskii
Avramiev
Urzha
Pskovsko-
Pecherskii
Kostroma
Makarev
Lovat
Uglichskii
Yaroslavl
Torzhok
Volga
Rostov
Nikolaevskii
Tikhonov
Polotsk
Pereslavl
Gorodetskii
Feodorovskii
Gorodets
Tver
Suzdal
Pecherskii
Nizhnii Novgorod
Volga
Troitsko-
Sergievskii
Iosifov-
Volokolamskii
Vladimir
Makaryevo
Kazan
Dvina
Zvenigorodskii
Gzhatsk
Moscow
Murom
Vyazma
Mozhaisk
Borovskii
Pafnutviev
Kolomenskii
Smolensk
Serpukhov
Oka
Nikolo
Radovickii
Kasimov
Minsk
Pustynskii
Kaluga
Golutvin
Ryazan
Bulgar
Kirov
Kozelskii
Tula
Saransk
Tikhvinskii
Kulikovo Pole
Odoyev
Don
Bolkhovskii
Penza

Inset map (bottom left) — Russian territories in the 14th century:

scale 1:15 000 000
0 — 300 km
0 — 200 mi

L Onega
Kargopol
Ustyug
NOVGOROD
TERRITORIES
GULF OF FINLAND
L Ladoga
OBONEGO
VIATKA
VODSKAIA
Vologda
Kirov
GRAND PRINCIPALITY
OF MOSCOW
Novgorod
Borovich
BEZHETSK
Galich
Kholm
SHELONSKAIA
Kostroma
DEREVSKAIO
Torzhok
Yaroslavl
PRINCIPALITY
OF TVER
Rostov
Tver
KHANATE
OF KAZAN
Polotsk
Mozhaisk
Suzdal
Nizhnii
Novgorod
Moscow
Vladimir
Kazan
White
Russian
Murom
Kolomna
Bulgar
GRAND PRINCIPALITY
OF LITHUANIA
Smolensk
Ryazan
Great
Russian
Kozelsk
Pronsk
Belev
Odoyev
PRINCIPALITY
OF RYAZAN
Gomel
Starodub
Novosil
Dankov
APANAGE
PRINCIPALITIES
Yelets
Novgorod
Severskii
Chernigov
Glukhov
Tatars
Volga
Kiev
Pereyaslav
Golden Horde
Dnieper
Little
Russian
Sarai
KHANATE OF
ASTRAKHAN
KHANATE OF
THE CRIMEA
Don
Russian territories in the 14th century
Azov
Great Russian dialect
SEA OF AZOV
Little
Russian
—— language divisions
——— limit of wooded steppe

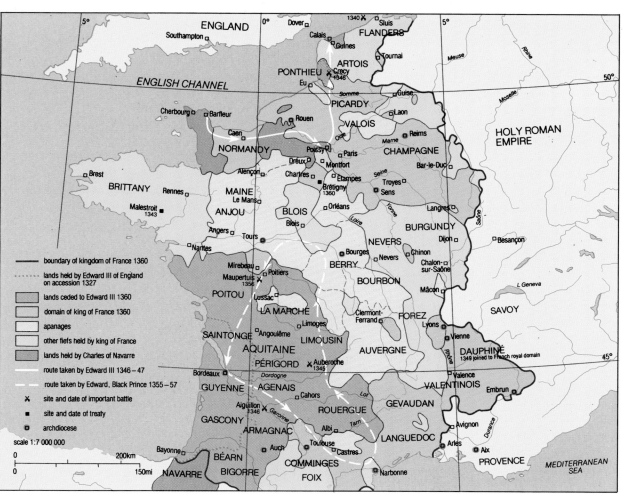

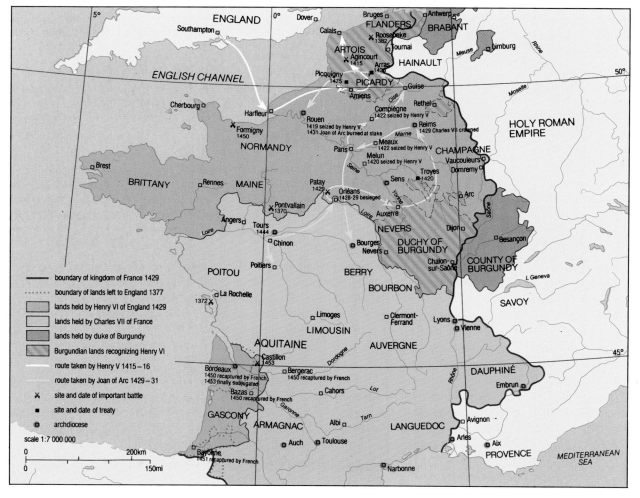

The Anglo-French war

When war between the kings of England and France broke out again in 1294 after 35 years of peace, it proved difficult to resolve the dispute, so war, though frequently suspended by truces, recurred again and again until the mid-15th century. Various attempts to find a way to peace by redefining the relationship of the English king as duke of Aquitaine with the king of France, including the formal claim to sovereignty in Aquitaine, or the even more radical attempt to unite the two kingdoms under Henry VI, failed to resolve the matter. Both parties sought foreign support. The impartiality of the papacy at Avignon was impugned, and when the Great Schism occurred (1378), this weakness of the church was exploited by both sides. The war therefore played its part in hampering religion, holding back crusader efforts and allowing heresies to burgeon. The kingdom of France, as the principal battleground, suffered from the presence of professional soldiers, both when they were employed by the contending parties during hostilities and after the proclamations of peace when they had to fend for themselves. The great princes of France were divided by doubts about the claims of the Valois dynasty to rule, about the competence of the individual kings and about alternative policies. The bitter feuds of the princes and nobles made this the most difficult period in the history of medieval France.

tributed to an intensification of Russian religious sentiment at this time and for Moscow to take the lead in religious matters inevitably had important consequences. The development of Russian monastic life, particularly by St Sergius of Radonezh, was particularly important for its contribution to Russian culture, through religious literature and painting, for its links with the Orthodox monasteries on Mount Athos and for a new awareness of the Orthodox mystical Hesychast movement. The monks also obtained favors from the Tatar overlords such as the privilege of not paying tribute from their estates. The monks endorsed the submissive, respectful attitude towards the Tatars and this helped the rulers of the dynasty to maintain peaceable relations with their masters. Ivan Kalita I (1328–41) was the first ruler of Moscow to obtain from the Tatars the right to act as their tax collector from the Christians and in this way used the Tatar dominion as a means of getting influence with all the Russians. Ivan passed his authority to his son. It is probably important for the continuity of Russian history that there was no failure of sons in each generation and that these rulers of Moscow were individually and successively long-lived: there were only six rulers between 1359 and 1584.

The position obtained by Tatar favor was of course threatened when the Tatar empire began to weaken, as it did after the Ming dynasty put an end to the Mongol government of China in 1386. But the Tatars were still capable of being aggressive for about a century. Their defeat at Kulikovo Pole in 1380 was more symbolic than decisive. From their khanate at Kazan (established by 1445) they were able to create trouble for Moscow until the city was taken in 1535. The Tatars even took Vasili (Basil) II himself prisoner in 1445, though he was admittedly rather a weak ruler. The princes of Moscow also faced contests for leadership of the Russians with other rulers, like those of Tver, not finally stilled until 1484. They had to fight the Lithuanians, against whose campaign of 1368 the walls of a stone citadel – the Kremlin – were first raised in Moscow, with Tugtamish, vassal general of Timur the Lame (1382), and against the boyars of the principality who three times deposed Vasili II from power. Yet Vasili II survived the most turbulent reign of his family and called himself sovereign of the whole Russian land. It was in his time that the first autocephalous metropolitan of the church was established, when the Russians refused to recognize the formal union of Orthodox and Latins agreed at the Council of Florence in 1438. When Constantinople itself was captured by the Ottomans, Ivan III was ready to consider himself the proper heir of Rome and imitate the political examples of his wife's family, Sophia Palaeologi. But the development of czarist Russia – the power of the landlord and the serfdom of the peasantry – belongs properly to the subsequent history of Russia. By the end of the 15th century the Russians thought less of the evils to come than the miseries that were past. In the two centuries of the Mongol domination Russia had been thoroughly transformed in response to that pressure, rather than by direct Mongol rule. The Russians had not suffered the fate of the Chinese in the same period. Their prospects for the future were, however, quite unsuspected, either in the east or in the west.

Western dynasties and the hundred years' war

The very real importance of the histories of the different peoples of eastern Europe in this period, and the new significance of the whole region at this time, indicate to some extent the positive, if checkered, achievements of the 14th century. Reverting to the west with fresh ideas about dynasties, nobles, towns and nations, we may even be able to consider the great war between the kings of England and France in less anachronistic terms than have often been employed. The great eminence achieved by the last Capetian kings of France was not dependent on their real strength, but on the luck of being the first continental rulers to achieve institutional sophistication and in having unstinted papal support. Philip IV (king 1285–1314), the most aggressive of these Capetian rulers, had however to meet the challenge of his most powerful vassal, the duke of Aquitaine, Edward king of England, as well as the challenge of Pope Boniface VIII, who was exasperated to find that his defense of the clergy forced him to rebuke Philip. The papacy's enmity was however short-lived, and a succession of southern French popes in residence at Avignon gave French kings for many decades the comfort of an even closer special relationship with popes. Peace was now patched up between Philip and Edward by the pope himself, but their successors found it impossible to keep the peace for long and times of peace remained belligerent in thought if not in deed. The resources of the two kings were quite unequal, so that the power of the king of England to renew the war rested on his finding willing allies within the French kingdom for his interventions. The military front shifted according to circumstances and the objectives varied from the English king claiming a better title to the throne of France than that of its Valois incumbent, to more moderate and equally unacceptable demands for recognition of their sovereign status in their feudal holdings. At stake in both cases was the unitary state that had developed unchallenged up to the time of Philip IV. This was proving irksome, not simply to the duke of Aquitaine, but even more oppressively to the count of Flanders in the beginning and to others, like the dukes of Brittany and Burgundy, later on. The great princes of France, including the Flemish and the English, were all related to one another. The success of the apanage system in France had in the first generation or two worked to the advantage of the king, but in due course inevitably gave rise to distinct branches of the royal house. Rivalries rather than diversities brought conflicts, not so much with the intention of dismembering the kingdom but to allow the princes more freedom of action than the king's own growing army of servants wished to allow. The kings of England, who made the French war popular with their subjects, both high and low, remained to the end deeply committed to what they saw as their role within the French kingdom and the French ruling house. For them the war could never become the national cause that it sometimes seemed to their subjects and that it became in legend. England itself suffered directly from the war only to the extent of raids and plunder in coastal areas and in the ever-troubled border regions. The war was fought in France and written about by writers of French – of whom the most distinguished, Jean Froissart, came

from Hainault. In the writings of this famous author of poetry and romance the history of the war became a nostalgic lament for chivalry.

The long period over which successive generations of English kings renewed the war makes it probable that it had profound consequences on English social and political development but it is difficult to isolate the precise consequences of the war on events when so many other factors also had time to operate. The most important outcome was that the English king eventually lost every scrap of his French land except Calais (taken for England in 1347) and for the French king this represented therefore a triumph. He had expelled his most truculent vassal and added vast new territories to his state. He had also, in the final stages of the war, achieved the means of both taxing his kingdom and maintaining a standing army. This gave him unprecedented leverage in the kingdom. The monarchy of St Louis was transformed into a state ready for war. The even more vast extent of his domains had however made the task of governing them all the more complicated. The monarchy had to share some of its powers, if not with feudal vassals, then with corporations of lawyers, office-holders and army captains. The apanage princes were eased out or absorbed into the monarchy at the convenient extinction of their dynasties, but the privileges of the provinces were graciously confirmed by kings to rally support in the regions. The triumphant monarchy of Charles VII (king 1422–61) was not therefore a mere restoration of Philip IV's style of government. And if the king of England had been expelled from the kingdom, the province of Flanders, that Philip IV himself had sweated blood to obtain, still eluded royal control. Lastly, France itself had also suffered recurrent invasions, pillage, sackings and devastations. France had above all lost its preeminent position in Europe. The Franco-papal alliance, which had served the French kings so well

in the 13th century, gave the French king during the Great Schism no more help in Christendom than his own secular allies did, and with the coming of the Renaissance papacy the French kings enjoyed no special favors. The decades of war therefore had very profound consequences for the French kingdom. The experience of war, disorder, defeat and dismemberment left only the Valois dynasty itself as a guarantee of continuity. Few of its representatives were personally equal to their responsibilities, but when God appeared to send Joan of Arc to secure the coronation at Reims of the pitiful Charles VII (1429), French loyalty to the dynasty revived. Faith in God's providential provision of a male successor to the crown thereafter guaranteed the survival of the kingdom. It was not the French nation that was created by the war: it was the royal dynastic principle itself that had been vindicated.

Above left Feudal nobility before the walls of Paris, an illustration from Froissart's chronicles which cover events in western Europe, and especially those of the Anglo-French war, from 1325 to 1400.

Above Calais was for more than two centuries in English hands and by the 16th century, when this drawing was made, the only territory left to the English in France. The picture gives a good impression of the town's appearance in the Middle Ages with its fortifications, the harborside and the narrow entry to the port channel.

Left This copy of the Latin text of the *Trial of Joan* gives the legalistic evidence for her life and career which, for all its manifest bias, constitutes the bulk of the only reliable information still available to historians. The illustrated initial is no more than a token representation of events and has no claim to be considered lifelike, though the records were copied by scribes who sat in court with her for many days.

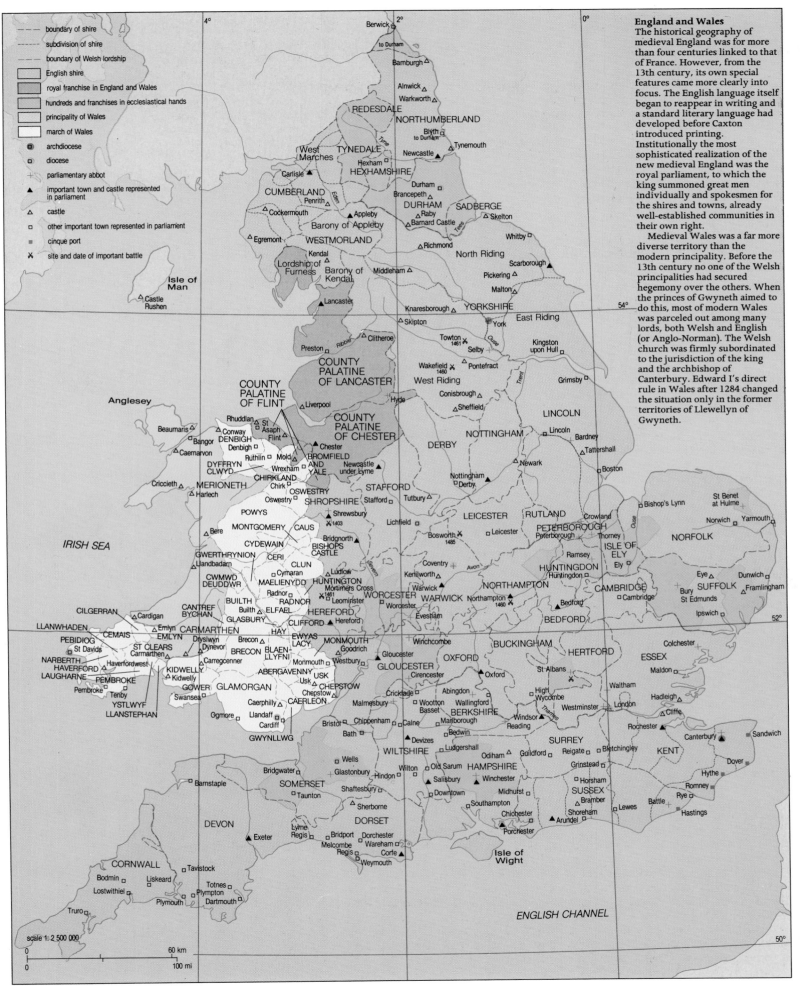

England and Wales
The historical geography of medieval England was for more than four centuries linked to that of France. However, from the 13th century, its own special features came more clearly into focus. The English language itself began to reappear in writing and a standard literary language had developed before Caxton introduced printing. Institutionally the most sophisticated realization of the new medieval England was the royal parliament, to which the king summoned great men individually and spokesmen for the shires and towns, already well-established communities in their own right.

Medieval Wales was a far more diverse territory than the modern principality. Before the 13th century no one of the Welsh principalities had secured hegemony over the others. When the princes of Gwyneth aimed to do this, most of modern Wales was parceled out among many lords, both Welsh and English (or Anglo-Norman). The Welsh church was firmly subordinated to the jurisdiction of the king and the archbishop of Canterbury. Edward I's direct rule in Wales after 1284 changed the situation only in the former territories of Llewellyn of Gwyneth.

Map legend:
- ----- boundary of shire
- ----- subdivision of shire
- ----- boundary of Welsh lordship
- English shire
- royal franchise in England and Wales
- hundreds and franchises in ecclesiastical hands
- principality of Wales
- march of Wales
- ⊚ archdiocese
- ◻ diocese
- + parliamentary abbot
- ▲ important town and castle represented in parliament
- △ castle
- ◻ other important town represented in parliament
- ■ cinque port
- ✕ site and date of important battle

For England the other outstanding result of the war with France was the survival of the independent kingdom of Scotland. In the second half of his reign Edward I of England (king 1272–1307) had several times arranged the government of Scotland according to his own will, but despite his apparent success in imposing his solutions, his power proved illusory. His grandson Edward III (king 1327–77) also tried briefly to make himself master of Scotland, but such English intentions for Scotland were resisted by the Scots' determination to manage their own affairs. In this the Scots showed a similar spirit to that displayed by the other smaller "nations" of Europe that resisted all attempts to incorporate them into dynastic empires.

The Scots were not however a well-developed nation by 1300. Only in the previous generation had their king obtained from the Norwegians the overlordship of the Highlands and Islands. The strength of the monarchy lay in the coastal plain, in the narrow belt of land between the Clyde and the Forth, spilling over north into Perthshire and south into the valleys of the Borders. This land had been transformed into a feudalized monarchy in the early 12th century and its most powerful ruler, David I (king of Scotland 1124–53), had temporarily extended its southern frontier to include Northumbria, Cumbria and Lancashire to the Ribble. These encroachments had naturally pro-

voked the English king to retaliate. Victories by Henry II and John had both resulted in formal submissions of the Scots king to the English king which became the basis of Edward I's claim to the overlordship of Scotland. The Scottish bishoprics needed a special relationship with Rome to rescue them from attempts by the archbishop of York to make them part of his province. Many English barons held lands in southern Scotland. Had Edward I not been so eager to define and assert his role, the prospects of the two kingdoms merging were good. But his peremptory manner with the Scots caused resentment. When Robert Bruce (king 1306–29) offered the Scots effective leadership they welcomed the chance to fend off the English and consolidate an independent tradition.

Scotland was too remote from the English king's bases in the south; it was too poor to be an attractive land for English barons looking for the rewards of military adventure. Far more interest was lavished on the wars with France. Scotland, which clung to the French alliance, was able to continue the struggle despite its own weaknesses. Under the new Stewart dynasty (1371), with its own archbishops, St Andrews (1472), Glasgow (1492), its own universities (St Andrews founded in 1410, Glasgow 1451, Aberdeen 1495), though still poor, it was willing or able to resist English domination. It was only united with England when its own Protestant king,

Below The castle at Eileen Donan, built by Alexander II in 1220 on the site of a preexisting fortification, affirmed the royal presence in the Highlands at a critical point opposite Skye where three lochs meet.

Scotland

In the Middle Ages, as now, the population of Scotland settled most densely in the lowland zone. The disturbances of the borders created a region of recurrent warfare in the 14th and 15th centuries, where previously feudal lordships had stabilized a frontier, formally defined in 1249. About the same time the disintegration of the Norse empire brought the Scottish king into direct lordship of the Highlands and Islands. But medieval Scotland was made by the people of the central zone, where the king had his castles, and where the clergy, towns and sheriffs were concentrated. Its political independence became linked to its alliance with France against England, which required the east coast ports to keep open the maritime routes. The persistence of the war with the English gave the Scots confidence in their chances of holding off English conquest and over the decades they built up their institutions.

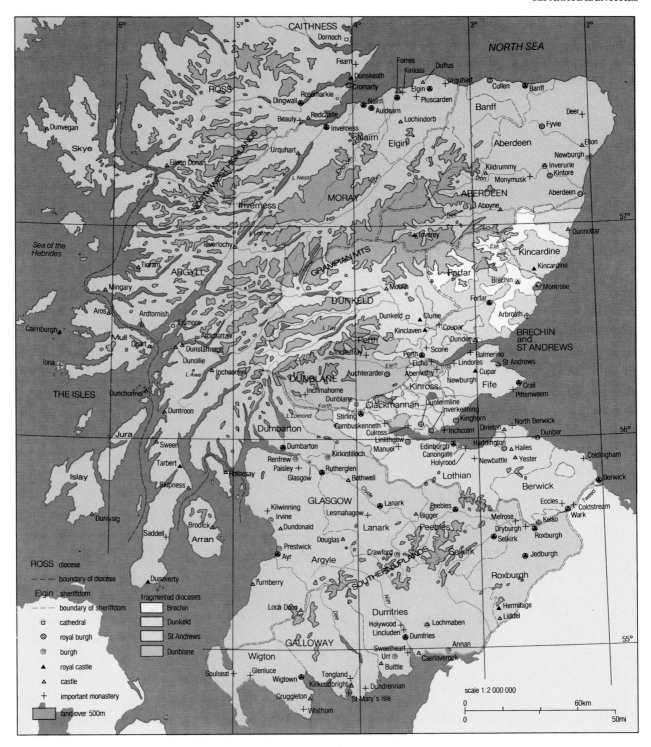

ROSS diocese
— — — boundary of diocese
Elgin sheriffdom
— — — boundary of sheriffdom
▫ cathedral
◉ royal burgh
◉ burgh
▲ royal castle
△ castle
✛ important monastery
land over 500m

fragmented dioceses
Brechin
Dunkeld
St Andrews
Dunblane

scale 1:2 000 000
0 ____ 60km
0 ____ 50mi

Norse speaking

Gaelic speaking

English speaking

approximate division

James VI, inherited the southern crown in 1603.

As a result of all these activities across Europe during the 14th and early 15th centuries, it became clear that there was a widespread capacity for smaller nations to resist the most powerful kings of the day, so that instead of a few great continental empires emerging in Europe, as happened in the 18th century, political units remained, on the whole, small and numerous. Some of these states were no larger than cities which, usually because of their maritime positions, proved to be large enough to preserve their independence by virtue of the extra strength found in commerce. But most states needed a large enough territory to provide the necessary resources for their populations, and the homogeneity that came from common legal and religious institutions. Some of them banded together under joint rulers, provided that their separate identities were not impaired. The religious impulse in both Catholicism and Orthodoxy encouraged the use of the local vernacular languages for prayer and devotions, so that literature in these languages began to fortify these peoples by defining them as cultural groups. The dominant position assumed by the Latin clergy as masters of their flocks was however, in due course, inevitably challenged by pieties of another kind accessible to laymen. Kings and nobles had never been as numerous or colorful as they were in this period, but they jostled for attention with hosts of others no less proud of their achievements. It was an age that respected social hierarchies still, but gloated too in the common sinfulness of all humanity, accepting that popes and emperors could be as wicked as the rest. There is therefore an element of realism about this time that made the effectiveness of power more important than nominal ideals. Few of the states of this period worried much about the legalities of their positions. In Italy, notably, the city-states expanded their frontiers as they could and acquired titles, if at all, only later. During the Great Schism Christendom lacked a universally accepted arbiter and mediator. What could not be settled by arms had therefore to be argued about and negotiated. As a result, the well-being of Christendom fell into the hands of many and could not be retained by the few traditional authorities. Europe had become a highly complex and intricate political society.

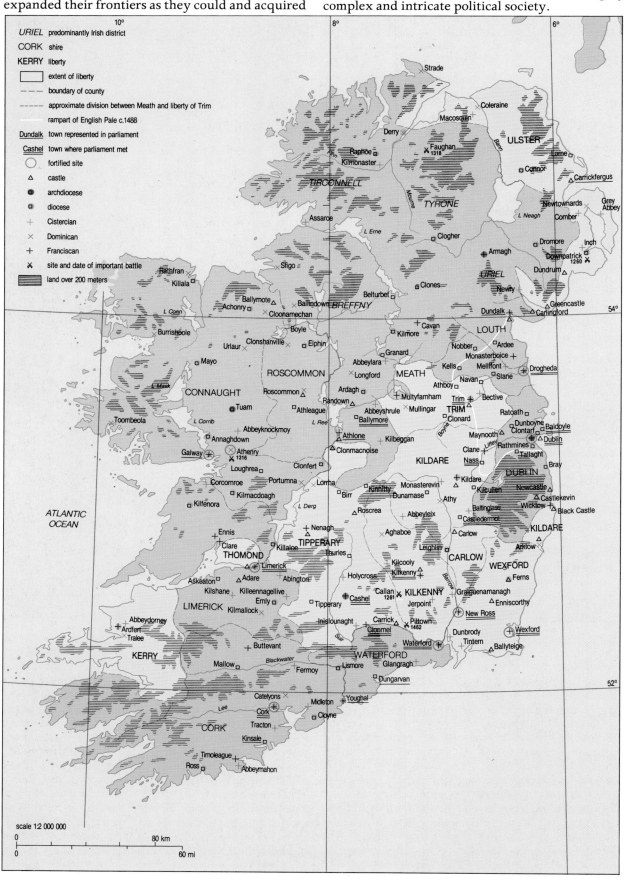

Left: Ireland
The conquests which enabled Henry II to claim the lordship of Ireland in 1162 were never sufficiently exploited to give the English king control of all Ireland. After John only one English medieval king, Richard II, ever went there. Many descendants of the original Anglo-Norman settlers lost interest too. English lordship over the Gaels was more nominal than real. In the least accessible areas, the north and the west, Gaelic Ireland retained its separate identity and gradually encroached into English areas. Warfare was endemic, but so also was intermarriage between the Gaels and indigenous Anglo-Irish families, whose loyalties, even as families, were frequently divided. The most trusted, however, later served terms as chief governors of the lordship, with an administration based in Dublin but largely itinerant. Irish parliaments also met in several different places. By 1485 the area of effective English control was limited to the so-called Pale around Dublin. Ecclesiastical geography is hardly more precise, though four provinces were formally established in the 12th century. Except in Tuam, many of the later bishops were English or Anglo-Irish rather than Gaels.

Right: The German empire in the late Middle Ages
Although the empire was ruled in fact, almost without exception, by members of the Luxembourg (1346–1437) and Hapsburg (1438–) families, the electoral formalities of the empire also acknowledged the real powers enjoyed by the great princes, on whose behalf the prince electors cast their votes. The impartibility required of the electoral estates (1356) duly influenced the other secular princes to give up dividing their inheritances. Gradually the family lands were reunited and distinctive states could emerge. The mosaic of German states in this period was however chiefly due to the many ecclesiastical domains of bishops and monasteries, and to the compact lands of the many imperial towns. In the 14th century the fragmentation of their family holdings gave individuals even of distinguished families very little power to overawe others. Notably in this period the Swiss could inflict several crippling defeats on their Hapsburg enemies. At the same time the different states of the Low Countries passed away from the empire and fell into the hands of the French dukes of Burgundy. The disintegration of the old kingdom of Burgundy in the west, which benefited the king of France most, was later paralleled in the northeast by the assertion of Polish sovereignty over land of the Teutonic Order. The erosion on the periphery did not however herald the disintegration of the German empire itself. The vitality of German culture, economy and religion at this time suggests that the loose political structure actually served Germans well.

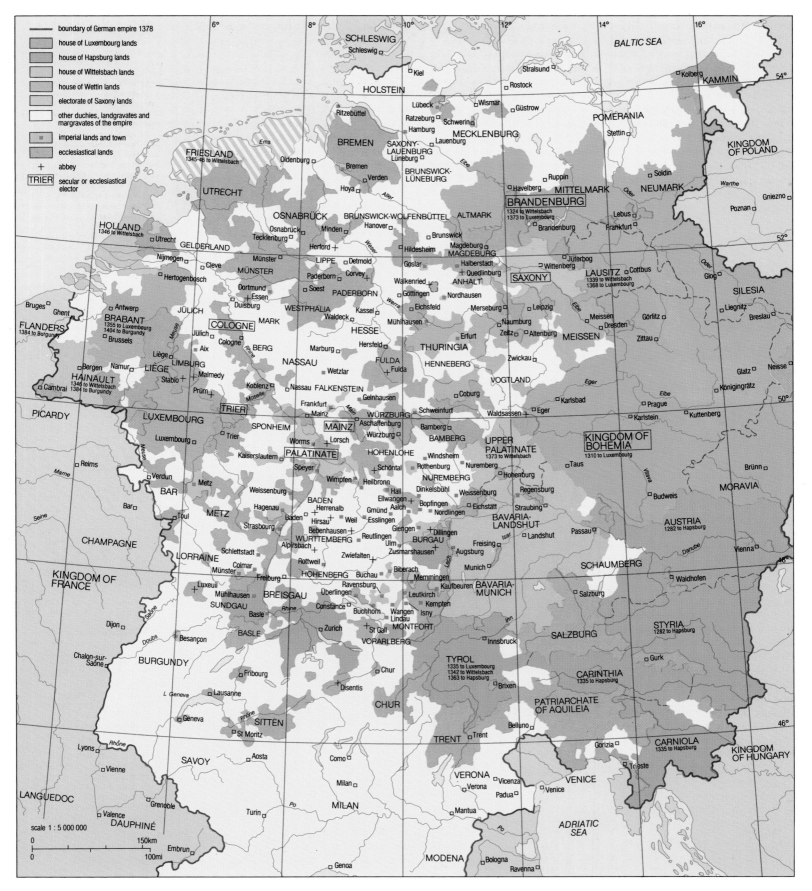

Legend:

- boundary of German empire 1378
- house of Luxembourg lands
- house of Hapsburg lands
- house of Wittelsbach lands
- house of Wettin lands
- electorate of Saxony lands
- other duchies, landgravates and margravates of the empire
- imperial lands and town
- ecclesiastical lands
- + abbey
- TRIER secular or ecclesiastical elector

scale 1 : 5 000 000

0   150km
0   100mi

Petrarch: The First Humanist

Petrarch was renowned in his own lifetime as a poet and man of letters. He exercised no important public functions, though he was courted by many persons of political importance and acted as adviser, negotiator and spokesman on their behalf. His historical importance, however, derives from the fact that he was the first man to be so completely absorbed by an interest in his own character and by the problem of how to lead his life for his own satisfaction that he left an abundance of written material from which his personal life can be reconstructed in unprecedented detail. The style of this life was so exceptional at the time that his contemporaries were struck by it and, ever since, his example has exerted a powerful attraction in European culture.

Hitherto human social life had been organized in such a way as to oblige all men to cooperate in their working lives. All men belonged to and clung to the communities they were born in or entered into voluntarily. The only exceptions were the hermits, who deliberately turned their back on organized society to live in the wilderness. Petrarch enjoyed living in the country and enjoyed his own company, but he was no hermit. He needed books to read and friends to talk with; he loved to write and receive letters, he advocated the value of literature and the study of the past, and he used his personal influence and talents to serve his friends and the peoples he lived with. He valued his independence but he never contemplated cutting himself off from the world at large. His ability to live privately for himself was not due to the possession of a private income. His father's legacy enabled him only to complete his student days at leisure. Petrarch's father had been a Florentine notary, driven into exile at the same time as Dante by the victorious Black Guelf faction in 1302, so that Petrarch himself was brought up to consider himself as shut out of his proper home. This was the decisive influence that deprived him of the natural social or political affiliations enjoyed by most of his contemporaries. Trained as a lawyer in the most famous universities of his day (Montpellier and Bologna), he cultivated rather a love of literature and, when he had to earn his living, became a copyist of manuscripts at Avignon. He accepted the patronage of a great Roman cardinal, Giovanni Colonna, whose household chaplain he became in 1330, and thereafter his income was derived from the canonries of cathedral churches at Lombez, Pisa, Parma and Padua. Such offices were commonly held by men in the service of great prelates and did not commit him to any pastoral responsibilities. What was exceptional about Petrarch was that within a few years he began to live away from his patron in Avignon and to give himself up mainly to his literary interests, with the blessing of his ecclesiastical superiors. Thus his ability to lead a private life in fact owed a great deal to the development of the new Italian town that had exiled his family, to the residence of the papal court

Left Portrait miniature by Altichiero. Petrarch is one of the first medieval men known to have been painted from the life to satisfy the wish to have a likeness of him, itself a tribute to his reputation. Altichiero painted a fresco portrait for Francesco da Carrara shortly after the poet's death, which has much deteriorated.

Below Simone Martini's illustration to Petrarch's Virgil. Petrarch's main intellectual interests focused on Roman antiquities but he also appreciated contemporary art, and particularly the work of Martini, who painted this frontispiece for his Virgil c. 1338, according to Petrarch's own detailed instructions. This text had once been his father's and Petrarch freely annotated it.

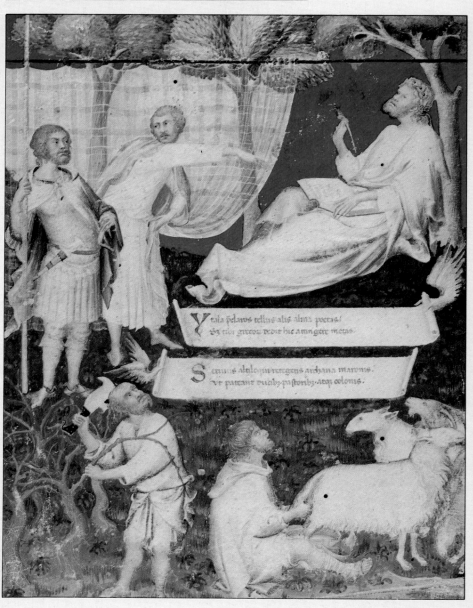

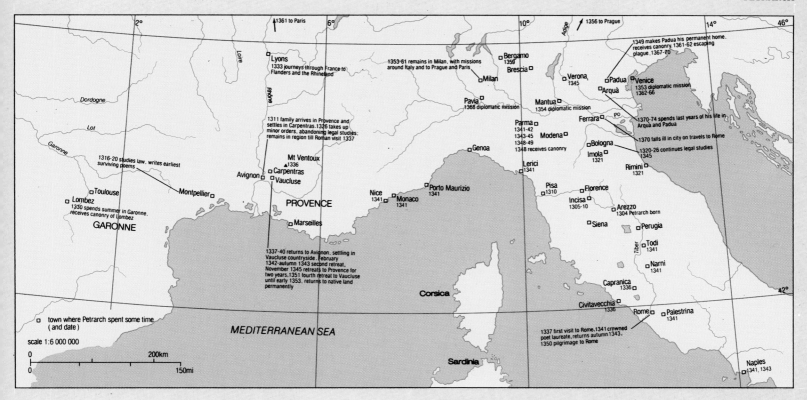

The following labels appear on the map:

- 1361 to Paris
- 1356 to Prague
- Lyons 1333 journeys through France to Flanders and the Rhineland
- 1353-61 remains in Milan, with missions around Italy and to Prague and Paris
- Bergamo 1359
- Brescia
- Milan
- Verona 1345
- Padua
- Venice 1353 diplomatic mission 1362-66
- 1349 makes Padua his permanent home. receives canonry. 1361-62 escaping plague. 1367-70
- Arquà
- Pavia 1368 diplomatic mission
- Mantua 1354 diplomatic mission
- Dordogne
- Lot
- Loire
- Rhône
- Adige
- Po
- 1370-74 spends last years of his life in Arquà and Padua
- Ferrara
- Parma 1341-42 1343-45 1348-49 1348 receives canonry
- Modena
- Bologna
- 1370 falls ill in city on travels to Rome
- 1320-26 continues legal studies 1345
- Garonne
- 1311 family arrives in Provence and settles in Carpentras. 1326 takes up minor orders, abandoning legal studies: remains in region till Roman visit 1337
- 1316-20 studies law, writes earliest surviving poems
- Genoa
- Lerici 1341
- Imola 1321
- Rimini 1321
- Toulouse
- Lombez 1330 spends summer in Garonne. receives canonry of Lombez
- Montpellier
- Avignon
- Mt Ventoux 1336
- Carpentras
- Vaucluse
- PROVENCE
- Nice 1341
- Monaco 1341
- Porto Maurizio 1341
- Pisa 1310
- Florence
- Incisa 1305-10
- Arezzo 1304 Petrarch born
- Siena
- Perugia
- GARONNE
- Marseilles
- 1337-40 returns to Avignon, settling in Vaucluse countryside. February 1342-autumn 1343 second retreat, November 1345 retreats to Provence for two years. 1351 fourth retreat to Vaucluse until early 1353, returns to native land permanently
- Tiber
- Todi 1341
- Narni 1341
- Capranica 1336
- Civitavecchia 1336
- Rome
- Palestrina 1341
- Corsica
- 1337 first visit to Rome. 1341 crowned poet laureate, returns autumn 1343. 1350 pilgrimage to Rome
- MEDITERRANEAN SEA
- □ town where Petrarch spent some time (and date)
- scale 1:6 000 000
- 0 200km
- 0 150mi
- Sardinia
- Naples 1341, 1343

Above The map clearly reveals the range of Petrarch's movements, mainly either side of the Alps within a narrow belt of latitude. It is possible to establish his movements year by year from his extensive correspondence. His ability to live in a number of different places for long periods reflects conditions of medieval life that encouraged mobility among professional as well as aristocratic individuals. In Petrarch's case it was countered by a strong inclination to acquire a permanent home of his own, where he could house his library and tend his garden.

at Avignon and to the enlightened patronage of princes of the church who appreciated the value of literature and scholarship.

Petrarch's dedication to scholarship was total. It focused on the great Latin writers, Cicero and Livy, and involved traveling in search of manuscripts, correspondence with other scholars and the preparation of critical editions. In all this Petrarch was a pioneer of later Renaissance scholarship. By his day the universities had become places for the mastery of technical subjects, law, medicine, logic or theology, so that literature was either neglected or considered merely ancillary. Petrarch and his patrons had no program for rehabilitating it as a scholarly discipline; nor did they seek to justify his activities. Whatever explanations may be offered for their own obvious enthusiasm, it was their discovery of how much benefit they derived from their studies that initially encouraged others to take up and continue their work. Out of his scholarly labors Petrarch developed particular interests in the study of Roman history. He himself wrote biographies of famous men and a great Latin epic poem on the Roman hero Scipio Africanus. Petrarch is perhaps best known to us for his vernacular poems, works in a tradition known also to Dante and cultivated as a literary genre both by the Italians around the papal court and by the Provençaux with whom they mingled. Petrarch's reputation as a poet, however, then rested on his Africanus and for this a poetic crown was conferred on him in Rome on 8 April 1341 by Robert, king of Naples.

Petrarch's concern for the greatness of the Roman past made him zealous to restore Rome in his own day. He pleaded with popes and emperors to serve the city; he applauded Cola di Rienzo, another enthusiast for ancient Rome; by his writings he strove to revive appreciation of what Rome had stood for. Increasingly during the 1340s he turned back to Italy as his homeland, leaving his country house at Vaucluse for the last time in 1353. Still working at literature, in the long term to revive Italian interest in the past glories of the Latin race, at the same time he was often brought in to help appease the quarrels of the Italians of his own day by virtue of his personal reputation. As he grew older his commitment to religion also became more profound, but he rejected any temptation to follow his brother into the Carthusian order. Faithful to his view that his life was to be led to his own satisfaction, he stood out against the exclusive demands of religious reformers. His own sense of the greatness of the Roman (pagan) past made him much more anxious to stress the common humanity that linked him, for example, to Cicero than the differences between them in terms of religious belief. The emphasis was more on the moral virtues of religion and philosophy, as shown in his last major work *De Remediis Utriusque Fortunae* which occupied him over about 12 years (1354–66).

Petrarch was always busy with writing and scholarship but he was not a man to complete one work and move on to another. He was constantly revising and repolishing and some of his works were never completed. But his life was itself full and satisfying, giving pleasure and enlightenment to his many friends, and he himself continued to find happiness and instruction in nature and in books, retiring again from the town to a country house at Arquà where he died in 1374. For more than 40 years the inspiration of his lyric verse was the Laura he had seen at Avignon in 1327, a vision to which he constantly returned. But despite the liaisons that gave him two children, Petrarch's style of life necessarily made him a solitary figure. He had no strong family ties, belonged to no communities and had no formal pupils to continue his work. He lived according to certain ideals, and by his dedication to them helped to make them real to others. Apart from his influence on later culture it is important to notice how his style of life was made possible by the new conditions of his own times.

THE AXIS OF WESTERN EUROPE

Tradition and new growth in the 15th century

The multiplicity of kingdoms established by the 14th century gave greater institutional variety to Europe but complicated international relations. Thus the war between England and France had served not only to save Scotland and strengthen French provincial aspirations, as in Flanders or Brittany, but it spread into Spain, where Pedro I welcomed English support against his half-brother Henry of Trastamara and where the French, called in by Henry, ultimately established him. In due course Castilian superiority provoked Portuguese resistance and this in turn obtained English support. To the east Germany could not avoid the repercussions of the war, even if its divisions made it less important for either side to acquire friendship there. During the war the moral support of the Avignon popes had served French interests well, so that when a schism occurred in the church in 1378 it was rather unscrupulously exploited by both sides in the war to divide Christendom along familiar lines and to excuse further campaigning with the pretence of combating schismatics.

These excuses never looked very convincing and from the beginning efforts were made to heal the schism, but this proved very hard to do. Genuinely ecclesiastical problems had emerged and many clergy became reluctant to restore a united papacy before taking advantage of its embarrassments to secure reforms. Even to settle the schism between two popes confident of their unimpeachable authority would require novelty and ingenuity. The church had relied for so long on the papacy making ultimate decisions that it faltered when the papacy itself could not, as in this case, decide. In Bohemia the breakdown of papal authority coincided with the inadequacies of King Wenceslas, who allowed dissident religious opinion to stampede the clergy. Elsewhere heresy did not so easily triumph and the schism was eventually healed when the scandal of division shamed Christendom into restoring unity without requiring too much agreement on reform: the formal unity of Christendom mattered much. In practice the regional variations of the churches were best protected by rulers who duly negotiated concordats with the papacy if deemed necessary.

The 15th century seems, historically, to wear a deceptive cloak of show, with its great aristocrats, its extravagant pieties, its international church, its traditional revival of the old order. Historians detect beneath the appearances the brutal vigor of new monarchies in the making, the first signs of radical religious teaching, a warfare of cannon and pikemen rather than of chivalrous cavalry, an economic reality of money, trade and industry rather than of aristocratic landlords. Historians have long thought of the 16th century as a period of new growth. Thus the 15th century, which seems to be teetering on the brink of novelty, incurs criticism for its refusal to hasten forward the moment, as though the panoply of aristocratic government were an offensive deceit. From this point of view the duke of Burgundy, living with chivalrous medieval display, and the Florentines, trying to write, think and live like Romans of the Republic, both indicate how unable or reluctant men were to face their own realities.

For the most part Europeans had in the 14th century suffered from such prolonged and painful disorders that many of them did welcome some restoration of a familiar legitimate order, like that of the papacy (1417) for the universal church, or the crowning of Charles VII at Reims in 1429 for France. In the empire itself legitimacy rather than election prevailed when the succession passed from Sigismund of Luxembourg (emperor 1411–37) to his Hapsburg son-in-law Albert II (emperor 1438–39) and thereafter to the Hapsburgs for centuries (1439–1806). In the east the Jagellons gave new power to Poland-Lithuania and offered the potential of dynastic union with Hungary and Bohemia. The revival of Ottoman power in the Balkans under Murad II (sultan 1421–51) did not immediately inspire dread of the consequences for Constantinople, and when the city fell to Sultan Mehmet II in 1453 this did not hinder the Europeans from continuing with their own preoccupations. They had had their fill of troubles and were desperately trying to find their way back to a new order. In their buildings, paintings and sculpture the level of their success can be measured. Politically they cared less for the reforming programs of intellectuals, as formulated for example in the Council of Basle (1431–49), than for the formula of aristocratic government, where one lordship could bring into one state many rival territories. When, after the Anglo-French wars, the French king made peace in his own kingdom, soldiers of fortune naturally turned elsewhere for employment. For their own safety other states also had to discipline themselves. After 1494 international wars began in Italy, showing the potential dangers for the rest of Europe when ambitious kings managed to impose peace at home. But it is probably true that, however dreadful later wars between rulers became, there was less sheer indiscriminate slaughter, more chance of bringing warfare under control and indeed of using diplomacy to arrest it altogether. Towns were protected by massive new walls and fortresses, built to withstand cannon-fire – not until the 19th century were these walls demolished to allow urban expansion. The days of freebooting soldiers were over and the cost of warfare gave advantage to the defense rather than the oppressor. Little by little, experience of the truth of this in the 15th century probably encouraged men to place their hopes in princes' government and to become more optimistic about the future of their peoples.

The undeniable advantages brought by peace and princes to some extent excuse the emphasis

The Arnolfini Marriage (1434) by Jan van Eyck (c. 1390–1441). This famous painter, friend and counsellor of Duke Philip the Good, lived at Bruges for the last 12 years of his life. He was the first Flemish painter to sign his work, and with him the reputation of Flemish painting became international.

given here to political developments. Yet the 15th century belongs culturally to men like Johann Gutenberg, the great Flemish and Italian painters, the musicians John Dunstable and Guillaume Dufay, and the eccentric genius like Leonardo da Vinci or Christopher Columbus. The patronage of rulers mattered to the success of their enterprises, but the inspiration and the technical mastery they learned had nothing to gain from politics at all, except that the interaction of courts and craftsmen seems essential to their work. The political situation had created societies able to benefit from such skills. It is no mere chance that printing should be developed in the German Rhenish towns, or that it was in Florence, rather than Siena or Milan, that architecture, sculpture and figure painting were "renewed" in the early 15th century. The success of printing is also a reminder that here the princes counted for little. It was the "mass" demand for printed books, pamphlets and pictures that mattered and it was therefore where literate "masses" were numerous that printing met a need. Contrariwise, in such societies mariners and visionaries could not find backers. Neither the Genoese nor even the English could have taken any advantage of Columbus's discoveries, had they been undertaken in either of their names. One of the strengths of Europe in this period was that its political units, though comparable, differed considerably in composition. The diversity of European culture has remained one of its strengths as well as one of its more exasperating features.

A new presence in western Europe: Burgundy

The seemingly traditional appeal to aristocratic rule in this period must not, however, be allowed to obscure the degree of political innovation displayed in the 15th century. The most spectacular European rulers of the mid-15th century were without question the dukes of Burgundy. Yet Burgundy was not really the basis of their power, and their ducal title, within the French kingdom, misrepresents their sovereign character. They were real aristocrats, descended from the French royal house and wedded in every generation to aristocratic princesses, yet they were also considerable innovators. Their fortunes were originally made by Charles V of France, who obtained the hand of the heiress of Flanders for his youngest brother Philip of Burgundy, mainly to prevent the heiress being married by an enemy of his kingdom (1369). Philip of Burgundy (the Bold) played his role loyally enough, but events in the French kingdom itself nonetheless frustrated the ultimate hopes of Charles V with regard to the Low Countries. Instead of being effortlessly absorbed over the generations as a way of continuing the policy of Philip IV by other means, the Low Countries were in effect united by Philip's son John (the Fearless) and turned into a powerful independent state. The inability of King Charles VI to govern his kingdom had given Philip of Burgundy an additional burden which he conscientiously shouldered with dignity, but after his death his son, John, expected to succeed to his role in the kingdom and not surprisingly Charles VI's brother, Louis of Orléans, challenged his claims. The political loyalties of the Burgundians and Armagnacs (the royal party led by the count of Armagnac) divided the kingdom, as a result of

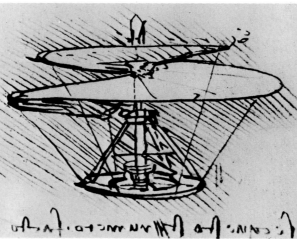

Left The genius of Leonardo da Vinci frequently led him into flights of aerial fantasy as with this sketch of an early helicopter of 1486–90.

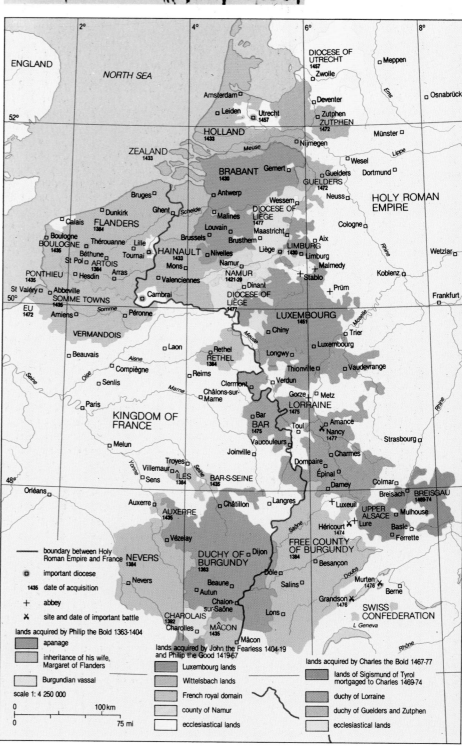

Above The assassination of John the Fearless in 1419 on the bridge at Montereau, illustrated here in a mid-15th-century manuscript of the *Chronicle of Enguerrand de Monstrelet*, was vengeance exacted for the murder of Duke Louis of Orléans in 1407. Its immediate consequence was the Burgundian alliance with Henry V of England which opened the way for English control of northern France.

Left: The Low Countries under the dukes of Burgundy
Before the middle of the 15th century the dukes of Burgundy succeeded in uniting under their control the much-divided Low Countries. By this means they frustrated the hopes of several other great European families, notably the Wittelsbachs and Luxembourgs, to do the same, and even more important cheated the kings of France of possession of Flanders, a royal fief. Apart from recovering the Somme towns in 1477, Louis XI could subsequently do nothing to stop the united Low Countries from passing to the Hapsburgs. The four dukes of Burgundy who thus transformed the political geography of the Rhine estuary lands originally worked in the well-established family tradition of the counts of Flanders of using marriage alliances to build inheritances. The apanage of the duchy of Burgundy itself, given by King Charles V of France to his brother Philip, was adjacent to the county of Nevers, inherited by Philip's wife from her grandmother. To fling the dynastic net so wide as to include both Burgundy and the Low Countries did not in the end prove to be so presumptuous, as the lands between them began to fall under the Burgundian spell. Though disappointed in the end of a crown and an enduring dynasty of their own, the dukes in their lifetime enjoyed a merited respect, patronized culture and learning on an unparalleled scale and wrought a permanent change in political geography.

which the duke of Burgundy became a highly controversial figure and was driven to taking up a much more independent position. He withdrew from Paris to fall back on the Low Countries as his own power base. Murdered by the Armagnac party in 1419, John was avenged by his son Philip (the Good) making an alliance with Henry V of England that enabled that king to impose his terms on Charles VI. The Anglo-Burgundian alliance lasted until 1435. It was bitterly resented in the part of France that eluded English control. Philip meanwhile used those years to extend his political hold on the Low Countries.

The beginning of a movement to create a sovereign power in the Low Countries can however be traced back to Philip the Good's great grandfather, Louis de Mâle, who demonstrated that as count of Flanders he had recovered enough authority to deal with his townsmen. He not only aided the patricians in the towns against popular movements, but also encouraged rural industries to weaken the towns' economic strength. Above all, by setting up a supreme court of appeal (1369) he offered the advantages of all extensive political authorities: an end to local particularisms and the effective enforcement of standard rules of law within his territories. He and his heirs, the dukes of Burgundy, regarded claims of municipal independence as incompatible with their own political objectives. The weakening position of the cloth trade at Bruges in the late 14th century made it easier for the duke to impose ducal regulations on the traders. What they lost by submission to his authority they made up for by the fact that his own jurisdiction in the Low Countries began to grow. To his own estates in France (the duchy of Burgundy, the counties of Mâcon, Auxerre and Bar-sur-Seine) Philip the Bold added Nevers which his wife at last inherited from her grandmother (died 1382). Her legacy included the lands of Artois to augment his dominions in the Low Countries. In 1392 Philip bought the county of Charolais.

The dispute with the Orléans party for a time brought the Burgundians claims on the duchy of Luxembourg, where they had to contend with local aristocratic resistance, supported by the Luxembourg emperor Sigismund. Only under John's successor Philip did the duke acquire the hereditary rights of Elizabeth of Görlitz and again receive the submission of the Luxembourgers (1451). The bishopric of Liège also felt the weight of Burgundian influence from the time of John the Fearless, but John's grandson, Charles the Bold, was still obliged to deal ruthlessly with the Liègeois (the city was sacked in 1468) and his heiress renounced her rights on the prince-bishopric in 1477. The status of the principality saved its nominal independence, though in practice later bishops collaborated with the rulers of the Low Countries.

Philip the Good (duke 1419–67) did most to consolidate the Low Countries, not so much by inheritance but by outright conquests and bullying. He obtained the reversion of Alsace from his aunt in 1420, bought Namur in 1421–29, asserted his claim on Holland and Hainault (together with Friesland and Zealand) in 1433, and succeeded to Brabant-Limburg in 1430. For making peace with the king of France and setting aside his vengeance for his father's murder, he obtained the recovery of some of his grandfather's lands and the Somme towns with Ponthieu and Boulogne-sur-Mer (1435). He successfully established his claims on Luxembourg. His son Charles the Bold actually obtained Alsace in return for military help to Sigismund of Hapsburg and became committed to Lorraine in 1473–75. He took Guelders and Zutphen by force in 1472. The duke also appointed the bishops of Utrecht, Cambrai, Tournai and Thérouanne.

Thus the dukes deliberately and systematically brought under one lord the various territories of the Low Countries. Formerly fragmented and disorderly, they were now united under the dukes' rule. Though no attempt was made to iron out local traditions, outright resistance such as was put up at the towns of Bruges (1436–37) and Ghent (1450–53) proved unavailing. The commercial possibilities of Antwerp were encouraged from 1442; nothing could now prevent the decline of Bruges itself which was caused basically by the silting of the port. The prosperity of the region as a whole enabled the dukes to improve their own financial position. In 1455 their revenues are estimated to have been 900 000 ducats a year, about the same as those of Venice, but twice those of the papacy or the dukes of Milan, their nearest rivals. Apart from their political ambitions the dukes were lavish and discriminating patrons of music and painting. Though in the end Burgundian power did not create a lasting autonomous state, the nucleus of power in the Low Countries inherited by the Hapsburgs gave the emperor Charles V, born at Ghent, the resources to dominate Europe in his heyday (emperor 1519–56). And the leading position of the Low Countries was only compromised, not shattered, by the later wars of religion.

A new force in western Europe: the Swiss
Charles the Bold of Burgundy was checked in his military exploits by the Swiss, who by his day had demonstrated that despite their small numbers they were a force to be reckoned with. If the glories of the 15th century owe much to the Burgundians, the Swiss must also count the 15th century as one of their greatest.

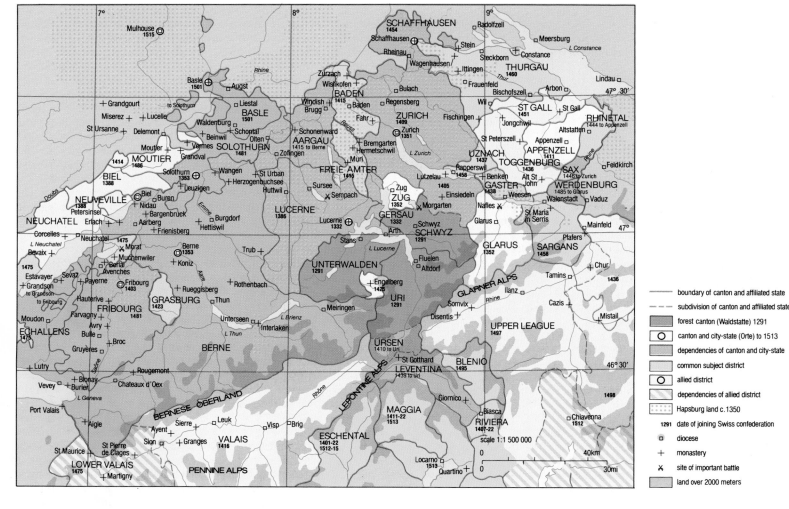

The map legend reads:

— boundary of canton and affiliated state
--- subdivision of canton and affiliated state
forest canton (Waldstätte) 1291
◯ canton and city-state (Orte) to 1513
dependencies of canton and city-state
common subject district
◯ allied district
dependencies of allied district
Hapsburg land c.1350
1291 date of joining Swiss confederation
◻ diocese
+ monastery
✕ site of important battle
land over 2000 meters

scale 1:1 500 000
0 40km
0 30mi

Switzerland is the most extraordinary political state of Europe and came into unexpected existence during the 14th and 15th centuries. In 1291 the commune of Schwyz, the valley community of Uri and the Mountaineers of the Unterwalden swore a fellowship whereby they promised mutual help and succor, and agreed to refuse the jurisdiction of any judges in seignorial courts who had bought their offices. Two centuries later from this modest beginning they had created a political community of 10 linked cantons recognized as virtually independent of the German empire. How had this come about?

All the territory of modern Switzerland lay within the bounds of the German empire from 1037 and the fortunes of the empire therefore affected its development. Neither the area's established bishoprics nor its monasteries had become genuinely independent; the fate of the territory seemed rather to depend on the energies of a few ambitious noble families. By the 13th century as elsewhere in the empire they were taking advantage of their opportunities to consolidate their holdings and build durable states. They also promoted the growth of towns. During the 13th century the number of Swiss towns rose from 16 to 80. Though the number proved to be excessive, it is certain that the economic life of the country developed rapidly during this period. In particular the routes between the Rhine and northern Italy across the St Gotthard pass opened up central Switzerland for the first time. This focused attention on the passage up to the Stätt pass, through the valleys of the Aare and the

Reuss and across Lake Lucerne (Vierwaldstättersee) with its rural settlements, Schwyz, Uri and Unterwalden, where Switzerland, *Die Schweiz*, began. At the northern end the most remarkable member of the Hapsburg family, Count Rudolf IV, had already consolidated his territorial hold on the region at the time of his election as king of the Romans in 1273. Though this opened the way for the subsequent glory of his house with the acquisition of Austria (1282), it distracted him from his original ambitions in Switzerland and so gave the Swiss their opportunity. The Hapsburgs' failure to keep Rudolf's crown also enabled the Swiss to seek support against the Hapsburgs by obtaining confirmation of their privileges from other kings. For a long period the Hapsburg family's position in the empire nevertheless gave them advantages in dealing with the Swiss and the confederation grew slowly and uncertainly.

The Uri valley community had obtained from Frederick II in 1231 a privilege whereby it was placed immediately subject to the empire, probably in recognition of the importance of the passage to the St Gotthard. In practice this came to mean that after Frederick's death, at least, the valley community itself appointed its own judges. By a privilege for the Schwyz granted in 1240 Frederick also removed the jurisdiction of the Hapsburg family and placed that valley community directly under the empire. The Hapsburg family did not recognize this royal act because it was made after Frederick's quarrel with the papacy. In practice they were unable to prevent that valley community from also managing its own legal affairs, until Rudolf IV's election to the kingship restored the possibility of his interfering by virtue of his royal powers. Just how Rudolf's government bore oppressively on these cantons is not clear. Before he died in 1291 he promised to appoint no man of servile origin to judge the free men of Schwyz, and a few months later after his death the three forest states (Schwyz, Uri and Unterwalden) swore their permanent pact for mutual assistance against all their enemies. They added a clause declaring that no judge who bought office or who was not from the valley would be recognized. The pact is not explicitly directed against the Hapsburgs and may be a renewal of a pact made earlier, but this agreement is usually taken to be the first step towards the formation of the Swiss confederation (the Eidgenossenschaft).

The belief of the valley communities in their traditional rights to justice as freemen and the constitutional character of their imperial privileges naturally drove them to seek further royal confirmations of the position from the Hapsburgs' rivals for the empire, Adolf of Nassau (1297), Henry of Luxembourg (1309), with Unterwalden thenceforward included with the others, and all now referred to collectively as the *Waldstätte* (forest cantons). If the Hapsburgs could not overtly resist these developments they certainly did not give up their ambitions in the region and could not foresee that the *Waldstätte* had a real political future. The Hapsburgs had bought the lordship of Fribourg (1277), the town of Lucerne (1264/88) and Zug. The opportunity for a showdown with the confederation came in 1315 at a time when Frederick of Hapsburg was engaged in a struggle with Louis the Bavarian for the German crown. Frederick's brother Leopold planned and led a campaign against Schwyz to punish them for an attack on the monastery of Einsiedeln (of which the Hapsburgs were protectors) arising out of a long-standing dispute over grazing rights in the mountains. Leopold's host was decisively defeated by the footmen of Schwyz and Uri at Morgarten. This gave the Swiss an international reputation and prompted them to draw up a new statement of their confederation in German, in which the perpetual alliance for the first time explicitly denied Hapsburg seignorial rights in the territory of the confederation. This clear indication of their aim and demonstration of their military capacity to defeat a powerful noble army enabled the confederation to survive the succeeding years of uncertainty. The Hapsburgs, humiliated but not resigned, had no need to fear active royal support for the Swiss, who saw that they would have to look after their own interest. To do so they needed to enlarge the size of the confederation if it was not to be stifled between Lucerne and the St Gotthard.

The first step was clearly to secure the adherence of Lucerne itself. In 1332 it became a perpetual ally of the confederation and at this point the Vierwaldstätter first combined together, though Lucerne did not cease to be a Hapsburg possession or change its own laws in order to enter the confederation's community of justice. The Hapsburgs did not challenge this strange pact of their town with their sworn enemies and it remained a Hapsburg town until 1385. The rural confederation thus showed that it could add to its

strength by finding an urban ally and could do so without having to incorporate its acquisition formally. Still more strange was the alliance struck with Zurich in 1351. This imperial city had fallen into the hands of Rudolf Brun, appointed as perpetual burgomaster in 1336. Forced into war with the Hapsburgs in 1350 by the efforts of some exiled citizens, he made a pact with the confederation as avowed Hapsburg enemies. In the war that followed, both the Hapsburg territories of Glarus and Zug also joined the allies against their lord. At the peace of Regensburg in 1355, though these two reverted to Hapsburg dominion, the Hapsburgs had to recognize the existence of the confederation. If the latter seemed to have gained little territorially by Zurich's alliance of expediency, it had nonetheless survived to be accorded grüdging recognition by its original enemy. At the same period the expanding city-state of Berne to the west found it advantageous to enter into a perpetual pact in 1353 in order to neutralize the Swiss from aiding Berne's subject peasantry in the valleys of the Lütschine and Bodeli. Neither Zurich nor Berne, which had their own traditions of urban independence, regarded their part in the confederation as more than opportunist and they were far from regarding the Hapsburgs as their own inveterate enemies. Nevertheless in 1382 Berne called on the confederation for military assistance in its war against Rudolf II of Keburg-Burgdorf, a kinsman of the Hapsburgs. As a result Berne found its territories were now adjacent to the Hapsburg lands to the north. When Lucerne too took advantage of the situation in 1385 to build up a territory for itself by seizing Hapsburg lands and throwing off Hapsburg claims on the city, Leopold III decided that the moment of decisive intervention had come, if his lordship was not to be eroded utterly. The four forest cantons beat his army and killed Leopold himself at the battle of Sempach in July 1386. An avenging army led by Albert III of Austria, Leopold's brother, was also defeated by the peasants of Glarus in 1388 at Nafels. Berne took advantage of the situation to acquire the Hapsburg lordships of Büren and Nidau. A truce negotiated in 1389 was prolonged till 1415. The confederation had now become a powerful force and comprised eight *Orte* (territories): Schwyz, Uri, Unterwalden, Lucerne, Zurich, Berne, Glarus and Zug.

The confederation still lacked common institutions and this defect was not remedied, but it had acquired a sense of achievement and commitment that was to carry it forward for the next century as the confederation moved from a defensive to a more aggressive position. Thus the peasants of Appenzell were accepted as allies after obtaining their independence from the abbot of St Gall (1411). Four years later Berne took the lead in subjecting the Hapsburg Aargau to Swiss control. This land was not divided among the members but administered jointly. Despite this common commitment members of the confederation had too little motive to secure much agreement on policy. The interests of the towns in particular conflicted with those of the valleys. Thus in the middle of the 15th century the ambitions of Zurich to build a city-state of comparable importance to that of Berne to the west foundered on the resistance of Schwyz and Glarus. The war brought Swiss fighting qualities to

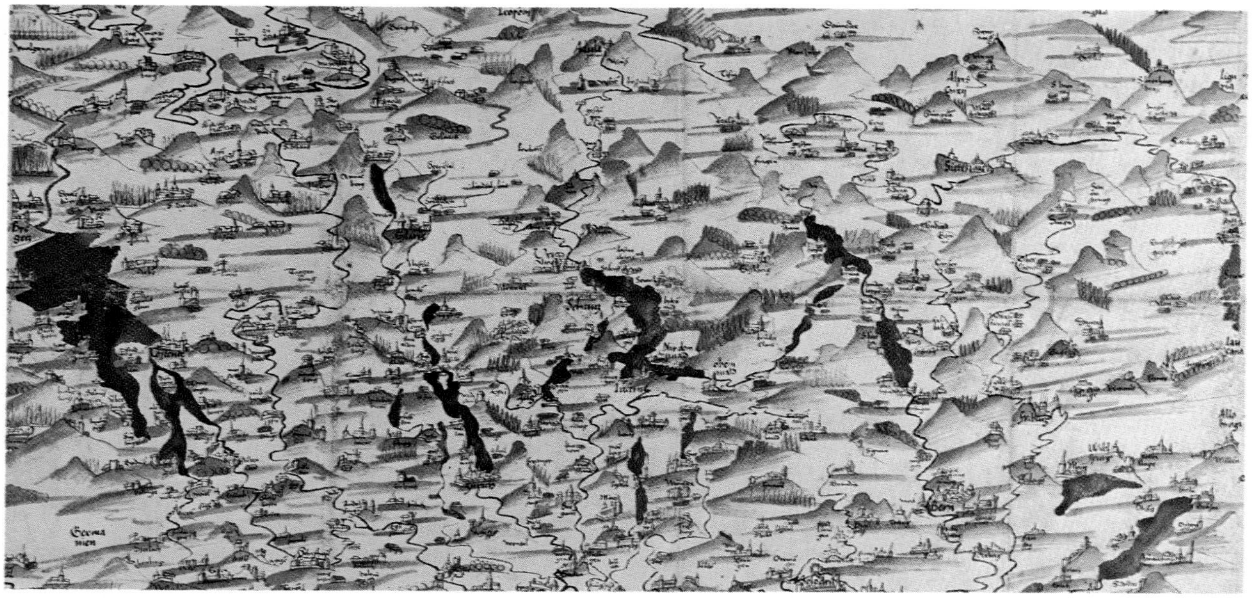

Left A map of Switzerland by Konrad Türst, c.1497. Southeast is to the top with Lake Constance on the left. Each town is drawn with an attempt at realism.

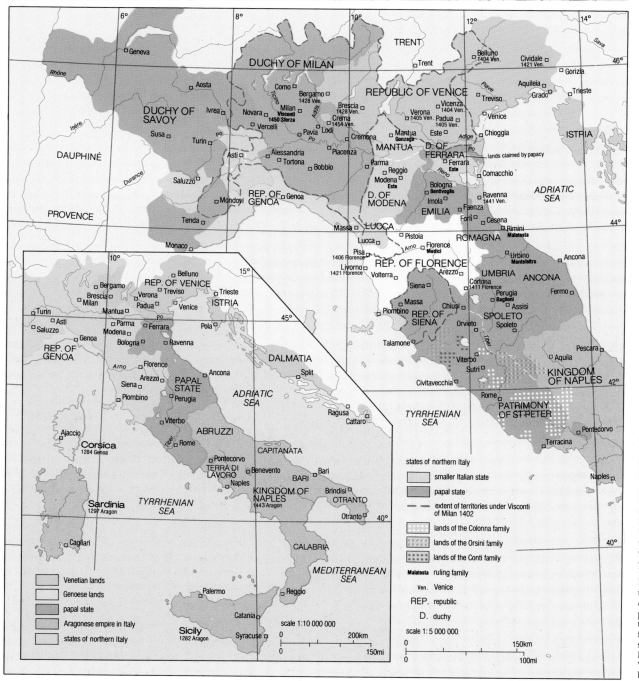

Italy in the 15th century

At the time of Frederick II's death in 1250 the effective collapse of imperial authority enabled many Italian cities to exercise practical independence. Few of the many places thus saddled with sovereignty succeeded in preserving their freedoms till the 15th century. Italy had by then become dominated by several powerful dynasties, of which the most conspicuously successful was the Visconti of Milan, whose duchy passed to the Sforzas in 1450. The state with greatest reserves and potential seemed, however, to be Venice, which had added an Italian territory to its existing colonial empire after 1402. Venice was a republic with an aristocratic doge elected as ruler for life. The papal state also had an elected head. In the Florentine republic the elected committees of the government after 1434 barely disguised the real power exercised by the Medici. In the course of this century the boundaries of these states might be contested, but the states themselves had acquired a durable shape and a balance of power was designed to preserve the status quo and keep foreigners at bay. When this scheme broke down in 1494, Italy's states, great and small, Venice excepted, felt the bitterness of foreign domination.

Map labels (large map)

TRENT
DUCHY OF MILAN
REPUBLIC OF VENICE
DUCHY OF SAVOY
DAUPHINÉ
PROVENCE
REP. OF GENOA
MANTUA
D. OF FERRARA
D. OF MODENA
EMILIA
ISTRIA
ADRIATIC SEA
LUCCA
ROMAGNA
REP. OF FLORENCE
REP. OF SIENA
UMBRIA
ANCONA
SPOLETO
PATRIMONY OF ST PETER
KINGDOM OF NAPLES
TYRRHENIAN SEA

Geneva, Aosta, Como, Bergamo 1428 Ven., Trent, Belluno 1404 Ven., Cividale 1421 Ven., Gorizia, Aquileia, Trieste, Grado, Treviso, Vicenza 1404 Ven., Verona 1405 Ven., Padua 1405 Ven., Venice, Chioggia, Ivrea, Novara, Milan, Visconti 1450 Sforza, Brescia 1428 Ven., Crema 1454 Ven., Vercelli, Pavia, Lodi, Cremona, Mantua Gonzaga, Este, Susa, Turin, Asti, Alessandria, Tortona, Piacenza, Parma, Reggio, Modena Este, Ferrara Este, Comacchio, Bologna Bentivoglio, Ravenna 1441 Ven., Saluzzo, Mondovi, Genoa, Bobbio, Imola, Faenza, Forli, Cesena, Rimini Malatesta, Tenda, Massa, Lucca, Pistoia, Florence Medici, Arno, Urbino Montefeltro, Ancona, Monaco, Livorno 1421 Florence, Pisa 1406 Florence, Volterra, Siena, Arezzo, Cortona 1411 Florence, Perugia Baglioni, Assisi, Piombino, Chiusi, Spoleto, Fermo, Massa, Talamone, Orvieto, Tiber, Pescara, Civitavecchia, Viterbo, Sutri, Aquila, Rome, Terracina, Pontecorvo, Naples

lands claimed by papacy

states of northern Italy (legend)

- smaller Italian state
- papal state
- --- extent of territories under Visconti of Milan 1402
- lands of the Colonna family
- lands of the Orsini family
- lands of the Conti family
- **Malatesta** ruling family
- Ven. Venice
- REP. republic
- D. duchy

scale 1:5 000 000

| 0 | | 150km |
| 0 | 100mi |

Inset map labels

REP. OF VENICE
ISTRIA
REP. OF GENOA
DALMATIA
PAPAL STATE
ADRIATIC SEA
ABRUZZI
CAPITANATA
TERRA DI LAVORO
KINGDOM OF NAPLES 1443 Aragon
BARI
OTRANTO
CALABRIA
TYRRHENIAN SEA
MEDITERRANEAN SEA

Belluno, Bergamo, Treviso, Brescia, Verona, Milan, Padua, Venice, Trieste, Turin, Mantua, Asti, Saluzzo, Parma, Ferrara, Pola, Genoa, Modena, Bologna, Ravenna, Arno, Florence, Ancona, Split, Arezzo, Siena, Perugia, Ragusa, Piombino, Viterbo, Cattaro, Ajaccio, Rome, Pontecorvo, Benevento, Naples, Bari, Brindisi, Otranto, Cagliari, Reggio, Palermo, Catania, Syracuse, Terracina, Pontecorvo

Corsica 1284 Genoa
Sardinia 1297 Aragon
Sicily 1282 Aragon

Inset legend

- Venetian lands
- Genoese lands
- papal state
- Aragonese empire in Italy
- states of northern Italy

scale 1:10 000 000

| 0 | 200km |
| 0 | 150mi |

the notice of the French king which drew the Swiss into international affairs. They became aware of their own strength and had no scruples about using it. Thurgau was occupied in 1460 and in 1466 Berne agreed to make a defensive alliance with the imperial city of Mülhausen (Mulhouse) which feared for its independence at the hands of Duke Sigismund of Austria. In this way the Swiss became involved again with the Hapsburgs, and Sigismund in turn with the duke of Burgundy, Charles the Bold. The Swiss defeat of Charles at the battle of Morat in 1476 demonstrated Swiss military superiority over the finest soldiers in Europe. This decisive defense of Swiss independence opened the way for the acceptance of Fribourg and Solothurn as additional members of the confederation by the agreement of Stans (1481). When under Maximilian the confederation had to fight against the Swabian league, the result was a final showdown with the empire that gave the Swiss political independence in all but name (1499). Immediately afterwards Basle and Schaffhausen joined the confederation (1501) and Appenzell became a full sovereign member in 1513. The pacific reputation of the Swiss in modern times, backed up though it is by the burdensome military service still demanded of Swiss citizens, makes it difficult to recall the 15th-century reputation of the Swiss mountain-men. Had they been more united among themselves at that stage, they might have ventured to use their military strength on their own account to build up an empire, as the Swedes did in the 17th century. The local character of their cantonal government instead kept their ambitions within bounds and set Europe a different example. Challenged by the changing conditions of the day, they responded by insisting on their own independence and by so doing added their own indispensable voice to the complicated harmonies of Europe.

Rival states of the Italian peninsula

In contrast with Burgundy and Switzerland, 15th-century Italy appears to offer political states established in a much more traditional mold, but appearances can be misleading. For example, the largest of the Italian states, the kingdom of Naples, dated from 1130. It was far from presenting a picture of stable continuity however. After 1282 Sicily was separated from the mainland and ruled by princes from Aragon. After 1343 and for nearly a century Naples knew no stable government at all. First it was the turn of Joanna I and a succession of husbands, and eventually pretenders. Not until Ladislas II took charge of government was there some continuity in policy, but Ladislas behaved more like a contemporary leader of *condottieri* (mercenary adventurers) than a king and his position was made more difficult by the Roman papacy being preoccupied at that time by the need to put an end to schism in the church. When Ladislas II died suddenly in 1414, it was the turn of his sister, Joanna II, and her succession of husbands to give government to Naples. Most of this time the ruler of Sicily, King Alfonso V of Aragon, aspired to reunite the two parts of the old kingdom. This he accomplished in 1442. Naples, his main center, was nonetheless only one part of domains that stretched across the whole western Mediterranean. When he died his bastard son Ferrante was left with Naples,

while his brother Juan II ruled Sicily as well as the other states of the kingdom. In effect, therefore, the kingdom of Naples, the largest and most established state of Italy, was in the 15th century subjected to the most bizarre and arbitrary changes in its style of rule. Not surprisingly it seemed to others to be most in need of nursing. At the end of the century the rival claims of the kings of France and Spain to the succession of Ferrante ushered in the period of foreign domination in Italy. The anxieties of Italians about Naples were not, after all, groundless.

The papacy was the neighboring state of Naples and nominally its overlord. As an ecclesiastical principality its political aspirations varied more than those of most states because it depended on a ruler elected for life, which precluded the continuity elsewhere provided by family interests. In addition, at the beginning of the 15th century, the pope was distracted from Italian politics by the Great Schism. After its resolution in 1417 a pope from the powerful Colonna family (Martin V, 1417–31) faced the state's political problems in the practical manner characteristic of Roman aristocratic families. His Venetian successor, a former Cistercian abbot, Eugenius IV, was not so well placed to continue such a policy, particularly as he was obliged to deal with the new Council at Basle which proved troublesome. He was actually driven out of Rome itself, and was only able to return in 1444. The stage was now set for the famous last act of the medieval church, the Renaissance papacy: 10, mainly short, controversial pontificates in which political considerations and indeed worldly pursuits often appeared to blot out any other considerations, until Martin Luther appeared on the scene. The popes did not necessarily please even the other Italian states of the day, but gave every sign of being equal to the burdens of their office and their own personal reputations did not at the time damage respect for Rome abroad. Their concern for the papal state itself naturally seemed in Italy to be complying with a legitimate duty of the papacy and the steps taken to restore the city of Rome by new building were inspired by the newest intellectual enthusiasms of 15th-century Italians.

The popes of the late 15th century who set about dominating Italian politics to restore respect for the church's position had to contend with other states that had much less historical justification or tradition behind them. The most powerful and respected was Venice, but in the past Venice had been an isolated city-state with a growing maritime empire down the Adriatic and in the Aegean; only in the 15th century had the Venetians ventured to acquire an extensive dominion in Italy itself. Its earlier contest with Genoa at sea had left it so weak that when peace was finally concluded in 1380 it played no effective part in attempting to limit Milanese ambitions in the next decade. However the danger they presented was so clear that, given their chance when Duke Gian Galeazzo died in 1402, the Venetians immediately seized Padua and Verona, territories of the former Carrara family. Having taken the plunge the Venetians committed themselves to further conquests and pushed their frontier against Milan as far as the Adda by 1429. Fifteenth-century Venice was therefore really a new Italian power, emerging from its exotic, Byzantine past, a fact of Italian political life, unknown,

Overleaf The doge's palace, Venice. When the Sala del Maggior Consiglio was enlarged in the middle of the 14th century, it became necessary to rebuild the loggias beneath. Later a balcony onto the piazzetta was added, and finally after 1424 the facade of the palace was extended towards San Marco. The result is a building of unrivaled greatness, with a massive upper story relieved by the delicate patterning of the stonework, by the two loggias of different rhythms below and by the almost Islamic decoration of the skyline.

untested and feared. Many Venetians were also uneasy about this new commitment to landed instead of maritime interests, but, as Doge Foscari pointed out, the Venetians no longer had the choice of opting out of Italy. Their old security had depended upon the divisions of the mainland and the inability of any one power either to present a united front or to cut Venetian commercial arteries through the Po valley or across the Alpine passes. The success of Milanese expansion in the late 14th century threatened to put Venetian prosperity at their mercy. The Venetians had either to reimpose their own control by restoring the status quo ante or to resign themselves to decline. The Venetians accepted the risk of going forward into the unknown and agreed to make changes in their own order of priorities. They had in particular to learn how to administer Italian towns and territories where their experience in the past had all been in governing Greek or Slav peoples.

The local government of Italian states in this period has not been much studied, though there are grounds for believing that different styles prevailed across the peninsula. More important than the variations is the fact that local "self"-government of the towns everywhere suffered direction from a handful of great "metropolitan" centers, which in effect created several regional states so that Venice was in this respect not alone in facing new problems. Communal independence, as it had been fought for in the 12th century, no longer served. A dozen towns at most became capitals of small states of various sizes, normally under a ruling dynasty. The most powerful dynasty was the Visconti family of Milan who had outdistanced the rival Torriani family in their race to prevail over the greatest city of the Italian mainland. Milan had been an imperial capital in the 4th century and its archbishop was the most powerful Italian prelate north of Rome. Its advantageous position for Italian commerce bound for the north had guaranteed its success. The German kings had seen in Milan their chief enemy in Lombardy but even razing the town to the ground had not proved more than an ephemeral act of revenge. With the Visconti firmly in the saddle, Milan appeared certain to unite all northern Italy, at least, in one great state. Gian Galeazzo Visconti, who obtained the whole of the Visconti domain for himself in 1385, rapidly extended his rule by taking the Carrara state of Verona and Padua, and acquired the suzerainty of Tuscan towns as well, like Siena and Pisa (both in 1399). To confirm the position openly he bought the title "Duke of Milan" from the German king. Yet when he died unexpectedly in 1402 his empire collapsed – briefly.

Venice had taken advantage of its opportunity to thwart any subsequent Milanese ambitions before the duchy was revived by Filippo Maria Visconti. Gian Galeazzo had perhaps overreached himself. He certainly alarmed those states like Venice and Florence which had faith in their power to defend their independence. From being the potential force for unity in the north Milan became a feared tyrant, pushed onto the defensive if it were to hold onto a position of any consequence at all. When Filippo Maria (duke 1412–47) did restore some of his father's state, his neighbors watched him. Having no son of his own, Filippo eventually became indifferent to the future. Yet the logic of Milan's

position drew north Italians back into a regional government and after Filippo Maria's death, his son-in-law, Francesco Sforza, a great *condottiere* captain, exacted obedience from the subject territories. The new dynasty (1450–99) became a conservative force in peninsular politics.

In this bid to retain the power of the Milanese state Sforza was assisted by Cosimo de' Medici, the senior of Florence's politicians, who abandoned the old Florentine policy of hostility to Milan, recognizing that times had changed and that Milan no longer threatened Florence's own independence. A greater danger to Italian security as a whole would probably have followed a dismemberment of the Milanese state. Florence too had changed. In 1450 Cosimo enjoyed a preeminence in political life which owed nothing to any official position. In Gian Galeazzo's time Florence had been ruled by committees regularly elected every few months from the leading guildsmen in order to prevent any one individual acquiring excessive powers. Cosimo's "tyranny" was neither obtrusive nor oppressive, but his real power was acknowledged in Florence, though the complicated apparatus of elective committees was retained to maintain a republican fiction. The reasons for this institutional change in Florence are complex and controversial, but among them must be placed the new responsibilities of the city-state for a number of hitherto independent neighboring cities, like Arezzo (obtained in 1384) or Pisa (1406), acquisitions to improve Florence's defensive position in wars and its economic well-being, particularly for guaranteeing for Florence itself supplies of food and raw materials. Better known perhaps than either of these developments in early 15th-century Florence was a remarkable burst of creative energy, shown by the bold scheme of Filippo Brunelleschi for the completion of the cathedral with a great dome, and the contemporary work of the sculptors Donatello and Lorenzo Ghiberti and the young painter Masaccio, not to speak of the scholarly innovations of Florence's humanist chancellors, Coluccio Salutati, Leonardo Bruni and Poggio Bracciolini. Even at that time Florence began to draw artists and scholars from all over Italy, eager to learn new techniques and to explore a new dimension in human consciousness. And in retrospect the dazzling achievements of Florence have tended to blind men to the contributions in art and scholarship made by other Italians of the time. Milan cathedral, for example, planned by Gian Galeazzo Visconti and the center of an international debate about the technical problems involved, was an impressive 15th-century building that might have had profound influence upon other Italians. But Milanese fortunes had collapsed and Florence increased its lead over other Italian cultural centers, by usurping the place of the papacy as patron of the arts during the darkest days of the schism and the conciliar movement. But all the capital cities of the Italian states became centers of art and culture. Enriched by their own standing in their regions and beautified in honor of their rulers, these new towns also served to impress or overawe subjects of doubtful loyalty. The new rulers who took advantage of favorable circumstances to make their fortunes quickly discovered the possibilities of their roles, and the culture of their courts and the rebuilding of their chief city became favored priorities. All Italian capital cities still show the marks of this policy, but it was Rome itself that was most affected by it. Though it was the last city to benefit from the movement, the pontiffs, when they became patrons of building, were able to import their artists and architects from the established centers, particularly Florence, men who were then at the height of their creative powers.

Europe's major kingdoms in the shadows

The striking nature of events in the area of the old Middle Kingdom, Burgundy and Italy, in the 15th century might give a somewhat misleading impression of the future of this region. In the 16th century it was to be politically overshadowed, if not actually overrun, by the great powers from outside it — from Spain, from the Hapsburgs and from France. By the end of the 15th century the great powers were ready to take the stage, but for most of the century they were reduced to making noises off, and showed little sign of having potential to do more. The later strength of Spain for example rested on the united monarchy of Castile and Aragon, brought about by marriage (1479), and on the riches of America, still unsuspected even after the discovery of the New World in 1492. Europe was quite unprepared for Spanish preeminence. Only England's kings in the recent past had, because of their interests in Gascony, consistently taken care to cultivate Spain's rulers. Admittedly, since the Sicilian Vespers (1282), Italy had had experience of Aragonese intervention, which was in one sense only part of the general Catalan share in Mediterranean politics. As far as Italy was concerned this was, however, only the mildest of warnings. Sicily, separated from Naples, hardly constituted much danger for the rest of the peninsula. Moreover, during the 14th century Sicily had rulers of its own, drawn from the ruling house of Aragon, but sovereign, though when the Sicilian line died out (1409) the king of Aragon himself came to rule Sicily directly. The new Aragonese dynasty from Castile, which ruled after 1413, was also (apart from Alfonso V) more interested in the affairs of the Iberian peninsula than in continuing the old Catalan policies in the Mediterranean. Alfonso's brother Juan II had

perforce to deal with serious unrest in Catalonia, particularly in Barcelona. Spanish affairs were too complex before the conquest of Granada (1492) for Spanish monarchs to deal single-mindedly with foreign affairs, as King Ferdinand showed himself able to do in the last 20 years of his remarkable life.

Similarly, Germany in the 15th century turned in on itself. Between the period when the conciliar movement excited great hopes for ecclesiastical renewal and that of the wild exhilaration released by Martin Luther, German religious life was probably less volatile, but it was still sufficiently intense to react bitterly at the failure of the kingdom's princes to obtain papal support for attacking ecclesiastical abuses. Some German idealism at this time was directed into secular channels, for individual princely houses and for the state of the empire itself. The military weaknesses of the emperor Sigismund in dealing with the Muslim Turks and the heretic Hussites became a matter of shame to respectable Germans, but projects of reform got nowhere, particularly because the long-lived emperor Frederick III of Hapsburg concentrated his energies on reuniting the scattered lands of his house. Notable among the contributions made by the princes to the development of Germany at this time was the foundation of many universities, from Vienna (1365) and Heidelberg (1385) down to Tübingen and Mainz (1476). As a result every major German principality acquired its own university and this had both immediate and long-term consequences for the Germans.

Even if the nature of the studies there was not radically new and graduates were intended for the service of their local princes and prelates, the increase in the number of educated persons throughout the country and the new kind of corporations created in a dozen leading towns helped to prepare for a unique German cultural blossoming. The printing press aptly brought together skilled craftsmen and scholars who valued the multiplication of books and who worked to get editions prepared. Nuremberg in this period became the greatest commercial center north of the Alps and east of the Rhine, birthplace and school of Albrecht Dürer (1471–1528), the only northern artist comparable to Leonardo da Vinci. Here too were found the great cartographers and cosmographers, not because they were at the center of the discoveries themselves but because they could assemble books from all the known world and digest their information as they appeared.

The power of France by the end of the 15th century was strikingly demonstrated by Charles VIII's triumphal progress through Italy in 1494. Until that time however the 15th-century kings of France had been taken up with the problems of keeping on top of their relations and vassals, of whom the greatest, the dukes of Burgundy and Aquitaine, were independent princes outside the kingdom. The physical and psychological failings of Charles VI (king 1380–1422) allowed disorder to prevail in his later years. Even before his death the king of England invaded France (1415) and after it open warfare between the partisans of his son, Charles VII, and his grandson, Henry VI of England, prolonged the agony. Charles VII won back the position piecemeal, by renewed assaults on the English holdings in France and by improving the

Left Christ from *Assignment of the Keys* (c.1430) by Donato di Nicolò (Donatello) (1386–1466). The many works of figure sculpture in bronze and marble executed by Donatello had a profound influence upon Florentine 15th-century painting. In this bas relief Donatello himself achieved a painterly effect in marble. Most of his work was destined for ecclesiastical patrons. Despite the classical influences upon him there is no whiff of paganism about the greatest sculptor of the age.

Right Albrecht Dürer's (1471–1528) portrait of his father (detail), painted in 1497, is uncompromisingly Germanic in style and bears no trace of any influence the painter may have derived from his recent visit to Italy.

qualities of his military forces. In the meantime the powers of the princes could not be checked. The end of the war with England (1453) overlapped with continuing domestic disputes. Charles VII's successor, Louis XI (king 1461–83), made himself master of the kingdom by slow degrees. His chief enemy, Charles the Bold of Burgundy, succumbed not to Louis's direct onslaught but to his own rashness in getting involved with the Swiss. Luckily for Louis various branches of his own family died out in his reign, so that their apanages fell to the crown as escheats. His sickly heir, Charles VIII (king 1483–98), not the most likely ruler to impress Europe with the renewed strength of the French monarchy, was quite simply the first king, for more than a century and a half, to be free to initiate policy rather than react to it. His personal insignificance demonstrated even more impressively that the king's resources in men, money and ambition counted for more than any personal qualities.

The power of the great nations after 1494 should not be allowed to overshadow the great contributions made by the peoples of the Middle Kingdom – aristocrats, peasants and citizens, occupying the lands across Christendom from the North Sea to the Mediterranean – who constituted the axis of Europe in the 15th century. From these lands their achievements passed to their neighbors on both sides, except to the southeast where the Ottomans had established the frontier. These peoples neither formed a single political unit nor had wide political powers, but they had helped Europe to become what it was; they built on the work of their predecessors as they provided a basis for later building by others. It is not important whether by convention their achievements should be called medieval or whether by our appropriation of them they should be called modern. They prove only that at the end of the Middle Ages there was no faltering in inspiration or accomplishment.

The Invention of Printing

By the late 14th century with the general availability of paper it became possible to produce religious pictures in large quantities by using wood blocks, some carrying carved letters. The success of this stimulated craftsmen to devise a means for multiplying copies of written texts. The early stages of the experiments, which cannot be traced in detail, established how to cast the individual letters from an identical mold and what metal to use for them, as well as how to set up the typeface. The combination of talents involved obliged craftsmen to collaborate and the speculative character of the business certainly led to disputes. The name of Gutenberg, the probable inventor of the movable type for printing, appeared in one of these. The earliest datable printed book is the Mainz Psalter of 1457. Strasbourg and Bamberg were the only other towns where printing was carried on before 1460; in the next decade the skill appeared in several more German towns, and enterprising German craftsmen introduced the craft in some foreign places like Venice, Rome and Paris. By 1500 there were over 250 European towns with presses but the invention was most successful in the great commercial cities like Venice or Nuremberg where the expertise of merchants obviously mattered more than the skills of the craftsmen. The rapid development of printing proves how great was the demand for printed matter.

Of the 15 European towns where over 1000 incunabula were issued, eight were German, five Italian and two French, so the Germans retained their head start by a narrow margin. The concentration of printing in great centers like Venice, with 150 presses, or Paris, with 50 presses, reflects the importance of distribution rather than actual manufacture for commercial success. The idea of printing was also rapidly extended, most notably by the use of woodcut illustration. The earliest illustrated book, the *Edelstein*, came out at Bamberg in 1462. Engraving was also used and the presses brought out printed maps in several German centers and in Venice. Much more specialized books, like those of ancient authors or Bibles in Latin or in the vernacular, which required scholarly assistance for their production, benefited more discriminating purchasers. The scholarly traditions of 15th-century Italy explain why printers in a few towns there cut Greek type for books. The printing of Hebrew texts in Italian and Spanish towns, some of them otherwise without presses, also reflects a rather specialized local market. The great number of Dutch editions of classical texts and other school-

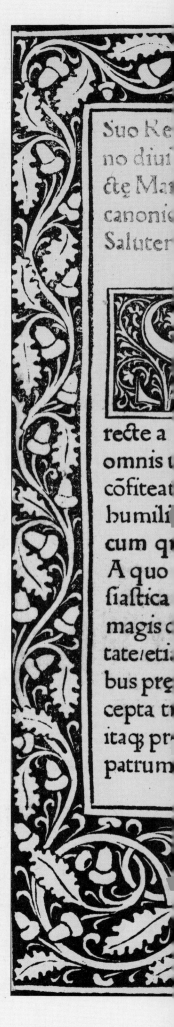

Above right This illustration of the printer's press, dated 1520, was used by the Parisian printer Jodocus Badius of Assche as his printer's mark. It derived from a satirical drawing made by Dürer in 1511 where he showed three craftsmen with the printer in the middle, busily engaged in their trade.

Right St Christopher, 1423. This is the second-oldest dated woodcut known and illustrates one of its most popular early uses: the multiplication of pictures of saints printed on paper to be sold to meet the demand for cheap devotional images. It was produced at Buxheim in Bavaria.

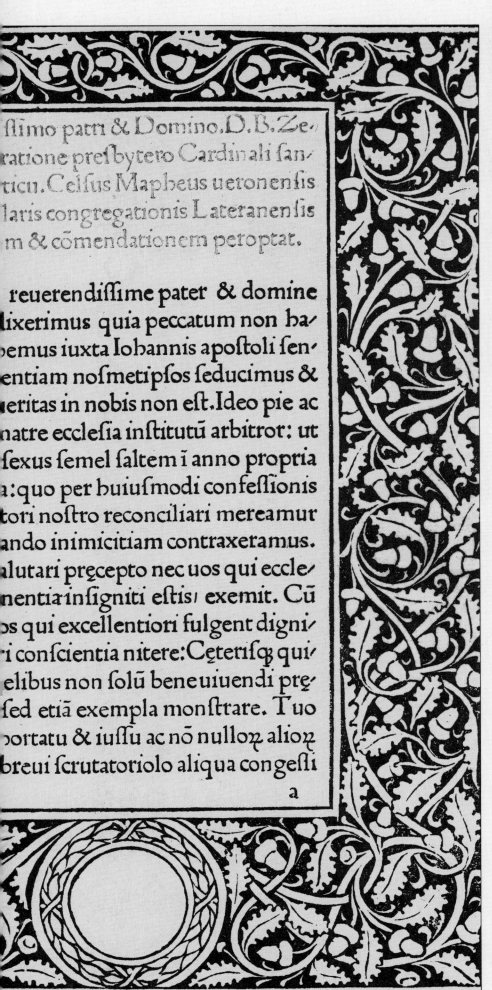

ſſimo patri & Domino.D.B.Ze
ratione preſbytero Cardinali ſan
ticu.Celſus Mapheus ueronenſis
laris congregationis Lateranenſis
m & cōmendationem peroptat.

reuerendiſſime pater & domine
lixerimus quia peccatum non ha
emus iuxta Iohannis apoſtoli ſen
entiam noſmetipſos ſeducimus &
eritas in nobis non eſt.Ideo pie ac
natre eccleſia inſtitutū arbitror: ut
ſexus ſemel ſaltem ī anno propria
a:quo per huiuſmodi confeſſionis
tori noſtro reconciliari mereamur
ando inimicitiam contraxeramus.
alutari preçepto nec uos qui eccle
nentiaīnſigniti eſtis, exemit. Cū
s qui excellentiori fulgent digni
i conſcientia nitere:Ceteriſq; qui
elibus non ſolū beneuiuendi pre
ſed etiā exempla monſttare. Tuo
ortatu & iuſſu ac nō nulloꝛ alioꝛ
breui ſcrutatoriolo aliqua congeſſi

a

Left Celso Maffei's (1425–1508) *Monumentum*, printed at Venice in 1478. The woodcut border, designed by Bernhard of Augsburg, adapts the decorative style of manuscript illumination for the press. The typeface was derived from Italian humanist handwriting, itself modeled on Carolingian script (see p. 56).

Below These playing cards, printed by Jean de Dale of Bresse in Lyons c. 1470, are from a set of 56 which form one of the most important collections of cards surviving from the 15th century. The press is here providing frivolous goods in contrast to its original devout products.

books arose from the importance of the educational reforms started there.

The printers' success was mainly due to their ability to provide for an apparently unsatisfied demand for works of a religious character, from complete Bibles down to single-page woodcuts of pious subjects. Surprising perhaps is the great number of vernacular Bibles that appeared in the 15th century, 18 editions in Germany, 16 in Italy, as well as Catalan, Czech and Dutch versions. The greatest demand in Bibles, however, was for Vulgate Latin versions (133 editions, of which 71 were German) at tempting prices and with accurate texts. Much less important commercially were the vernacular books that appealed to literate but not very scholarly clients.

Whereas the demand for Latin texts is predictable, the vernacular texts put out by the printers attract more modern attention for the clues they give as to the nature of the popular culture at the time. In general the prose romances, Italianized tales from the French, scored best. However in Italy the three great Tuscan writers, Dante, Petrarch and Boccaccio, sold well (though not nearly as well as Cicero). Other standard titles were of the popular encyclopedic kind like Brunetto Latini's *Tesoro* or the more recent allegorical epic by Federico Frezzi, now forgotten. Vernacular titles in Spain actually outnumbered the Latin ones, with Castilian texts three times more common than Catalan ones. Religious works in the vernacular amount to a quarter of the whole. In French the market was supplied not merely from Paris and Lyons and other centers in France, but also from Geneva and Bruges. There were presses that produced law books of local customs or lives of local saints. In Rouen the taste was for local history. The readiness to produce books for the market is best suggested by the activities of the presses in the Low Countries, where books appeared in Flemish, French, English and Frisian. In England itself the presses of Caxton and his successors produced more vernacular texts than were found anywhere else in Europe.

Medieval Mapmaking

It was during the 14th and 15th centuries that the desire and the ability to make maps appeared; without some sense of their use the age of discoveries that begins with Columbus is inconceivable. It is not difficult to perceive the importance of this change in European culture and admire the evidence for improvements in technique, the most conspicuous evidence for which is provided by the revival of interest in the work of Ptolemy of Alexandria. His *Geography* was translated from Greek into Latin by Jacopo d'Angelo of Scarperia working in Rome in 1406 and shortly afterwards new maps were drawn for this translation on the basis of another Greek text obtained from Constantinople. Nearly 50 manuscripts of this translation are now known from the 15th century, all Italian, and it was first published in 1475, and with maps in 1477. The profusion of Italian editions confirms the importance of the text in Italy itself, but interest in Germany is also shown by the Ulm edition of 1482, for which special new maps were commissioned. Ptolemy's *Cosmographia* was used to teach the art of making maps by mathematical means and students showed every intention of applying their learning for the benefit of their contemporaries and not merely as antiquarians. It is believed that Ptolemy was taken up in circles interested in the applications of mathematics, which in 15th-century Italy naturally included the artists of Florence. The skills of artist, draftsman and eventually (for printing) engraver were closely connected; artists had an important part to play in mapmaking at the time, though in due course the demand for maps created the more specialized profession of cartographer.

The earliest maps, designed to convey accurate information as to distance and direction, appeared in the 13th century as aids to navigation at sea, almost certainly in connection with the use of the magnetic compass. This was known in western Europe at least by the late 12th century when it was first described by scholars. In 1270 Louis IX of France at sea in Cagliari bay asked fretfully about his position, which was pointed out to him on a map. As it happens, the oldest surviving nautical chart known to us was made at Pisa about 1275, but the sophistication of its workmanship makes it likely that the technique of compiling such a chart had been refined for several years before that. To compile it the cartographer needed access to a work of reference listing the ports of the Mediterranean with their estimated bearings from one another and the distances. Such a book, called *Lo Compasso da navigare*, was written c. 1250. It is probably therefore in the mid-13th century that the modern mapmaker's art was devised for sailors who needed to find their way.

From ancient times they had in the fairly predictable conditions of the Mediterranean learned the lore of the winds and the stars. They apparently had no charts at that time, and Muslim sailors used

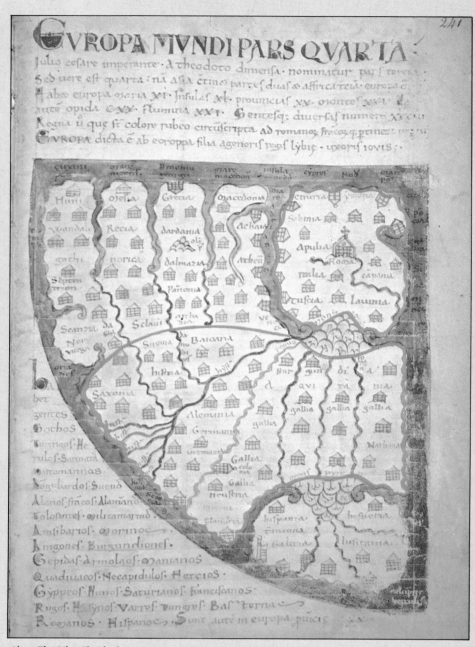

Above The *Liber Floridus* by Lambert of Ardres, c. 1120. According to the author, Europe constituted a quarter of the earth, Africa another quarter and Asia a half, hence the quadrant shown here. Though very schematic, the distribution of the provinces bears some relation to the facts.

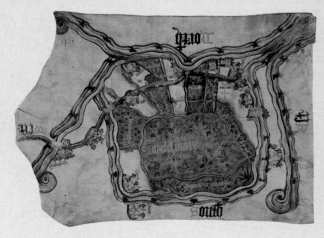

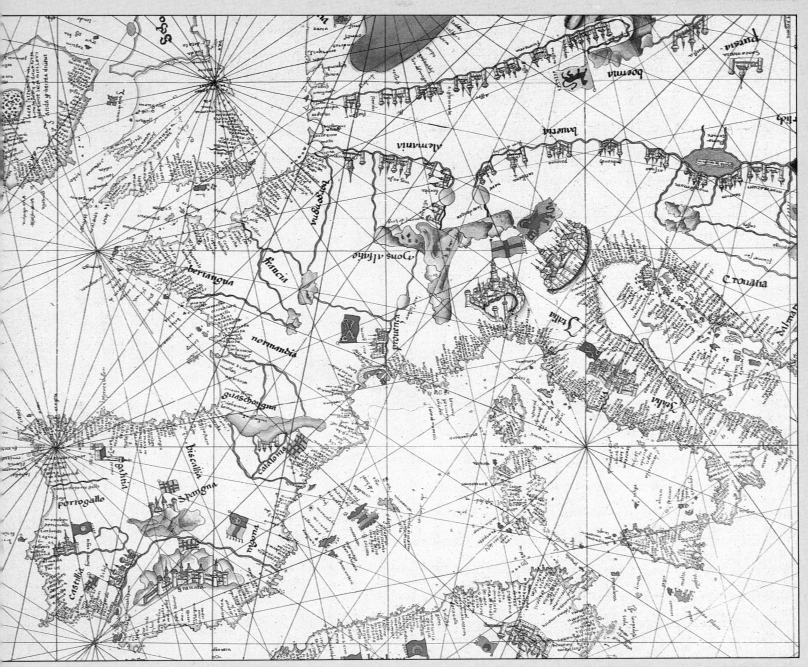

Above A Portolano chart of 1497 by Freducci d'Ancona. The map, a late example of its kind, creates a recognizable impression of western Europe but one where the coastline is given more attention than the interior.

Left The original of this picture map of Inglemoor was first drawn for a lawsuit about peat-cutting rights in 1405/8. The rivers which form the boundaries of this marshy district are clearly shown, though the names are written in such a way as to involve turning the map frequently. Within the enclosed area may be discerned bridges, villages, wayside crosses and fenced enclosures and the moor is decorated with flowers to suggest its aspect as a meadow. The technique is similar to that shown on the Canterbury waterworks plan of the 12th century (see p. 84).

none. It must have been the discovery of the uses of the magnetic compass that prompted the invention of a precise chart to be used in conjunction with it, complete with an indication of scale. To use it effectively the steersman would, however, need to know enough mathematics to make simple calculations, and to use a ruler and a pair of dividers. Not surprisingly it was in Italy that these conditions were met earliest, but the Catalans, particularly those of Majorca, also soon acquired a great reputation as mapmakers. The earliest surviving atlas with several maps was made in Majorca for King Charles V of France in 1375. This presentation copy had a better chance of surviving than the single membranes of sheepskin used by Mediterranean pilots until, presumably, they fell to pieces from excessive use. There are nonetheless enough examples of earlier charts to show how the techniques were experimented with and improved on through the 14th century. Both in Venice and in Genoa, as might have been expected, ambitious maps were drawn by specialized cartographers. The

Venetian Marino Sanudo, who wrote about the problem of recovering the Holy Land from the Muslims, sent his book to the pope together with a set of appropriate maps made by Pietro Visconte (c. 1320). It was the recognition of how much had to be learned about mapmaking by using tables of coordinates for different places that drove men of learning back to Ptolemy, for he had faced the same problem. Little by little the makers of land maps learned how to proceed from the presentation of small surveyable areas to the mapping of regions and whole countries. From Ptolemy too they learned about making world maps, and as the voyages of discovery in the 15th century brought new lands to notice, so they duly appeared on the maps; for example the Canaries are shown on the Laurentian Portolano of 1351, and the west coast of Africa appears on the map made by the Venetian Andrea Bianco at London in 1448. Likewise navigators had to learn how to record accurate observations of the places they visited if the mapmakers were to incorporate their discoveries on their maps.

EPILOGUE: EUROPE DISCOVERS THE WORLD

Before the end of the 15th century some Europeans had already found their way by sea to India and America. Europeans face-to-face with peoples of quite different cultures did not thereupon put aside their own former disputes and preoccupations to concentrate on exploiting these discoveries, but European history had all the same to live thereafter in a new dimension. If the Middle Ages are deemed to end here, let it not be supposed that it is because the age of discoveries had finally demonstrated the foolishness of medieval fears about falling off the edge of the earth. The age of discoveries was rather one of the consequences that flowed from the promotion of every kind of human skill known in the Middle Ages across the whole continent. Medieval craftsmanship had not been reserved for the universal empire, or for elite patrons. It marketed its goods and in such diverse settings that there were always good chances for worthwhile projects. With the discoveries, the Mediterranean, at least symbolically, lost its millennia-long pre-eminence. Europeans no longer looked inwards to the maritime basin for their cultural inspiration. They had become bold enough to up anchor and leave its shores altogether. For a thousand years men had striven to adapt classical culture for northern consumption. No more fitting conclusion to this period could be found than for the torch of exploration to be handed from such peoples as the Genoese, Majorcans and Catalans to the Portuguese, Spaniards, Bretons, English and Dutch. Explorers departed from Atlantic ports to visit all the corners of the earth. The first circumnavigation was completed by the expedition led by the Portuguese Magelhães (Ferdinand Magellan) in 1519.

The great empire built by the Portuguese from the 16th century raised a small kingdom with no remarkable past to the status of a great power, which is itself a commentary on the kind of society to be found in medieval Europe. Despite its shape as the southwest peninsula of Europe, Iberia is not geographically well designed for political unity. Apart from its experience under the Romans (when it constituted five provinces) the peninsula has only ever enjoyed unitary government for 60 years (1580–1640). In the Middle Ages it was normally divided into several kingdoms, with people speaking and writing many different languages and worshiping in at least three religious traditions: Christian, Muslim and Jewish. No other territory of the former Roman empire enjoyed such an enduring multiplicity of cultures, able to hold their own against one another without the country ever breaking down to the institutional level of the municipality, as happened in Italy, and always preserving some balance of interests between town and country and between land and sea.

Among the great maritime powers of Europe, Portugal was almost the last to take shape just as it was the last kingdom to appear in Spain itself. However if Portugal had to wait till the 12th century for its first king (Afonso-Henry, 1109–85), a county of Portugal existed within the kingdom of León from the late 10th century and the origin of the county goes back another hundred years still, when Christians first recovered the land from the Muslims. Initially a marcher land, it did not consolidate its hold south of the Douro river until the 11th century. By that time the county had been held for several generations by one family from Galicia with claims on the benevolence of the kings of León. After the conquest of the town of Coimbra (1064) the county became much more extensive. It passed through the hands of several counts nominated by the kings, before Alfonso VI set it up as the dowry for his daughter Teresa when she married the Burgundian count Henry c. 1095. From this union descended the first nine kings of Portugal. The kingdom was extended by wars against the Muslims. In 1147, with the help of English crusaders bound for the Holy Land, Lisbon was captured. Not until a century later, when the kingdom was extended still further south to include the province of Algarve and reach the southern coast a mere 160 kilometers away, did Lisbon emerge as the kingdom's leading city. At its greatest extent Portugal remained a small kingdom (though not the smallest in the peninsula), hemmed in between Castile and the sea. To investigate the possibilities of its maritime situation it was obliged to come to terms with the Atlantic Ocean, the only Iberian state in such a position.

Until the end of the 14th century there was no impetus to overcome an age-old antipathy to the stormy seas to the west. At this stage the Portuguese embarked on a course of national rejuvenation in consequence of the efforts of the Trastamara dynasty of Castile to incorporate the Portuguese kingdom on the death of the last legitimate ruler of the Burgundian royal family. Because Castile was in alliance with France, the Portuguese received help from England in their battles to maintain independence, an alliance that went back at least two centuries. The successful outcome of the war not only forced Portugal to turn its back on the rest of the peninsula, but the dislocation of political, social and economic life in the generation after the crucial victory of Aljubarrota (1386) brought to power behind the Avis dynasty men willing to support independence with arms and money and eager to take advantage of their new opportunities. The first proof of the new spirit was the campaign for the capture of Ceuta (1415) and the subsequent acquisition of lands in North Africa, where sugar cultivation could be developed. More enterprising still, the Portuguese began to settle a few years later in Madeira (discovered less than a century before), cultivating sugar and cereals to supplement the resources of their beleaguered homeland. They were also short of manpower. Slaves were first seized in the Canaries, then obtained as a result of wars in Morocco. North Africa was, however, seen

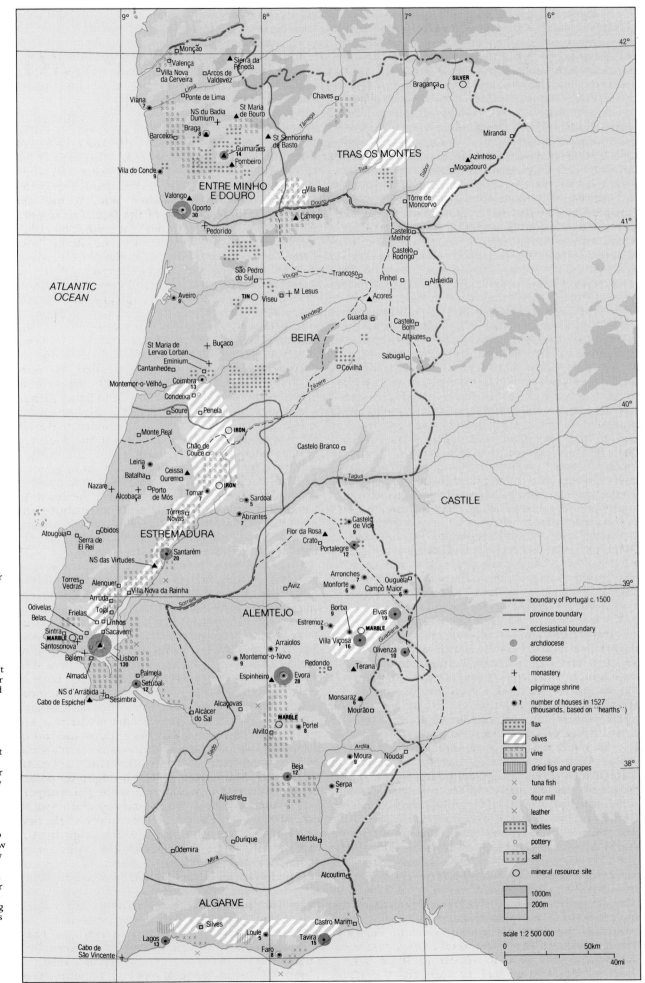

Portugal
Few of the feudal states to appear in the 11th century managed to survive and become sovereign states, as Portugal did. The special circumstances of Christian involvement with the reconquest of Spain from the Muslims originally gave the counts of Portugal their chance to make themselves a kingdom. It was ruled by a single dynasty for over two centuries. When it died out, Portugal nearly succumbed to Castilian conquest but was saved in part by finding an ally in England, drawn into Spain to counteract French influence on Castile. The defiant Portugal that affirmed its independence at Aljubarrota (1386) became under the new Avis dynasty like a new state. Isolated from the rest of Spain by Castilian hostility, the Portuguese turned their zeal outwards, first to Morocco against the Muslims, and then to colonization in Madeira. The new dynasty which brought in a new aristocracy also won support in the towns. Portuguese valor and enterprise equipped Portugal for its imperial century. Despite the survival of crusading zeal among the nobles, the 15th century was for the kingdom one of novelty and invention. The Portuguese became the first nation on the Atlantic seaboard to seek its destiny confidently across the ocean.

boundary of Portugal c.1500
province boundary
ecclesiastical boundary
archdiocese
diocese
monastery
pilgrimage shrine
number of houses in 1527 (thousands, based on "hearths")
flax
olives
vine
dried figs and grapes
tuna fish
flour mill
leather
textiles
pottery
salt
mineral resource site
1000m
200m
scale 1:2 500 000
0   50km
0   40mi

to be also an important source of gold. Though as Christians the Portuguese regarded the Muslims there as their principal enemies and had no scruples about fighting to obtain what they wanted, they were also prepared to track down the origin of the gold. For these reasons the Portuguese began to take an interest in the exploration of the Atlantic coast in search of the golden river (Senegal) whence gold departed across the Sahara en route for North Africa. After the failure of King Duarte's imposing military expedition against Tangiers in 1437, the main thrust of expansion for the next few years was naturally by colonization, commerce and discovery, rather than by military means. The most famous promoter of exploration is Prince Henry the Navigator. He was in fact deeply committed to the program of military conquests in Morocco, and as a

patron of exploration between 1415 and 1460 he actually played a less important role than either his brother, the regent Pedro, or private merchants and other lords. Portuguese efforts in this direction did not therefore depend on one man's vision. There was a broadly based realization of the advantages Portugal might legitimately expect.

Systematic exploration down the coast was at first undertaken in quite small ships. They succeeded in rounding Cape Bojador by 1431. For this purpose sailors had to learn how to return home by forsaking the coastal currents and winds; they found their way by going far out into the ocean to pick up the return currents near the Azores (rediscovered in 1427). Over the years Portuguese sailors learned how to do this with confidence and precision. By 1445 the whole operation had become

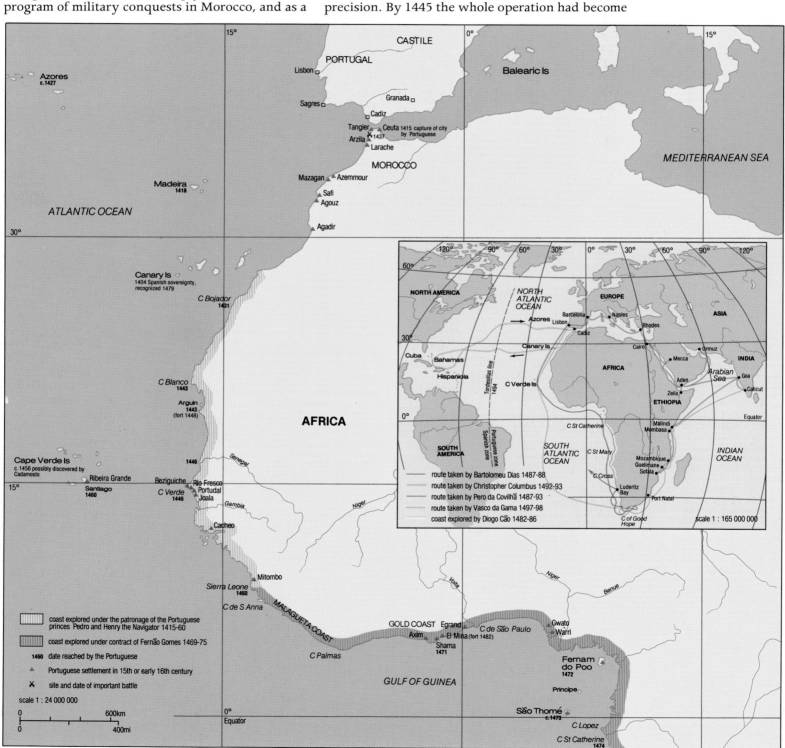

Left: Discoveries in the 15th century

The discovery of America (1492) and the Portuguese arrival in India (1498) were the culmination of voyages of discovery launched with an accelerating confidence and enthusiasm throughout the 15th century. The history of the enterprise needs to take into account even earlier plans, like that of the Genoese in 1291 to send ships to the Far East around the coast of Africa. The Muslim revival in the Levant encouraged hopes of finding an alternative southern route to India before the size of the African continent was realized. Catholic recovery of the Balearic Islands stimulated confidence in their powers of navigation and established important contacts with the results of Muslim geographical research. Sailors ventured far enough out into the Atlantic to find both the Canary Islands and Madeira. Iberian sailors from the Atlantic ports familiar with northern sailing ships were even better equipped than the Mediterranean navigators to take up the ocean challenge: their navigational technique and their craft were in better shape. Both military and economic motives encouraged the Portuguese, in particular, to get the better of their Muslim enemies in northwest Africa by craftily outdistancing them at sea. Even after the development of the new caravel sailing ship it took another half-century for the sailors to reach India. Throughout that period the basis of reliable knowledge of the winds, tides, southern stars as well as the peoples of Africa was duly laid, as the Portuguese acquired increasing confidence in their own seamanship.

much more easy, due to the use of the caravel, introduced c. 1440. This ship could easily be maneuvered by skilled men and their knowledge of the winds and currents could be put to better use.

About the same time the Portuguese brought back the first black African slaves, from their raiding in northern Mauritania (at about 20° N), though not until they entered the Gulf of Guinea in the early 1460s did the slave trade become really big business. By that time the king of Castile, Juan II, began to take an interest in these discoveries, but as his successor Henry IV (1454–74) did not pursue this challenge to Portugal, it was not until the time of Isabella (queen of Castile 1474–1504) that Castilians and Portuguese started fighting in the Gulf of Guinea. These disputes came eventually to settlement, whereby in return for surrendering their claims on the Canary Islands, the Portuguese obtained from Castile recognition of their monopoly to explore and trade with all lands south of Canary, a treaty ratified by the pope in 1481. The church was deeply committed to all projects that weakened the Muslims in Africa and hopeful that exploration would soon provide easy access to African Christians, thought to flourish under Prester John. Harmonizing Iberian quarrels to hasten this Christian work, the papacy did not regard itself as dividing up the world for Christian exploitation.

Whereas Afonso V (king 1438–81) had taken most interest in chivalrous campaigning both in Morocco and in Castile, his son and successor, John II (1481–95), took up the royal patronage of discovery in a determined and systematic way. Even before his accession he had planned voyages to find a maritime route to Asia. At this time explorers had already found that the coast of Africa turned south, instead of continuing due east from the Gulf of Guinea. John's explorers spent several years

pushing south, leaving inscribed stones at vantage points to mark their advances. Finally, in 1488, Bartolomeu Dias rounded the Cape of Good Hope. In the same year as Dias left Portugal, another royal expedition set out to find the overland route to Ethiopia. Pero da Covilhã did eventually get there, but only after writing back to the king from Cairo to describe a no less incredible journey, disguised as a merchant, from Egypt to Aden and on to India. By the 1490s therefore the Portuguese had devised a means of entering the Indian Ocean and by their intelligence work had anticipated how they could use the network of Arab navigation for their own purposes. In this way the expedition led by Vasco da Gama in 1498 took Arab pilots from the east coast of Africa on its way to Calicut.

By that time John II had long since rejected the fanciful schemes of Columbus for reaching India by sailing west, for he was confident that Portuguese plans to reach India by sailing around Africa were close to being realized. Columbus took his ideas to Castile and America was therefore discovered and claimed on behalf of Spain. Before his death in 1495, John II obtained from the Borgia pope Alexander VI another papal ruling about the respective claims of Spain and Portugal, so that the Spaniards were left with the mysterious lands to the west of the meridian passing 370 leagues beyond the Cape Verde Islands, and Portugal with the rights to the known riches of the east. For the Spaniards this proved to be a risk worth taking. But in 1494 the Portuguese could feel fully satisfied that their king had successfully protected their interests and their years of effort. The Portuguese had equipped themselves with ships, maps, instruments and skills to meet the rest of the world. Drawing upon the resources of the Middle Ages, Portugal had led Europe into modern history.

GLOSSARY

Alamans The people of "all the men," as they were called by others, who appear to have preferred to call themselves Swabians. They tried to penetrate the Roman frontier in the Rhine-Danube area from the early 3rd century. The pressure to colonize was maintained for several centuries, but the opposition of the Franks in particular deflected their efforts and concentrated their strength across the Rhine in the region of Alsace.

Alans A people known originally in Turkestan, their empire in the region of the Caspian Sea was destroyed by the Huns in 375. The remnant fled to the west, where bands under different chiefs either served the Roman empire or made common cause with other barbarians, as with the Vandals in Spain (409). In both cases their distinctive character was lost during the 5th century.

Albigensians Cathar heretics of southern France, so called from Albi, the earliest of their "bishoprics" (founded 1167). Ecclesiastical efforts to convert them eventually provoked the murder of the papal legate Peter of Castelnau in 1208 which led to the preaching of a crusade against them. These wars were concluded in 1229 but the Catholic victory was incomplete. The Inquisition was established to hunt down heretics but it was another century before all heresy was finally suppressed.

Angles People from the "Angel" country on the east coast of Schleswig, similar to Saxons with whom they invaded and settled in the Roman province of Britain in the middle of the 5th century.

apanage Originally a territory assigned to provide for the maintenance of a younger brother of the king of France, from the 13th century onwards.

Arianism The heresy derived from the teaching of the 4th-century Alexandrian Arius who held that Christ was not of the same substance as the Father.

Avars A nomadic people from the region north of the Caspian Sea who sought refuge in the west from the Turks. They eventually succeeded in establishing a base for their operations in the middle Danube, taking Sirmium in 582. The formation of the Slav and Bulgar states limited their activities, but their raiding was still so troublesome in the late 8th century that Charlemagne was provoked to annihilate their power.

banate The district ruled by a ban who held military responsibilities in certain Slavonic areas dependent on the kingdom of Hungary.

barbarian A Greek term originally designating all non-Greek peoples, it was adopted by the Romans to mean all peoples outside the Roman empire.

Bogomil From the Bulgar *bogu-mil*, "dear to God," used to describe the dualist heretics who were prominent in Bulgaria in the 10th century. They spread throughout the Balkans despite ecclesiastical persecution and only disappeared after the Ottoman conquests of the 14th century.

Burgundians Originally from Scandinavia, these people had established some links with the Roman empire by a long sojourn in Germany before they joined the barbarian invasion force of 406. They soon became Roman auxiliaries and only obtained a kingdom of their own between Lyons and Geneva at the end of the 5th century. The kingdom succumbed, however, to the Catholic Merovingians in 533-34.

burh A fortress or walled settlement used as a refuge in wartime.

caliph The title taken by those who succeeded (or claimed to succeed) to the role of Muhammad as ruler of Islam.

cañada (Spanish) Glen or dale, used for the sheep walks across the Spanish peninsula in transhumance pastoralism.

canton The term generally used to describe the individual member states of the Swiss confederation.

catepan The title used to describe the governor of a theme (or province) of the east Roman empire until the 11th century when it designated only the subordinates of the governor, now called *dux*.

Cathars Term derived from the Greek *katharos*, "pure" or "perfect," and used to describe dualist heretics, inspired by Bogomil teaching. They were found in several parts of western Europe in the 12th and 13th centuries, under a variety of local names such as Albigeois in southern France and Patarini in northern Italy.

Cinque Port Originally one of the five ports (Hastings, Dover, Sandwich, Romney and Hythe) which enjoyed special privileges in return for providing naval service to English kings.

commune A municipal corporation established by sworn oaths, originally occurring in northern Italy from the 11th century.

crusade The military expeditions preached in the west after 1095 to provide aid for eastern Christians were originally called "pilgrimages." The term "crusade" became established out of the habit of sewing cloth crosses to the military pilgrims' clothing – such men were "crossed" (*croisés* in French).

demesne The lord's own estate as distinct from land granted to vassals of which the lord remained nominal "owner."

diocese Originally a district of the Roman empire normally styled province, the term "diocese" came to be used for the much smaller territories ruled ecclesiastically by bishops, several of whom were found in any one imperial province, which was itself ruled ecclesiastically by the metropolitan or archbishop.

elector By 1273 the election of German kings by the princes of the empire was formally managed by a few of the most prominent. In 1356 they were declared to be the archbishops of Cologne, Trier and Mainz, the king of Bohemia, the Count Palatine of the Rhine, the duke of Saxony and the margrave of Brandenburg.

exarch The governor of a province of the eastern empire, most particularly of Italy from the 6th century.

fief A lordship held by feudal law in return for military service.

franchise A legal immunity from royal jurisdiction enjoyed by a favored lord or bishop or the equivalent.

Franks Germanic people of the middle and lower Rhineland, known from the 3rd century, who only won special renown in the late 5th century and who established their special eminence in the barbarian world by the early acceptance of Catholic Christianity.

Frisians Western neighbors of the Saxons and Angles along the southern coast of the North Sea who played some uncertain part in the settlement of Britain but who appear to have preferred to concentrate their own expansion into the continental lands vacated by the Saxons.

Germans Term used by the Romans to describe the various barbarian peoples they encountered in the Rhineland, implying a cultural or linguistic unity not actually perceived by the people themselves, until *Deutsche* was used in the 8th century to distinguish "Germans" from "Romans" in the Carolingian empire.

Goths The most important of the barbarian peoples whose destiny brought them into contact with the Roman empire across the Danube until 376 when they demanded refuge within the empire from the Huns. The Visigoths (west Goths) won important political power in the western empire in the 5th century; the Ostrogoths (east Goths) eventually won a kingdom in Italy (493-534), but the Arianism of both barbarian peoples prevented the consolidation of their states among their Catholic subjects.

Guelf Party label used especially in Italy to signify pro-papal and anti-imperial political sentiments. It was, however, derived from the feud between German princes which made the Welf dukes of Bavaria the leading opponents of the Hohenstaufen emperors from the second quarter of the 12th century.

guild Originally a society of merchants with the monopoly of rights to trade in the town. Later craft guilds appeared as confraternities of specific commercial activities.

heresy Theological opinion maintained in opposition to "orthodox" or "catholic" doctrine.

Huns The Huns' defeat of the Alans and Goths in 374-75 established the reputation of these steppe peoples who continued to be feared, particularly by other barbarians, until the death of their most famous leader Attila in 453.

Hussites Term used by foreigners to describe the Bohemians who opposed the authority of the church and the king after the execution of the theological reformer John Hus by the Council of Constance in 1415. This opposition was, in fact, far from united in its views or in its sympathy for Hus himself.

iconoclasm Image smashing, particularly the movement to suppress reverence for holy images in the Orthodox church, initiated by the Isaurian emperors and lasting from 725 to 842.

Jutes People said by Bede to have settled in Kent, the Isle of Wight and parts of Hampshire from Jutland. This testimony has provoked much comment, and the Jutes remain an obscure people for historians.

knight A term originally meaning an attendant; it came to carry a more specific sense of royal servant, a man of military rank serving with horse and superior armament; ultimately it described a man of superior social rank, a gentleman of less than noble standing, and one formally "created" a knight when he became of suitable age and proven military capacity.

kontore Commercial depot, warehouse or store belonging to German merchants abroad or away from their home town and constituting a foreign branch of their business.

landgrave The count (*Graf*) of a province (*Land*), as distinct from a county, who enjoyed a wider jurisdiction giving him authority over other counts.

liberty A liberty was equivalent to a **franchise**. Great lords customarily enjoyed many exemptions by virtue of royal concessions and from the 12th century often needed to obtain confirmation of their liberties (in the plural) from kings, not with any claim to philosophic rights, but with traditional privileges in view.

Lombards These were the last important group of barbarians to enter the Roman empire. They created a kingdom for themselves in Italy (568) in the wake of the troubles rising out of the imperial reconquest. Their kingdom lasted until it was conquered by Charlemagne in 774.

march A frontier territory often entrusted to a vice-regent with special military responsibilities, where laws appropriate to a mixed population and unsettled conditions prevailed.

margravate A march territory ruled by a count, comparable to a landgravate but with the additional responsibility of defending the border.

mayor of the palace The Frankish majordomo of the palace, who in effect ran the king and kingdom of the later Merovingian dynasty.

Merovingians Meroveus was, according to Gregory of Tours, the father of Childeric, father of Clovis, the first Catholic Frankish king, whose career launched his people's historical reputation. The Merovingians designate Clovis's family of rulers and, by extension, the Frankish peoples they ruled. But Meroveus himself is more likely to have been the eponymous hero of myth than a historical ruler.

metropolitan Bishop having oversight of an ecclesiastical province; in the western church he was an archbishop; in the eastern church he was superior in rank to an archbishop but below the patriarch.

monophysitism A theological belief that Jesus Christ had only one (divine) nature and not two, widely accepted in the Syrian and Coptic churches in the 5th century.

Ostrogoths *See* **Goths**.

pale A term used to describe a district with agreed bounds, applying a distinct law, as with the English government at Calais and Dublin, found from the end of the 15th century and used for convenience for earlier periods.

parlement A place for talking, discussion and decision which in the French kingdom came to be the chief royal court of law, unique at Paris till the 15th century when provincial *parlements* also came into being.

parliament The French term *parlement* was used in England to describe assemblies where political discussions, which developed out of legal proceedings, gradually became more important. The royal courts of justice had developed earlier, but parliament has never lost its status as the high court of the realm.

parliamentary abbot Originally all English prelates were summoned to the king's court when he required, but during the 14th century the burden of attendance at parliament was limited to bishops and certain abbots, mainly Benedictine of ancient foundations.

patriarch The title of the bishops of Antioch, Alexandria and Rome, subsequently granted also to those of Constantinople and Jerusalem.

Pentapolis This imperial province of Italy was occupied by the Lombards in 752 and given by Pepin to the papacy after his Italian campaign. It corresponded more or less to Flaminia and comprised the five coastal bishoprics of Rimini, Pesaro, Fano, Senigallia and Ancona but was also on occasion described as extending from Rimini to Gubbio, and so included other bishoprics of the interior: Urbino, Fossombrone, Cagli, Iesi, Osimo, Gubbio, Perugia and Numana.

Saracens The term used in the Roman empire and the Latin west for the nomadic peoples of the Syrian-Arabian desert, and by extension in the crusading period for the Arabs and all Muslims.

Saxons The Saxons had established themselves in lower Saxony by the middle of the 3rd century and their raids on Britain required the organization of special imperial defenses long before they certainly began to colonize. In the 7th century, after the conversion of the English, ties of sentiment with old Saxony inspired English missionary activity on the continent, so the Saxon emigrants cannot have altogether lost contact with their original homeland.

schism A disruption of the visible unity of the church, most blatantly between the Latin (Catholic) and eastern churches, but also within the medieval Latin church, as in disputes about the legitimate succession to the bishopric of Rome.

see The seat or residence of a bishop, as distinct from the diocese which he ruled.

seigneur A feudal lord.

sheriff The reeve of the shire, that is the royal official who managed the royal interest in each county and carried out royal orders within his territory.

Sicilian Vespers Insurrection begun on Easter Monday, 31 March 1282, in Palermo against the French government of the island maintained by Charles of Anjou. It soon brought Peter III, king of Aragon, to Sicily and led to the partition of the former Norman kingdom into the separate kingdoms of (Angevin) Naples and (Aragonese) Sicily.

strategus A military commander in the east Roman empire.

Suevi The Suevi were a fragmented people by 406 when they joined with other barbarians in crossing the Rhine. Their most conspicuous achievement thereafter was to share with the Vandals in the conquests of Spain. After the Vandals moved into North Africa, the Suevi extended their Spanish kingdom from its base at Braga, but they could not prevent the Visigoths from acquiring a kingdom in Spain in 456. They retained their own separate kingdom in Galicia, however, until the Visigoths annexed it in 585.

summa A comprehensive treatise giving the sum total of knowledge about the matter in question.

Taborites A group of Bohemian religious dissenters of radical beliefs among the Hussites whose center was at Mount Tabor, south of Prague.

taifa From Arabic *tawa'if* meaning faction or party, used for the small kingdoms founded in Islamic Spain after the collapse of the caliphate at Cordoba in 1031; Almeria, Valencia, Denia and the Balearics, Granada, Málaga, Algeciras, Carmiona, Ronda, Moron, Huelva-Settes, Niebla, Silver, Santa Maria de Algarve, Albarracia, Seville, Badajoz, Toledo, Saragossa, Murcia, Cordoba.

theme After Heraclius the provincial government of the east Roman empire was administered through themes, each of which was responsible for raising military contingents.

Vandals These people crossed the Rhine in 406 and, having traversed Gaul, entered Spain in 409 to avoid an imperial counterattack. After 20 years of pillage they passed into North Africa where they set up a kingdom that lasted until Belisarius arrived in 533 to reestablish imperial authority.

vassal Originally a servant or dependant, it came to mean the servant of a great lord, from whom he commonly held lands on conditions of honorable service.

Visigoths *See* **Goths.**

LIST OF ILLUSTRATIONS

180tr. St Omer Psalter: British Library, London Ms. Yates Thompson 14.
180c. Book of Kells, Trinity College, Dublin Ms. 58, f. 34: Phaidon Press Picture Archive, Oxford.
180bl. St Luke's Gospel: Pierpont Morgan Library, New York Ms. 806, f. 96.
180bc. Bible of St Martial de Limoges: Bibliothèque Nationale, Paris Ms. Lat. 254, f. 10.
180br. *Historia Naturalis* of Pliny the Elder: Victoria and Albert Museum, London A.L. 1504–1896.
181. Printing scene, title-page of *Hegesippus*, printed in 1511 by J. B. Ascensius: Mary Evans Picture Library, London.
183t. Palace of the popes, Avignon: Leonard von Matt, Buochs.
183b. Bridge at Karitaina: Graham Speake, Oxford.
186. Castle of the knights of St John, Rhodes: Ekdotike Athenon, S.A., Athens.
187. Frangocastello, Crete: Zefa, London.
191. Krakow cathedral: Giraudon, Paris.
193t. Doorway, Ják abbey: Michael Dixon, Dover.
193c. Ottoman siege of Belgrade, miniature: Topkaki Museum, Istanbul (photo Sonia Halliday, Weston Turville).

194. Cathedral at Suzdal: Robert Harding Associates, London.
195. Novgorod icon, the divine fatherhood: Tretyakov Gallery, Moscow.
198tl. View of Paris from Froissart's chronicles: Bibliothèque Nationale, Paris Ms. Fr. 2645, f. 321v.
198tr. Calais from the sea: British Library, London Cotton Ms. Aug. I. ii. 70.
198c. Trial of Joan of Arc: Bibliothèque Nationale, Paris Ms. Lat. 5969, f. 1.
200. Castle at Eileen Donan: Sonia Halliday, Weston Turville.
204t. Portrait of Petrarch: Bibliothèque Nationale, Paris Ms. Lat. 6069 A v.
204b. Frontispiece of Petrarch's Virgil illustrated by Simone Martini: Biblioteca Ambrosiana, Milan S.P. 10/27.
207. *Arnolfini Marriage* by Jan van Eyck: National Gallery, London.
208. Helicopter design by Leonardo da Vinci: Institut de France, Paris Ms. B, f. 83v.
209. Assassination of John the Fearless, duke of Burgundy: Bibliothèque Nationale, Paris Ms. 5084, f. 1.
212. Map of Switzerland by Konrad Türst from *De Situ Confoederatum Descriptio*: Zentralbibliothek, Zurich.

214. Doge's palace, Venice: Scala, Florence.
216. Christ from *Assignment of the Keys* by Donatello: Victoria and Albert Museum, London.
217. Portrait of the artist's father, (detail) by Albrecht Dürer: National Gallery, London.
218t. Printer with closed press from a drawing by Dürer: Mary Evans Picture Library, London.
218b. Buxheim, St Christopher: John Rylands Library, Manchester.
219l. Page from Celsus Maffeus, *Monumentum*: British Library, London.
219tr. Playing cards signed by J. de Dale: Bibliothèque Nationale, Paris.
220t. Map of Europe from *Liber Floridus* by Lambert of Ardres: University Library, Ghent Ms. 92, f. 241r.
220b. Copy of map of Inglesmoor, Yorkshire (now Lincolnshire): Public Record Office, London M.P.C. 56.
221t. Portolano chart by Freducci d'Ancona: Royal Geographical Society, London.
225tl. Henry the Navigator, detail from St Vincent triptych by Nuno Gonçalves: Museu Nacional de Arte Antiga, Lisbon (photo Giraudon, Paris).
225tr. Woodcut illustrating Columbus's voyage to the West Indies: Elsevier Archives, Amsterdam.

BIBLIOGRAPHY

Historical Atlases
J. Engel (ed.), *Grosser historischer Weltatlas, ii, Mittelalter*, 4th edn, Munich 1981.
R. I. Moore (ed.), *The Hamlyn Historical Atlas*, London 1981.
R. L. Poole, *Historical Atlas of Modern Europe from the Decline of the Roman Empire*, Oxford 1902.
K. von Spruner and T. Menke, *Handatlas für die Geschichte des Mittelalters und der neueren Zeit*, 3rd edn, Gotha 1880.

General Accounts
J. W. Barker, *Justinian and the Later Roman Empire*, Madison, Wisc. 1966.
P. Brown, *The World of Late Antiquity: from Marcus Aurelius to Muhammed*, London 1971.
Cambridge Medieval History (8 vols.), Cambridge 1911–36.
C. Courtois, *Les Vandales et l'Afrique*, Paris 1955.
J. Hale, J. R. L. Highfield and B. Smalley (eds.), *Later Medieval Europe*, London 1965.
J. Huizinga (trans. F. Hopman), *The Waning of the Middle Ages*, London 1924.
A. H. M. Jones, *The Later Roman Empire 284–602: a social, economic and administrative survey* (3 vols.), Oxford 1964.
D. Matthew, *The Medieval European Community*, London 1977.
H. St. L. B. Moss, *The Birth of the Middle Ages 395–814*, Oxford 1935.
L. Musset (trans. E. and C. James), *The Germanic Invasions: the making of Europe AD 400–600*, London 1975.
C. D. Smith, *Western Mediterranean Europe: a historical geography of Italy, Spain and southern France since the Neolithic*, London 1979.
R. W. Southern, *The Making of the Middle Ages*, London 1953.
E. A. Thompson, *The Early Germans*, Oxford 1965.
—— *A History of Attila and the Huns*, Oxford 1948.
—— *The Visigoths in the Time of Ulfila*, Oxford 1966.
J. M. Wallace-Hadrill, *The Barbarian West 400–1000*, London 1967.

The Western Church, the Papacy and Monasticism
G. Barraclough, *The Medieval Papacy*, London 1968.
R. Brentano, *Two Churches: England and Italy in the 13th century*, Princeton, N.J. and Oxford 1968.
—— *Rome before Avignon: a social history of 13th-century Rome*, London 1974.
H. Chadwick, *The Early Church*, Harmondsworth 1967.
C. H. Dawson (ed.), *The Mongol Mission: narratives and letters of the Franciscan missionaries in Mongolia and China in the 13th and 14th centuries*, London 1955.
A. Fliche and V. Martin, *Histoire de l'église* (21 vols. in 24), Paris 1934–.

H. Jedin and J. P. Dolan (eds.), *History of the Church* (3 vols.), New York 1980.
H. Jedin, K. Latourette and J. Martin, *Atlas zur Kirchengeschichte*, Freiburg 1970.
M. D. Knowles, *Christian Monasticism*, London 1969.
—— *The Monastic Order in England*, Cambridge 1962.
—— *The Religious Orders in England* (3 vols.), Cambridge 1948–59.
K. Latourette, *History of the Expansion of Christianity: Thousand Years of Uncertainty 500–1500 AD*, New York 1971.
L. J. Lekai, *The Cistercians: ideals and reality*, Kent, Ohio 1977.
G. Mollat, *The Popes at Avignon 1305–78*, London 1963.
J. R. H. Moorman, *A History of the Franciscan Order from its Origins to the Year 1517*, Oxford 1968.
P. Partner, *The Lands of St Peter*, London 1972.
R. W. Southern, *Western Society and the Church in the Middle Ages*, Harmondsworth 1970.
W. Ullmann, *The Growth of Papal Government in the Middle Ages*, London 1955.
F. van der Meer, *Atlas de l'ordre cistercien*, Brussels 1965.
D. P. Waley, *The Papal State in the 13th Century*, London 1961.

The East Roman Empire
T. S. R. Boase (ed.), *The Cilician Kingdom of Armenia*, Edinburgh 1978.
R. Browning, *The Byzantine Empire*, London 1980.
G. F. Hill, *A History of Cyprus* (4 vols.), Cambridge 1940–52.
R. J. H. Jenkins, *Byzantium: the imperial centuries 610–1071*, London 1966.
D. M. Lang, *Armenia: cradle of civilization*, London 1978.
—— *The Georgians*, London 1966.
C. A. Mango, *Byzantium: the empire of new Rome*, London 1980.
W. Miller, *The Latins in the Levant: a history of Frankish Greece*, London 1908.
D. Obolensky, *The Byzantine Commonwealth: eastern Europe 500–1453*, London 1971.
—— *Byzantium and the Slavs*, London 1971.
G. Ostrogorsky (trans. J. M. Hussey), *History of the Byzantine State*, Oxford 1968.
K. M. Setton, *Catalan Domination of Athens 1311–88*, Cambridge, Mass. 1948.
P. Sherrard, *Constantinople*, Oxford 1965.

Islam
W. C. Brice, *An Historical Atlas of Islam*, Leiden 1981.
C. Cahen, *Pre-Ottoman Turkey*, London 1968.
K. A. C. Creswell, *Early Muslim Architecture* (2 vols.), Oxford 1932, 1940.
—— *The Muslim Architecture of Egypt* (2 vols.), Oxford 1952, 1959.
P. K. Hitti, *History of the Arabs*, London 1970.

M. G. S. Hodgson, *Venture of Islam* (vols. 1 and 2), Chicago, Ill. 1974.
H. Inalcik (trans. N. Itzkowitz and C. Imber), *The Ottoman Empire: the classical age 1300–1600*, London 1973.
G. Le Strange, *Baghdad during the Abbasid Caliphate*, Oxford 1900.
R. Le Tourneau, *The Almohad Movement in North Africa in the 12th and 13th Centuries*, Princeton, N.J. 1969.
A. Miquel, *L'Islam et sa civilisation*, Paris 1977.
W. Popper (ed.), *Egypt and Syria under the Circassian Sultans 1382–1468 AD, Systematic Notes to Ibn Taghri Birdi's Chronicle of Egypt*, Berkeley, Calif. 1955.
M. Rogers, *The Spread of Islam*, Oxford 1976.
J. J. Saunders, *A History of Medieval Islam*, London 1965.
—— *The History of the Mongol Conquests*, London 1971.
S. Vryonis, *The Decline of Medieval Hellenism in Asia Minor and the Process of Islamization from the 11th through to 15th Century*, Berkeley, Calif. 1971.

Bohemia
F. G. Heymann, *George of Bohemia, King of Heretics*, Princeton, N.J. 1965.
—— *John Zizka and the Hussite Revolution*, Princeton, N.J. 1955.
H. Kaminsky, *A History of the Hussite Revolution*, Berkeley, Calif. 1967.

Bulgaria
R. Browning, *Byzantium and Bulgaria: a comparative study across the early medieval frontier*, London 1975.
D. M. Lang, *The Bulgarians from Pagan Times to the Ottoman Conquest*, London 1976.
J. C. S. Runciman, *A History of the First Bulgarian Empire*, London 1930.

Crusader States
T. S. R. Boase, *Castles and Churches of the Crusading Kingdom*, London 1967.
H. E. Mayer (trans. J. B. Gillingham), *The Crusades*, Oxford 1972.
J. Prawer, *The Latin Kingdom of Jerusalem: European colonialism in the Middle Ages*, London 1972.
J. C. S. Runciman, *A History of the Crusades* (3 vols.), Cambridge 1951–54.
K. M. Setton (ed.), *A History of the Crusades* (4 vols.), Madison, Wisc. 1969–77.

England
Bede (trans. L. Sherley-Price), *A History of the English Church and People*, Harmondsworth 1970.
J. Campbell (ed.), *The Anglo-Saxons*, Oxford 1982.
R. G. Collingwood and J. N. L. Myres, *Roman Britain and the English Settlements*, Oxford 1937.
D. C. Douglas, *William the Conqueror*, London 1964.
M. E. Falkus and J. B. Gillingham (eds.), *Historical Atlas*

of Britain, St Albans 1981.
D. Hill, *An Atlas of Anglo-Saxon England*, Oxford 1981.
E. F. Jacob, *The Fifteenth Century*, Oxford 1961.
W. Kapelle, *The Norman Conquest of the North*, London 1980.
M. McKisack, *The Fourteenth Century*, Oxford 1959.
D. J. Matthew, *The Norman Conquest*, London 1966.
H. Mayr-Harting, *The Coming of Christianity to Anglo-Saxon England*, London 1977.
A. L. Poole, *From Domesday Book to Magna Carta*, Oxford 1951.
F. M. Powicke, *The Thirteenth Century*, Oxford 1962.
F. M. Stenton, *Anglo-Saxon England*, Oxford 1971.
C. Thomas, *Christianity in Roman Britain to AD 500*, London 1981.
W. L. Warren, *Henry II*, London 1973.

France
G. Duby and R. Mandrou (trans. J. B. Atkinson), *A History of French Civilisation*, London 1966.
K. Fowler, *The Age of Plantagenet and Valois: the struggle for supremacy 1328–1498*, London 1967.
J. Froissart (trans. G. Brereton), *Chronicles*, Harmondsworth 1968.
Gregory of Tours (trans. L. Thorpe), *The History of the Franks*, Harmondsworth 1974.
E. M. Hallam, *Capetian France 987–1328*, London 1980.
C. Higounet (ed.), *Histoire de l'Aquitaine*, Toulouse 1971.
W. C. Jordan, *Louis IX and the Challenge of the Crusade*, Princeton, N.J. 1979.
M. W. Labarge, *St Louis: the life of Louis IX of France*, London 1968.
R. Latouche, *Caesar to Charlemagne: the beginnings of France*, London 1968.
J. F. Lemarignier, *Le Gouvernement royal aux premiers temps capétiens 987–1108*, Paris 1965.
P. S. Lewis, *Late Medieval France: the polity*, London 1968.
E. C. Lodge, *Gascony under English Rule*, London 1926.
A. Longnon, *Atlas historique de la France* (3 vols.), Paris 1885–89.
M. Rouche, *L'Aquitaine des Visigoths aux Arabes 418–718*, Paris 1977.
E. Salin, *La Civilisation mérovingienne* (4 vols.), Paris 1950–9.
J. R. Strayer, *The Albigensian Crusades*, New York 1971.
P. Tucoo-Chala, *Gaston Fébus, un grand prince d'occident au xive siècle*, Paris 1976.

Germany and the German Empire
G. Barraclough, *The Origins of Modern Germany*, Oxford 1973.
C. C. Bayley, *The Formation of the German College of Electors in the mid-13th Century*, Toronto 1949.
D. A. Bullough, *The Age of Charlemagne*, London 1965.
E. Christiansen, *The Northern Crusades: the Baltic and the Catholic frontier 1100–1525*, London 1980.
H. J. Cohn, *The Government of the Rhineland Palatinate in the 15th Century*, London 1965.
P. Dollinger (trans. D. S. Ault and S. H. Steinberg), *The Hansa*, London 1970.
J. Fleckenstein (trans. B. S. Smith), *Early Medieval Germany*, Amsterdam 1978.
R. Folz (trans. S. A. Ogilvie), *The Concept of Empire in Western Europe from the 5th to the 16th Century*, London 1969.
Frederick II (trans. C. A. Wood and F. M. Fyfe), *De Arte Venandi*, Stanford, Calif. 1943.
L. Halphen (trans. G. de Nie), *Charlemagne and the Carolingian Empire*, Amsterdam 1977.
K. Hampe, *Germany under the Salian and Hohenstaufen Emperors*, Oxford 1973.
E. H. Kantorowicz (trans. E. O. Lorimer), *Frederick II 1194–1250*, London 1931.
A. W. A. Leeper, *A History of Medieval Austria*, Oxford 1941.
K. Leyser, *Rule and Conflict in an Early Medieval Society: Ottonian Saxony*, London 1979.
P. Munz, *Frederick Barbarossa: a study in medieval politics*, London 1969.
G. Strauss (ed.), *Pre-Reformation Germany*, London 1972.
J. E. Tyler, *The Alpine Passes: the Middle Ages*, Oxford 1930.
T. C. van Cleve, *The Emperor Frederick II of Hohenstaufen*, Oxford 1972.

Hungary
D. J. Maenchen-Helfen, *The World of the Huns: studies in their history and culture*, Berkeley, Calif. 1973.
E. Pamlenyi (trans. L. Boros *et al.*), *A History of Hungary*, London 1975.

Ireland
L. Bieler, *Ireland: harbinger of the Middle Ages*, Oxford 1963.

R. D. Edwards, *Atlas of Irish History*, London 1981.
R. Frame, *Colonial Ireland 1169–1369*, Dublin 1981.
J. F. Kenney, *The Sources for the Early History of Ireland*, New York 1968.
J. Lydon, *Ireland in the Later Middle Ages*, Dublin 1973.
A. J. Otway-Ruthven, *A History of Medieval Ireland*, London 1968.
J. Watt, *The Church in Medieval Ireland*, Dublin 1972.

Italy
P. Burke, *Culture and Society in Renaissance Italy*, London 1972.
F. Chalandon, *Histoire de la domination normande en Italie et en Sicile*, Paris 1907.
D. C. Douglas, *The Norman Achievement 1050–1100*, London 1969.
—— *The Norman Fate 1100–1154*, London 1976.
T. Hodgkin, *Italy and her Invaders*, Oxford 1885–99.
J. K. Hyde, *Society and Politics in Medieval Italy: the evolution of the civil life 1000–1350*, London 1973.
F. C. Lane, *Venice: a maritime republic*, Baltimore, Md. 1973.
J. Larner, *Culture and Society in Italy 1290–1420*, London 1971.
P. Toubert, *Les Structures du Latium médiéval* (2 vols.), Rome 1973.
C. J. Wickham, *Early Medieval Italy: central power and local society 400–1000*, London 1981.

Low Countries
P. J. Blok *A History of the People of the Netherlands: part one, from the earliest times to the beginning of the 15th century*, New York 1898.
D. E. W. Cartellieri (trans. M. Letts), *The Court of Burgundy*, London 1929.
H. Pirenne, *Histoire de Belgique des origines à nos jours* (7 vols.), Brussels 1907–26.
R. Vaughan, *Charles the Bold: the last Valois duke of Burgundy*, London 1973.
—— *John the Fearless: the growth of Burgundian power*, London 1966.
—— *Philip the Bold: the formation of the Burgundian state*, London 1962.
—— *Philip the Good: the apogee of Burgundy*, London 1970.

Poland
N. Davies, *God's Playground: a history of Poland* (vol. 1), Oxford 1981.
W. F. Reddaway (ed.), *The Cambridge History of Poland* (vol. 1), Cambridge 1941.

Portugal
A. H. de Oliveira Marques (trans. S. S. Wyatt), *Daily Life in Portugal in the Later Middle Ages*, Madison, Wisc. 1971.
—— *A History of Portugal*, New York 1976.
V. Magalhães Godinho, *L'Economie de l'empire portugais aux xve et xvie siècles*, Paris 1969.

Russia
J. Blum, *Lord and Peasant in Russia from the Ninth to the Nineteenth Century*, Princeton, N.J. 1961.
J. L. I. Fennell, *The Emergence of Moscow 1304–59*, London 1969.
M. L. Freishin-Chirovskii, *A History of the Russian Empire: grand-ducal Vladimir and Moscow*, London 1973.
G. Vernadsky, *A History of Russia* (vols. 2–4), New Haven, Conn. 1944.

Scandinavia
H. R. Ellis Davidson, *The Viking Road to Byzantium*, London 1976.
T. K. Derry, *A History of Scandinavia*, London 1979.
G. Jones, *The Norse Atlantic Saga*, Oxford 1964.
E. Jutikkala, *A History of Finland*, London 1979.
L. Musset, *Les Peuples Scandinaves au moyen âge*, Paris 1951.
P. H. Sawyer, *The Age of the Vikings*, London 1971.

Scotland
G. W. S. Barrow, *The Anglo–Norman Era in Scottish History*, Oxford 1980.
—— *The Kingdom of the Scots*, London 1973.
A. A. M. Duncan, *Scotland: the making of the kingdom*, Edinburgh 1975.
P. MacNeill, *An Historical Atlas of Scotland*, St Andrews 1975.
R. G. Nicholson, *Scotland: the later Middle Ages*, Edinburgh 1974.

Slav Lands
F. W. Carter, *Dubrovnik (Ragusa): a classic city-state*, London 1972.
S. Clissold (ed.), *A Short History of Yugoslavia from Early*

Times to 1966, Cambridge 1968.
F. Dvornik, *The Slavs: their early history and civilisation*, Boston, Mass. 1959.
J. V. A. Fines, *The Bosnian Church*, New York 1975.
M. Gimbutas, *The Slavs*, London 1971.
R. Portal (trans. P. Evans), *The Slavs*, London 1969.
H. W. V. Temperley, *A History of Serbia*, London 1917.
A. P. Vlasto, *The Entry of the Slavs into Christendom: an introduction to the medieval history of the Slavs*, Cambridge 1970.

Spain
R. I. Burns, *Islam under the Crusaders: colonial revival in the 13th-century kingdom of Valencia*, Princeton, N.J. 1973.
H. J. Chaytor, *A History of Aragon and Catalonia*, London 1933.
J. N. Hillgarth, *The Spanish Kingdoms 1250–1516* (2 vols.), Oxford 1976, 1978.
James I of Aragon (trans. J. Forster), *The Chronicle*, London 1883.
J. Klein, *The Mesta: a study in Spanish economic history 1273–1836*, Cambridge, Mass. 1920.
P. A. Linehan, *The Spanish Church and the Papacy in the 13th Century*, Cambridge 1971.
D. W. Lomax, *The Reconquest of Spain*, London 1978.
A. Mackay, *Spain in the Middle Ages: from frontier to empire 1000–1500*, London 1977.
R. Menéndez-Pidal (trans. H. Sunderland), *The Cid and his Spain*, London 1934.
—— *Historia de España* (vols. 4, 5, 6, 7, 14, 15), Madrid 1950–.
J. Orlandis-Rovira, *España Visigotica*, Madrid 1977.
P. E. Russell, *The English Intervention in Spain and Portugal in the Time of Edward III and Richard II*, Oxford 1955.
J. Shneidman, *The Rise of the Aragonese-Catalan Empire 1200–1350*, New York, 1970.
M. Stokstad, *Santiago de Compostella*, Norman, Ok. 1979.
E. A. Thompson, *The Goths in Spain*, Oxford 1969.
J. Vicens-Vives, *Approaches to the History of Spain*, Berkeley, Calif. 1970.
P. Vilar, *La Catalogne dans l'Espagne moderne*, Paris 1962.

Switzerland
F. Bonjour, H. S. Offler and G. R. Potter, *A Short History of Switzerland*, Oxford 1952.

Wales
R. R. Davies, *Lordship and Society in the March of Wales 1282–1400*, Oxford 1978.
J. E. Lloyd, *A History of Wales from the Earliest Times to the Edwardian Conquest*, London 1912.
W. Rees, *Historical Atlas of Wales*, Cardiff 1951.

Urban Society, Trade and Industry
M. W. Barley (ed.), *European Towns: their archaeology and early history*, London 1977.
C. M. Cipolla, *Before the Industrial Revolution: European society and economy 1000–1700*, London 1976.
—— *Guns and Sails in the Early Phases of European Expansion 1400–1700*, London 1966.
—— *Money, Prices and Civilisation in the Mediterranean World 5th–7th Century*, Princeton, N.J. 1956.
E. Ennen (trans. N. Fryde), *The Medieval Town*, Amsterdam 1977.
D. Nicholas, *Town and Countryside: social, economic and political tensions in 14th-century Flanders*, Ghent 1971.
I. Origo, *The Merchant of Prato*, London 1960.
C. Phythian-Adams, *Desolation of a City: Coventry and the urban crisis of the late Middle Ages*, Cambridge 1976.
C. Platt, *The English Medieval Town*, London 1976.
M. Postan (ed.), *Economic Organisation and Policies in the Middle Ages*, Cambridge 1963.
—— (ed.) *Trade and Industry in the Middle Ages*, Cambridge 1952.
S. M. G. Reynolds, *An Introduction to the History of English Medieval Towns*, Oxford 1977.
F. Rörig (trans. D. Bryant), *The Medieval Town*, London 1967.
R. Unger, *The Ship in the Medieval Economy*, Montreal 1980.

Rural Society and the Agrarian Economy
R. H. Bautier, *The Economic Development of Medieval Europe*, London 1971.
M. Bloch (trans. L. A. Manyon), *Feudal Society*, London 1961.
—— (trans. J. Sondheimer), *French Rural History: an essay on its basic characteristics*, London 1966.
J. Critchley, *Feudalism*, London 1978.
G. Duby (trans. C. Postan), *Rural Economy and Country Life in the Medieval West*, London 1968.
M. Postan (ed.), *The Agrarian Life of the Medieval West*, Cambridge 1966.

Education and Intellectual Life

C. N. L. Brooke, *The Twelfth-Century Renaissance*, London 1969.

H. J. Chaytor, *From Script to Print*, Cambridge 1945.

F. C. Copleston, *Aquinas*, Harmondsworth 1955.

E. Gilson, *A History of Christian Philosophy in the Middle Ages*, London 1955.

D. Hay, *The Italian Renaissance in its Historical Background*, Cambridge 1977.

M. D. Knowles, *The Evolution of Medieval Thought*, London 1962.

C. Morris, *The Discovery of the Individual 1050–1200*, London 1972.

A. Murray, *Reason and Society in the Middle Ages*, Oxford 1978.

B. Radice (trans. and ed.), *The Letters of Abelard and Heloise*, Harmondsworth 1974.

H. Rashdall (ed. F. M. Powicke and A. B. Emden), *The Universities of Europe in the Middle Ages*, Oxford 1936.

P. Riche, *Education and Culture in the Barbarian West*, Columbia, S.C. 1978.

E. H. Wilkins, *Life of Petrarch*, Chicago, Ill. 1961.

—— *Studies in the Life and Work of Petrarch*, Cambridge, Mass. 1955.

Science, Medicine and Technology

L. C. Arano (ed.), *Tacuinum Sanitatis: medieval health handbook*, New York 1976.

F. Klemm, *A History of Western Technology*, London 1959.

J. F. D. Shrewsbury, *A History of Bubonic Plague*, Cambridge 1970.

A. P. Usher, *A History of Mechanical Inventions*, Cambridge, Mass. 1954.

The Visual Arts

J. Acland, *Medieval Structure: the Gothic vault*, Toronto 1973.

J. J. G. Alexander, *The Decorated Letter*, London 1978.

—— *Insular Manuscripts, 6th–9th Century*, London 1978.

M. Baxandall, *The Limewood Sculptors of Renaissance Germany*, London 1980.

—— *Painting and Experience in 15th–Century Italy*, Oxford 1972.

K. J. Conant, *Carolingian and Romanesque Architecture 800–1200*, Harmondsworth 1959.

C. R. Dodwell, *Painting in Europe 800–1200*, Harmondsworth 1978.

J. Fitchen, *The Construction of Gothic Cathedrals; a study of medieval vault erection*, Oxford 1961.

H. Focillon, *The Art of the West in the Middle Ages* (2 vols.), London 1963.

P. Frankl, *Gothic Architecture*, Harmondsworth 1963.

H. J. Hansen (ed.), *Architecture in Wood*, London 1971.

J. H. Harvey, *The Master Builders: architecture in the Middle Ages*, London 1971.

W. Hohnquist, *Germanic Art during the First Millennium*, Stockholm 1955.

J. James, *Chartres*, London 1979.

C. M. Kauffmann, *Romanesque Manuscripts 1066–1190*, London 1975.

E. Kitzinger, *Early Medieval Art*, London 1940.

F. Klingender, *Animals in Art and Thought to the end of the Middle Ages*, London 1971.

R. Krautheimer, *Early Christian and Byzantine Architecture*, London 1965.

—— *Rome: profile of a city 312–1308*, Princeton, N.J. 1980.

P. Lasko, *Ars Sacra 800–1200*, Harmondsworth 1973.

J. D. le Couteur, *English Medieval Painted Glass*, London 1926.

E. Panofsky (ed.), *Abbot Suger on the Abbey Church of St Denis and its Art Treasures*, Princeton, N.J. 1946.

—— *Early Netherlandish Painting: its origin and character* (2 vols.), Cambridge, Mass. 1964.

—— *The Life and Art of Albrecht Dürer*, Princeton, N.J. 1955.

J. Pope-Hennessy, *Italian Gothic Sculpture*, London 1972.

G. L. Remnant, *Catalogue of Misericords in Great Britain*, Oxford 1969.

L. Salzman, *Building in England down to 1540*, Oxford 1952.

J. Strzygowski, *Early Church Art in Northern Europe*, London 1928.

R. M. Tovell, *Flemish Arts of the Valois Counts*, Toronto 1950.

E. von Witzleben, *French Stained Glass*, London 1968.

M. Whinney, *Early Flemish Painting*, London 1968.

J. E. L. T. White, *Art and Architecture in Italy 1250–1400*, London 1966.

R. Wittkower, *Architectural Principles in the Age of Humanism*, London 1962.

Music

J. Caldwell, *Medieval Music*, London 1978.

F. Harrison, *Music in Medieval Britain*, London 1958.

R. Hoppin, *Medieval Music*, New York 1980.

G. Reese, *Music in the Middle Ages*, London 1941.

O. Strunk, *Source Readings in Music History: I Antiquity and the Middle Ages*, London 1981.

Literature

M. Alexander (trans. and ed.), *Beowulf*, Harmondsworth 1973.

E. Auerbach, *Mimesis: the representation of reality in western literature*, Princeton, N.J. 1968.

E. R. Curtis, *European Literature and the Latin Middle Ages*, London 1953.

Dante (trans. J. Sinclair), *The Divine Comedy* (3 vols.), Oxford 1971.

R. S. Loomis, *Arthurian Literature in the Middle Ages*, Oxford 1959.

D. D. R. Owen, *The Legend of Roland*, London 1973.

F. J. E. Raby, *A History of Secular Latin Poetry in the Middle Ages*, Oxford 1957.

E. Vinaver, *The Rise of Romance*, Oxford 1971.

Castles and Warfare

W. F. d'E. Anderson, *Castles of Europe from Charlemagne to the Renaissance*, London 1970.

H. M. Colvin, *The History of the King's Works* (6 vols.), London 1963–76.

D. Macgibbon and T. Ross, *Castellated and Domestic Architecture of Scotland from the 12th to the 18th Century* (5 vols.), Edinburgh 1887–92.

C. L. Salch and J. Burnouf, *Atlas des châteaux-forts*, Strasbourg 1977.

—— and —— *Atlas des villes fortifiées*, Strasbourg 1978.

J. F. Verbruggen, *The Art of Warfare in Western Europe*, Amsterdam 1976.

Printing

L. P. V. Febvre (ed. G. Nowell-Smith and D. Wootton), *The Coming of the Book: the impact of printing 1450–1800*, London 1976.

A. M. Hind, *A History of Engraving and Etching*, London 1923.

—— *An Introduction to a History of Woodcut*, London 1935.

Mapmaking

P. D. A. Harvey, *The History of Topographical Maps*, London 1980.

G. H. T. Kimble, *Geography in the Middle Ages*, London 1938.

N. A. E. Nordenskiöld, *Facsimile Atlas to the Early History of Cartography*, Stockholm 1889.

GAZETTEER

Arelate *see* Arles
Arezzo (Italy), 43°28′N 11°53′E, 109, 165, 204
Argenteuil (France), 48°57′N 2°15′E, 75
Argos (Greece), 37°38′N 22°43′E, 184, 185
Argyle* 201
Argyll* 201
Ariano Irpino (Italy), 41°09′N 15°05′E, 96
Arklow (Irish Republic), 52°48′N 6°09′W, 202
Arles (Arelate), (France), 43°41′N 4°38′E, 18, 28, 36, 40, 52, 80, 94, 118, 164, 187, 196
Armagh (UK), 54°21′N 6°39′W, 48, 98, 202
Armagnac* 98, 118, 196
Armenia* 19, 50, 90, 112
Arnhem (Netherlands), 52°00′N 5°53′E, 128
Arpino (Italy), 41°38′N 13°37′E, 109
Arquà (Italy), 45°16′N 11°44′E, 204
Arraiolos (Portugal), 38°44′N 7°59′W, 223
Arran (Isl), (UK), 55°35′N 5°15′W, 201
Arras (France), 50°17′N 2°46′E, 40, 52, 75, 118, 196, 208
Arronches (Portugal), 39°08′N 7°16′W, 223
Arruda (Portugal), 38°59′N 9°04′W, 223
Arta (Greece), 39°10′N 20°59′E, 184
Arth (Switzerland), 47°03′N 8°32′E, 210
Artois* 75, 118, 196, 208
Arundel (UK), 50°51′N 0°34′W, 199
Arzua (Spain), 42°55′N 8°10′W, 104
Aschaffenburg (W Germany), 49°58′N 9°10′E, 203
Ascoli (Italy), 42°52′N 13°35′E, 43, 96, 109
Askeaton (Irish Republic), 52°36′N 8°58′W, 202
Assisi (Italy), 43°04′N 12°37′E, 109, 165, 212
Asti (Italy), 44°54′N 8°13′E, 43, 80, 94, 212
Astorga (Spain), 42°27′N 6°23′W, 70, 114
Asturias* 70
Aswan (Egypt), 24°00′N 32°58′E, 50, 69, 112
Athboy (Irish Republic), 53°37′N 6°55′W, 202
Athenry (Irish Republic), 53°18′N 8°45′W, 202
Athens (Greece), 38°00′N 23°44′E, 12, 18, 19, 28, 36, 67, 112, 133, 184, 185, 187
Athleague (Irish Republic), 53°34′N 8°15′W, 202
Athlone (Irish Republic), 53°25′N 7°56′W, 98, 202
Athy (Irish Republic), 52°59′N 6°59′W, 98, 202
Atouguia (Portugal), 39°20′N 9°20′W, 223
Attalia *see* Antalya
Attigny (France), 49°28′N 4°35′E, 52, 75
Auch (Elimberris), (France), 43°40′N 0°36′E, 18, 40, 98, 104, 118, 196
Augsburg (W Germany), 48°21′N 10°54′E, 80, 94, 165, 203
Augst (Switzerland), 47°32′N 7°44′E, 210
Augusta Treverorum *see* Trier
Auldearn (UK), 57°34′N 3°48′W, 201
Auimay (France), 46°01′N 0°20′W, 104
Aureliani *see* Orléans
Aurillac (France), 44°56′N 2°26′E, 104, 118
Austrasia* 18, 40, 52
Autun (France), 46°58′N 4°18′E, 40, 52, 75, 118, 208
Auvergne* 40, 75, 98, 118, 196
Auxerre (France), 47°48′N 3°35′E, 40, 52, 75, 104, 118, 165, 208
Avaricum *see* Bourges
Avellino (Italy), 40°49′N 14°47′E, 96
Avenches (Switzerland), 46°53′N 7°03′E, 210
Aversa (Italy), 40°58′N 14°13′E, 96, 109
Avignon (France), 43°56′N 4°48′E, 75, 80, 94, 118, 165, 187, 196, 204
Ávila (Spain), 40°39′N 4°42′W, 70, 114, 165
Aviz (Portugal), 39°03′N 7°54′W, 223
Avranches (France), 48°42′N 1°21′W, 75, 98, 118
Axminster (UK), 50°47′N 3°00′W, 48
Ayent (Switzerland), 46°17′N 7°25′E, 210
Ayr (UK), 55°28′N 4°38′W, 98, 201
Azov (USSR), 47°06′N 39°26′E, 19, 63, 185, 195

Badajoz (Spain), 38°53′N 6°58′W, 70, 114
Baden (Switzerland), 47°28′N 8°19′E, 210
Baden (W Germany), 48°45′N 8°15′E, 203
Baeza (Spain), 38°00′N 3°28′W, 70, 114
Baghdad (Iraq), 33°20′N 44°26′E, 50, 69, 111
Balla (Irish Republic), 53°45′N 9°10′W, 48
Ballymore (Irish Republic), 53°29′N 7°40′W, 202
Ballymote (Irish Republic), 54°06′N 8°31′W, 202
Ballyteige (Irish Republic), 52°12′N 6°45′W, 202
Balmerino (UK), 56°25′N 3°02′W, 201
Baltinglass (Irish Republic), 52°57′N 6°42′W, 48, 202
Bamberg (W Germany), 49°54′N 10°54′E, 80, 94, 165, 203
Bamburgh (UK), 55°36′N 1°42′W, 199
Banff (UK), 57°46′N 2°31′W, 201
Bangor (UK), 54°40′N 5°40′W, 48
Bangor (UK), 53°13′N 4°08′W, 48, 199
Banja Luka (Yugoslavia), 44°47′N 17°11′E, 184
Banwell (UK), 51°20′N 2°52′W, 48
Bar (Antivari), (Yugoslavia), 42°05′N 19°06′E, 184, 203, 208
Barbastro (Spain), 42°02′N 0°07′E, 70, 114
Barcelona (Spain), 41°25′N 2°10′E, 12, 18, 19, 28, 52, 70, 114, 133, 165, 187, 224
Barcelos (Portugal), 41°32′N 8°37′W, 223
Bardney (UK), 53°12′N 0°21′W, 48, 199
Bardsey (UK), 52°46′N 4°48′W, 48
Barfleur (France), 49°40′N 1°16′W, 98, 196
Bari (Italy), 41°07′N 16°52′E, 67, 96, 212
Barking (UK), 51°33′N 0°06′E, 48
Bar-le-Duc (France), 48°46′N 5°10′E, 196
Barletta (Italy), 41°20′N 16°17′E, 96
Barnard Castle (UK), 54°33′N 1°55′W, 199
Barrow (UK), 53°41′N 0°23′W, 48
Bar-sur-Aube (France), 48°14′N 4°43′E, 75
Bar-sur-Seine (France), 48°07′N 4°23′E, 75, 208
Barukhan* 185
Basle (Switzerland), 47°33′N 7°36′E, 80, 94, 165, 203, 208, 210
Basra (Iraq), 30°30′N 47°50′E, 50, 69, 111
Batalha (Portugal), 39°40′N 8°56′W, 165, 223
Bath (UK), 51°23′N 2°22′W, 48, 98, 118, 199
Battle (UK), 50°55′N 0°29′E, 199
Batum (USSR), 41°37′N 41°36′E, 112, 185
Baulmes (Switzerland), 46°48′N 6°32′E, 40
Bautzen (E Germany), 51°11′N 14°29′E, 188
Bavaria* 18, 40, 52, 80, 188, 203
Bayeux (France), 49°16′N 0°42′W, 75, 98, 118, 165
Bayonne (France), 43°30′N 1°28′W, 70, 98, 118, 165, 196
Baza (Spain), 37°30′N 2°45′W, 70, 114
Bazas (France), 44°26′N 0°12′W, 40, 98, 118, 196
Béarn* 98, 118, 196
Beaucaire (France), 43°48′N 4°37′E, 118, 133
Beaulieu (France), 47°33′N 2°48′E, 40
Beauly (UK), 57°29′N 4°29′W, 201
Beaumaris (UK), 53°16′N 4°05′W, 98, 165, 199
Beaune (France), 47°02′N 4°05′E, 208
Beauvais (France), 49°26′N 2°05′E, 52, 75, 118, 165, 208
Bebenhausen (W Germany), 48°33′N 9°05′E, 203
Beckford (UK), 52°01′N 2°02′W, 48
Bective (Irish Republic), 53°36′N 6°42′W, 202
Bedford (UK), 52°08′N 0°29′W, 199
Beinwil (Switzerland), 47°17′N 8°12′E, 210
Beirut (Lebanon), 33°52′N 35°30′E, 12, 50, 90, 133
Beja (Portugal), 38°01′N 7°52′W, 70, 114, 223
Bela Crkva (Yugoslavia), 44°54′N 21°25′E, 184
Belas (Portugal), 38°46′N 9°15′W, 223
Belém (Portugal), 38°41′N 9°12′W, 114, 165, 223
Belgrade (Yugoslavia), 44°50′N 20°30′E, 12, 18, 19, 36, 67, 133, 184, 185, 192
Belin (France), 44°29′N 0°47′W, 104
Bellême (France), 48°22′N 0°34′E, 75
Belley (France), 45°46′N 5°41′E, 118
Bellinzona (Switzerland), 46°12′N 9°02′E, 43, 78
Belluno (Italy), 46°08′N 12°13′E, 203, 212
Belorado (Spain), 42°25′N 3°11′W, 104
Benevento (Italy), 41°08′N 14°46′E, 18, 19, 43, 52, 96, 109, 212
Benken (Switzerland), 47°39′N 8°39′E, 210
Berantevilla (Spain), 42°41′N 2°50′W, 70
Berg* 203
Bergamo (Italy), 45°42′N, 9°40′E, 43, 78, 80, 94, 204, 212
Bergen (Netherlands), 51°36′N 6°02′E, 203
Bergen (Norway), 60°23′N 5°20′E, 19, 63, 128, 133
Bergerac (France), 44°50′N 0°29′E, 104, 196
Berkley (UK), 51°42′N 2°27′W, 48
Berkshire* 199
Berlin (Germany), 52°32′N 13°25′E, 12, 128, 188
Bernau (E Germany), 52°41′N 13°36′E, 188
Berne (Switzerland), 46°57′N 7°26′E, 12, 78, 94, 165, 208, 210
Beroea *see* Aleppo
Beroun (Czechoslovakia), 49°58′N 14°05′E, 188
Berry* 75, 196
Berwick (UK), 55°46′N 2°00′W, 98, 199, 201
Besalú (Spain), 42°12′N 2°42′E, 70, 114
Besançon (Besontio), (France), 47°14′N 6°02′E, 18, 40, 52, 80, 94, 118, 196, 203, 208
Besau* 187
Besontio *see* Besançon
Béthisy (France), 49°17′N 2°48′E, 75
Béthune (France), 50°32′N 2°38′E, 208
Beverley (UK), 53°51′N 0°26′W, 48, 165
Bèze (France), 47°28′N 5°16′E, 40
Béziers (France), 43°21′N 3°13′E, 98, 118
Bialystok (Poland), 53°09′N 23°10′E, 190
Biasca (Switzerland), 46°22′N 8°58′E, 210
Biberach (W Germany), 48°21′N 8°02′E, 203
Biel (Switzerland), 47°09′N 7°16′E, 210
Bielefeld (W Germany), 52°02′N 8°32′E, 128
Bigorre* 98, 118, 196
Bijeljina (Yugoslavia), 44°46′N 19°14′E, 184
Bilbao (Spain), 43°15′N 2°56′W, 70
Birka (Sweden), 59°23′N 17°56′E, 63
Birr (Irish Republic), 53°05′N 7°54′W, 48, 98, 202
Bisaccia (Italy), 41°02′N 15°23′E, 96
Bisceglie (Italy), 41°14′N 16°31′E, 96
Bischofszell (Switzerland), 47°30′N 9°15′E, 210
Bishops Castle* 199
Bishopston (UK), 51°35′N 4°03′W, 48
Bishops Waltham (UK), 50°58′N 1°12′W, 48
Bisignano (Italy), 39°31′N 16°17′E, 43, 96
Bitetto (Italy), 41°02′N 16°45′E, 96
Bithynia* 185
Bitola (Monastir), (Yugoslavia), 41°01′N 21°21′E, 184, 185
Bitonto (Italy), 41°07′N 16°41′E, 96
Black Castle (Irish Republic), 52°58′N 6°03′W, 202
Blackwater (Irish Republic), 52°26′N 6°20′W, 202
Blaenllyfni* 199
Blaye (France), 45°08′N 0°40′W, 104
Bledzew (Poland), 52°31′N 15°23′E, 188, 190
Blekinge* 63
Blenio* 210
Blois (France), 47°36′N 1°20′E, 75, 98, 118, 196
Blonay (Switzerland), 46°28′N 6°54′E, 210
Blyth (UK), 55°07′N 1°30′W, 199
Bobbio (Italy), 44°46′N 9°23′E, 43, 52, 80, 94, 109, 212
Bochnia (Poland), 49°59′N 20°25′E, 190
Bodmin (UK), 50°29′N 4°43′W, 48
Bohemia* 19, 52, 80, 94, 188, 190, 192, 203
Boiano (Italy), 41°28′N 14°20′E
Boleslawiec (Poland), 51°16′N 15°34′E, 188, 190
Bologna (Italy), 44°30′N 11°20′E, 78, 94, 109, 133, 165, 203, 204
Bolzano (Italy), 46°30′N 11°22′E, 43, 78
Bône *See* Annaba
Bonn (W Germany), 50°44′N 7°06′E, 12
Bopfingen (W Germany), 48°52′N 10°22′E, 203
Borba (Portugal), 38°48′N 7°28′W, 223
Bordeaux (Burdigala), (France), 44°50′N 0°34′W, 18, 36, 40, 52, 98, 104, 118, 133, 165, 187, 196
Borglum (Denmark), 57°22′N 9°51′E, 63
Bosanska Krupa (Yugoslavia), 44°53′N 16°10′E, 184
Bosnia* 19, 52, 184, 185, 192
Boston (UK), 52°59′N 0°01′W, 128, 199
Bosworth (UK), 52°42′N 1°23′W, 199
Bougie (Algeria), 36°49′N 5°03′E, 69, 133, 187
Boulogne (France), 50°43′N 1°37′E, 40, 52, 75, 98, 208
Bourbon* 75, 118, 196
Bourges (Avaricum), (France), 47°05′N 2°23′E, 18, 40, 52, 75, 98, 104, 118, 165, 196
Bova (Italy), 38°00′N 15°56′E, 96
Bovino (Italy), 41°15′N 15°20′E, 96
Boyle (Irish Republic), 53°58′N 8°18′W, 165, 202
Brabant* 80, 94, 98, 196, 203, 208
Brač (Isl), (Yugoslavia), 43°20′N 16°40′E, 184
Bradford (UK), 51°22′N 2°15′W, 48
Bradwell (UK), 51°44′N 0°54′E, 48
Braga (Portugal), 41°32′N 8°26′W, 70, 104, 114, 223
Bragança (Portugal), 41°47′N 6°46′W, 70, 114, 223
Brancepeth (UK), 54°44′N 1°39′W, 199
Brandenburg (E Germany), 52°25′N 12°34′E, 19, 80, 94, 128, 188, 190, 203
Braniewo (Braunsberg), (Poland), 54°24′N 19°50′E, 128, 190
Braslav (USSR), 55°34′N 27°06′E, 190
Bratislava (Pressburg), (Czechoslovakia), 48°10′N 17°10′E, 94, 165, 188, 192
Brattahlid (Greenland), 61°00′N 45°25′W, 63
Braunsberg *see* Braniewo
Brechin (UK), 56°44′N 2°40′W, 201
Brecon (UK), 51°57′N 3°24′W, 199
Bredon (UK), 52°02′N 2°07′W, 48
Breffny* 202
Bregenz (Austria), 47°31′N 9°46′E, 78
Breisach (W Germany), 48°02′N 7°36′E, 208
Breisgau* 208
Bremen (W Germany), 53°05′N 8°48′E, 63, 80, 94, 128, 133, 203
Bremgarten (Switzerland), 47°21′N 8°21′E, 210
Brescia (Italy), 45°33′N 10°13′E, 43, 78, 80, 94, 109, 212
Breslau (Wroclaw), (Poland), 51°05′N 17°00′E, 128, 133, 165, 188, 203
Brest (France), 48°23′N 4°30′W, 196
Breteuil (France), 49°38′N 2°18′E, 75
Brétigny (France), 48°37′N 2°19′E, 196
Bréval (France), 48°57′N 1°32′E, 75
Bridgnorth (UK), 52°33′N 2°25′W, 199
Bridgwater (UK), 51°08′N 3°00′W, 199
Brienne (France), 48°24′N 4°32′E, 75
Brindisi (Italy), 40°37′N 17°57′E, 43, 67, 96, 212
Bristol (UK), 51°27′N 2°35′W, 165, 199
Brittany* 40, 52, 98, 118, 196
Brive-la-Gaillarde (France), 45°09′N 1°32′E, 165
Brixen (Italy), 46°43′N 11°40′E, 80, 94, 203
Brixworth (UK), 52°20′N 0°54′W, 48
Brno (Brünn), (Czechoslovakia), 49°13′N 16°40′E, 188, 192, 203
Broc (Switzerland), 46°37′N 7°07′E, 210
Brod (Yugoslavia), 45°09′N 18°00′E, 184
Bromfield and Yale* 199
Bromyard (UK), 52°11′N 2°30′W, 48
Bruges (Belgium), 51°13′N 3°14′E, 75, 94, 118, 128, 133, 165, 196, 203, 208
Brugg (Switzerland), 47°29′N 8°13′E, 210
Brumath (France), 48°44′N 7°43′E, 52
Brünn *see* Brno
Brunswick (W Germany), 52°15′N 10°30′E, 80, 94, 128, 165, 203
Brussels (Belgium), 50°50′N 4°21′E, 12, 75, 133, 165, 203, 208
Brusthem (Belgium), 50°48′N 5°13′E, 208
Brzeg (Poland), 50°52′N 17°27′E, 188, 190
Bucharest (Romania), 44°25′N 26°07′E, 12, 185, 192
Buckingham* 199
Buda *see* Budapest
Budapest (Ofen), (Hungary), 47°30′N 19°03′E, 12, 19, 63, 94, 133, 165, 192
Budweis *see* Ceské Budějovice
Builth (UK), 52 09′N 3°24′W, 98, 199
Bukhara (USSR), 39°47′N 64°26′E, 50, 69, 111
Bukowo (Poland), 54°20′N 16°20′E, 190
Bulach (Switzerland), 47°32′N 8°32′E, 210
Bulle (Switzerland), 46°37′N 7°04′E, 210
Burdigala *see* Bordeaux
Buren (Switzerland), 47°08′N 7°23′E, 210
Burgas (Bulgaria), 42°30′N 27°29′E, 185
Burgau* 203
Burgdorf (Switzerland), 47°03′N 7°38′E, 210
Burgos (Spain), 42°21′N 3°41′W, 70, 104, 114, 118, 165
Burgundy* 18, 19, 40, 43, 52, 75, 80, 94, 98, 118, 196, 203, 208
Bursa (Turkey), 40°12′N 29°04′E, 133, 185
Bury St Edmunds (UK), 52°15′N 0°43′E, 48, 98, 199
Busra (Syria), 32°30′N 36°29′E, 36, 50, 112
Butera (Italy), 37°12′N 14°12′E, 96
Buxtehude (W Germany), 53°29′N 9°42′E, 128
Bytom (Poland), 50°21′N 18°51′E, 188, 190

Cabra (Spain), 37°28′N 4°28′W, 70
Cacabelos (Spain), 42°36′N 6°44′W, 104
Cáceres (Spain), 39°29′N 6°23′W, 70
Cádiz (Spain), 36°32′N 6°18′W, 36, 70, 114, 133, 224
Caen (France), 49°11′N 0°22′W, 75, 98, 165, 196
Caerleon* 199
Caernarvon (UK), 53°08′N 4°16′W, 98, 165, 199
Caerphilly (UK), 51°35′N 3°14′W, 199
Caerwent (UK), 51°37′N 2°46′W, 48
Caesarea (Algeria), 36°36′N 2°11′E, 36
Caesarea (Israel), 32°30′N 34°54′E, 50, 67, 90
Caesarea (Turkey), *see* Kayseri
Caesarodunum *see* Tours
Cagli (Italy), 43°33′N 12°38′E, 43
Cagliari (Italy), 39°13′N 9°08′E, 43, 187, 212
Cahors (France), 44°28′N 0°26′E, 40, 75, 98, 104, 118, 133, 165, 196
Caiazzo (Italy), 41°10′N 14°22′E, 96
Cairo (Fustat), (Egypt), 30°03′N 31°15′E, 19, 50, 69, 111, 112, 133
Caistor (UK), 53°30′N 0°20′W, 48
Calabria* 43, 67, 96, 212
Calahorra (Spain), 42°19′N 1°58′W, 70, 114
Calais (France), 50°57′N 1°52′E, 19, 196, 208
Calatayud (Spain), 41°21′N 1°39′W, 70, 114
Callinicum *see* Raqqa
Calne (UK), 51°27′N 2°00′W, 199
Caltabellotta (Italy), 37°35′N 13°13′E, 96
Caltagirone (Italy), 37°14′N 14°31′E, 96
Caltavuturo (Italy), 37°49′N 13°54′E, 96
Camaldoli (Italy), 43°43′N 11°46′E, 80, 94, 109
Cambrai (France), 50°10′N 3°14′E, 40, 75, 80, 94, 118, 203, 208
Cambridge (UK), 52°12′N 0°07′E, 165, 199
Camerino (Italy), 43°08′N 13°04′E, 43, 94, 109
Campagna* 43
Candia (Greece), 35°20′N 25°08′E, 133, 184, 185
Canfranc (Spain), 42°42′N 0°31′W, 104
Cangás de Onis (Spain), 43°21′N 5°08′W, 70
Canosa (Italy), 41°13′N 16°04′E, 43, 96
Cantanhede (Portugal), 40°20′N 8°36′W, 223
Canterbury (UK), 51°17′N 1°05′E, 48, 63, 98, 118, 165, 199
Cantref Bychan* 199
Capaccio (Italy), 40°24′N 15°05′E, 96
Cappadocia* 36, 67
Capranica (Italy), 42°15′N 12°11′E, 204
Capri (Isl), (Italy), 40°34′N 14°15′E, 96
Capua (Italy), 41°06′N 14°13′E, 43, 96, 109
Caput Vada (Tunisia), 35°10′N 11°06′E, 36
Caracuel (Spain), 38°50′N 4°04′W, 70
Caransebes (Romania), 45°23′N 22°13′E, 184
Carcassonne (France), 43°13′N 2°21′E, 70, 118, 165, 187
Cardiff (UK), 51°30′N 3°13′W, 199
Cardigan (UK), 52°06′N 4°40′W, 98, 199
Carinola (Italy), 41°12′N 13°59′E, 96
Carinthia* 18, 52, 80, 192, 203
Carlisle (UK), 54°54′N 2°55′W, 48, 63, 98, 165, 199
Carlow (Irish Republic), 52°50′N 6°55′W, 202
Carmarthen (UK), 51°52′N 4°20′W, 199
Carmona (Spain), 37°28′N 5°38′W, 70
Carniola* 52, 80, 94, 203
Carpentras (France), 44°03′N 5°03′E, 204
Carrhae (Harran), (Turkey), 36°51′N 39°01′E, 36
Carrick (Irish Republic), 54°39′N 8°38′W, 202
Carrickfergus (UK), 54°43′N 5°49′W, 202
Carrión (Spain), 42°20′N 4°37′W, 70, 104
Cartagena (Carthago Nova), (Spain), 37°36′N 0°59′W, 18, 36, 114, 187
Carthage (Tunisia), 36°54′N 10°16′E, 18, 28, 36, 50
Carthago Nova *see* Cartagena
Casablanca (Morocco), 33°39′N 7°35′W, 12
Caserta (Italy), 41°04′N 14°20′E, 96
Cashel (Irish Republic), 52°31′N 7°53′W, 48, 98, 165, 202
Caslav (Czechoslovakia), 49°56′N 15°24′E, 188
Caspe (Spain), 41°14′N 0°03′W, 114
Cassano Ionio (Italy), 39°47′N 16°20′E, 96
Cassel (France), 50°48′N 2°29′E, 75
Castel del Monte (Italy), 41°05′N 16°15′E, 165
Castellammare (Italy), 40°47′N 14°29′E, 96, 187
Castellaneta (Italy), 40°38′N 16°57′E, 96
Castellón (Spain), 39°59′N 0°03′W, 70, 114
Castelo Branco (Portugal), 39°50′N 7°30′N, 114, 223
Castelo de Vide (Portugal), 39°25′N 7°27′W, 223
Castile* 19, 70, 98, 114, 187, 223, 224
Castillon (France), 42°55′N 1°01′E, 196
Castledermot (Irish Republic), 52°55′N 6°50′W, 48, 202
Castor (UK), 52°35′N 0°20′W, 48
Castres* 118
Castro (Italy), 40°00′N 18°26′E, 96
Castrogeriz (Spain), 42°17′N 4°09′W, 104
Castro Marim (Portugal), 37°13′N 7°26′W, 223
Catania (Italy), 37°31′N 15°06′E, 43, 67, 96, 165, 187, 212
Catalaunian Plains (France), 48°44′N 3°30′E, 28
Catalonia* 187
Cattaro (Yugoslavia), 42°27′N 18°46′E, 185, 212
Caus* 199
Cavaillon (France), 43°50′N 5°02′E, 40
Cavan (Irish Republic), 54°00′N 7°21′W, 202
Cazis (Switzerland), 46°44′N 9°26′E, 210
Cefalú (Italy), 38°03′N 14°03′E, 96
Celano (Italy), 42°06′N 13°33′E, 96
Cemais* 199
Centuripe (Italy), 37°37′N 14°44′E, 96
Cephalonia (Isl), (Greece), 38°28′N 20°30′E, 184
Cerami (Italy), 37°48′N 14°31′E, 96
Cerdana* 70, 187
Cerenzia (Italy), 39°14′N 16°47′E, 96
Ceri* 199
Cerigo (Isl), (Greece), 36°09′N 23°00′E, 184, 185
Cerne (UK), 50°49′N 2°29′W, 48
Cervatos (Spain), 42°17′N 4°45′W, 70
Cesena (Italy), 44°09′N 12°15′E, 43, 109, 212
Ceské Budějovice (Budweis), Czechoslovakia), 48°58′N 14°29′E, 188, 203
Ceský Brod (Czechoslovakia), 50°05′N 14°52′E, 188
Cetinje (Yugoslavia), 42°25′N 18°56′E, 184
Ceuta (Sp), (Morocco), 35°53′N 5°19′W, 18, 50, 69, 114, 133, 224
Chalcedon (Turkey), 40°59′N 29°02′E, 36, 184
Châlons-sur-Marne (France), 48°58′N 4°22′E, 40, 52, 75, 118, 208
Chalon-sur-Saône (France), 46°47′N 4°51′E, 40, 75, 118, 196, 203, 208
Champagne* 75, 98, 118, 196, 203
Charenton (France), 46°44′N 2°38′E, 40
Charlieu (France), 46°10′N 4°10′E, 118
Charolais* 208
Charolles (France), 46°26′N 4°17′E, 208
Charroux (France), 46°09′N 0°25′E, 75, 118
Chartres (France), 48°27′N 1°30′E, 40, 52, 75, 104, 118, 165, 196
Chartreuse (France), 43°15′N 6°25′E, 88
Château d'Oex (Switzerland), 46°29′N 7°08′E, 210
Châteaudun (France), 48°04′N 1°20′E, 75
Châteaufort (France), 48°45′N 2°05′E, 75
Château Gaillard (France), 49°15′N 1°23′E, 98, 165
Châteauroux* 118
Châtellerault (France), 46°49′N 0°33′E, 75
Châtillon (France), 46°59′N 1°11′E, 75
Châtillon (France), 47°52′N 4°35′E, 208
Chaumont (France), 47°37′N 1°54′E, 75
Chaves (Portugal), 41°44′N 7°28′W, 223
Cheb *see* Eger
Chelles (France), 48°53′N 2°35′E, 40, 52
Chelmno (Poland), 53°20′N 18°25′E, 128, 165, 190
Chepstow (UK), 51°39′N 2°41′W, 199
Cherbourg (France), 49°38′N 1°37′W, 98, 196
Chernigov (USSR), 51°30′N 31°18′E, 190, 195
Chertsey (UK), 51°23′N 0°30′W, 48
Chester (UK), 53°12′N 2°54′W, 98, 199
Chiavenna (Italy), 46°19′N 9°24′E, 43, 78, 210
Chichester (UK), 50°50′N 0°48′W, 98, 118, 199
Chiemsee (W Germany), 47°53′N 12°27′E, 80
Chieti (Italy), 42°21′N 14°10′E, 43, 96, 109
Chinon (France), 47°10′N 0°15′E, 75, 98, 196
Chioggia (Italy), 45°13′N 12°17′E, 43, 109, 212
Chios (Isl), (Greece), 38°27′N 26°09′E, 184, 185
Chippenham (UK), 51°28′N 2°07′W, 199
Chirk (UK), 52°56′N 3°03′W, 199
Chiusi (Italy), 46°38′N 11°34′E, 43, 212
Chomutov (Czechoslovakia), 50°27′N 13°25′E, 188
Chrudim (Czechoslovakia), 49°57′N 15°47′E, 188
Chur (Switzerland), 46°52′N 9°32′E, 78, 80, 94, 203, 210
Cieszyn (Poland), 49°45′N 18°35′E, 188, 190
Cilgerran* 199
Cilicia* 67, 185
Cirencester (UK), 51°44′N 1°59′W, 199

234

Monselice (Italy), 45°14′N 11°46′E, 43
Montalbán (Spain), 40°50′N 0°48′W, 70, 114
Montauban (France), 44°01′N 1°20′E, 75
Monte Cassino (Italy), 43°21′N 13°26′E, 43, 52, 96, 109
Montecorvino (Italy), 40°43′N 14°57′E, 96
Montemarno (Italy), 40°54′N 14°59′E, 96
Montemor-o-Novo (Portugal), 38°38′N 8°13′W, 223
Montemor-o-Vélho (Portugal), 40°11′N 8°41′W, 223
Montenegro* 184, 185, 192
Monte Sant'Angelo (Italy), 41°43′N 15°58′E, 96
Monteverde (Italy), 41°00′N 15°32′E, 96
Montfort (France), 45°18′N 5°55′E, 75, 118, 196
Montgomery* 199
Montier-en-Der (France), 48°29′N 4°46′E, 40, 75
Montpellier (France), 43°36′N 3°53′E, 98, 104, 118, 133, 165, 187, 204
Montreuil (France), 48°52′N 2°28′E, 75
Montrose (UK), 56°43′N 2°29′W, 201
Mt St Michel (France), 48°38′N 1°30′W, 98, 118, 165
Monymusk (UK), 57°14′N 2°32′W, 201
Monza (Italy), 45°35′N 9°16′E, 43, 109
Morat *see* Murten
Moravia* 80, 188, 192, 203
Moray* 201
Morea* 185
Morella (Spain), 40°37′N 0°06′W, 70
Morimond (France), 48°02′N 5°41′E, 88
Mortagne (France), 48°32′N 0°33′E, 75
Mortain (France), 48°39′N 0°56′W, 75
Moscow (USSR), 55°45′N 37°42′E, 12, 19, 63, 133, 195
Mostar (Yugoslavia), 43°20′N 17°50′E, 184
Mottola (Italy), 40°38′N 17°02′E, 96
Moudon (Switzerland), 46°41′N 6°48′E, 210
Moura (Portugal), 38°08′N 7°27′W, 223
Mourao (Portugal), 38°22′N 7°20′W, 223
Moutier (Switzerland), 47°18′N 7°23′E, 210
Much Wenlock (UK), 52°36′N 2°34′W, 48
Mühlhausen (Mulhouse), (W Germany), 49°45′N 10°47′E, 94, 203, 208, 210
Mulhouse *see* Mühlhausen
Mullingar (Irish Republic), 53°32′N 7°20′W, 202
Munich (W Germany), 48°08′N 11°35′E, 12, 94, 165, 203
Munster (W Germany), 51°58′N 7°37′E, 80, 94, 98, 128, 133, 203, 208
Murcia (Spain), 37°59′N 1°08′W, 70, 114
Muri (Switzerland), 47°16′N 8°21′E, 210
Muro Lucano (Italy), 40°45′N 15°29′E, 96
Murten (Morat), (Switzerland), 46°56′N 7°07′E, 208, 210
Muscat (Oman), 23°37′N 58°38′E, 50, 69
Myra (Turkey), 36°17′N 29°58′E, 67, 184
Mytilene (Greece), 39°06′N 26°34′E, 67, 184

Naas (Irish Republic), 57°13′N 6°39′W, 48
Nairn (UK), 57°35′N 3°53′W, 201
Naissus *see* Niš
Nájera (Spain), 42°25′N 2°45′W, 70, 104
Namur (Belgium), 50°28′N 4°52′E, 203, 208
Nancy (France), 48°42′N 6°12′E, 208
Nantes (France), 47°14′N 1°35′W, 40, 52, 98, 118, 133, 165, 196
Naples (Neapolis) (Italy), 40°50′N 14°15′E, 12, 18, 19, 36, 43, 96, 109, 133, 165, 187, 204, 212, 224
Narberth* 199
Narbo *see* Narbonne
Narbonne (Narbo) (France), 43°11′N 3°00′E, 18, 28, 36, 40, 50, 52, 70, 94, 98, 118, 133, 165, 187, 196
Narni (Italy), 42°31′N 12°31′E, 43, 109, 204
Našice (Yugoslavia), 45°29′N 18°04′E, 184
Nassau (W Germany), 50°18′N 7°49′E, 203
Naumburg (E Germany), 51°09′N 11°48′E, 33, 80, 165, 203
Naupactus (Lepanto), (Greece), 38°23′N 21°50′E, 67, 184, 185
Nauplia (Greece), 38°23′N 21°50′E, 185
Navarre* 19, 70, 98, 118, 187, 196
Naxos (Isl), (Greece), 37°05′N 25°30′E, 184, 185
Neapolis *see* Naples
Neisse (Poland), 50°30′N 17°20′E, 94, 188, 203
Nenagh (Irish Republic), 52°52′N 8°12′W, 202
Neocaesarea (Turkey), 40°35′N 36°59′E, 67
Nesle (France), 49°45′N 2°55′E, 75
Neuchâtel (Switzerland), 46°59′N 6°55′E, 210
Neumark* 128, 188, 203
Neuss (W Germany), 51°12′N 6°42′E, 208
Neustria* 18, 40, 43, 52
Neuveville* 210
Nevers (France), 47°00′N 3°09′E, 40, 75, 94, 104, 118, 196, 208
Nevesinje (Yugoslavia), 43°15′N 18°07′E, 184
Newark (UK), 53°05′N 0°49′W, 199
Newburgh (UK), 57°19′N 2°01′W, 201
Newcastle (Irish Republic), 53°18′N 6°30′W, 202
Newcastle (UK), 54°59′N 1°35′W, 98, 199
Newcastle under Lyme (UK), 53°00′N 2°14′W, 199
New Ross (Irish Republic), 52°24′N 6°56′W, 202
Newry (UK), 54°11′N 6°20′W, 202
Nicaea (Turkey), 40°27′N 29°43′E, 36, 67, 184
Nicastro (Italy), 38°59′N 16°20′E, 96
Nice (France), 43°42′N 7°16′E, 80, 94, 187, 204
Nicomedia (Turkey), 40°47′N 29°55′E, 36, 67, 184, 185
Nicopolis (Nikopol), (Bulgaria), 43°41′N 24°55′E, 36, 67, 184, 185, 192
Nicosia (Cyprus), 35°09′N 33°21′E, 12, 184
Nicosia (Italy), 37°45′N 14°24′E, 96
Nicotera (Italy), 38°33′N 15°56′E, 96
Nidaros *see* Trondheim
Nidau (Switzerland), 47°07′N 7°15′E, 210
Niebla (Spain), 37°22′N 6°40′W, 70
Nijmegen (Netherlands), 51°50′N 5°52′E, 40, 80, 94, 128, 203, 208
Nikopol *see* Nicopolis
Nikšić (Yugoslavia), 42°48′N 18°56′E, 184
Nîmes (France), 43°50′N 4°21′E, 40, 98, 104, 118
Niort (France), 46°19′N 0°27′W, 75
Niš (Naissus) (Yugoslavia), 43°20′N 21°54′E, 28, 36, 67, 133, 184, 185, 192
Nishapur (Iran), 43°20′N 21°54′E, 50, 69, 111
Nisibis *see* Nusaybin
Nitra (Czechoslovakia), 48°19′N 18°04′E, 188, 192
Nivelles (Belgium), 50°36′N 4°20′E, 40, 208
Nivernais* 98
Nizhnii Novgorod *see* Gorki
Nobber (Irish Republic), 53°49′N 6°45′W, 202
Nocera (Italy), 43°06′N 12°47′E, 43, 96
Nogent-le-Roi (France), 48°39′N 1°32′E, 118
Nogent-le-Rotrou (France), 48°19′N 0°50′E, 75
Noirmoutier (France), 47°01′N 2°15′W, 40
Nola (Italy), 40°55′N 14°32′E, 96
Nonantola (Italy), 44°41′N 11°03′E, 43, 80, 94
Nordalbing* 52
Nordgau* 52, 80
Nordhausen (E Germany), 51°31′N 10°48′E, 203
Nordlingen (W Germany), 48°51′N 10°31′E, 133, 203
Norfolk* 199
Noricum* 43
Normandy* 75, 98, 118, 196
Northampton (UK), 52°14′N 0°54′W, 199
North Berwick (UK), 56°04′N 2°44′W, 201
Northeim (W Germany), 51°43′N 9°59′E, 128
Northumberland* 199
Northumbria* 18, 63
Norwich (UK), 52°38′N 1°18′E, 63, 98, 165, 199
Nottingham (UK), 52°58′N 1°10′W, 63, 98, 199
Novae *see* Svishtov
Novara (Italy), 45°27′N 8°37′E, 43, 78, 94, 212
Novgorod (USSR), 58°30′N 31°20′E, 19, 63, 128, 133, 195
Noyon (France), 49°35′N 3°00′E, 40, 52, 75, 118, 165
Numedia* 36
Nuremberg (W Germany), 49°27′N 11°05′E, 94, 133, 165, 203
Nusaybin (Nisibis), (Turkey), 37°05′N 41°11′E, 36, 67, 112

Oberwesel (W Germany), 50°06′N 7°44′E, 94
Obrovac (Yugoslavia), 44°11′N 15°41′E, 184
Ochrida (Yugoslavia), 41°06′N 20°49′E, 67, 184, 185
Odemira (Portugal), 37°35′N 8°38′W, 223
Odense (Denmark), 55°24′N 10°25′E, 63, 165
Oderzo (Italy), 45°47′N 12°29′E, 43
Odessa (USSR), 46°30′N 30°46′E, 12
Odiham (UK), 51°15′N 0°57′W, 199
Odivelas (Portugal), 38°47′N 9°11′W, 223
Ogmore (UK), 51°29′N 3°37′W, 199
Oldenburg (W Germany), 53°08′N 8°13′E, 80, 94, 203
Old Killcullen (Irish Republic), 53°07′N 6°45′W, 48
Old Sarum (UK), 51°06′N 1°49′W, 199
Oléron Ile d' (France), 45°55′N 1°16′W, 118
Olivenza (Spain), 38°51′N 7°06′W, 70, 223
Olmutz *see* Olomouc
Olomouc (Olmutz), (Czechoslovakia), 49°38′N 17°15′E, 33, 80, 188, 192
Oloron (France), 43°12′N 0°35′W, 98, 118
Olten (Switzerland), 47°22′N 7°55′E, 210
Opava (Czechoslovakia), 49°58′N 17°55′E, 188, 190
Opol and Ratibor* 94
Oporto (Portugal), 41°09′N 8°37′W, 12, 70, 114, 223
Oppido Mamertina (Italy), 38°17′N 15°59′E, 96
Opsikion* 67
Optimaton* 67
Oradea (Nagyvarad), (Romania), 47°03′N 12°55′E, 192
Oran (Algeria), 35°45′N 0°38′W, 133
Orange (France), 44°08′N 4°48′E, 40, 75, 118, 165
Orense (Spain), 42°20′N 7°52′W, 70, 114
Oricum *see* Vlóre
Oriens* 18
Orihuela (Spain), 38°05′N 0°56′W, 70, 114
Oristano (Italy), 39°54′N 8°36′E, 187
Orléans (Aureliani), (France), 47°54′N 1°54′E, 18, 19, 28, 40, 52, 75, 98, 118, 104, 133, 165, 196, 208
Ormuz (Iran), 27°31′N 54°56′E, 69, 111, 224
Orvieto (Italy), 42°43′N 12°06′E, 109, 165
Osimo (Italy), 43°28′N 13°29′E, 43, 109
Oslo (Norway), 59°56′N 10°45′E, 12, 63, 128, 133
Osma (Spain), 42°52′N 3°03′W, 70, 114
Osnabrück (W Germany), 52°17′N 8°03′E, 80, 94, 128, 165, 203, 208
Osterberg (E Germany), 52°48′N 11°45′E, 128
Ostuni (Italy), 40°44′N 17°35′E, 96
Oswestry (UK), 52°52′N 3°04′W, 199
Otranto (Italy), 40°08′N 18°30′E, 19, 43, 67, 96, 185, 187, 212
Oundle (UK), 52°29′N 0°29′W, 48
Ourique (Portugal), 37°38′N 8°13′W, 114, 223
Oviedo (Spain), 43°21′N 5°50′W, 18, 70, 104, 114
Oxford (UK), 51°46′N 1°15′W, 48, 98, 165, 199

Paderborn (W Germany), 51°43′N 8°44′E, 52, 80, 94, 128, 165, 203
Padrón (Spain), 42°44′N 8°40′W, 70, 104
Padstow (UK), 50°33′N 4°56′W, 48
Padua (Italy), 45°24′N 11°53′E, 43, 78, 80, 94, 109, 165, 203, 204, 212
Paisley (UK), 55°50′N 4°26′W, 201
Palas de Rey (Spain), 42°51′N 7°52′W, 104
Palatinate (Rhineland)* 203
Palencia (Spain), 41°01′N 4°32′W, 70, 104, 114, 165
Palermo (Italy), 38°08′N 13°23′E, 12, 43, 96, 133, 165, 187
Palestrina (Italy), 41°50′N 12°54′E, 204
Pallars* 70, 187
Palma (Spain), 39°35′N 2°39′E, 70, 114, 133, 165, 187
Palmela (Portugal), 38°34′N 8°54′W, 223
Pamplona (Spain), 42°49′N 1°39′W, 70, 104, 114, 165, 187
Pannonia* 18, 36, 52
Paris (France), 48°52′N 2°20′E, 12, 18, 19, 28, 40, 52, 75, 88, 94, 98, 104, 118, 133, 165, 196, 208
Parium (Turkey), 40°25′N 27°04′E, 184
Parma (Italy), 44°48′N 10°19′E, 43, 78, 94, 109, 204, 212
Paros (Isl), (Greece), 37°04′N 25°06′E, 184
Parthenay (France), 46°39′N 0°14′W, 75
Partney (UK), 53°12′N 0°06′E, 48
Pašman (Yugoslavia), 43°58′N 15°20′E, 184
Passau (W Germany), 48°35′N 13°28′E, 80, 94, 188, 203
Patay (France), 48°03′N 1°42′E, 196
Paterno (Italy), 37°34′N 14°55′E, 96
Patras (Greece), 38°14′N 21°44′E, 67, 184
Patti (Italy), 38°08′N 14°58′E, 96
Pavia (Italy), 45°12′N 9°09′E, 28, 43, 52, 78, 80, 109, 165, 204, 212
Payerne (Switzerland), 46°49′N 6°57′E, 210
Peć (Yugoslavia), 42°40′N 20°19′E, 184
Pechina (Spain), 36°55′N 2°25′W, 70
Pécs (Hungary), 46°04′N 18°15′E, 165, 192
Peebles (UK), 55°39′N 3°12′W, 201
Peking (China), 39°55′N 116°25′E, 111
Peloponnesus* 67
Pembroke (UK), 51°41′N 4°55′W, 63, 98, 199
Penally (UK), 51°40′N 4°44′W, 48
Penela (Portugal), 40°02′N 8°23′W, 223
Penne (Italy), 42°27′N 13°56′E, 43, 96, 109
Penrith (UK), 54°40′N 2°44′W, 199
Pentapolis* 43, 109
Penthièvre* 98
Perche* 118
Perge (Turkey), 36°59′N 30°46′E, 36
Périgord* 75, 98, 118, 196
Périgueux (France), 45°12′N 0°44′E, 52, 98, 104, 118
Péronne (France), 49°56′N 2°57′E, 40, 208
Perpignan (France), 42°42′N 2°54′E, 70, 114, 165
Persarmenia* 36
Pershore (UK), 52°07′N 2°05′W, 48
Perth (UK), 56°24′N 3°28′W, 201
Perugia (Italy), 43°07′N 12°23′E, 94, 109, 165, 204
Pesaro (Italy), 43°54′N 12°54′E, 43, 109
Pescara (Italy), 42°27′N 14°13′E, 43, 96, 109, 212
Pescina (Italy), 42°02′N 13°40′E, 96
Pest *see* Budapest
Peterborough (UK), 52°35′N 0°15′W, 48, 165, 199
Petra (USSR), 41°37′N 41°36′E, 36
Petralia (Italy), 37°48′N 14°07′E, 96
Pfafers (Switzerland), 47°01′N 9°30′E, 210
Philadelphia (Turkey), 38°22′N 28°32′E, 185
Philippi (Greece), 41°05′N 24°19′E, 67, 184
Philippopolis *see* Plovdiv
Phocaea (Turkey), 38°39′N 26°46′E, 185
Piacenza (Italy), 45°03′N 9°41′E, 43, 78, 80, 94, 109, 165, 212
Picardy* 196, 203
Picenum* 43
Pickering (UK), 54°14′N 0°46′W, 199
Picquigny (France), 49°57′N 2°09′E, 196
Pilos (Greece), 36°53′N, 21°42′E, 184
Piltown (Irish Republic), 52°21′N 7°25′W, 202
Pinhel (Portugal), 40°47′N 7°03′W, 114, 223
Piombino (Italy), 42°56′N 10°32′E, 212
Pisa (Italy), 43°43′N 10°24′E, 19, 43, 80, 94, 133, 165, 187, 204, 212
Pistoia (Italy), 43°56′N 10°55′E, 109
Pithiviers (France), 48°10′N 2°15′E, 75
Plasencia (Spain), 40°02′N 6°05′W, 114
Pljevlje (Yugoslavia), 43°21′N 19°21′E, 184
Plovdiv (Philippopolis), (Bulgaria), 42°08′N 24°45′E, 28, 36, 67, 133, 184, 185
Plymouth (UK), 50°23′N 4°10′W, 199
Plympton (UK), 50°24′N 4°03′W, 199
Poblet (Spain), 38°56′N 3°59′W, 114, 165
Poissy (France), 48°56′N 2°02′E, 75, 196
Poitiers (France), 46°35′N 0°20′E, 18, 19, 40, 52, 75, 98, 104, 118, 133, 165, 196
Poitou* 75, 98, 118, 196
Pola (Yugoslavia), 44°52′N 13°52′E, 43, 212
Policastro (Italy), 40°04′N 15°37′E, 43, 96
Polignano (Italy), 40°59′N 17°13′E, 96
Polotsk (USSR), 55°30′N 28°43′E, 63, 128, 190, 195
Poltava (USSR), 49°35′N 34°35′E, 63, 190
Pomerania* 19, 94, 190, 203
Ponferrada (Spain), 42°33′N 6°35′W, 104
Pontecorvo (Italy), 41°27′N 13°40′E, 212
Pontefract (UK), 53°42′N 1°18′W, 98, 199
Ponthieu* 118, 196, 208
Pontigny (France), 47°55′N 3°43′E, 88, 118
Pontlevoy (France), 47°24′N 1°15′E, 75
Pontoise (France), 49°03′N 3°05′E, 75
Pontvallain (France), 47°45′N 0°11′E, 196
Portalegre (Portugal), 39°17′N 7°25′W, 114, 223
Portel (Portugal), 38°18′N 7°42′W, 223
Portumna (Irish Republic), 53°06′N 8°13′W, 202
Porvoo (Finland), 60°24′N 25°40′E, 165
Potées* 118
Potenza (Italy), 40°38′N 15°48′E, 96
Poznan (Poland), 52°25′N 16°53′E, 19, 133, 165, 190, 203
Pozzuoli (Italy), 40°49′N 14°07′E, 96
Prague (Czechoslovalia), 50°05′N 14°25′E, 12, 19, 80, 94, 128, 165, 188, 192
Prato (Italy), 43°53′N 11°06′E, 109, 165
Prémontré (France), 49°33′N 3°24′E, 88, 118
Prenzlau (E Germany), 53°19′N 13°52′E, 165, 188
Pressburg *see* Bratislava
Preston (UK), 53°46′N 2°42′W, 199
Prestwick (UK), 55°30′N 4°37′W, 201
Prijedor (Yugoslavia), 45°00′N 16°41′E, 184
Prijepolje (Yugoslavia), 43°23′N 19°39′E, 184
Prilep (Yugoslavia), 41°20′N 21°32′E, 184
Priština (Yugoslavia), 42°39′N 21°10′E, 184
Pritzwalk (E Germany), 53°09′N 12°11′E, 128
Prizren (Yugoslavia), 42°12′N 20°43′E, 184
Provence* 28, 40, 52, 94, 187, 196, 204, 212
Provins (France), 48°34′N 3°18′E, 75, 165
Prüm (W Germany), 50°12′N 6°25′E, 52, 80, 94, 203, 208
Puente de la Reina (Spain), 42°40′N 1°49′W, 104
Puertomarin (Spain), 42°48′N 7°37′W, 104

Quedlinburg (E Germany), 51°48′N 11°09′E, 80, 203
Quercy* 98
Quimper (France), 48°00′N 4°06′W, 98, 118, 165

Rabanal (Spain), 42°28′N 6°17′W, 104
Racibórz (Poland), 50°05′N 18°10′E, 190, 192
Radicofani (Italy), 42°54′N 11°46′E, 109
Radolfzell (W Germany), 47°44′N 8°59′E, 210
Raetia* 43, 52
Ragusa (Dubrovnik), (Yugoslavia), 42°40′N 18°07′E, 43, 67, 96, 133, 184, 185, 187, 192
Ragusa (Italy), 36°55′N 14°44′E, 96
Ramsey (UK), 52°27′N 0°07′W, 199
Randers (Denmark), 56°28′N 10°03′E, 63
Raphoe (Irish Republic), 54°52′N 7°36′W, 48, 202
Rapolla (Italy), 40°58′N 15°41′E, 96
Rapperswil (Switzerland), 47°14′N 8°50′E, 210
Raš (Yugoslavia), 43°17′N 20°37′E, 184
Raška* 184
Rathvilly (Irish Republic), 52°53′N 6°41′W, 48
Ratiaria (Bulgaria), 43°49′N 22°55′E, 36
Ratoath (Irish Republic), 53°31′N 6°24′W, 48, 202
Ratzeburg (W Germany), 53°42′N 10°46′E, 80, 94, 203
Ravello (Italy), 40°38′N 14°36′E, 96
Ravenna (Italy), 44°25′N 12°12′E, 18, 28, 36, 40, 43, 52, 78, 80, 94, 109, 203, 212
Ravensburg (W Germany), 47°47′N 9°37′E, 203
Reading (UK), 51°28′N 0°59′W, 199
Rebais (France), 48°51′N 3°15′E, 40
Recanati (Italy), 43°24′N 13°32′E, 109
Reculver (UK), 51°23′N 1°12′E, 48
Redcastle (UK), 57°31′N 4°22′W, 201
Redesdale* 199
Redondo (Portugal), 38°38′N 7°32′W, 223
Regensberg (Switzerland), 47°29′N 8°26′E, 210
Regensburg (W Germany), 49°01′N 12°07′E, 18, 19, 52, 80, 94, 165, 188, 203
Reggio di Calabria (Italy), 36°06′N 15°39′E, 28, 43, 67, 96, 212
Reggio nell'Emilia (Italy), 44°42′N 10°37′E, 43, 78, 109, 165, 212
Rehme (W Germany), 52°13′N 8°49′E, 52
Reichenau (W Germany), 47°41′N 9°03′E, 52, 80
Reims (France), 49°15′N 4°02′E, 18, 19, 40, 52, 75, 94, 98, 118, 133, 165, 196, 203, 208
Remagen (W Germany), 50°34′N 7°14′E, 94
Remiremont (France), 48°01′N 6°35′E, 40, 52
Renfrew (UK), 55°53′N 4°24′W, 201
Rennes (France), 48°06′N 1°40′W, 52, 98, 118, 196
Repton (UK), 52°50′N 1°32′W, 48
Rethel (France), 49°31′N 4°22′E, 75, 118, 196, 208
Reutlingen (W Germany), 48°30′N 9°13′E, 203
Reval (USSR), 59°22′N 24°48′E, 128, 133
Rheinau (Switzerland), 47°43′N 8°37′E, 210
Rhethymnon (Greece), 35°23′N 24°28′E, 184
Rhinetal* 210
Rhodes (Isl) (Greece) 36°15′N 28°10′E, 19, 67, 185, 224
Rhuddlan (UK), 53°18′N 3°27′E, 98, 199
Ribagorza* 70, 187
Ribe (Denmark), 55°20′N 8°47′E, 63
Ribémont (France), 49°48′N 3°28′E, 75
Richmond (UK), 54°24′N 1°44′W, 98, 199
Rieti (Italy), 42°24′N 12°51′E, 43, 96, 109
Rievaulx (UK), 54°15′N 1°07′W, 165
Riga (USSR), 56°53′N 24°08′E, 12, 19, 128, 133, 190
Rimini (Italy), 44°03′N 12°34′E, 80, 94, 109, 204
Ringsted (Denmark), 55°28′N 11°48′E, 63
Ripoll (Spain), 42°12′N 2°12′E, 114, 118
Ripon (UK), 54°08′N 1°31′W, 48, 165
Risan (Yugoslavia), 42°32′N 18°42′E, 184
Rocamadour (France), 44°48′N 1°36′E, 104
Rochester (UK), 51°24′N 0°30′E, 48, 98, 165, 199
Rodez (France), 44°21′N 2°35′E, 40, 75, 98, 118, 165
Rogaland* 63
Romagna* 94, 109, 212
Rome (Italy), 41°53′N 12°30′E, 12, 18, 19, 28, 36, 43, 52, 67, 94, 96, 109, 133, 165, 187, 204, 212
Romsey (UK), 59°59′N 1°30′W, 48
Roncesvalles (Spain), 43°0′N 1°19′W, 52, 70, 104
Ronda (Spain), 36°45′N 5°10′W, 70
Roosebeke (Belgium), 50°50′N 4°51′E, 196
Roscommon (Irish Republic), 53°38′N 8°11′W, 202
Roscrea (Irish Republic), 52°57′N 7°47′W, 48, 202
Roskilde (Denmark), 55°39′N 12°07′E, 63, 128, 165
Rosnay (France), 46°42′N 1°12′E, 75
Ross (UK), 51°55′N 2°35′W, 48, 202
Rossano (Italy), 39°35′N 16°38′E, 96
Rostock (E Germany), 54°06′N 12°09′E, 128, 165, 203
Röthenbach (Switzerland), 46°52′N 7°45′E, 210
Rothenburg (W Germany), 49°23′N 10°13′E, 165, 203
Rothesay (UK), 55°51′N 5°03′W, 201
Rotomagus *see* Rouen
Rottweil (W Germany), 48°10′N 8°38′E, 203
Roucy* 118
Rouen (Rotomagus), (France), 49°26′N 1°05′E, 18, 40, 52, 75, 98, 118, 133, 196
Rouergue* 75, 196
Rougemont (France), 47°29′N 6°21′E, 75
Roussillon* 70, 98, 118, 187
Roxburgh (UK), 55°34′N 2°30′W, 98, 201
Royat-Chamalières (France), 45°45′N 3°03′E, 40
Rüeggisberg (Switzerland), 46°49′N 7°27′E, 210
Rumelia* 19, 185
Rutherglen (UK), 55°50′N 4°12′W, 201
Ruthwell (UK), 55°00′N 3°26′W, 48
Rutland* 199
Ruvo (Italy), 41°07′N 16°29′E, 96
Rye (UK), 50°57′N 0°44′E, 199

Sabina* 109
Sablé (France), 47°50′N 0°20′W, 75
Sabugal (Portugal), 40°20′N 7°05′W, 223
Sacavém (Portugal), 38°47′N 9°06′W, 223
Sahagún 42°23′N 5°02′W, 70, 104, 114
Sahla* 70
St Albans (UK) 57°46′N 0°21′W, 48, 98, 199
St Andrews (UK), 56°20′N 2°48′W, 165 201
St Asaph (UK), 53°16′N 3°26′W, 48, 98, 199
St-Benoit-sur-Loire (France), 47°48′N 2°18′E, 75
St Bertrand-de-Comminges (France), 43°02′N 0°34′E, 40, 118
St Brieuc (France), 48°31′N 2°45′W, 98, 118
St Calais (France), 47°55′N 0°45′E, 40
St Clair (France), 49°11′N 1°03′W, 118
St Clears* 199
St Cloud (France), 48°51′N 2°12′E, 75
St David's (UK), 51°54′N 5°16′W, 48, 98, 118, 199
St Denis (France), 48°56′N 2°21′E, 40, 52, 75, 165
St Dié (France), 48°17′N 6°57′E, 40
St Emmeram* 52
Saintes (France), 45°44′N 0°38′W, 40, 98, 104, 118
St Evroult (France), 48°47′N 0°28′E, 118
St Gall (Switzerland), 47°25′N 9°23′E, 40, 52, 78, 80, 94, 203, 210
St Germain-en-Laye (France), 48°53′N 2°04′E, 75
St Germans (UK), 50°24′N 4°18′W, 48
St Gilles (France), 43°40′N 4°26′E, 104
St Gotthard (Switzerland), 46°34′N 8°31′E, 78, 210
St Jean-d'Angély (France), 45°47′N 0°31′W, 104
St Jean-de-Maurienne (France), 45°17′N 6°21′E, 40
St Jean-Pied-de-Port (France), 43°10′N 1°14′W, 104
St Kew (UK), 50°33′N 4°45′W, 48
St Léonard-de-Noblat (France), 45°50′N 1°29′E, 104
St Lizier (France), 43°01′N 1°07′E, 40
St Malo (France), 48°39′N 2°00′W, 98, 118
St Maur des Fossés (France) 48°48′N 2°29′E, 40, 75

St Maurice (Switzerland) 46°14′N 7°01′E, 210
St Mesmin (France), 48°32′N 1°58′E, 40
St Michael's Mount (UK), 50°06′N 5°29′W, 48
St Moritz (Switzerland), 46°30′N 9°51′E, 52, 80, 94, 203
St Omer (France), 50°45′N 2°15′E, 52, 75, 118
Saintonge* 98, 118, 196
St Paul (France), 44°21′N 4°46′E, 40
St Peterszell (Switzerland), 47°19′N 9°11′E, 210
St Pierre le Moutier (France), 46°48′N 3°06′E, 118
St Pol (France), 50°23′N 2°20′E, 75, 208
St Pol de Léon (France), 48°42′N 4°00′W, 98, 118
St Quentin (France), 40, 52, 75, 165
St Riquier (France), 50°09′N 1°58′E, 40, 52, 75
St Sauveur (France), 47°37′N 3°12′E, 75
St Savin (France), 45°09′N 0°26′W, 98
St Sever (France), 43°45′N 0°34′W, 104
St Urban (Switzerland), 47°14′N 7°51′E, 210
St Ursanne (Switzerland), 47°23′N 7°09′E, 210
St Valéry (France), 50°11′N 1°38′E, 40, 75, 208
St Wandrille (France), 49°32′N 0°45′E, 52
Salamanca (Spain), 40°58′N 5°40′W, 70, 114, 133, 165
Salerno (Italy), 40°40′N 14°46′E, 43, 96, 109, 165
Salins (France), 45°12′N 2°22′E, 208
Salisbury (UK), 51°05′N 1°48′W, 98, 118, 165, 199
Saluzzo (Italy), 44°39′N 7°29′E, 80, 94, 212
Salzburg (Austria), 47°54′N 13°03′E, 52, 80, 94, 133, 165, 203
Salzwedel (E Germany), 52°51′N 11°10′E, 128
Samarkand (USSR), 39°40′N 66°57′E, 50, 69, 111
Samnium* 43
Samogitia* 128, 190
Samos (Isl), 37°42′N 26°59′E, 67, 184, 185
Samothrace (Isl), 40°29′N 25°32′E, 185
Samsun (Turkey), 41°17′N 36°22′E, 112, 185
San Biagio Platani (Italy), 37°31′N 13°32′E, 96
Sancerre (France), 47°20′N, 2°50′E, 75, 118
San Clemente di Casauria (Italy), 42°14′N 13°55′E, 96
Sandwich (UK), 51°17′N 1°20′E, 199
San Gimignano (Italy), 43°28′N 11°02′E, 165
San Giuseppe Iato (Italy), 37°58′N 13°11′E, 96
Sangüesa (Spain), 42°34′N 1°17′W, 104
San Marco Argentano (Italy), 39°33′N 16°07′E, 96
San Marco d'Alunzio (Italy), 38°09′N 14°42′E, 96
San Sebastián (Spain), 43°19′N 1°59′W, 104, 114
San Severo (Italy), 41°41′N 15°23′E, 96
Sant' Agata de Goti, 41°05′N 14°30′E, 96
Santa Maria de la Huerta (Spain), 41°15′N 2°10′W, 165
Santa Maria di Leuca (Italy), 39°48′N 18°23′E, 12
Santander (Spain), 43°28′N 3°48′W, 70, 104, 114
Sant' Angelo dei Lombardi (Italy), 40°55′N 15°11′E, 96
Santarém (Portugal), 39°14′N 8°40′W, 70, 114, 223
Santa Severina (Italy), 39°08′N 16°55′E, 67, 96
Santiago de Compostela (Spain), 42°52′N 8°33′W, 70, 104, 114, 165
Santillana del Mar (Spain), 43°24′N 4°06′W, 70, 104
Santo Domingo de la Calzada (Spain), 42°26′N 2°57′W, 104
Saragossa (Spain), 41°39′N 0°54′W, 18, 19, 52, 69, 70, 114, 133, 165, 187
Sarajevo (Verbosna), (Yugoslavia), 43°52′N 18°26′E, 184, 185, 192
Sardes (Turkey), 38°28′N 28°02′E, 36, 67
Sardica (Sofia), (Bulgaria), 42°40′N 23°18′E, 18, 19, 67
Sargans* 210
Sarno (Italy), 40°48′N 14°37′E, 96
Sassari (Italy), 40°43′N 8°34′E, 187
Satriano di Lucania (Italy), 40°32′N 15°38′E, 96
Saumur (France), 47°16′N 0°05′W, 75
Šavnik (Yugoslavia), 42°59′N 19°05′E, 184
Savona (Italy), 44°18′N 8°28′E, 43, 187
Savoy* 94, 118, 196, 203, 212
Sax* 210
Saxony* 18, 40, 52, 80, 94, 188, 203
Scalea (Italy), 39°49′N 15°47′E, 96
Scania* 63, 128
Scarborough (UK), 54°17′N 0°24′W, 199
Schaffhausen (Switzerland), 47°42′N 8°38′E, 210
Schaumberg* 203
Schleswig (W Germany), 54°32′N 9°34′E, 80, 203
Schlettstadt (France), 48°16′N 7°27′E, 203
Schönenwerd (Switzerland), 47°23′N 8°01′E, 210
Schöningen (W Germany), 52°08′N 10°58′E, 52
Schöntal (W Germany), 49°20′N 9°33′E, 203, 210
Schwäbisch Gmünd (W Germany), 48°49′N 9°48′E, 165, 203
Schweinfurt (W Germany), 50°03′W 10°16′E, 203
Schwerin (E Germany), 53°38′N 11°25′E, 80, 203
Schwerte (W Germany), 51°26′N 7°34′E, 128
Schwyz (Switzerland), 47°02′N 8°34′E, 210
Scodra *see* Scutari
Scutari (Scodra), (Albania), 42°03′N 19°01′E, 36, 184, 185
Sebastea *see* Sivas
Seckau (Austria), 47°14′N 14°50′E, 80, 94
Sées (France), 48°36′N 0°10′E, 118
Segorbe (Spain), 39°51′N 0°30′W, 114
Segovia (Spain), 40°57′N 4°07′W, 70, 114, 165
Selby (UK), 53°48′N 1°04′W, 199
Selestat (France), 48°16′N 7°28′E, 52
Seleucia *see* Silifke
Selkirk (UK), 55°33′N 2°50′W, 201
Selsey (UK), 50°44′N 0°48′W, 48
Semigallia* 190
Sempach (Switzerland), 47°13′N 8°12′E, 210
Senigallia (Italy), 43°43′N 13°13′E, 43
Senlis (France), 49°12′N 2°35′E, 75, 118, 165, 208
Sens (France), 48°12′N 3°18′E, 40, 52, 75, 118, 165, 196, 208
Septimania* 40, 52
Serpa (Portugal), 37°56′N 7°36′W, 70, 114, 223
Serra de el Rei (Portugal), 39°20′N 9°20′W, 223
Serrastretta (Italy), 39°01′N 16°25′E, 96
Sesimbra (Portugal), 38°26′N 9°06′W, 223
Sessa Aurunca (Italy), 41°14′N 13°56′E, 96, 109
Sesto (Italy), 46°42′N 12°22′E, 43
Setúbal (Portugal), 38°31′N 8°54′W, 70, 223
Seville (Spain), 37°24′N 5°59′W, 19, 50, 69, 70, 114, 133, 165
Sheffield (UK), 53°23′N 1°30′W, 199
Sherborne (UK), 50°57′N 2°31′W, 48, 199
Shiraz (Iran), 29°38′N 52°34′E, 50, 69, 111
Shoreham (UK), 51°20′N 0°10′E, 199
Shrewsbury (UK), 52°43′N 2°45′W, 98, 199
Shropshire* 199
Sibenik (Yugoslavia), 43°45′N 15°55′E, 165, 184, 192
Side (Turkey), 37°22′N 27°42′E, 67
Siena (Italy), 43°19′N 11°19′E, 43, 94, 109, 165, 187, 204, 212
Sierre (Switzerland), 46°18′N 7°33′E, 210
Sigtuna (Sweden), 59°36′N 17°44′E, 63
Sigüenza (Spain), 41°04′N 2°38′W, 70, 114, 165, 187
Silesia* 94, 188, 190, 192, 203
Silifke (Turkey), 36°22′N 33°57′E, 36, 67, 185
Silistria (Bulgaria), 44°06′N 27°17′E, 36, 67, 185
Silvan (Turkey), 38°08′N 41°00′E, 36
Silves (Portugal), 37°11′N 8°26′W, 114, 223
Simancas (Spain), 41°35′N 4°50′W, 70
Sinope (Turkey), 42°02′N 35°09′E, 18, 50, 63, 112, 133, 184, 185
Sintra (Portugal), 38°48′N 9°22′W, 223
Sion (Sitten), (Switzerland), 46°14′N 7°22′E, 80, 94, 165, 203, 210
Siponto *see* Manfredonia
Sirmione (Italy), 45°29′N 10°36′E, 43
Sirmium *see* Sremska Mitrovica
Sisak (Yugoslavia), 45°30′N 16°22′E, 184
Sitia (Greece), 35°13′N 26°06′E, 184
Sitten *see* Sion
Sivas (Sebastea), (Turkey), 39°44′N 37°01′E, 18, 36, 50, 67, 111, 112, 133, 185
Skalholt (Iceland), 64°08′N 20°31′W, 63
Skanör (Sweden), 55°24′N 12°50′E, 133
Skara (Sweden), 58°23′N 13°25′E, 63, 165
Skellig Michael (Isl), (Irish Republic), 51°47′N 10°32′W, 48
Skipton (UK), 53°58′N 2°01′W, 199
Skiros (Isl), (Greece), 38°55′N 24°34′E, 184, 185
Skopje (Scupi, Uskub), (Yugoslavia), 42°00′N 21°28′E, 36, 133, 184, 185
Slagelse (Denmark), 55°24′N 11°23′E, 63
Slane (Irish Republic), 54°43′N 6°33′W, 48, 202
Slavinia* 94
Slawno (Poland), 54°21′N 16°40′E, 128
Slieve League (Irish Republic), 54°39′N 8°42′W, 48
Sligo (Irish Republic),54°17′N 8°28′W, 202
Sluis (Netherlands), 51°18′N 3°23′E, 196
Slupsk (Poland), 54°28′N 17°00′E, 128, 190
Smaland* 63, 128
Smolensk (USSR), 54°49′N 32°04′E, 19, 63, 133, 190, 195
Smyrna (Turkey), 38°25′N 27°10′E, 18, 19, 50, 67, 184, 185
Sobrarbe* 70, 187
Söderköping (Sweden), 58° 28′N 16°20′E
Sodermanland* 63, 128
Soest (W Germany), 51°34′N 8°06′E, 128, 165, 203
Sofia (Sardica, Sredec), (Bulgaria), 42°40′N 23°18′E, 12, 184, 185, 192
Soissons (France), 49°23′N 3°20′E, 40, 52, 75, 118, 165
Solignac (France), 45°45′N 1°16′E, 40
Solin (Yugoslavia), 43°33′N 16°30′E, 184
Sollentuna (Sweden), 59°26′N 17°56′E, 63
Solothurn (Switzerland), 47°13′N 7°32′E, 94, 210
Somerset* 199
Somma (Italy), 42°40′N 12°44′E, 109
Somvix (Switzerland), 46°43′N 8°55′E, 210
Sora (Italy), 41°43′N 13°37′E, 96, 109
Sorde (France), 43°32′N 1°03′W, 104
Soria (Spain), 41°46′N 2°28′W, 70, 114
Sorrento (Italy), 40°37′N 14°23′E, 96, 109
Souillac (France), 44°53′N 1°29′E, 98
Soure (Portugal), 40°04′N 8°38′W, 223
Southampton (UK), 50°55′N 1°25′W, 98, 196, 199
Southwell (UK), 53°05′N 0°58′W, 165
Spalato *see* Split
Speyer (W Germany), 49°18′N 8°26′E, 52, 80, 94, 133, 203
Split (Spalato), (Yugoslavia), 43°31′N 18°28′E, 18, 43, 67, 184, 192, 212
Spoleto (Italy), 42°44′N 12°44′E, 43, 52, 94, 96, 109, 212
Sponheim* 203
Squillace (Italy), 38°46′N 16°31′E, 43, 96
Srebrenica (Yugoslavia), 44°06′N 19°20′E, 184
Sredec *see* Sofia
Sremska Mitrovica (Sirmium), (Yugoslavia), 44°59′N 19°39′E, 18, 67, 184, 192
Stablo (Stavelot), (Belgium), 50°23′N 5°56′E, 40, 52, 80, 94, 203, 208
Stade (W Germany), 53°36′N 9°28′E, 128
Stafford (UK), 52°48′N 2°07′W, 199
Stamford (UK), 52°39′N 0°29′W, 63
Stans (Switzerland), 46°58′N 8°22′E, 210
Stargard (Poland), 53°21′N 15°01′E, 128
Stavanger (Norway), 58°58′N 5°45′E, 63
Steckborn (Switzerland), 47°44′N 8°60′E, 210
Stein (Switzerland), 47°33′N 7°58′E, 210
Stendal (E Germany), 52°36′N 11°52′E, 128
Stettin (Szczecin), (Poland), 53°25′N 14°32′E, 128, 133, 165, 190, 203
Štip (Yugoslavia), 41°44′N 22°12′E, 184
Stirling (UK), 57°28′N 1°48′W, 201
Stobi (Yugoslavia), 41°33′N 21°59′E, 36
Stockholm (Sweden), 59°20′N 18°95′E, 12, 19, 128, 133, 165
Ston (Yugoslavia), 42°50′N 17°42′E, 184
Stralsund (E Germany), 54°18′N 13°06′E, 128, 165, 203
Strasbourg (France), 48°35′N 7°45′E, 40, 52, 80, 94, 133, 165, 203, 208
Stratford (UK), 52°12′N 1°41′W, 48
Straubing (W Germany), 48°53′N 12°35′E, 203
Strongoli (Italy), 39°16′N 17°03′E, 96
Strumica (Yugoslavia), 41°26′N 22°39′E, 184
Studenica (Yugoslavia), 43°21′N 20°35′E
Styria* 80, 94, 192, 203
Sudak (USSR), 44°52′N 34°57′E, 133
Suez (Egypt), 29°58′N 32°33′E, 112
Suffolk* 199
Sulmona (Italy), 42°03′N 13°56′E
Sundgau* 203
Surrey* 199
Sursee (Switzerland), 47°11′N 8°07′E, 210
Susa (Italy), 45°08′N 7°02′E, 78, 212
Sussex* 199
Sutri (Italy), 42°14′N 12°14′E, 43, 94, 109, 212
Svendborg (Denmark), 55°04′N 10°38′E, 128
Svishtov (Novae), (Bulgaria), 43°36′N 25°22′E, 36
Swabia* 80, 94
Swansea (UK), 51°38′N 3°57′W, 199
Sween (UK), 55°59′N 5°38′W, 201
Swidnica (Poland), 50°51′N 16°29′E, 188, 190
Syracuse (Italy), 37°04′N 15°18′E, 19, 36, 43, 67, 96, 133, 165, 187, 212
Szczecin (Stettin), (Poland), 53°25′N 14°32′E, 128, 133, 165, 190, 203
Székesfehérvar (Hungary), 47°11′N 18°22′E, 192

Tabor (Czechoslovakia), 49°25′N 14°40′E, 188
Tabriz (Iran), 38°05′N 46°18′E, 50, 69, 111
Tafalla (Spain), 42°32′N 1°41′W, 70
Tagliacozzo (Italy), 42°05′N 13°15′E, 96, 109
Talavera (Spain), 39°57′N 4°50′W, 70
Tamins (Switzerland), 46°50′N 9°25′E, 210
Tangermünde (E Germany), 52°34′N 11°58′E, 128
Tangier (Morocco), 35°48′N 5°45′W, 18, 19, 36, 50, 69, 70, 114, 133, 224
Taormina (Italy), 37°51′N 15°17′E, 43, 67, 96
Tara (Irish Republic), 53°35′N 6°35′W, 48
Taranto (Italy), 40°28′N 17°15′E, 43, 96, 133
Tarazona (Spain), 41°54′N 1°44′W, 114, 187
Tarbes (France), 43°14′N 0°05′E, 98, 118
Tardajos (Spain), 42°21′N 3°49′W, 104
Tarentaise (France), 45°35′N 6°53′E, 80, 94, 203
Taron* 67
Tarraco *see* Tarragona
Tarragona (Spain), 41°07′N 1°15′E, 18, 52, 70, 114, 165, 187
Tarsus (Turkey), 36°52′N 34°52′E, 19, 36, 50, 67, 112, 133, 185
Tartu (USSR), 58°20′N 26°44′E, 195
Tattershall (UK), 53°07′N 0°11′W,199
Taus (Czechoslovakia), 49°28′N 13°00′E, 188, 203
Tavira (Portugal), 37°07′N 7°39′W, 223
Teano (Italy), 41°15′N 14°05′E, 96, 109
Tecklenburg (W Germany) 52°13′N 7°49′E, 203
Tegernsee (W Germany), 47°42′N 11°46′E, 80, 94
Tekke* 185
Telese (Italy), 41°13′N 14°31′E, 96
Temesvar (Romania), 45°45′N 21°13′E, 192
Tenby (UK), 51°41′N 4°43′W, 199
Tenedos (Isl), (Turkey), 39°49′N 26°03′E, 185
Teramo (Italy), 42°40′N 13°43′E, 96, 109
Termoli (Italy), 42°00′N 15°00′E, 96
Terracina (Italy), 41°17′N 13°15′E, 96, 109
Terra di Lavoro* 212
Teruel (Spain), 40°21′N 1°06′W, 70, 114, 187
Tetbury (UK), 51°39′N 2°10′W, 48
Tewkesbury (UK), 51°59′N 2°09′W, 48
Thasos (Isl), (Greece), 40°46′N 24°42′E, 185
Thebes (Greece), 38°19′N 23°19′E, 67, 184
Thelepte (Tunisia), 35°04′N 8°38′E, 36
Theodosiopolis *see* Erzurum
Thermopylae (Greece), 38°50′N 22°35′E, 36
Thérouanne (France), 50°38′N 2°15′E, 75, 118, 208
Thessalonica (Greece), 40°38′N 22°58′E, 18, 19, 28, 36, 67, 112, 133, 184, 185
Thessaly* 184, 185
Thiers (France), 45°51′N 3°33′E, 75
Thionville (France), 49°22′N 6°11′E, 208
Thomond* 202
Thorney (UK), 52°37′N 0°07′W, 199
Thouars* 75, 118
Thrace *see* Heraclea
Thracesion* 67
Threekingham (UK), 52°55′N 0°23′W, 48
Thun (Switzerland), 46°46′N 7°38′E, 78, 210
Thurgau* 210
Thuringia* 40, 52, 80, 94, 203
Thurles (Irish Republic), 52°41′N 7°49′W, 202
Thykkvibaer (Iceland), 63°44′N 20°35′W, 63
Tilbury (UK), 51°28′N 0°23′E, 48
Timahoe (Irish Republic), 52°58′N 7°12′W, 48, 98
Timoleague (Irish Republic), 51°38′N 8°46′W, 202
Tinchebrai (France), 48°46′N 0°44′W, 98
Tineo (Spain), 43°20′N 6°24′W, 70
Tintagel (UK), 50°40′N 4°45′W, 48
Tintern (UK), 51°43′N 2°41′W, 202
Tipperary (Irish Republic), 52°29′N 8°10′W, 202
Tirconnell* 202
Tisbury (UK), 51°04′N 2°03′W, 48
Tivoli (Italy), 41°58′N 12°48′E, 43, 94, 96, 109
Tlemcen (Algeria), 34°53′N 1°21′W, 50, 69, 133
Todi (Italy), 42°47′N 12°24′E, 43, 109, 204
Toggenburg* 210
Toledo (Spain), (Toletum), 39°52′N 4°02′W, 18, 19, 28, 36, 50, 69, 70, 114, 133, 165
Toletum *see* Toledo
Tolosa (Spain), 43°08′N 2°04′W, 18, 165
Tomar (Portugal), 39°36′N 8°25′W, 70, 114, 165, 223
Tongland (UK), 54°52′N 4°02′W, 201
Tonnerre (France), 47°51′N 3°59′E, 75
Tönsberg (Norway), 59°16′N 10°25′E, 128
Tordesillas (Spain), 41°30′N 5°00′W, 70
Toro (Spain), 41°31′N 5°24′W, 70
Torre de Moncorvo (Portugal), 41°10′N 7°03′W, 233
Torres (Italy), 40°50′N 8°23′E, 43
Torres Novas (Portugal), 39°28′N 8°32′W, 223
Torres Vedras (Portugal), 39°05′N 9°15′W, 223
Tortona (Italy), 44°54′N 8°52′E, 43, 94, 212
Tortosa (Spain), 40°49′N 0°31′E, 69, 70, 114, 165, 187
Torun (Poland), 53°01′N 18°35′E, 28, 133, 165, 190
Tory (Isl), (Irish Republic), 55°16′N 8°13′W, 48
Toul (France), 48°41′N 5°54′E, 94, 118, 203, 208
Toulon (France), 43°07′N 5°55′E, 94
Toulouse (France), 43°33′N 1°24′E, 18, 19, 28, 36, 40, 52, 70, 75, 98, 104, 118, 133, 165, 187, 196, 204
Touraine* 75, 98, 118
Tournai (Belgium), 50°36′N 3°24′E, 40, 75, 98, 118, 165, 196, 208
Tournus (France), 46°33′N 4°55′E, 75
Tours (Caesarodunum), (France), 47°23′N 0°42′E, 18, 36, 40, 52, 75, 98, 104, 118, 133, 165, 196
Trainopolis (Greece), 40°57′N 25°56′E, 36, 67
Tralee (Irish Republic), 52°16′N 9°42′W, 202
Trancoso (Portugal), 40°46′N 7°21′W, 223
Trani (Italy), 41°17′N 16°25′E, 96
Transylvania* 192
Trápani (Italy), 38°02′N 12°32′E, 96, 187
Traungau* 80
Travnik (Yugoslavia), 44°13′N 17°40′E, 184
Trebinje (Yugoslavia), 42°44′N 18°20′E, 184
Trebizond (Trabzon), (Turkey), 41°00′N 39°43′E, 18, 19, 36, 50, 67, 111, 112, 185
Tréguier (France) 48°47′N 3°14′W, 98, 118
Trelleborg (Sweden), 55°22′N 13°10′E, 63
Trenčin (Czechoslovakia), 48°53′N 18°00′E, 188, 192
Trent (Italy), 46°04′N 11°08′E, 43, 80, 94, 203, 212
Trevico (Italy), 41°03′N 15°14′E, 96
Treviso (Italy), 45°40′N 12°15′E, 43, 94, 165, 212
Triacastela (Spain), 42°45′N 7°14′W, 104
Trier (Augusta Treverorum), (W Germany), 49°45′N 6°39′E, 18, 28, 40, 52, 80, 94, 133, 165, 203, 208
Trieste (Italy), 45°39′N 13°47′E, 43, 192, 203, 212
Trim (Irish Republic), 53°34′N 6°47′W, 48, 165, 202
Tripoli (Lebanon), 34°27′N 35°50′E, 91, 111
Tripoli (Libya), 32°58′N 13°12′E, 69, 133
Tripolitania* 36
Trivento (Italy), 41°47′N 14°33′E, 96
Troia (Italy), 41°32′N 15°19 E, 96
Trondheim (Nidaros), (Norway), 63°36′N 10°23′E, 63, 165
Tropea (Greece), 37°43′N 21°57′E, 96, 187
Troyes (France), 48°18′N 4°05′E, 40, 75, 94, 98, 118, 133, 165, 196, 208
Trub (Switzerland), 46°57′N 7°54′E, 210
Trujillo (Spain), 39°28′N 5°53′W, 70
Truro (UK), 50°16′N 5°03′W, 199
Tuam (Irish Republic), 53°31′N 8°50′W, 48, 98, 202
Tübingen (W Germany), 48°32′N 9°04′E, 165
Tudela (Spain), 42°04′N 1°37′W, 70, 114, 165
Tulle (France), 45°16′N 1°46′E, 118
Tunis (Tunisia), 36°50′N 10°13′E, 12, 19, 50, 69, 133, 187
Turenne (France), 45°04′N 1°34′E, 98, 118
Turin (Italy), 45°04′N 7°40′E, 12, 43, 78, 80, 94, 165, 187, 203
Turku (Finland), 60°27′N 22°15′E, 165
Turnovo (Bulgaria), 43°04′N 25°39′E, 185
Turnu Severin (Romania), 44°36′N 22°39′E, 184, 192
Tursi (Italy), 40°14′N 16°29′E, 96
Tuscany* 94, 109
Tuscia* 43
Tutbury (UK), 52°52′N 1°40′W, 199
Túy (Spain), 42°03′N 8°39′W, 70, 114
Tyana (Turkey), 37°48′N 34°36′E, 36, 67
Tynedale* 199
Tynemouth (UK), 55°01′N 1°24′W, 48, 199
Tyre (Lebanon), 33°16′N 35°12′E, 67, 91
Tyrol* 203

Überlingen (W Germany), 47°46′N, 9°10′E, 203
Uclés (Spain), 39°58′N 2°52′W, 114
Uelzen (W Germany), 52°58′N 10°34′E, 128
Ugento (Italy), 39°55′N 18°10′E, 96
Ulm (W Germany), 48°24′N 10°00′E, 52, 80, 94, 96, 165, 203
Umbria* 43, 212
Umbriatico (Italy), 39°21′N 16°55′E, 96
Uncastillo (Spain), 42°21′N 1°08′W, 70
Unterseen (Switzerland), 46°41′N 7°46′E, 210
Unterwalden* 210
Upper Alsace* 208
Upper Lorraine* 80, 94
Upper Palatinate* 188, 203
Uppland* 63, 128
Uppsala (Sweden), 59°55′N 17°38′E, 63, 165
Urbino (Italy), 43°43′N, 12°38′E, 43, 109, 212
Urfa (Edessa), (Turkey), 37°08′N 38°45′E, 36, 67, 90, 111
Urgel (Spain), 42°21′N 1°28′E, 70, 114, 118
Uri* 210
Uriel* 202
Urr (UK), 55°09′N, 3°56′W, 201
Ursen* 210
Usedom (E Germany), 53°53′N 13°55′E, 128
Usk (UK), 51°43′N 2°54′W, 199
Uskub *see* Skopje
Utrecht (Netherlands), 52°06′N 5°07′E, 52, 80, 94, 203, 208
Uzès (France), 44°01′N 4°25′E, 118, 198
Užice (Yugoslavia), 43°51′N 19°51′E, 184

Vadstena (Sweden), 58°26′N 14°55′E, 63, 165
Vaduz (Liechtenstein), 47°08′N 9°32′E, 210
Vaison (France), 44°14′N 5°04′E, 40
Valais* 210
Valcarlos (Spain), 43°05′N 1°18′W, 104
Valença (Portugal), 42°02′N 8°38′W, 223
Valence (France), 44°56′N 4°54′E, 40, 75, 80, 94, 118, 165, 196, 203
Valencia (Spain), 39°28′N 0°22′W, 12, 18, 19, 50, 69, 70, 114, 133, 165, 187
Valenciennes (France), 50°22′N 3°32′E, 52, 208
Valentinois* 196
Valeria* 43
Valladolid (Spain), 41°39′N 4°45′W, 70, 114, 165
Vallentuna (Sweden), 59°32′N 18°05′E, 63
Vallombrosa (Italy), 43°44′N 11°34′E, 109
Valmaseda (Spain), 43°11′N 3°11′W, 70
Valmiera (USSR), 57°32′N 25°29′E, 128
Valois* 75, 118, 196
Valona *see* Vlóre
Valonga (Portugal), 40°37′N 8°27′W, 223
Vannes (France), 47°40′N 2°44′W, 52, 98, 118
Varberg (Sweden), 57°06′N 12°15′E, 128
Varmland* 63, 128
Varna (Bulgaria), 43°12′N 27°57′E, 185, 192
Vaspurkan* 67
Vasteras (Sweden), 59°36′N 16°32′E, 63
Vaucluse (France), 43°55′N 5°08′E, 204
Vaucouleurs (France), 48°36′N 5°40′E, 196, 208
Velay* 98
Vendôme (France), 47°48′N 1°04′E, 75, 165
Venice (Italy), 45°26′N 12°20′E, 18, 19, 43, 78, 80, 94, 109, 111, 133, 165, 187, 203, 204, 212
Venosa (Italy), 40°57′N 15°49′E, 96
Ventimiglia (Italy), 43°47′N 7°37′E, 43
Verberie (France), 49°18′N 2°45′E, 52
Vercelli (Italy), 45°19′N 8°26′E, 43, 78, 80, 94, 165, 212
Verden (W Germany), 52°56′N 9°14′E, 52, 80, 94, 165, 203
Verdun (France), 49°10′N 5°23′E, 40, 52, 75, 80, 98, 118, 203, 208
Vermandois* 75, 98, 118, 208
Verona (Italy), 45°26′N 11°00′E, 28, 43, 78, 80, 94, 109, 133, 165, 203, 204, 212
Vestfold* 63
Vestmanland* 12, 128
Vevey (Switzerland), 46°28′N 6°51′E, 210
Vexin* 75
Vézelay (France), 47°28′N 3°43′E, 104, 118, 165, 208
Viborg (Denmark), 56°28′N 9°25′E, 63, 128
Vicenza (Italy), 45°33′N 11°33′E, 43, 78, 94, 109, 165, 203, 212

INDEX

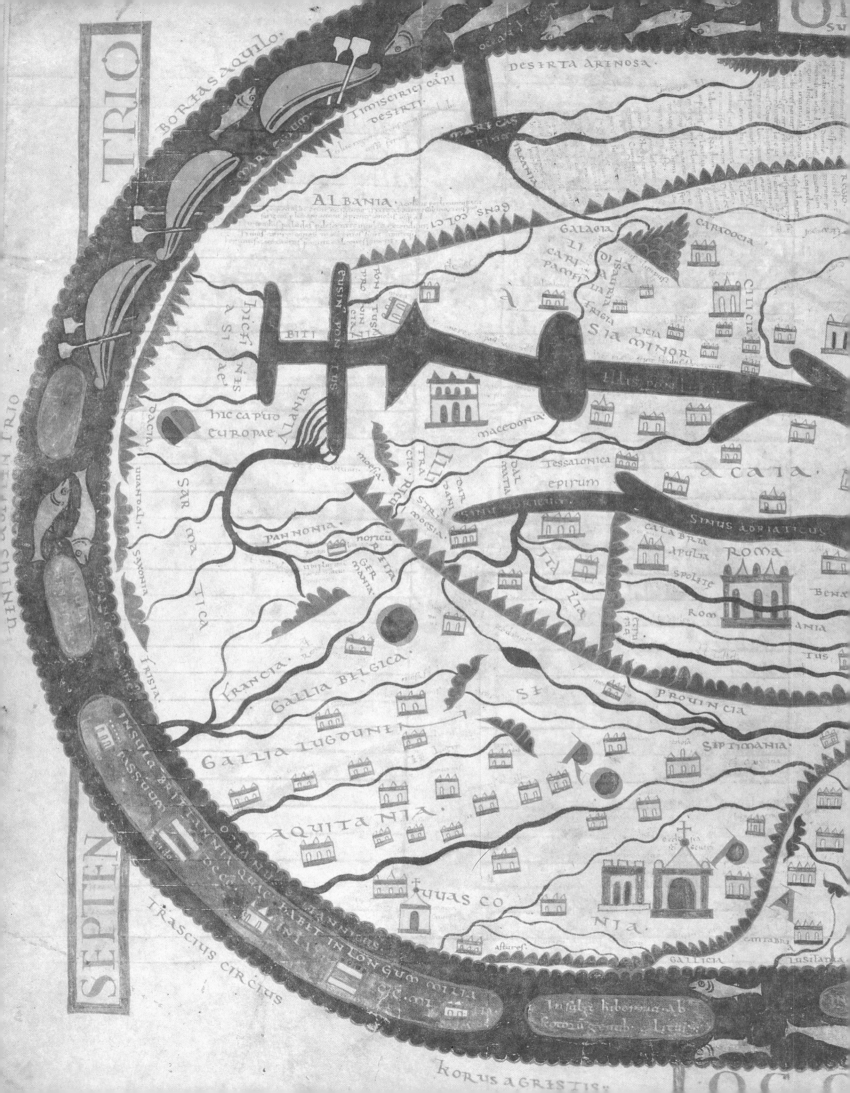

SEPTENTRIO

TRIO

BORIAS AQUILO.

OCEANUS AQUILONIS IN TRIO

DESERTA ARENOSA.

TIMISCIRICI CAPI DESERTI.

MARICIS

URCANIA

ALBANIA

GENS COLCI

GALACIA

CAPADOCIA

LIDIA ISAURIA CARIA PAMPILIA FRIGIA

CILICIA

EUSINUS PONTUS

PONTUS PROUINCIA

BITINIA

DICINIS ASIAE

SIA MINOR

ILLIS prov

ALANIA

HIC CAPUD EUROPAE

MACEDONIA

ACAIA

DACIA

SARMANOALI

moesia

TRACIA TRACIA RICU moesia

DALMACIA

TESSALONICA EPIRUM

SINUS ADRIATICUS

UUANOALI

SAXONIA

PANNONIA

noricu RETIA GERMANIA

ITALIA

CALABRIA APULIA SPOLITE ROM

ROMA

FRISIA

SARMATICA

FRANCIA

GALLIA BELGICA

SI

PROUINCIA

TANIA

BENE

TUS

INSULA BRITANNIA ASSIDUM ORIANT GERMANNIAE QUAE TABET IN LONGUM MILIA DCCC

GALLIA LUGDUNE

SIPTIMANIA

TRASCIUS CIRCIUS

AQUITANIA

UUAS CO NIA

ecclesia ISTI

asturcs

Insula hibernia ab horou Zecundo licuit

GALICIA

CANTABRIA

LUSITANIA

KORUS AGRISTIS

OC